Qualitative Research Methods in Education and Educational Technology

Qualitative
Research Methods
in Education and
Educational Technology

by

Jerry W. Willis, PhD
Manhattanville College

INFORMATION AGE PUBLISHING, INC.
Charlotte, NC • www.infoagepub.com

Library of Congress Cataloging-in-Publication Data

Willis, Jerry, 1942-
  Qualitative research methods in education and educational technology / by
Jerry W. Willis.
      p. cm.
  Includes bibliographical references.
  ISBN 1-930608-54-3 (pbk.) – ISBN 1-930608-55-1 (hardcover)
  1. Education–Research. 2. Educational technology–Reserach. 3.
Research–Methodology. I. Title.
  LB1028.W51918 2009
  370.72–dc22

                                                2008042374

Printed in the United States of America

CONTENTS

SECTION 1
FOUNDATIONS

SECTION 2
PATHWAYS TO UNDERSTANDING

SECTION 3
PATHWAYS TO UNDERSTANDING:
THE METHODS OF RESEARCH AND SCHOLARSHIP

SECTION 4

DISSEMINATION OF RESULTS

SECTION 1

FOUNDATIONS

CHAPTER 1

WOLVES, LAMBS, AND LIONS—ROAMING THE RESEARCH RANGE

Norman Lederman, a professor at Illinois Institute of Technology, has written several papers on the nature of research in both education in general and the field of educational technology in particular (Lederman, 2003; Lederman and Flick, 2003). Lederman's (2003) paper on ways of thinking about and doing research on educational/instructional technology begins with a commentary on the movie, *Never Cry Wolf.* The movie is based on a book by the Canadian author, Farley Mowat, and it stars Charles Martin Smith as the young researcher, Tyler, who comes to the Artic to get proof that wolves are the major reason for the decline in caribou herds. Smith is better known for his role as "Toad" in the movie *American Graffiti* and as one of the Crickets in *The Buddy Holly Story.* However, as Tyler, he is part of a story that tells us a lot about the issues and problems of doing research today.

For our present discussion, there are two important implications of the movie. The first is that *ideology guided the research project.* As a young scientist Tyler was commissioned to do a certain research study because his mentor already "knew" what the results would be (that Arctic wolves were killing caribou and causing a significant and dangerous decline in the population). The researcher's main job was to provide empirical evidence to support that known fact and then come up with ways of reducing the wolf

Qualitative Research Methods in Education and Educational Technology, pages 3–26
Copyright © 2008 by Information Age Publishing
3

population in order to save the caribou population. The research thus began with a preconceived notion about the place of wolves in the Arctic ecosystem along with a very detailed set of assumptions about their hunting and eating patterns as well as their family structure.

We could speculate for a long time on why the mentor was so sure wolves were the cause of the caribou problem. Perhaps it goes back to the steady diet of Disney movies that many of us were exposed to while we were growing up. Predators like wolves don't get much good press in those movies. And then there is the Big Bad Wolf fairy tale and the use of the term wolf to mean a sexually predatory male on the prowl (this is a particularly egregious stereotype given that male wolves have a much better track record as fathers and husbands than many human males). No, wolves don't get an even shake in the children's media, and things aren't much better for them when it comes to coverage in adult media. Of course, we don't have to develop a theory about cultural bias against wolves to explain the mentor's ideas. He could have simply based his belief on sound experience. Perhaps all his experience in the field pointed to wolves as the culprits and the research was just a formality in establishing a truth that everyone in the field knew already.

That is not what happened, however. Tyler does not gather data that confirms what everyone already knows. Our young researcher begins his lonely research in the Arctic by observing wolves, and as he gathers data he gradually comes to realize that wolves aren't the source of the caribou decline. They mostly eat mice and other small rodents, which the researcher also samples to test their edibility. Wolves do sometimes bring down a caribou but they mostly catch the weak and the ill which means they probably enhance the survival probabilities of healthy caribou rather than reducing them.

The movie is based on a true story and it is hard not to wonder how this could happen. How could the mentor have been so wrong? We will probably never know why but we can be sure that this was not the first time research refuted a sure thing, nor will it be the last. We do research because we want to know more about the world we live in and sometimes the results give us more confidence in what we believed in the first place. Sometimes the results cause us to question our closely held beliefs and even to reject them in favor of another way of explaining the world. That is the purpose of research.

A second aspect of the study in *Never Cry Wolf* is that the standard criteria of what is generally called the Scientific Method were violated many times. The researcher did not begin by stating a hypothesis, then gather data, and finally analyze the data to determine if the hypothesis was supported or not. Tyler, the researcher, changed his research method several times, and he also changed the focus and purpose of his research. Though his research was successful—peers in his field agreed that he had discovered something about an important relationship that was not known before—it did not meet the criteria for "valid" research that tens of thousands of college students are taught in undergraduate and graduate research courses every year.

What are those standards? Here is my list of essential characteristics of research that follows the scientific method.

1. *Objective*—you must approach the question of the research in an objective way and avoid interjecting any form of subjectivity into your research because that can lead to bias. Tyler actually began the study with one subjective bias, borrowed from his mentor. He expected a certain set of results and he set up a study to get those results. Then, as the study progressed his subjective bias shifted to the opposite conclusion and he began to gather data that would support the opposite of his original belief.

2. *Empirical*—gather quantitative data and analyze it according to established statistical methods so that your conclusions are based on data that can be replicated and tested by other researchers. Tyler's most important data was not a set of numbers he could analyze with a standard statistical procedure such as a t-test or analysis of variance. Instead, it was his observations that were most important. His data was predominately qualitative, not quantitative.

3. *Linear, Preplanned, and Structured*—design your study beforehand and then execute it according to your plan. Once the data has been gathered, analyze it according to your plan and report the results. Tyler was a dismal failure at following this rule. The original research plan was jettisoned and replaced by a series of new plans. Even the purpose of the research changed and that called for new methods and new types of data.

4. *Prefer Controlled Experimental Methods*—while other methods are acceptable it is always best to conduct experiments under controlled conditions. Where that is not possible, use quasi-experimental methods that attempt to stay as close to real experimental methods as possible. And where that is not possible use co-relational methods that give you a statistic indicating the degree of relationship between two or more variables. Tyler could not do a true experimental study where he randomly assigned caribou to one of two living situations—with packs of wolves in the area or without wolf packs. He could not even do a quasi-experimental study in which he found two naturally existing caribou herds—one with wolves in the area and one without—to study. The best he might

have done would have been to study many caribou herds and also count the number of wolves in each herd's region. A correlation of, say, –.78, would indicate that the more wolves around the more caribou were killed and eaten by wolves. Even that weaker type of empirical research was probably not possible. Instead, Tyler used a method called case study. Case studies are considered one of the least useful types of research by traditional advocates of the scientific method when trying to establish a cause and effect relationship. In essence, Tyler conducted what anthropologists would call ethnographic research and what educational researchers would describe as a case study. He used one of the weakest forms of research according to the rules of the scientific method. However, I suggest you watch the movie to see how well the "fit" was between the methods he used and the questions he wanted to answer. The fit was very good even though his research methodology violated some of fundamental rules for scientific research.

5. *Search for Universals: Laws, Rules of Behavior*—When using the scientific method, the purpose of research in the social sciences is to predict and control behavior. You do that through discovering universal laws of behavior that allow us, if we know the context, to predict how an organism will behave. This is the only one of the six characteristics of the scientific method that actually fits Tyler's research. He was looking for a general answer to the question of whether wolves are responsible for the decline in the caribou population.

6. *Research is Separate From, and Superior to, Practice*—In the traditional scientific method, research is a complex and sophisticated activity that must be done by specialists, called researchers, in controlled contexts. Once the researcher has discovered universal laws, the implications of those laws are communicated to practitioners. "Good practice" in this model involves doing what researchers say you should do. Tyler comes close to meeting this criterion. He was a specially trained researcher and he did draw conclusions from his research that was intended to guide practitioners. However, in this case he was not simply a researcher. He was both a researcher and a practitioner. He played both roles just as an instructional technologist who designs an instructional package and evaluates its quality plays both roles. Also, Tyler did not work in a controlled environment. He did his research in the natural environment and sacrificed the strict control of a laboratory. But in doing so he gained a great deal. For example, he did not have to generalize from the behavior of wolves in captivity to wolves in the wild—he was studying in the very environment he wanted to generalize too!

SCIENTIFIC METHODS, NOT METHOD!

Never Cry Wolf is a movie that could be profitably viewed in many types of research classes. It illustrates the folly of teaching "the scientific method." As Lederman points out, there is not one scientific method, there are many. Different fields of scholarship do not all adhere to the same scientific method. Rather, different disciplines have developed their own approach to research. In the twentieth century, for example, many American psychologists used tightly controlled experiments in artificial environments to study how children learn. At the same time, Jean Piaget in Switzerland was studying the behavior of his own children in semi- or uncontrolled contexts. Instead of preplanning his research Piaget would often adapt his method and procedure based on the behavior of the children and he often gathered qualitative data, such as comments from children about their learning, in preference to the quantitative data that American psychologists valued. Also in the 20th century, Margaret Mead changed our perceptions of other cultures with reports of her ethnographic research in exotic Pacific island cultures where she used participant observation as her primary research method. Her research environment was not even semi controlled. It was the natural context, and thousands of researchers have followed in her footsteps to study everything from the Fox Indians in Iowa to the behavior of teachers and students in inner city schools.

All of the scholars mentioned in the previous paragraph have had a major impact on how we think about society, schools, and learning. Their descendants have contributed to our growing knowledge about technology and education. Consider the six characteristics of the traditional scientific method:

- Objective
- Empirical
- Linear and preplanned
- A preference for experimental methods
- Search for universals
- A research–practice relationship in which research dominates practice

There is not a single one that is common to all, or even most, of the research that has influenced education and the social sciences over the past 100 years. Not a one! Every one of these "requirements" has been ignored, violated, and directly opposed by thousands of scholars, in many disciplines, who have produced useful research that influenced teachers, administrators, and policy makers. In spite of that, most "educational research" and most "doing research in educational technology" textbooks and courses continue to hold out the scientific method, as described above, as the best and most appropriate way for us to learn more about education and the best roles for educational technology in learning.

The list of characteristics that defines the scientific method is, at best, the guidelines for doing psychological research that were advocated by most of the major American centers of psychological research for part of the twentieth century. And even while that model dominated American psychology, there were advocates of other approaches. As early as 1948, Kurt Lewin, for example, began talking about action research methods that were based on work in real world settings and that encouraged the participation of many stakeholders.

THE MAIN ISSUE: WARRANT

Lederman's main point is that projects like the U.S. Department of Education's What Works Clearinghouse (WWC) attempt to select and disseminate information about how we should teach and learn. That advice comes from research based on variations of the scientific method. WWC and similar efforts thus attempt to create a classical link between research and practice. Researchers discover the truth through controlled experiments and pass on the implications to practitioners. Those practitioners are good practitioners to the extent that they follow the directives of the researchers. Lederman believes WWC is flawed for at least two reasons. First, he criticizes the underlying assumption of the project: that "scientific" evidence can only be provided by causal research designs (aka The Scientific Method). I applaud and agree with Lederman's suggestion that we use a much wider range of research methods and that we always keep in mind the foundational assumptions of the research frameworks we use. Further, Lederman argues that the WCC assumes "research findings from studies of teaching and learning can be generalized freely across contexts and situations if derived from studies following causal designs." This does, indeed, seem to be a foundational assumption of WCC—that universals, once discovered, can be widely applied. This is one of the major rocks upon which naive positivism in the form of the Vienna Circle foundered. Naïve positivism as advocated by a group known as the Vienna Circle, assumed that proper research using the scientific method could show us the Truth about human behavior and reveal universal laws of human behavior. However, the results of any particular study may be due to many factors—problems in instrumentation, a failure to separate theory from observation, measurement error, experimental bias, sampling error—that have nothing to do with the truth of the hypothesis under study. This led Sir Karl Popper to formulate an approach now called postpositivism that rejected some of the confidence of the Vienna Circle's logical empiricism (also called logical positivism) but maintained most of the tenets and strategies of the scientific method. This kinder, gentler positivism still dominates much of American experimental psychology but today there are at least a hundred alternatives, including postmodern psychology, that are based on different paradigms, ask different questions, and use different research methods. That pattern is also reflected in educational technology where critical theory, postpositivism, and interpretivism are movements that guide the research of many groups of scholars.

To this point I agree with much of what Lederman has said but I think he has not gone far enough. He presents the issues before us as a problem of limits. Some groups want to restrict our sources of information to the results of research based on "The Scientific Method" and Lederman believes there are many other valid and useful sources of knowledge. I agree, but I think this issue is not the core one. The core is how we decide what warrants our attention and our acceptance.

With hundreds of thousands of studies published about education and educational technology every year there has to be a way of deciding what to pay attention to and what not to pay attention to. By limiting their focus to "scientific" studies, especially experimental and quasi-experimental research, WCC has effectively eliminated about 97% of the educational literature. It can then concentrate on the remaining 3% and confidently report results that should be generalizable. What could be simpler? Base your directions to practitioners on the results of well done "scientific research"!

As Lederman points out there are many reasons to consider this approach simplistic. However, if we stop at this point in the analysis we miss two more important points. One is that ideology guides most decisions about what constitutes both acceptable research and acceptable practice. The other is that different audiences for research have different ways of deciding what warrants their attention.

IDEOLOGY: WE ARE SELF CONFIRMING ORGANISMS

In my early years as a professor I was unwittingly a participant in a study of how a scholar's beliefs influence decisions about whether an article should be published or not. Professors from two theoretical camps received a paper that supposedly had been submitted to an annual that would be published in a few months. They were asked to review the paper and recommend whether it should be included or not. There were two versions of the paper. In one, the theoretical beliefs of Reviewer Group A were supported by the results. In the other version the beliefs of Group B were supported. The results of the study indicated that reviewers who read the version supporting their beliefs were more likely to recommend acceptance while the opposite was true of reviewers who read a version with data that did not support their beliefs. Today there are hundreds of studies of reviewer bias that indicate the ideology of the reviewer is a significant influence on whether a paper is accepted to a journal or not. This is a specific example of what may be a general characteristic of humans—we have lower standards for information that confirms beliefs we already hold and higher standards for accepting information that disconfirms our beliefs.

That characteristic is a foundational issue when it comes to research. Whether we are researchers, editors, reviewers, or consumers of research, we prefer studies that tell us we are right and our opponents are wrong. Our ideology is a basic, primitive source of guidance when we do research and when we select what warrants our attention. Put another way, we don't decide what type of research we will consume and then develop our ideology, our beliefs, from reading research. Instead, we begin with our ideology and then we select research based on our ideology. Do you doubt this assertion? Consider this quote from Todd Oppenheimer (1997) in an influential article he wrote for *The Atlantic Monthly:*

> There is no good evidence that most uses of computers significantly improve teaching and learning, yet school districts are cutting programs—music, art, physical education—that enrich children's lives to make room for this dubious nostrum, and the Clinton Administration has embraced the goal of "computers in every classroom" with credulous and costly enthusiasm.

Oppenheimer is an outspoken critic of computers in schools and his reading of the research literature is that computers are a "dubious nostrum." Another critic, Larry Cuban (2001) wrote a book titled *Oversold and Underused: Computers in the Classroom,* and after reviewing the research he concluded that computers in schools have had very little impact.

In another book, titled *The Child and the Machine: How Computers Put Our Children's Education At Risk,* Armstrong and Casement (2000) said they "discovered that what had been excluded from the debate was scientific evidence. Proponents often claimed this research bolstered the argument for computer-based education, but in reality it struck a far more cautious, if not critical note. . . . So far the most that can be said about computer-based instruction is that vast sums have been lavished on a technology whose educational potential has yet to be proven" (p. xii).

I have cited three extensive studies of the research on computers in education that conclude we simply do not have the evidence that computers do anything good in education. Does that settle the matter? No. Consider these quotes from surveys of the literature on the use of computers in education.

Recent research consistently demonstrates the value of technology in enhancing student achievement. (Sivin and Bialo, 1994)

A meta-analysis of the research literature found "computer-assisted instruction in science education" is effective. (Bayraktar, 2002)

A review of the research on "computers as learning tools" concluded they are effective. (Schacter, 1999)

A meta-analysis concluded computers are powerful tools for reading instruction. (Soe, Koki, and Chang, 2000)

How can these two sets of conclusions be valid when they are supposedly based on the same research literature? The answer is complex but it is also simple. Simply put, we are self-confirming organisms and we tend to find what we expect to find when we select research that warrants our attention. In one review of all the studies of peer review that could be located, J. Scott Armstrong (1997) at the Wharton School of Business, concluded that:

Peer review improves quality, but its use to screen papers has met with limited success. Current procedures to assure quality and fairness seem to discourage scientific advancement, especially important innovations, because findings that conflict with current beliefs are often judged to have defects. (p. 63)

If supposedly objective and experienced journal reviewers have trouble keeping their particular biases and ideological preferences out of the reviewing process, it is likely that this is a problem for most researchers and practitioners as well. If I am correct, research will never "settle" disagreements about issues such as whether computers are effective in schools or any of a thousand other questions about teaching and learning. However, research will often be used to support established positions. This is amply illustrated in the current literature and I will cite only one example. In their book on how to fix American education, two conservative critics David Kearns and James Harvey (2000), who have connections to recent Republican administrations, advocate their solution—standards and testing. As authors of *A Legacy of Learning: Your Stake in Standards and New Kinds of Public Schools* they repeatedly say their solutions are based on research. However, at about the same time this book was published by the Brookings Institution Press in Washington, Howard Sacks (1999) wrote *The Higher Price of America's Testing Culture and What We Can Do to Change It.* In that book Sacks concluded that "The evidence revealed the very troubling and costly effects of our growing dependence on large-scale mental testing to assess the quality of schools, one's merit for college, and a person's aptitude for many different jobs. In light of the evidence, I was dumbfounded that mental testing was continuing to carve out an increasingly entrenched and unquestioned position in our schools, colleges, and workplaces" (p. xi). Sacks was dealing with the same issues and he sometimes used the same evidence, but the conclusions he drew from his review of the research are the opposite of Kearns and Harvey. Sacks is a liberal and Kearns and Harvey are conservatives. The difference in the two books was not research; it was the ideology of the authors.

If you still have doubts about the central role of ideology in the debates about education and educational technology I urge you to read Gerald Bracey's (2002) book about the attack on American public education. Bracey is a liberal commentator and the book is a direct attack on the conservative Republican view of American education as broken and in need of fixing. Bracey goes to great pains to point out how the Republicans misinterpret research, suppress and reject research that goes against their education ideology, and ignore published studies that contradict beloved policy. Once you have read Bracey, read Finn and Ravitch (1996) and learn how liberal teacher education professors have scorned good research on a group of teaching methods Finn and Ravitch call "instructivism" and instead adopt the unproved and ill conceived ideas of Dewey and constructivists. Bracey, Finn, and Ravitch present their views of American education as established Truths supported by research that proves they are correct and their opponents wrong.

Again, it is important to say that research is not the center of our major debates in education today. Ideology is. And, while both the major sides—liberals and conservatives—accuse the other of ignoring or misconstruing the available research, that does not mean research is at the center of the debate. It is often simply a weapon to advance one side over another.

BRIDGING THE GAP

American education today is a battle ground for two major ideologies—one conservative and one liberal (with a third, critical theory, playing a lesser role in the public debate). Advocates believe their side is right and the other wrong, and much of the debate, especially at the policy level, is couched in those terms. I am reminded however, of two poems by Robert Blake.

The Lamb

Little Lamb, who made thee?
Dost thou know who made thee,
Gave thee life, and bid thee feed
By the stream and o'er the mead;
Gave thee clothing of delight,
Softest clothing, woolly, bright;
Gave thee such a tender voice

Making all the vales rejoice;
Little Lamb who made thee?
Dost thou know who made thee?

The Tyger

Tyger! Tyger! burning bright,
In the forests of the night,
What immortal hand or eye
Could frame thy fearful symmetry?
In what distant deeps or skies
Burnt the fire of thine eyes?
On what wings dare he aspire?
What the hand dare sieze the fire?
And what shoulder, & what art,
Could twist the sinews of thy heart?
And when thy heart began to beat,
What dread hand? & what dread feet?
What the hammer? what the chain?
In what furnace was thy brain?
What the anvil? what dread grasp
Dare its deadly terrors clasp?
When the stars threw down their spears,
And water'd heaven with their tears,
Did he smile his work to see?
Did he who made the Lamb make thee?
Tyger! Tyger! burning bright
In the forests of the night,
What immortal hand or eye
Dare frame thy fearful symmetry?

The excerpts from Blake's poems suggest he was reflecting on how different the creatures of nature are, yet they are all part of nature. In the current context of education in America, perhaps it is also possible that the major ideologies—that sometimes seem as different as Blake's tiger and lamb, have something important to say to American education. There are numerous ongoing debates today that reflect underlying differences in preferred ideology. The debates are about basic as well as somewhat more complicated issues as illustrated by current issues in just one field of education—instructional technology:

- What do we mean when we use the term "educational technology"? (Luppicini, 2005)
- Are traditional, systematic, structured instructional design models are to be preferred over the newly developed "constructivist" ID models? (Willis, 1995; Willis, 2000)

- Does the increased use of "educational technology" in education improve the quality of learning? (Schacter, 1999)
- Is educational technology, as currently used in American schools, a significant tool in the "deskilling" of teachers? (Apple, 1994; Hellman, 2003)
- Should the traditional paradigms and ideologies used in the field (behaviorism, information processing theory, and cognitive science) be replaced with newer frameworks such as cognitive constructivism or social constructivism? (Albirini, 2007)

The list above is only a sample of the many, many debates that are ongoing in education. Most are important, and many scholars and researchers believe that when we get "a little more good research" the current debates will be conclusively settled and we can move on to other issues and questions. I am arguing that research cannot do that because many of these debates are not, at their core, debates about research results. Instead, they are debates about which paradigm or ideology is the "best" and research is only a tool to influence others to think the way proponents do.

At this point, further discussion is needed. If research cannot "prove" anything, if ideology is at the heart of most debates, why do research at all? Why even read research? I think there are many reasons. Research is a vehicle for influencing how others think about the issues that are important to you. Research is thus one of several channels of influence that can have an impact on other people's ideologies as well as professional practices. Thus, while research is not the Holy Grail or the sword in the stone in the legend of King Arthur and Excalibur, it is an important way of influencing others and it is worth doing. In addition, both reading the research of others and doing research yourself, can have a major impact on your beliefs as well as the way you practice your profession. Research is guided by, and used to defend ideology, but it is a two-way street. If you make the effort to remain open to alternative explanations and meanings, research can influence your ideologies as well.

SELECTING YOUR ROLE IN THE IDEOLOGY AND RESEARCH CONTEXT

You will find that different researchers and scholars adopt different roles as they do research. I think there are five main options and it is important to think about which of these roles fits you best because they call for somewhat different forms of research practice and also different types of knowledge and skills.

Radical Advocates (Political Officer)

In the movie *The Hunt for Red October,* the dual command structure of the Soviet military was highlighted. The Captain of the submarine Red October was the ranking naval officer but there was a *political officer* who also had considerable power. This pattern was also highlighted in Boris Pasternak's classic Russian novel, *Dr. Zhivago* when the military commander and the political commander of a Red Army unit disagree on whether Zhivago should be allowed to return home. The political officer was responsible for representing the "party line" and seeing to it that decisions were made according to party beliefs. In today's discussions about education and educational technology many of us will play the role of political officer. We will adhere to the party line of our preferred ideology, express our views in terms of what the party says we should do, and advocate the views of the party. Four scholars mentioned earlier in this chapter fit this model. Finn and Ravitch as well as Kearns and Harvey are political officers (though all four would probably have been in the White rather than the Red Army had they lived in Russia in 1920). However, Bracey and Sacks are also political officers but they represent another ideology. Much of the sound and fury about education today comes from political officers who are the radical advocates of a particular orthodoxy. Their research, and their interpretation of other people's research, reflects their role as radical advocates.

There are, however, four other roles you can play.

Opportunists

When I work in former Soviet Union countries I often come in contact with educators and politicians who have become ardent capitalists as well as advocates of Western education methods. For some of them this is a true conversion as well as an opportunity to express ideas that had been suppressed or hidden during the Soviet era. For others it simply reflects their lack of commitment to the foundational beliefs of the former system. If things change again, they will quickly and comfortably convert to the newest ideology because they have no depth of conviction and no investment in any particular ideology. They are willing to "go along to get along" and that is not necessarily a terrible philosophy of life unless you are a radical advocate. For still others, however, it is opportunism. The wind changed and so did the loyalties of the opportunists. Some of these people were devoted Young Communists a few years ago and when that era passed they took off their scarves with Lenin's picture and their red enameled hammer and sickle pins that were awarded to high achievers. Not long after that they were dressed in the power suits and ties of capitalism and were looking for deals.

Any change will attract opportunists. I suspect that some of the interest in integrating technology into teacher education during the 1990s was because the large PT3 grant programs from the U.S. Department of Education made it profitable. Now that the money has run out, many opportunists will drop that topic and move on to the next one with money behind it. I am not even sure that is bad. Opportunists work within the existing structure and manage to get resources to do things that might be impossible without their ability to take advantage of changing situations.

Pragmatists and Needs-Based Scholars

There is also another group of scholars who can be difficult to distinguish from opportunists. Some scholars look at their field and make a conscious decision to conduct research on a particular topic, or in a particular way, because they believe it is the most important thing to do at that moment in the development of their discipline or profession. In four or five years they may be doing something entirely different, but the reasons for doing the new research are the same as it was for the old research—it is what they believe is needed at that point. This is a rather large group in educational technology and there is much to be said for this approach. As new issues and problems arise, this group of scholars may be in the forefront of research and scholarship about them.

In my experience this group is also pragmatic. They consider not only what their profession or discipline needs; they also consider what is possible. For example, if one of their high need topics is "fundable" (e.g., grants are available), they may develop a program of research and scholarship on that topic. Later, if funding priorities change, the pragmatic needs-based scholar may shift to another topic he or she also considers a high need. This approach also has the advantage of keeping a scholar focused on topics that are at the forefront of concern in the field (critics might say it this amounts to "chasing fads" and "climbing on bandwagons").

Specialists

Specialist researchers generally focus on a particular topic—distance education, charter schools, staff development, the impact of simulations, problem-based learning, multimedia, technology applications in early childhood, organizational change strategies, or any of a thousand other topics. A specialist may also be an opportunist or a radical advocate but many are not. They are specialists because they have a strong interest in a particular type of information technology, a level of education such as higher education, a particular subject matter such as literacy or chemistry or foreign languages, or a teaching method such as anchored instruction or collaborative learning. Specialists are often relatively flexible in terms of their willingness to use different research methods and to work with diverse and even contradictory ideologies and paradigms if they can see that it may advance work in their particular specialty.

Translators and Interpreters

Another significant role to consider is that of translator and interpreter. Members of ideological camps tend to talk to each other and to read research that supports their views. They often find research from other traditions hard to follow and understand. Just as two people who speak different languages need a translator to communicate, sometimes different ideological groups need translators and interpreters to communicate. Two conservatives talking about accountability and how computers can help make schools accountable for learning probably will not have difficulty communicating with each other. Adding a political agent from the liberal camp to the conversation is more likely to bring it to an abrupt halt than to advance understanding. What is needed is an interpreter who understands both ideologies and can translate concerns and research results from one camp into the language and context of the other. This is probably the most difficult of the five roles but it is probably the most important if we are to take advantage of all the knowledge and expertise in our field. Unfortunately, the role of translator/interpreter is likely to be the most unappreciated and most difficult to understand. It requires the widest range of skills and it may also call for a thick skin. On the other hand, successful interpreters are likely to find the role very rewarding.

AN OVERVIEW OF THE BOOK

Books on research come in many flavors, and each flavor is designed to meet the needs of a particular group of readers. There are, for example, detailed "how to" books on everything from action research in schools to the use of the SPSS computer software to analyze quantitative data. There are also hundreds of introductory books on the basic concepts of research in education with titles like *Introduction to Educational Research* and *Foundations of Educational Research*. There are also books on specialized research methods such as case studies or focus group research as well as books on research in a particular field such as nursing, or educational technology. The massive (1,224 pages) second edition of the *Handbook of Research on Ed-*

ucational Communications and Technology was published in 2003 by Lawrence Erlbaum Publishers and is an effort by the major professional organization to present the current state of this field. The equally massive, third edition of the *Handbook of Qualitative Research* that was published by Sage in 2005, is an example of a reference book on a particular group of methods and theories. These are two of the many handbooks and encyclopedias that are available to readers with a serious interest in a particular type of research methodology or doing research in a particular field. These reference books tend to be comprehensive and to assume the reader already knows at least the basics about the topic. The book you are reading now is both more modest in its goals and broader in its purpose. It was written for readers interested in exploring a wide range of approaches to research in education and educational technology.

Qualitative Research Methods for Education and Instructional Technology was written for students and scholars interested in applying qualitative research methods to education and one of the specialty disciplines in education—educational technology (aka instructional technology, educational computing). This book is not designed to be comprehensive or exhaustive. Instead, it was written to give readers a foundational understanding of the ideologies, the general procedures, and the qualitative methods that are particularly applicable to educational technology research. I have attempted to accomplish this through a combination of original material and through a selection of relevant articles and papers that extend the discussion of research methods or serve as good exemplars of a particular type or approach to educational technology research. Many of these readings are available online. Readings are introduced at the end of each chapter along with questions you may want to consider as you read the article. Developing your own answers to those questions will be one way you can extend your depth of understanding about qualitative research methods in education and educational technology.

The 12 chapters in this book are divided into four sections. A brief summary of each chapter is given below:

Section 1: Foundations

Chapter 1: Wolves, Lambs, and Lions—Roaming the Research Range. The chapter you are reading now.

Chapter 2: What Is Research? Introduces a broad definition of research that includes traditional quantitative and qualitative research as well as scholarly methodologies from the humanities, the arts, and philosophy.

Chapter 3: Typologies of Research and Scholarship. Looks at ways of organizing and categorizing qualitative research based on factors such as the type of data collected or the guiding paradigm or ideology. Introduces two traditions in Western scholarship: Aristotle's empiricism and Plato's rationalism and points out how they have influenced Western thinking for over 2000 years. In this chapter you will be introduced to some of the foundational frameworks for thinking about research as well as some of the methods of research and scholarship including philosophical inquiry, theory-based research, Boyer's four types of scholarship (discovery, integration, application, and teaching), hermeneutics, phenomenology, and poststructuralism.

Chapter 4: More Greeks: Homer and the Sophists. Presents two more types of scholarship. One comes from the humanities traditions of Homer and the Greek poets; the other is a descendent of the sophists who were relativists to some degree and who taught the skills of rhetoric to their students. The chapter ends with an introduction to alternative sources of knowledge that range from professional practice knowledge to art and literature to rhetorical speeches and papers. More specifically, these alternative sources of knowledge include shared professional practice knowledge, narrative, auto-ethnography, rhetoric, qualitative case studies, design as research, clinical research, participatory action research, and professional discourse. There are also a number of non-traditional methods of disseminating the results of your work. They are introduced in this chapter as well: performance ethnography, documentary film, stories, and storytelling.

Section 2: Pathways to Understanding

Chapter 5: Purposes, Phronesis, and Bent Flyvbjerg. This chapter begins with an overview of the positivist/postpositivist models of research from the natural sciences and introduces Aristotle's three types of knowledge: episteme, techne, and phronesis. As a way of exploring the role of these three types of knowledge in the field of educational technology, I present a, perhaps, typical master's program in educational technology and look at the emphasis of the courses and experiences required, in terms of which type of knowledge is emphasized. The conclusion is that techne is, as might be expected of a discipline with technology in its name, a major focus. From this foundation, I explore the purposes of research using Aristotle's types of knowledge and Boyer's types of scholarship. The final section of the chapter is devoted to an exploration of Bent Flyvbjerg's radical proposal that the social sciences reconstitute themselves and become "phronetic social science." The implications of that for educational technology complete the chapter.

Chapter 6: Building Your Relationships With Research. This short chapter is an exploration of possible relationships with research and scholarship—from totally ignoring all forms on the one hand to, on the other, immersing oneself in one paradigm of research or scholarship and making it a life's work. The discussion divides the relationship into two parts—consuming research and doing research. As a consumer you should become a competent and qualified consumer of a variety of research that uses many methods and is based on many different theoretical and paradigmatic foundations. As a researcher/scholar, it is probably impossible for most of us to become a talented producer of research and scholarship across a very wide range of methods and paradigms. It might be better, through reading, mentorships, internships, and other forms of experience, to become good at a few methods and to become comfortable with a few guiding paradigms so that you are capable of contributing to the literature of your field. The last part of the chapter deals with the questions about disseminating your scholarship and addresses questions such as selecting your audience, deciding on a journal or other outlet, the format you will use, the importance of joining a community that shares your interests, and the question of open access journals.

Section 3: Pathways to Understanding: The Methods of Research and Scholarship

Chapter 7. Making Sense of the Forms of Research and Scholarship in Educational Technology. This chapter brings the disparate threads of the discussion together into a flexible but meaningful organizational structure that will help you understand the nature of the research enterprise in education and educational technology. The chapter begins with a discussion of the meaning of the terms research and scholarship. Then the chapter explores the major cultures of research and scholarship, from the humanities and philosophy to qualitative and quantitative research in the social sciences and education. The chapter ends with an exploration of the one of the major families of research methods: quantitative.

Chapter 8: Qualitative Research Methods. This chapter focuses on the second major family of research methods—qualitative. You will read about traditional qualitative methods such as observation, interviewing, and historiography in the first part of the chapter. Later sections look at applied qualitative research methods, and empowerment research methods such as participatory action research and emancipatory research.

Chapter 9: Methods of Scholarship from the Humanities. In this chapter you will explore a set of methods and theories that are increasingly used in education but are still rarely used in educational technology research. They are the methods, models, and theories that come from the humanities. The chapter begins with an exploration of the three major theoretical frameworks used to guide research in education today: positivism/postpositivism, critical theory, and interpretivism. Following that introduction you will study the major forms of humanities scholarship: hermeneutic inquiry, narrative inquiry, and post-structuralist inquiry. Within each of these broad families of scholarship, several members of the family will be discussed. For example, within hermeneutic inquiry there is critical hermeneutics, inter-pretivist/philosophical hermeneutics, and literary criticism/theory. The chapter ends with a discussion of how these methods and approaches can be used in educational technology research.

Chapter 10: Methods of Philosophical Inquiry. This chapter covers an often used but infrequently discussed form of scholarship. The first part of the chapter looks at methods associated with or related to philosophy. The three families of scholarship introduced here. There are many examples of these three forms of scholarship in the literature of education and edu-cational technology, but they are rarely covered in educational research courses. They are philosophical inquiry, theoretical scholarship, and rhe-torical inquiry.

Chapter 11: Design as Research. Instructional design was discussed brief-ly in earlier chapters, but it is the sole focus of this chapter. Instructional design, or ID, is one of the core activities of educational technologists and it is both a professional activity and a scholarly process that many educators, trainers, and educational technologists engage in regularly. It thus deserves its own chapter. That is particularly true today because ID is a very active area of scholarship, both as a topic of study itself and as a method for doing research. In this chapter you will study three traditions of ID scholarship—the Instructional Systems Design or ISD thread, the newer Design-Based Research (DBR) movement, and the young Constructivist Instructional De-sign (C-ID) initiative. However, before these three frameworks for doing ID research are discussed, the chapter begins with an issue that confounds and confuses many discussions of ID. That is the question of whether ID is primarily the activity of applying empirically derived rules of pedagogy to a particular teaching task (Pedagogy ID) or a process that guides us through a complex design procedure (Process ID).

Section 4: Dissemination of Results

Chapter 12: Forms of Communication and Conversation: Disseminating the Results of Scholarship. This brief chapter offers some advice on how to disseminate the findings of your research and scholarship. A few years ago the primary means of dissemination was the journal article but today there are many more options—including a growing number of print and online journals as well as blogs, wikis, digital video, and other forms of electronic communication.

Most readers of this book will already have completed at least one course on educational research and most will be familiar with both the standard topics covered in introductory courses as well as traditional quantitative and qualitative research designs such as control-experimental studies, correlational studies, and survey research. I also assume readers are familiar with basic statistical procedures such as means, standard deviations, t-tests, and basic analysis of variance. I have not attempted in this book to give you yet another introduction to those topics. Instead, the focus is on what I consider the most important "next level" topics that will help you move from novice and inexperienced researcher to a strong consumer of educational technology research as well as an informed beginning scholar who understands enough about the purposes, types, methods and procedures of qualitative research to make good decisions about what research to undertake and how to do it.

SUMMARY

Norman Lederman's paper *Never Cry Wolf* highlights a major issue not only in educational technology. It is one that resonates across the field of education. Research in the traditional "scientific method" mold is too narrow and limited to supply us with the rich and robust vein of understanding that we need. We must encourage and consume many forms of scholarship. However, I do not think research plays the central role in decision making that Leaderman implies. It is, instead, a tool, or weapon, that is used to support ideology. It is ideology that is at the core of many education debates today and the sooner we realize that, the sooner we can play a significant role in the determination of policy and practice. As ideology changes, research will also change. However, the conduct and dissemination of research is one of many influences that can change ideology. Learning to do good qualitative research in education and the field of educational technology will give you one more way of influencing the thinking and actions of others.

REFERENCES

Albirini, A. (2007). The crisis of educational technology, and the prospect of reinventing education. *Educational Technology & Society, 10*(1), 227–236.

Apple, M. (1994, Spring). Computers and the Deskilling of Teaching, *CPSR Newsletter, 12*(2), 3–5.

Armstrong, J. S. (1997). Peer review for journals: Evicence on quality control, fairness, and innovation. *Science and Engineering Ethics, 3,* 63–84.

Bayraktar, S. (2002). A Meta-analysis of the effectiveness of computer-assisted instruction in science education. *Journal of Research on Technology in Education, 34*(2), 18–32.

Bracey, G. (2002). *What you should know about the war against America's public schools.* Boston: Allyn and Bacon.

Cuban, L. (2001). *Oversold and underused: Computers in the classroom.* Cambridge: MA: Harvard University Press. Available: http://www.hup.harvard.edu/catalog/CUBOVE.html

Cuban, L. (1986). *Teachers and machines: The classroom use of technology since 1920.* New York: Teachers College Press.

Finn, C. & Ravitch, D. (1996). *Education reform 1995–1996.* Washington, DC: Thomas B. Fordham Foundation. Available: http://www.edexcellence.net/library/epctoc.html

Hellman, J. A. (December, 2003). An unquestionably positive step forward: distance education. *UN Chronicle.* Retrieved 4/18/2007 from http://findarticles.com/p/articles/mi_m1309/is_4_40/ai_114007096/pg_2

Kearns, D. & Harvey, J. (2000). A legacy of learning: Your stake in standards and new kinds of public schools. Washington, DC: Brookings Institution Press.

Lederman, N. G. (2003). What works: A commentary on the nature of scientific research. *Contemporary Issues in Technology and Teacher Education, 3*(1), 1–8.

Lederman, N. G. & Flick, L. B. (2003). Never cry wolf. *School Science and Mathematics, 103*(2), 61–65.

Luppicini, R. (2005). A systems definition of educational technology in society. *Educational Technology & Society, 8*(3), 103–109.

Oppenheimer, T. (1997, July). The computer delusion. *The Atlantic Monthly Online Edition.* Available: http://www.theatlantic.com/issues/97jul/computer.htm.

Sacks, P. (1999). *Standardized minds: The high price of America's testing culture and what we can do to change it.* Cambridge, MA: Perseus.

Schacter, J. (1999). *The impact of educational technology on student achievement: What the most current research has to say.* Santa Monica, CA: Milliken Family Foundation. Available: http://www.mff.org/publications/publications.taf?page=161

Sivin-Kachala, J. & Bialo, E. (1994). *Report on the effectiveness of technology in schools 1990–1994.* Conducted by: Interactive Educational Systems Design, New York, NY. Commissioned by: Software Publishers Association.

Soe, K., Koki, S. & Chang, J. (2000). *Effect of computer-assisted instruction (CAI) on reading achievement: A meta-analysis.* Honolulu: Pacific Resources for Education and Learning. Available: http://www.prel.org/products/Products/Effect-CAI.pdf.

Willis, J. (1995). A recursive, reflective instructional design model based on constructivist-interpretivist theory. *Educational Technology , 35*(6), 5–23.

Willis, J. (2000). The maturing of constructivist instructional design: Some basic principles that can guide practice. *Educational Technology, 40*(1), 5–16.

READINGS FOR CHAPTER 1

This book contains chapters written by the author as well as introductions to particularly important and relevant papers from the literature. The chapters written by the author provide an orientation and an introduction to qualitative research in educational technology, and the suggested readings from the literature expand on and add depth to the chapter material. Many of these readings are available online. When they are, the web address will be given in the citation. Most of the other papers and articles are available through widely used full text databases such as Academic Search Premier, ERIC, ProQuest Education Journals, PsycArticles, PsycInfo, and Sage Journals. These databases contain the full text of many journals. If your library has a subscription to these or other full text databases, you should be able to find most, if not all, of the readings that are not available directly from the Internet. You can then read them online or print them out for reading.

To help you orient yourself to the readings I will introduce each of them and pose questions that relate to both the content of the relevant chapter and the reading. The first reading is a paper by Abdulkafi Albirini who is at the University of Illinois.

Reading 1.1

Albirini, A. (2007). The crisis of educational technology, and the prospect of reinventing education. *Educational Technology & Society, 10*(1), 227–236.

This is a very ambitious paper, which is indicated by the title, "The crisis of educational technology, and the prospect of reinventing education." Do you agree with Albirini's chain of reasoning that goes from the assertion that information technology has had such a profound impact on society that it has sparked a crisis in education about "the place of modern technology in education" and that, in turn, has become a "crisis of educational technology?" How strong is his argument that this crisis is more theoretical and paradigmatic than practical (e.g., tied to issues such as inadequate teacher preparation, the digital divide, gender bias, and so on)? Do you agree with the history Albirini presents of computer applications in education and the underlying paradigms that guided them? Do you agree with the conclusion? "Instead of revolutionizing the educational system, educational technology has essentially reinforced the existing educational practices." If you do, why do you think the revolutionary visions of reformers supporting technology integration into schools were so different from the often bland and traditional ways computers were actually used in most schools during each era Albirina discusses? Finally, if Albirina's description of the crisis is correct and his explanation of why it has happened accurate, what do you think is more important—getting high quality computer resources and information technologies into schools or facilitating and encouraging a major shift in the theoretical and paradigmatic foundations of modern education?

Reading 1.2

Chris Johnson. (no date). *What is research in computing science?* Available: http://www.dcs.gla.ac.uk/~johnson/teaching/research_skills/research.html

Chris Johnson is a professor in the Department of Computer Science at Glasgow University. He is part of the Glasgow Interactive Systems Group and this paper is on the question of what is research in the field of computer science. I have included it in this book because the discipline of computer science shares many characteristics with educational technology. Perhaps more important that the fact both fields deal a lot with computer hardware and software is the relationship of computer science to other fields. Like educational technology, computer science creates products, ideas, and procedures that are used by professionals. The two fields also share a focus on design as a core professional activity and they both are currently debating the utility of "prototyping" or "rapid prototyping" in the design process. Also, computer science has tended to share a traditional research emphasis on methods that were borrowed from the natural sciences, again like educational technology.

As you read this paper ask yourself whether you are comfortable with Johnson's description of Empiricism? Do the research studies you read typically follow this model? Are they part of a process that fits the "dialectic of research?" What about Johnson's overview of hermeneutics and the use of this approach in computer science? Does it have a place? If so, what is it? And, would it also be useful in educational technology?

Reading 1.3

Willis, J. (2001). Foundational assumptions for information technology and teacher education. *Contemporary Issues in Technology and Teacher Education*, [Online serial], *1*(3). Available: http://www.citejournal.org/vol1/iss3/editorials/article1.htm

The final reading for Chapter 1 was written by me. It is an attempt to defined the "lay of the land" with regard to one important area of educational technology. That area is information technology and teacher education. In consists of a set of assumptions that can serve as a beginning point for thinking about scholarship, practice, and the interaction between the two. The assumptions are organized into three categories—assumptions about technology, about education, and about diffusion and organizational change. As you read this paper, consider each of the assumptions. Do you agree with each of them? Why? Do you have problems or issues with some? What are the issues or problems and how would you go about convincing someone that your viewpoint is more appropriate, accurate, or correct?

A broader question is what type of text this paper represents. It was printed in the journal as an "Editorial." Is the paper also scholarship? Research? How would you defend your answer?

Finally, the author makes a number of basic assumptions about the nature of technology, learning, and organizational change. Do these assumptions hang together across the three categories of assumptions? What, if anything, seems to be consistent across the three categories? Do the assumptions seem to be derived from a particular theoretical framework or paradigm? What makes you answer this last question the way you did?

CHAPTER 2

WHAT IS RESEARCH?

The term *research* is widely used in everyday conversation as well as in academic discourse. With such widespread use it seems odd to discover that there is considerable debate about just what research is. Are the two examples in the boxes below both research? Is one research but not the other? As you read these two summaries ask yourself what models, procedures, and assumptions are being used and made by the authors. When you finish, ask yourself whether either of papers are research and decide how you would defend your position. Finally, are you very confident that your position is the correct one? Or do you have doubts?

EXAMPLE 2–1

Glenn Gordon Smith, Sinan Olkun, and James Middleton (2003). Interactive versus observational learning of spatial visualization of geometric transformations. *Australian Educational Computing, 18*(1), 3–10.

The first author of this paper is currently a professor at the University of South Florida while Dr. Olkun is a professor at Abant Izeet Baysal University in Turkey, and Dr. Middleton is at Arizona State University. The authors were interested in several aspects of teaching geometry with the support of multimedia computer applications like Geometric Supposer, Geometer's Sketchpad, and Geometry Tutor. More specifically,

---

Qualitative Research Methods in Education and Educational Technology, pages 27–46
Copyright © 2008 by Information Age Publishing

they wanted to know if students who simply observed another student working at the computer on programs to develop spatial visualization learned better or worse than students who were actually using the programs themselves. Citing logical arguments and prior research they suggested there are reasons why Observation might be more effective than Interaction.

To address this question the authors divided 32 fifth grade students into two groups. One group played several computer games that should encourage the development of spatial relations. Some were similar to the popular video game Tetris and all required students to visualize and manipulate geometric figures in their head and then decide what to do next in the computer game. The table below illustrates the basic plan for the study.

Pretest	Treatment	Posttest
(Differential Aptitude Test Subscale)		DAT subscale
	Interaction Condition	
	High Visual Spatialization Students	
	Low Visual Spatialization Students	
	Observation Condition	
	High Visual Spatialization Students	
	Low Visual Spatialization Students	

Students in the Interaction Condition actually played the computer games while students in the Observation Condition watched students play the games over a video link from another room. Both groups— those playing the games (Interaction Condition) and those watching (Observation Condition) were asked to "think aloud" as the computer games progressed. Students in the Observation Condition could hear the student they were observing as he (all participants were male) "thought aloud."

Each of the experimental conditions had one group of students who were high scorers on a measure of visual spatialization skills (the Space Relations Subscale of the Differential Aptitude Test) and another group that scored low on the same measure.

The researchers calculated *t*-tests on the pretest and posttest scores of the Interaction and Observation groups. There were no significant differences between the groups on the pretest, the posttest, or the gains from pre- to posttest. However, when they looked at the performance of High and Low Visual Spatialization (HiVS, LoVS) students in the two treatment conditions they found that LoVS students in the Interaction Condition improved their scores from pre to posttest while the scores of LoVS students in the Observation Condition actually decreased. The reverse was true for HiVS group. Their scores tended to decrease in the Interaction Group and increase in the Observation Group.

The researchers also did a comprehensive analysis of the think-aloud data and the videotapes. From that data they developed some possible explanations for the differences between the HiVS and LoVS groups. For the LoVS groups they concluded that they "did not use strategies involving holistic mental rotation. They seemed not to have holistic mental rotation in their repertoire of spatial visualization strategies. . . . For these participants, the [Interaction Condition] allowed them to focus on the interactive transformation of individual shapes. [It] provided additional sense information (kinesthetic and proprioceptive) not present in the observational condition. While dragging or clicking the mouse, the [student in the Interaction Condition] experienced kinesthetic sense information from his fingers, hand and arm. Similarly, while manipulating the mouse, the pilot received proprioceptive sense information reflecting changes in positioning of his joints. . . . For some less skilled participants, the [Interactive Condition] encouraged the inclusion of holistic mental rotation in their repertoire of spatial visualization strategies. However, these less skilled participants were probably not sufficiently engaged by spatial visualization problems to benefit from the observation . . . condition."

"By contrast, [HiVS] participants . . . already had a more complete repertoire of spatial visualization strategies. Apparently, they had the required cognitive resources or motivation to deal with these problems. They had little to gain from [the Interaction Condition] and, in fact, [it] interfered with their subsequent performance on spatial visualization problems. [The Observation Condition], however, provided more skilled participants with a goal free situation where, unencumbered with interaction with the computer, they could focus on configurations and suggest hypothetical solutions" (p. 8)

The authors end their paper with a set of implications for practice based on their findings. For example, they suggest that "the decision of whether to use manipulatives and interactive computer programs for subjects involving spatial visualization, such as geometry and mathematics, should be made on the basis of individual differences among students. Less skilled students who do not have a full repertoire of spatial visualization strategies may benefit from interactive situations, but may be bored with more passive observation. In contrast, for more advanced students, interactive activities may actually interfere with pre-existing cognitive structures" (p. 8). The authors also recommended that teachers keep programs like Geometer's Sketchpad, WinGeom and Cabri in their classrooms because "a struggling student may greatly benefit from some theme-oriented interactive explorations or better yet some goal oriented tasks where interaction is part of the problem solving" (p. 9). However, for stronger students they recommended "being paired as a consultant with a weaker student who is actually operating the program" (p. 9). Finally, the authors draw implications for the design of educational software. They suggest that the think aloud procedure used to gather data in the study is a very good way to obtain information that would be useful in improving instructional material while it is being developed and they suggest that designers should consider including ways for software to decide what type of problems a student is having and create different remedial loops for different types of problems.

If you would like to read the full version of this paper it is available at http://www.acce.edu.au/journal/journals/vol18_1.pdf.

EXAMPLE 2–2

Bernard Poerksen. (2006). Digital Distinctions: An analytical method for the observation of WWW and the emerging worlds of communication. *Constructivist Foundations*, 2(1), 17–27.

Poerkesen is a professor at the University of Hamburg in Germany and his interest in this paper is on the growing conviction that information technologies, particularly the Internet, are not only changing themselves, they are also changing many, if not all, aspects of our lives. He cites new words such as cybercash, cybersex, cyburbia, and cyberpolitics as well as virtual neighborhood, virtual society, and teleshopping to illustrate the breadth of influence. He points out that there are many predictions about the future as well as many different ways of describing and organizing the current situation. He feels the need for some conceptual framework that will bring some clarity to what appears to be a rapid and chaotic transformation of both information technologies and virtually all elements of society. More specifically, he asks "How can the dynamics of the media evolution be monitored in a theory-guided way without elevating one's own approach to the only possible perspective for the observation of the world? In other words, is there a form of presentation, which in some way or other integrates the problem of its form, i.e., which remains aware of its own limitations and its intrinsically provisional character (particularly during a transitory phase of media evolution)" (p. 17)? He draws on radical constructivist philosophies of meaning and human behavior and proposes this solution: "A core element of the constructivist concept of observation can be used as a strategy of presentation and reflection. The approach provides a framework for sorting all the theses and predictions, for drawing up a comprehensive survey of all the valuations and speculations, and for probing future scenarios at least in a general way" (p. 17). Poerkesen uses a liberal but not quite radical form of constructivist theory as his foundation. He does not deny that there is an external reality that is outside the human mind. He does, however, deny that humans have any reliable means of directly accessing that reality. He and his group of constructivist theorists thus, "emphatically reject representationalist theories and realist conceptions of perception and share the conviction that objective knowledge is essentially unobtainable. They do not deny the existence of an external world; they negate, however, its unconditional cognitive accessibility and, therefore, insist on a critical examination of how concepts of reality are manufactured" (p. 18). He then goes on to insist that knowledge does not consist in a direct correspondence with an external reality (correspondence theory of truth) but exclusively and inevitably in the constructions of an observer, a knowing subject" (p. 18).

This is, essentially, a summary of a constructivist philosophy of science and of the constructivist foundations for research in the social sciences. It does not accept the idea that anyone can come in direct contact with the real world and thus, through special methods such as the scientific method, come to know exactly how the real world works. Thus, we do not "discover" the real world through careful and systematic research. Instead, we construct the real world by beginning to describe, and thus make distinctions. "What tends to be overlooked usually is that these distinctions are not out there in the world, are not properties of things and objects but properties of our descriptions of the world. The objects there will forever remain a mystery but their descriptions reveal the properties of observers and speakers, whom we can get to know better in this way" (von Foerster & Poerksen, 2002, p. 17). One of the major implications of the constructivist position is that "The claim of objectivity has to be given up because of the qualities of an objective description is that the properties of observers do not enter into it, do not influence and determine it" (p. 18). Poerksen then quotes Heinz von Foerster's definition of objectivity. "Objectivity is a subject's delusion that observing can be done without him."

From this perspective, Poerksen goes on to build a plan for developing a flexible and fluid way of understanding the digital world and the society it is helping to create. He proposes to use the "analytic method" which is, put simply, thoughtful and reflective observation of experience. Many case studies, for example, rely on the analytic method. It is holistic rather than particularistic, and it tends to make the author the "method" of the study because the author's background, experience, and knowledge is the framework from which the work is done. It is similar to Elliot Eisner's (1997) Conoisseurship model of scholarship.

Poerksen begins with the concept of distinctions—efforts to differentiate aspects of the world. He talks, for example, about distinctions such as data/information, education/e-learning, fact/fiction, heterarchy/hierarchy, literature culture/visual culture, online/offline, place/placelessness, and text/hypertext. Poerksen then proceeds to explore ways distinctions can be organized into groups or categories. The distinctions and broader categories are discussed in some detail but not with an eye toward declaring them THE distinctions of importance. Instead, he proposes a number of questions or issues that should be addressed relative to each distinction. One question, for example, relates to "the ontological status of the distinctions" and he points out that "the distinctions... do not have ontological correlates which can be proven in an ultimate sense. We are *not* dealing with distinctions to which truth is ascribed in any emphatic sense. This would contradict the constructivist position of the author" (p. 19). In other words, he does not claim that the fact/fiction distinction is somehow more basic or fundamental than a distinction you or I might propose. In fact, he acknowledges the "possible superficiality of some of the descriptions" and he invites others to enter a discourse. "The collection of guiding differences that delineate the contours of digital worlds of communication, which has been presented here, will no doubt require further extension"

If you would like to read the full version of this paper it is available at http://www.univie.ac.at/constructivism/journal/articles/2.1.poerksen.pdf

ARE THESE TWO PROJECTS BOTH RESEARCH?

The two examples were selected because they are so different. The first is a very traditional example of objectivist research based on a straightforward use of the scientific method. Figure 2.1 depicts the progression of the study in six steps.

Begin with a Theory. The goal of most traditional research is to test a theory and the first study is no exception. It does not matter where the theory comes from, but it is critical that a theory is the starting point because it is the theory you will use to make generalizations to situations beyond the experimental setting. In the report from the National Research Council titled *Scientific Research in Education* (Shavelson and Towne, 2002) one of the six principles of research in education was "Link Research to Relevant Theory". The Council proposed that because "It is the long-term goal of much of science to generate theories that can offer stable explanations of phenomena that generalize beyond the particular. Every scientific inquiry is linked, either implicitly or explicitly, to some overarching theory or conceptual framework that guides the entire investigation. Science generates cumulative knowledge by building on, refining, and occasionally replacing, theoretical understanding" (p. 3). This approach currently dominates defi-

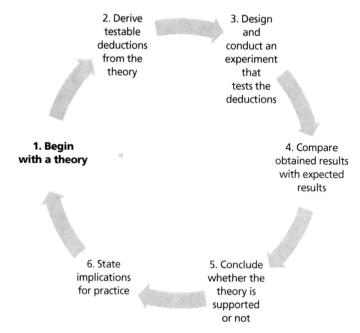

Figure 2.1 Diagram of the process of a traditional research study using the scientific method.

nitions of what "good" social science research is as well as good research in education and educational technology.

Derive Testable Deductions from the Theory. The spatial visualization study was applied research in the sense that it was attempting to answer very practical questions about whether interaction or observation of computer activities designed to support the development of spatial visualization are most effective. They were looking for broad and meaningful findings that applied to students in general but they hedged their bets by testing students for spatial visualization skills and dividing them into high and low groups. However, the goal was always to make predictions that were broadly applicable (e.g., not just applicable to the 5th grade students being studied).

Design and Conduct an Experiment that Tests the Deductions/Predictions. This is simple to say but difficult to do. There is a large and detailed set of requirements for acceptable experiments that can be trusted to provide tentative answers about whether deductions and predictions from theories are valid or not. Although there is a huge, healthy body of research in education and educational technology that relies on methods based on correlational statistics, the strongest proponents of the scientific method put control group—experimental group studies at the very top of the pantheon of research gods. And at that pinnacle the experimental studies that use random assignment of subjects to the experimental and control groups are the most highly valued. The Bush administration's Institute for Education Sciences considered random assignment so critical that it published a brochure titled *Random Assignment in Program Evaluation and Intervention Research: Questions and Answers* (available at http://www.ed.gov/rschstat/eval/resources/randomqa.pdf). There are many other requirements for good experimental research including the need to keep the conditions for experimental and control groups the same except for the one variable that is being tested.

Compare Obtained Results With Expected Results. Before the study has been conducted the researchers make theory-based predictions about the results. Once the actual data have been obtained, it can be compared to the predictions.

Conclude Whether the Theory is Supported or Not. If expected and obtained results are the same, then the theory is supported. Modern versions of the scientific method used in the social sciences and education, generally do not support the idea that a theory is "proven" because expected and obtained results are congruent. There is always the chance that the results were due to something other than the treatment conditions. It is thus, impossible to "prove" a theory in any absolute sense. Instead, if the results of an experimental study are positive, researchers conclude the theory was "supported" rather than proven.

State Implications for Practice. If a theory is supported, the last section of a research paper traditionally presents some implications for practice. Our spatial visualization study did just that. It offered a number of practical guidelines and suggestions for educators involved in teaching content such as geometry based on the findings of the study.

The first paper was relatively easy to diagram. It followed a linear, step-by-step process that is taught in thousands of research courses every year and used in hundreds of thousands of papers published and presented each year. Can we diagram the process and methodology of the second paper just as easily? No, not really. It is more difficult in part because the study does not follow a traditional procedure that is familiar to educational research-ers. Nevertheless, Figure 2.2 is an effort to visually represent the study:

There are several things to note about Figure 2.2. First, it is not intended to represent a linear process that begins with selecting an issue and ends with collaboration. Five layers of this triangle represent activities that may be done in any order. The process could, for example, begin with com-municating your perspective to others and move to selecting an issue. For example, collaborating and communicating with others may convince you that the issue you began with is not the most important one or the one that now interests you the most. Also, you do not necessarily work on just one of these actions at a time. You might be doing one, two, or more si-multaneously. It is thus a nonlinear process. It is also a recursive process, which is indicated by the symbol at the top of the pyramid (π). You do not

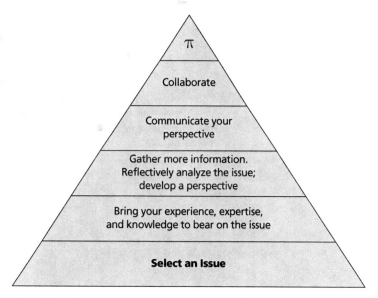

Figure 2.2 Visual illustration of the analytic method.

necessarily select an issue or gather more information only once. You may recycle through these actions many, many times. The recursive and nonlinear nature of the analytic process breaks some of the rules of the scientific method. For example, you are not allowed to select a different issue in the middle of a traditional research study. You must start over and gather new data. And, you are not permitted to change your hypotheses, or start with an interest in an issue, but no hypothesis, in traditional research. However, those sins are allowed, even encouraged, in many forms of qualitative and philosophical research. Finally, collaboration with others through sharing ideas, discussing, debating, reading, and problem-solving are important and essential ingredients of this method. That is, in part, because constructivists recognize the essentially social nature of knowledge. The traditional scientific method sees the role of others in your research somewhat differently. Others make value judgments about the quality of your work when you submit it for publication and they are expected to try and replicate your results (although this rarely happens) to test its dependability.

Now, after you have read the summaries of the two articles as well as my commentaries, are they both research? If you feel the first one is research but the second one is not, I have my work cut out for me because I believe both are research (or to use a broader term, both are scholarship). The issue boils down to this. Is there one relatively standard method of doing research that is common across all disciplines? The National Research Council answered that question with a resounding Yes! "At its core, scientific inquiry is the same in all fields. Scientific research, whether in education, physics, anthropology, molecular biology, or economics, is a continual process of rigorous reasoning supported by a dynamic interplay among methods, theories, and findings. It builds understandings in the form of models or theories that can be tested" (Shavelson & Towne, 2002, p. 2).

The remainder of this chapter will explore another option—that when used in education and educational technology, the term *research* (or the term *scholarship*) should be broadly interpreted to include many ways of coming to an understanding of the world around us.

As you read ask yourself what models, procedures, and assumptions are being used and made by the authors. When you finish, ask yourself whether either of the two papers are research and decide how you would defend your position. Finally, are you very confident that your position is the correct one? Or do you have doubts?

DEFINITIONS OF RESEARCH

Consider these definitions of research from James Cook University and from Universities Scotland:

Research encompasses activities that increase the sum of human knowledge. ...

Research and experimental development comprises:

- Creative work undertaken on a systematic basis in order to increase the stock of knowledge, including knowledge of humanity, culture and society, and the use of this stock of knowledge to devise new applications;
- Any activity classified as research and experimental development is characterized by originality; it should have investigation as a primary objective and should have the potential to produce results that are sufficiently general for humanity's stock of knowledge (theoretical and/or practical) to be recognizably increased. Most higher education research work would qualify as research and experimental development.

Research includes pure basic research, strategic basic research, applied research and experimental development.

Pure basic research is experimental and theoretical work undertaken to acquire new knowledge without looking for long-term benefits other than the advancement of knowledge.

Strategic basic research is experimental and theoretical work undertaken to acquire new knowledge directed into specified broad areas in the expectation of useful discoveries. It provides the broad base of knowledge necessary for the solution of recognised practical problems.

Applied research is original work undertaken primarily to acquire new knowledge with a specific application in view. It is undertaken either to determine possible uses for the findings of basic research or to determine new ways of achieving some specific and predetermined objectives.

Experimental development is systematic work, using existing knowledge gained from research or practical experience, that is directed to producing new materials, products or devices, to installing new processes, systems and services, or to improving substantially those already produced or installed.

The complementary activity of scholarship refers to possession of an extensive and profound knowledge of an academic discipline and the analysis and interpretation of existing knowledge aimed at improving, through teaching or by other means of communication, the depth of human understanding. (James Cook University (Australia), http://www.jcu.edu.au/office/research_office/researchdef.html)

* * *

Research is the creation of new knowledge. It can be categorised into three distinct types: basic, strategic and applied. Basic, or blue-sky research, is the pursuit of new knowledge without any assumptions about what it might lead to—essentially knowledge for its own sake. Strategic research is the pursuit of new knowledge which might, in principle, have a practical application but without a precise view of the timescale or nature of the application. Applied research is knowledge which is developed with a specific objective in mind, particularly the conversion of existing knowledge into products, processes and technologies.

Applied research may be the stage in which collaboration with industry is most likely, but basic and strategic research create pools of expertise and knowledge which benefit Scotland in many ways. Not only do breakthroughs with commercial potential first emerge from these types of research, but also the critical mass of knowledge needed to develop these breakthroughs into a marketable product is created here.

. . .

Often people think of research in terms of science and technology, but research takes place in every area of academic study. Research into our culture, our business practices or our economy can be as important as medical and scientific research. (Universities Scotland, http://www.universities-scotland. ac.uk/Facts_and_Figures/Research.pdf)

The first two of the definitions are relatively standard and traditional. At a very broad level they both define research as any activity that increases human knowledge. That sounds fine until you begin to explore what is meant by "increases human knowledge." Often the meaning applies only to the search for universal laws or rules. For example, the research question "Does the use of computer technology in schools increase the achievement level of students?" is stated in the tradition of new knowledge as a law-like conclusion. On the other hand, a question like, "Did the implementation of the new KBL early literacy program in the first three grades of the elementary schools in Elmore School District improve the reading and language arts performance of the students entering the fourth grade?" might be rejected as research. It is "program evaluation" and thus has only local implications rather than universal meaning. The definition from James Cook University states that the search for law-like knowledge is the goal of research when it states that research "should have the potential to produce results that are sufficiently general for humanity's stock of knowledge . . . to be recognizably increased." I will come back to this issue in a moment, but there are other issues with the first two definitions.

The James Cook University definition also makes a clear distinction between research and scholarship. Research is data collection and analysis for the purpose of finding law-like generalizations that can be applied broadly. Scholarship is "possession of an extensive and profound knowledge of an academic discipline and the analysis and interpretation of existing knowledge aimed at improving through teaching or by other means of communication, the depth of human understanding." This distinction is basically a distinction between someone gathering new data and analyzing it to come to conclusions about the world, and someone thinking about what they already know and coming to a conclusion. If we use this definition of research, then the study on spatial visualization described at the beginning of the chapter is clearly research while the second study is "only" scholarship.

The distinction between research and scholarship goes back at least to the Greeks. Aristotle was an empiricist because he gathered information about the world around him and used that data to draw conclusions about everything from animal behavior and astronomy to chemistry and zoology. Plato, on the other hand, was a rationalist. He relied much more heavily on rational thought and was suspicious of raw empirical data as a source of Truth. At James Cook University, Aristotle would be a researcher but Plato would be a scholar. The researcher/scholar distinction is widespread and commonly accepted. Robert Scholes, (2003), expressed the idea this way:

> Research, as I have said, is progressive; it involves invention or discovery of something new. And it often leads to new techniques or products, for which it is highly rewarded. Scholarship, by contrast, is more about recovery than discovery. It is about understanding more clearly or more richly the meaning of texts or events from the past, including how we got to our present cultural situation. And this is true whether the past is ancient, as in Nietzsche's Birth of Tragedy, or early modern, as in Michael McKeon's Origins of the English Novel, or quite recent, as in Jane Gallop's Around 1981. The end product of this scholarship is not new commercial processes or products; it is a pedagogy enhanced by the best knowledge available. Scholarship is learning in the service of teaching. In the humanities, we learn in order to teach. It is as simple as that.

But is it that simple? This approach to distinguishing between research and scholarship tends to encourage barriers between knowledge seekers in different disciplines. An English professor studying the writings of Tennessee Williams, for example, is a scholar while a chemist studying a new way to produce a heretofore expensive drug is a researcher. The distinction, which tends to run along disciplinary lines, might be satisfactory if there were not disciplines like education and educational technology that can benefit from both "research" and "scholarship." Education has traditionally cast its research lot with psychology (to be precise, American psychology) which means the scientific method of the natural sciences has been treated as the best, and sometimes the exclusive, source of new knowledge and understanding. In the field of educational technology there is a cost to be paid for the distinction between research and scholarship, especially when it involves a hierarchy of status with scholarship being considered of lesser value. The cost is that current and future researchers are generally restricted to learning a range of methodologies that do not include many of the procedures and methods used in the humanities, the arts, and fields like literary theory and philosophy. Yet, these methods can also provide important and valuable knowledge to the field. As a discipline we are weaker when these approaches are not available to researchers, either because they do not know them or because they do not consider them acceptable forms of research.

The definition from Universities Scotland is a bit more open than the one from James Cook University but it does not have the traction of Hull's definition of qualitative research.

In the last two decades, educational research has undergone a slow sea change as qualitative studies have gradually come into their own. Once rare, once reviled as unscientific or merely journalistic or too personal, or biased, or just "soft," such educational research now abounds in books, journals, and conferences, garnering at last considerable interest, respect, and even funding. The great strength of qualitative research is its "naturalism," its intimacy with real people in real situations, its concern for understanding human beings as they act in the course of their daily lives.

Qualitative researchers want to enter the worlds of the people they study, get to know them, and ultimately represent and interpret these worlds. It follows that qualitative writing tends to be rich with quotation, description, and narration, as researchers attempt to capture conversations, experiences, perspectives, voices, and meanings. This is research, it could be said, with words instead of numbers.

Although such research is wonderfully various, hailing from disparate disciplines and methodological traditions, qualitative researchers and the projects they undertake have some things in common. Qualitative researchers typically examine a small number of sites, situations, or people, and they usually do so over an extended period of time—weeks, months, or years. They gather their data by using themselves as instruments—observing, participating, interviewing. Although they formulate research questions to guide their inquiry, they expect their questions to change or sharpen as the study progresses. Qualitative researchers are interested in understanding the world from participants' frames of reference. Indeed, they want to take context fully into account, and to consider as well their own biases in their research. They assume reality to be multiple and shifting, and they see all inquiry as value laden and ideological. (Hull, 1997)

Hull does not try to create one definition that fits all research and she does not distinguish between research and scholarship. In addition, there is no talk of having to find law like generalizations that apply across many settings. Instead, she emphasizes the understanding of humans in local contexts as a goal or purpose, and she points out that while qualitative research may begin with a plan, that plan may well change many times over the course of the study. Hull's approach is similar to that of Christ Johnson who is in the Department of Computer Science at Glasgow University. In a paper titled "What is research in computing science?" that you read at the end of Chapter 1, Johnson (1996) argued that the reliance on empiricism and the scientific method is an issue in computer science because many of the problems in computer science do not lend themselves to that type of study. He recommends expanding the range of research methods used in the field to include approaches that would be considered "scholarship" rather than research by many. For example, he recommends hermeneutic methods which were originally developed studying the context in which sacred texts were written as well as the meaning of words and phrases in that context and in other writings of the same period. As Johnson points out, hermeneutic approaches "force researchers to observe the operation and use of an artifact within its intended working environments. The basic premise is that abstract models provide no substitute for real application. Similarly, the results of controlled experiments fail to provide generic results that can be accurately used to assess performance outside of those controlled settings. . . . Hermeneutic research, therefore, relies upon the interpretation of signs and observations in the working context rather than explicitly asking people about the performance of their systems. Hermeneutics techniques urge researchers to enter into the workplace."

Both Hull and Johnson offer a much broader and more inclusive definition of what research is. While the perspectives of Hull and Johnson suits my basic needs better than the first two definitions presented, there is another approach to what research is and how it is distinguished from scholarship that also has a great deal to offer.

The Boyer Report

For many years Ernest Boyer was President of the Carnegie Foundation for the Advancement of Teaching. From that position he led a number of studies on higher education. Before he died in 1995, he led an effort to redefine how research and scholarship was defined in American universities. *Scholarship Reconsidered: Priorities for the Professoriate* (Boyer, 1990) was an effort to redefine the work of professors and to bring different aspects of their work into closer harmony. Boyer described the proposal as an effort to "break out of the tired old teaching versus research debate and define, in more creative ways what it means to be a scholar" (Boyer, 1990, xii). Boyer redefined the term scholarship to include four types of work:

- The Scholarship of Discovery that is similar to traditional definitions of research. It is scholarship that adds to the "stock of human knowledge."

- The Scholarship of Integration that acknowledges the increasingly interdisciplinary nature of knowledge and recognizes as scholarship efforts to integrate knowledge across disciplines. As Boyer put it, the scholarship of integration involves "making connections across the disciplines, placing the specialties in larger context, illuminating data in a revealing way, often educating nonspecialists, too" (p. 18).
- The Scholarship of Application which involves the use of existing knowledge to solve social issues and problems. This type of scholarship is often practiced by educational technologists who use existing technologies and education methods to address significant issues in schools. The scholarship of application answers questions such as "How can knowledge be responsibly applied to consequential problems? How can it be helpful to individuals as well as institutions?" (p. 22). Boyer saw the Scholarship of Application as one way of breaking down the artificial and harmful distinction between research and practice. As he put it, "the one renews the other" (p. 23). Many of the service learning initiatives currently underway in American universities are supported and encouraged by the application of Boyer's idea of the Scholarship of Application.
- The Scholarship of Teaching is another type of scholarship that is often the focus of educational technologists. In defining work to improve the quality of teaching as an important form of scholarship, Boyer elevated it to a level it had rarely achieve in "research universities." Studying how to teach chemistry became research just as chemistry experiments had always been.

Boyer's four types of scholarship have a great deal to commend them and they have played a very important role in supporting expanded definitions of what counts as scholarship and research in many American universities. Twenty years ago, for example, a chemistry professor who developed an excellent multimedia computer program to support learning in introductory chemistry classes might have been given some credit in the service or teaching category when applying for tenure and promotion or when submitting her annual report for merit raises. Today that same professor would, at many research universities, be able to proudly include her software development work in her scholarship portfolio and also include the reviews and evaluations of her software just as she would reviews of books she had written.

Finally, although I will use the terms research and scholarship somewhat interchangeably in this book, the content of the following chapters will address ways of accomplishing all four types of scholarship as defined by Boyer.

SUMMARY

The question of what research is probably cannot be answered in any universal and definitive sense. This is particularly true when the term research is put up against the word scholarship. For some the term scholarship is broader than the term research and includes many ways of seeking knowledge that would not be considered research by those who reserve that term for studies based on the scientific method. For others, the two terms apply to what different disciplines do. English professors do scholarship, chemistry professors do research. Still others use the terms interchangeably.

Another important issue when deciding what research is relates to the question of whether the term applies only to the search for theoretical or basic knowledge, or can you do "applied" research that has a practical rather than a basic goal. Some groups try to distinguish between basic and applied work, and whether both types are called research or not depend on how ecumenical the group is. In education, there has been a tendency to use terms like "program evaluation" instead of "research" when the goal is to study something because the data is of local importance. It is only research when you are trying to generalize from the local study to other settings. This separation of research and evaluation has been called into question by interpretivist scholars because they also question the whole idea of doing studies to discover generalizable truths.

Perhaps Ernest Boyer's approach in the book *Scholarship Reconsidered* (1990) points us in the right direction. Scholarship is a broad and encompassing term that covers four major types of scholarship: the scholarship of discovery (e.g., traditional pure research), the scholarship of integration, the scholarship of application, and the scholarship of teaching. All these are critically important and worthy of effort and attention.

REFERENCES

Boyer, E. (1990). *Scholarship reconsidered: Priorities of the professoriate.* Princeton, NJ: Carnegie Foundation for the Advancement of Teaching.

Eisner, E. (1997). *The enlightened eye.* Englewood Cliffs, NJ: Prentice-Hall.

Hull, G. (1997). Research with words: Qualitative inquiry. *Focus on Basics, 1*(A). Retrieved April 18, 2007 from http://www.ncsall.net/?id=468

Johnson, C. (1989). *What is research in computing science?* Retrieved April 18, 2007 from http://www.dcs.gla.ac.uk/~johnson/teaching/research_skills/research.html

Scholes, R. (2003, Spring–Fall). Learning and teaching. *ADE Bulletin, 11*(16), 134–135. Retrieved April 18, 2007 from http://www.ade.org/ade/bulletin/n134/134011.htm

Shavelson, R. & Towne, L. (Eds) (2002). *Scientific research in education.* Washington, DC: National Academy Press.

Von Foerster, H. & Poerksen, B. (2002). *Understanding systems. Conversations on epistemology and ethics.* New Work: Kluwer Academic Publications/Plenum.

READINGS FOR CHAPTER 2

Reading 2.1

Thompson, A. (2005). Scientifically Based Research: Establishing a Research Agenda for The Technology in Teacher Education Community. *Journal of Research on Technology in Education, 37,* 331–337.

The first reading for Chapter 2 was written by Ann Thompson at Iowa State University. Dr. Thompson is one of the pioneers in educational technology and has been both a researcher and a journal editor. In this paper she looks at what the research agenda should be for the specialty area of technology and teacher education. However, many of the general conclusions and recommendations apply to educational technology and education in general.

Dr. Thompson wrote this paper near the end of the PT3 (Preparing Tomorrow's Teachers to Use Technology) grant program. It provided many millions of dollars to teacher education programs in the USA to integrate technology into those programs. A basic requirement of the grants was to conduct research/program evaluation to show what had been accomplished, and hundreds of papers and presentations were based on the work of scholars and practitioners working on PT3 grants. The recommendations in this paper come from a group of 60 leaders in the field who met in Washington, DC in 2003.

As you read the paper, please pay particular attention to the Primary Recommendations as well as the "Related Recommendations." Consider also, the relationship between them. For example, is the primary recommendation for "robust theoretical frameworks and models" compatible with the Related Recommendation that "both qualitative and quantitative methodologies are needed"? Some qualitative studies do not start with a theory and some do not plan to produce a theory or broad explanation as one of the results of the study. Some qualitative studies, for example, are efforts to develop an understanding of a particular context or project. Some simply "tell the story" of a project. Do they meet the primary recommendation criteria for "scientifically based research"?

What about another primary recommendation—"relevant predictions and careful generalizations." Should every study that qualifies as scientifically based research make predictions and generalizations based on the results? Why? Who should make generalizations in your opinion? Why?

Related Recommendation 2 asserts that research should "use multiple measures for formative and summative assessment." If you were justifying the extra effort and expense of gathering several types of data (e.g., test scores, interviews with teachers, parents and students, observations of classrooms) how would you justify using more than test scores? Could the study of a project to integrate technology into schools be focusing on a "bad" use of technology in schools even if test scores show an important increase in achievement? How? If you think this could happen, what other types of data could be gathered and analyzed to highlight this?

In your own field of interest, what question or topic could be approached using the recommendation that the methods of the study allow you to "disaggregate" the data?

Finally, in general, do you find papers like this helpful when you are thinking about research? Why?

Reading 2.2

Schrum, L., Thompson, A., Sprague, D., Maddux, C., McAnear, A., Bell, L., & Bull, G. (2005). Advancing the field: Considering acceptable evidence in educational technology research. *Contemporary Issues in Technology and Teacher Education* [Online serial], 5(3/4). Available: http://www.citejournal.org/vol5/iss3/editorial/article1.cfm

The second reading for Chapter 2 was written by the editors of some of the major journals in the field of educational technology. These editors developed a perspective on what types of research and scholarship are needed in educational technology, the appropriate methodologies for those studies, and the questions that need to be asked.

The paper addresses four issues:

1. What constitutes acceptable evidence?
2. How the field should be advanced?
3. How to facilitate effective research?
4. How to communicate and disseminate research results?

As you read the paper consider the answers the editors give to each of the four questions. Do you agree with the answers? Why? Do you find the answers comprehensive or do they highlight some solutions to the issue but ignore many others? If they are not comprehensive, what was left out?

Finally, of the recommendations in the paper (and recommendations not made but which you think are very important), which one is the most important to implement by the scholarly and professional organizations? The government? Editors? Graduate programs that prepare scholars and practitioners? Researchers and scholars? Schools and practitioners? Why?

Reading 2.3

Thomas Reeves. (current issue). *The scope and standards of the Journal of Interactive Learning Research.* Available: http://www.aace.org/PUBS/jilr/scope.html

The third reading is by Thomas Reeves at the University of Georgia. Dr. Reeves is Editor of the *Journal of Interactive Learning Research* (JILR) and a very active researcher himself as well as the author of many articles on research in educational technology.

This reading is actually the introduction to JILR but it is much more comprehensive than the typical overview of a journal at the front or back of each issue. Reeves situates JILR in the contemporary and historical context of scholarly publications and notes the critical role peer review has played in scholarly publishing as well as the central role of the concept of verifiability. What do you think of his way of both keeping these two important concepts—peer review and verifiability—while also expanding them through methods such as posting drafts of papers on the journal web site where others can critique them and discuss issues with the author? Why would this be useful to the author? To the field?

What do you think of the list of Old and New Assumptions about Learning? Consider the last ten decisions you have made about teaching/learning. Which ones were based on "old" assumptions and which on "new" assumptions?

Does the list of research goals cover the types of questions you want to find the answers to in the existing literature? In the research you want to do yourself? Can you think of other goals that are important in educational technology? What about instructional design work? Does it fit into one or more of the broad goals listed in Figure 2.1? What about the methods listed in Figure 2.2? Does instructional design obviously fit in one of those broad categories?

CHAPTER 3

TYPOLOGIES OF RESEARCH AND SCHOLARSHIP

This chapter builds on the previous chapter through an exploration of the many forms of research and scholarship that exist or can exist in the field of educational technology. The chapter is organized around ways of categorizing research and scholarship into different groups or families according to characteristics such as the methods used, and the theoretical framework. Boyer's four types of scholarship is, of course, one of the more popular organizing frameworks in common use today.

> Surely, scholarship means engaging in original research. But the work of the scholar also means stepping back from one's investigation, looking for connections, building bridges between theory and practice, and communicating one's knowledge effectively to students. Specifically, we conclude that the work of the professoriate might be thought of as having four separate, yet overlapping, functions. These are: the scholarship of *discovery*; the scholarship of *integration*; the scholarship of *application*; and the scholarship of *teaching*. (Boyer, 1990, p. 16)

All of Boyer's types of scholarship are routinely a part of the work of educational technology scholars and we often read papers in journals or listen to presentations at conferences that illustrate the vigor of all four of Boyer's forms of scholarship in our field.

Qualitative Research Methods in Education and Educational Technology, pages 47–81
Copyright © 2008 by Information Age Publishing
47

However, Boyer's categorical scheme is not the only way of organizing research and scholarship into groups or families. His types focus our attention primarily on the general purpose of scholarship:

- to discover basic knowledge about a topic,
- to integrate knowledge from several disciplines to address a problem, question, or issue,
- to apply knowledge to a real world problem,
- or to improve the quality of teaching and learning.

These broad purposes can also be broken down into more specific purposes, but there are times when other ways of thinking about research and scholarship are also important. One of those ways focuses on the methods used in the study.

METHODOLOGIES IN EDUCATIONAL TECHNOLOGY

Methodology is the general term for the procedures, steps, and actions of scholarship and research. For example, a sociologist may use interviews to gather data on the impact of computers in the homes of middle grades students. Interviewing is one popular methodology that has been used in many educational technology studies. On the other hand, psychologists often do experimental studies such as comparing the performance of students using a new computer-supported instructional method with students using a traditional method. There are many versions of the experimental method that can be used in instructional technology research, and some scholars argue that experiments are the only valid source of new knowledge and understanding. However, if you look at scholarly journals in education such as the *Journal of Philosophy of Education* or *Educational Philosophy and Theory*, you would not likely find a single article that uses any form of experimental method. Experimental scholarship is one, but only one, of many useful methods.

Below is a list of the articles published in the February, 2007 issue of the *Journal of Philosophy of Education:*

- *Knowledge and Skills for PISA—Assessing the Assessment* by Nina Bonderup Dohn. Uses conceptual, theoretical, and logical arguments to criticize a process for evaluating international students, the Programme for International Student Assessment (PISA) and concludes that it is very flawed.
- *Wellbeing and Education: Issues of Culture and Authority* by John White. The author critiques the philosophical foundations of arguments

that make definitions of wellbeing fixed and universal. He argues that they are actually culturally relative and thus products of culture. If that is true, he believes methods from the fields of aesthetics and art criticism are useful frameworks for thinking about wellbeing and that a democratic rather than elitist approach is most appropriate.

- *Disability, Dependency and Indebtedness?* By John Vorhaus. The paper explores the relationship between dependency and human learning. The author argues that dependency has been thought of mainly through attention to our most severe vulnerabilities and disabilities. He suggests that all humans are disabled and vulnerable in different ways in different stages of life and that these disabilities and dependencies should be built into theories and explanations of how humans learn and the relationship between learner and teacher.

- *Essentialism Regarding Human Nature in the Defence of Gender Equality in Education* by Katrinina Holma. This is a paper about the nature/ nurture question. The author reviews the major philosophies of human nature with a focus on what the ideal meaning of gender equality should be from the perspective of each philosophy of human nature. She identifies three alternative philosophies of human nature—essentialist, subjective, and cultural, and suggests that an essentialist account of human nature is the one most able "coherently to justify the educational pursuit of this ideal [of gender equality]. She describes the essentialist position as "the idea that there are some features common to all human beings (independent of individual, cultural and historical factors) that are conducive to a good life and human flourishing. She ends the paper with an explanation of how to deal with some of the major criticisms of essentialism, including the naturalistic fallacy (e.g., that what we see in nature is the norm and that it is therefore good).

- *How to Think about Environmental Studies* by Robert L. Chapman. Chapman traces the emergence of the discipline called Environmental Studies and explores the root causes of the lack of coherence and contradictory nature of the field. He rejects the idea that the discipline is in turmoil because it has adopted curricular universalism and thus does not have a unifying central concept that guides its development. He also rejects the explanation that other disciplines are resisting ceding territory to the new field (academic territorialism). Instead he believes problems such as lack of coherence are signs of a deeper problem that is, at its heart, philosophical. That problem, considered philosophically, is the failure to see that values are critical in shaping an emerging field. He suggests that values are a part of applied philosophy and that "Environmental Studies is inherently part of the philosophical enterprise, as such it belongs with the humanities."

- *Intersubjective Recognition and the Development of Propositional Thinking* by Krassimir Stojanov. The paper is an argument that the philosophy of education would be improved if new ways of thinking about propositional thinking that acknowledge the subjective nature of the process were given greater attention.
- *The Lure of Evil: Exploring Moral Formation on the Dark Side of Literature and the Arts* by David Carr and Robert Davis. This paper points out that the influence of art in society has been debated for ages. Plato, for example, wanted to exclude artists from his ideal state because they had a negative impact. The authors explore the relationship between the artistic, the aesthetic, and the moral (as well as the immoral and morally ambiguous). They suggest that the openness and freedom inherent in liberal-democratic societies comes with a concern that literary and artistic trends of an open society may actually have a corruptive influence on youth. One example of this is tension between openness and the "need" to protect children. The authors present arguments that efforts at "moralizing" are "mostly wrongheaded and unsustainable."
- *Lessons of Solitude: The Awakening of Aesthetic Sensibility* by Angelo Caranfa. The value of solitude as a part of learning is the focus of this paper with an emphasis on the need to provide a better balance between emotions on the one hand and intellect on the other, as well as between "action and contemplation." Caranfa believes the intellect and action components of experience and learning are emphasized today at the expense of emotion and contemplation. He proposes a method of instruction (aesthetic education) that will help students develop their "human qualities" by "paying attention to the things of Beauty." The approach "draws from theology, philosophy, the sciences and visual art; and, it is guided by an explanatory perspective that is constructive."

None of the papers in this issue of the journal are experimental or even quantitative. They are all reasoned arguments that use logic, analysis, reference to other ideas and concepts, and reflection to make the case for a particular belief, position, or assertion. The methodologies they use come from the methods of philosophical analysis supported by rhetorical skills, and the traditions of logic, argument, and discourse. Conducting this type of scholarship is rarely "taught" in educational technology graduate programs, yet you will find it in many educational technology journals and books. It is one of the dirty little secrets of our field that while we sometimes officially criticize this form of scholarship, it has actually been, and is, very influential in the field. Consider just two examples.

A THEORETICAL AND PHILOSOPHICAL BOOK

Thomas Duffy and David Jonassen (Eds), (1992). *Constructivism and the technology of instruction: A Conversation.* Mahwah, NJ: Lawrence Erlbaum.

This book, edited by Thomas Duffy at Indiana University and David Jonassen, now at the University of Missouri, was published in 1992. It would already be long out of print if it had been about the newest version of *Dreamweaver* or the best method of pressing educational laserdiscs. Even a book of research on educational technology would be showing its age 16 years later. However, this book has been, and continues to be, an influence in the field because it is a set of 12 chapters about the value and place of constructivist theory in educational technology. The chapters were written by some of the leading lights of our field, some staunch advocates of constructivism and some eternal opponents. A few of the authors cite some empirical research to argue for their particular position but the great majority do not. They use the same types of philosophical and theoretical arguments, links to other theories and concepts, and rhetorical tools that authors in the *Journal of Philosophy of Education* used. One of the best examples of this type of philosophical and theoretical argument is the second chapter in the book—*Theory into Practice. How Do We Link?* which was written by Anne Bednar, Donald Cunningham, Thomas Duffy, and J. David Perry. These authors make a reasoned and comprehensive argument for taking an epistemological and paradigmatic stand and then using it stand to guide practice. They argue for epistemological and paradigmatic purity (and that such purity should be based on a constructivist paradigm and constructivist epistemology) and against a promiscuous use of multiple, often conflicting, theories. While I do not completely agree with the position the authors take, their chapter is a very good example of the thoughtful, reflective type of philosophical and theoretical reasoning that Plato might have used.

A THEORETICAL AND PHILOSOPHICAL ARTICLE

William Winn. (1997, January/February). Advantages of a Theory-Based Curriculum in Instructional Technology. *Educational Technology,* 34–41.

Winn's article is a proposal to change the curricula of graduate programs in educational technology. He is particularly concerned with the balance of theoretical knowledge versus "how-to-do-it" knowledge. Winn believes there is too much how-to-do-it content in graduate programs and too little "why-do-it" or theoretical knowledge. As he put it, "Theory is played down in favor of being practical. . . . This is dangerous because it implies that instructional theory is finite and knowable" (p. 37). Winn believes that while educational technology is an applied field where graduates are expected to accomplish professional tasks when they graduate, students still need theory because the *how to* procedures they are taught "often don't work." Thus, students will need a framework for thinking about and resolving the inevitable problems that come up at work. Few, if any, of the rules of practice are so consistently and dependably true, and that means students need more than rules to follow if they are to avoid failure on a regular basis. He points out that even some supposedly well established laws of learning do not always apply—"knowing that providing knowledge of results may sometimes lead to better retention and comprehension and sometimes may not, there can be no valid prescriptive principles about providing knowledge of results in instruction" (p. 38). To deal with the unpredictability of the instructional design and deployment process Winn proposes his famous "first principles" which he acknowledges is similar to Donald Schon's "reflection in action." First principles are guiding ideas and concepts that are not prescriptions. Instead they are theory-based general guidelines that help the educational technologist decide what to do next. In Winn's words first principles require "the designer to reason to one step removed from the immediate problem at a more abstract level. For example, when an instructional prescription fails, the designer approaches the problem through learning theory. If knowledge of results (an instructional prescription) fails to produce learning, the designer does not try another instructional prescription but rather thinks through what processes are engaged (learning theory) when the student is processing the feedback. This knowledge may lead to the selection of an entirely new approach, perhaps without any feedback at all, rather than to an attempt to improve the feedback. It may lead to the invention, on the spot, of a new instructional principle" (p. 39). Because of his belief in the importance of theory, Winn argues that "any successful practitioner or researcher needs to be thoroughly versed in at least the immediately underlying discipline to his or her own. A good instructional designer knows psychology. A good architect knows engineering" (p. 40). Winn believes the courses in university graduate programs can be very good at teaching theoretical knowledge and First Principles. He believes they should focus on that and leave much of the how-to skills to internships, practica, and the employer. Winn is, in essence, proposing that graduate programs help students acquire theoretical knowledge and habits of thinking that prepare them to think on the job rather than simply apply prescriptions they have memorized. He illustrates how this can be done by describing classes he teaches and how he grades the papers produced. "Good grades go to students who say, 'I did it this way because Doe (1989) said it should be done this way.' Better grades go to those who say, 'in spite of what Doe (1989) said, I did it this way because.' The best grades go to those who say, 'In spite of what Doe (1989) said, I did it this way. Doe is wrong because and here is evidence of the greater effectiveness of my approach'" (p. 40). Winn's paper is a classic that will likely be read for many years.

TWO TRADITIONS: PLATO'S RATIONALISM AND ARISTOTLE'S EMPIRICISM

At its foundation, Winn's proposition is that empirical evidence is not likely to ever bring us to the point where we can confidently follow "evidence-based" prescriptions that have been developed to solve most of the presenting problems that face educational technologists. He argues that the ability to think rationally is a very important skill for the educational technologist. Winn's position requires attention to many forms of research and scholarship and to a thoughtful process of analysis and application in your particular work context. It contrasts with the more "recipe-like" approach of proponents of "evidence-based" educational technology practice where the responsibility of the educational technologist is to find the best "scientific" research and then follow the implications of that research. For more information on evidence-based educational technology practice see the article at http://eduscapes.com/tap/evidence.html. Also, the International Society for Technology in Education has established an online resource, the Center for Applied Research in Educational Technology (CARET) to help educational technologists locate research studies and information about conducting scientific research. The site is at http://caret.iste.org/ and while the Center does support the idea that scientific research is invaluable to the field, it includes many other forms of scholarship in its resources. In fact, the Center has developed an interesting typology to categorize useful papers. The structure below is from CARET's web site:

CARET: DEFINITION OF STUDY TYPES

Categorizing and Rating the Study: CARET has determined that there are four types of studies or information resources that are very relevant to educators who need to know more about the how electronic learning resources can be most effectively integrated into instruction and with the greatest impact possible on teaching and learning. Studies fall into four categories or types as follows:

A **General Articles and Expert Positions:** These are articles that describe processes, strategies, approaches, theoretical models, policies, curriculum or technology using standards, that may or may not allude to full-scale evaluation or empirical studies. Often such articles are based on experience, observations, and ideas proposed by the author(s). Examples include the ISTE standards, National or State technology plans, technology use planning guidelines and templates, testimony to commissions and legislative bodies, professional association platforms, etc. Type A information resources will be rated and designated a "level 1, 2, or 3" according to the following rubric:

  Level 1: The report is clearly documented by research or credible evaluations, provides clearly stated recommendations that can be easily applied in a wide variety of educational settings and would help inform educational technology planning and/or policy decisions to a wide audience.

  Level 2: The report is based on some type of consensus, discusses examples and shows awareness of available methods, research or evaluation studies on the topic, and would help inform educational decisions.

  Level 3: The report is basically one person's/one group's opinion/experience (e.g., outlining a theory or describing a methodology or analysis technique), may or may not be supported by documentation or research, is primarily of use in program implementation decisions.

B **Descriptive and Survey Studies:** These studies are descriptive research and typically use data derived from surveys, case studies, or more qualitative methods for gathering the information to inform the conclusions and recommendations of the study or report. Type B information is often data collection to yield new information, generate clearer questions or needs identification, and focus on specific projects or settings—the primary intent is to synthesize emerging patterns. Examples range from single project case studies to national studies such as the CEO Forum report, NCES Surveys on technology access in schools, meta-analysis reports of studies such as the recent SIIA report on technology effectiveness, state-wide or large scale needs assessments, Quality Educational Data (QED) and Market Data Retrieval (MDR) surveys, and many others.

Level 1: The data collection methods are clearly explained and credible with multiple measures, are current, could include strong mixed methods research, with adequate sampling and the data collected can easily justify the conclusions drawn from the study.

Level 2: The data collection methods are credible with validated surveys and/or other methods are clearly described such as observational strategies, case study methodologies, the data or information is current.

Level 3: The data collection—is focused on a limited sample of the population (e.g., single project case study)—and has minimal application in terms of generalizing the findings.

C   **Formal Evaluation Studies:** These are evaluation studies that assess the extent of implementation and impact of a specific program or project and usually emphasize needs assessment and/or formative evaluation methods designed to provide ongoing feedback to program or project managers. Impact or summative data is used to estimate the extent of change in the targeted population based on particular project or program interventions. Evaluation studies tend to focus on specific contexts of particular grants or projects with no attempt to generalize beyond the cases at hand. They often use a range of qualitative and quantitative tools but rarely use control or comparison groups and statistical methods to test specific hypotheses. Examples of such studies include evaluations of Technology Innovation Challenge Grants (TICG), Star Schools, Preparing Tomorrows Teachers for Technology (PT3), National Science Foundation (NSF) projects and programs, as well as a variety of state and privately supported programs, initiatives, and/or products.

Level 1: The evaluation includes and justifies valid and relevant measures and clearly describes the specific project interventions that contribute to the program or project outcomes and then provides sufficient contextual information for someone to generalize and possibly replicate the results by adopting the program in another location.

Level 2: The evaluation clearly describes design, the measures used and how they were developed or selected and analyzed to provide answers to specific evaluation questions that are directly related to the goals and objectives of the project.

Level 3: The evaluation is not thoroughly described in terms of theory base, design, methods, findings, and summary/recommendations. Rather, one or more of these components is emphasized in sufficient detail for replication or decision making.

D   **Formal Research Studies:** These studies are quantitative research studies, which incorporate a formal research design to test a hypothesis with validated measures. These studies should document that this research can be replicated or is generalizable to other settings. The criteria used for reviewers to judge the level or extent of validity of studies is adapted from the Fouts (1999) model for rating educational research according to level of depth and empirical validity. An example would include a study of a specific computer delivered curriculum in the area of primary level reading in comparison with a textbook delivered curriculum with variables such as curriculum content and student characteristics are held constant. The design allows for a statistical test of the specific differences found between the two groups on a validated measure that is relevant to the skills and knowledge intended to be developed.

Level 1: The study must incorporate a formal research design to test a hypothesis with validated quantitative measures. The study must clearly document that the results found in the initial evaluation or research have been, or have a high probability of being replicated in other settings, locations, or contexts.

Level 2: A level 2 study must incorporate a formal research design to test a hypothesis with validated quantitative measures and can be backed with qualitative measures to provide more descriptive information in describing the findings.

Level 3: This level of study would probably be described as research but upon closer inspection relies on surveys and measures that are not triangulated. This study tends to lack a clear relationship between the intervention studied and the outcomes attained due to inadequate research design.

The CARET system divides the useful literature into four broad categories that range essentially from "one person's opinions" to "formal research." Within each category papers can be graded for quality from 1 to 3 based on how well they meet the criteria developed for the category. CARET defines "research studies" as "quantitative research studies, which incorporate a formal research design to test a hypothesis with validated measures." CARET's ranking system clearly puts traditional "scientific research" at the pinnacle of the status hierarchy while other sources of knowledge are given much lower status. The CARET system also makes the traditional distinction between evaluation studies and research studies. Basically *evaluation studies* look at the effectiveness of a program or approach in one setting and tries to answer questions about whether "it works" in that setting. *Research studies* are conducted to answer more universal questions such as "does discrete phonics instruction supported by computer assisted instruction improve reading skills?" Such a question asks for an answer that transcends the particular context in which the study was conducted. It asks for answers that apply generally, not locally, and assumes that what researchers discover can be generalized to other settings. It is, in essence, a question about the laws of learning rather than the success of a local project. Most approaches within the qualitative framework have given up the idea that research can bring us to law-like conclusions that, once discovered, can be applied in recipe fashion to many other settings. Thus, the CARET system represents the traditional view of what "good" scholarship and research is. While it is more flexible than the standards for quality research adopted by the Bush administration's Institute for Education Sciences, it is clearly a member of the same family.

Winn's position is much broader and much more ecumenical. He would probably accept and value scholarship from all four of the CARET categories and he would not likely accept the hierarchical system inherent in the CARET typology that values experimental research over all other modes of scholarship.

Winn's position is both new and old. In one form or another it has been around for more than 2000 years. It has its origins with two giants of Greek intellectual thought. In the 19th century the English writer Samuel Taylor Coleridge proposed that "every man is either a Platonist or an Aristotelian" (quoted in Murphy, Katula, Hill, & Ochs, 1983, p. 28)

Aristotle and Plato took different sides on whether the royal road to knowledge is *empiricism* or *rationalism*. Aristotle believed in and applied the empirical approach. The best way to know more about the world was to study it systematically. In contrast to Aristotle's empiricism, Plato advocated rationalism. Informed thinking was his preferred way of discovering the Truth. These two approaches, empiricism and rationalism, are still with us today. Winn's paper is a plea for including more rationalism, more theory and thought, in educational technology graduate programs. He does this because, like Plato, he does not believe the empirical approach will ever give us precise, dependable and accurate prescriptions to deal with all the tasks and problems that arise in our professional lives. In contrast, the CARET typology is based on the traditions begun with Aristotle. The more quantitative, objective, and experimental the work, the higher its value. And the more rational and reflective, the lower its value.

While Aristotle's empiricism and Plato's rationalism are often presented as polar opposites, that is not really the case. There is rationalism in Aristotle's empirical way of knowing and empiricism in Plato's rational way of knowing. The difference is what they emphasize as the preferred and most dependable way of knowing. There are, of course, extremists, who see their preferred approach as the *only* valid approach, and they tend to try and convince others to become extremists too. The story of the horse's teeth, for example, was told by Francis Bacon to support his preference for the new scientific method over reliance on religious texts and other ancient sources. It is a story created to convince others that a new way of thinking is better than the old way:

> In the year of our Lord 1432, there arose a grievous quarrel among the brethren over the number of teeth in the mouth of a horse. For thirteen days the disputation raged without ceasing. All the ancient books and chronicles were fetched out, and wonderful and ponderous erudition such as was never before heard of in this region was made manifest. At the beginning of the fourteenth day, a youthful friar of goodly bearing asked his learned superiors for permission to add a word, and straightway, to the wonderment of the disputants, whose deep wisdom he sore vexed, he beseeched them to unbend in

a manner coarse and unheard-of and to look in the open mouth of a horse and find answer to their questionings. At this, their dignity being grievously hurt, they waxed exceeding wroth; and, joining in a mighty uproar, they flew upon him and smote him, hip and thigh, and cast him out forthwith. For, said they, surely Satan hath tempted this bold neophyte to declare unholy and unheard-of ways of finding truth, contrary to all the teachings of the fathers. After many days more of grievous strife, the dove of peace sat on the assembly, and they as one man declaring the problem to be an everlasting mystery because of a grievous dearth of historical and theological evidence thereof, so ordered the same writ down. (Francis Bacon, 1592)

This passage is widely attributed to Bacon, one of the founders of modern science, but there is considerable evidence that he read this story in another source and was simply repeating it. Similar and even better criticisms of rationalism are still made today. In his defense of science against the "anti-science" movement Gerald Holton (1992) used several sophisticated arguments to defend the traditional scientific method against criticism from many sources. He lumped opponents into a host of groups including Luddites, mystics, clairvoyants, astrologers, Stalinist scientists, magicians, Lysenkoism, Protestant Fundamentalism, Nazism, Romanticism, "a type of modern philosopher," "a new wing of sociologists of science," alienated intellectuals like Arthur Koestler, New Age thinkers, Eastern mysticism, Humanism, the 1960s counter-culture, scholars like Sandra Harding who propose alternative, feminist approaches to research and scholarship, and the American tendency to be suspicious of anything that is big and powerful which now includes science. He also suggested that a major reason why Americans do not support science and the scientific method today is "rampant scientific illiteracy", quoting scientific research that suggests less than 7% of adults in the U. S. are scientifically literate even when very liberal and flexible standards are used. He concluded that while the anti-science movement is not that powerful today, "it is prudent to regard the committed and politically ambitious parts of the anti-science phenomenon as a reminder of the Beast that slumbers below" (p. 125).

Arguments about what methods are appropriate for scholarship often have the ring of theological debates between hard line fundamentalists from opposing religious movements, and the sound and fury has not all come from supporters of a narrow definition of the scientific method. Vigorous criticisms of a purely empirical approach have also been made for centuries.

My view is that both sources of knowledge—rationalism and empiricism-are worthwhile and useful. Most debates about how to do research and scholarship come down to what the precise mix of empiricism and rationalism should be, not whether one should be used exclusively. If you look at journals on educational technology you will see that different patterns are preferred:

Educational Technology Research and Development tends to prefer *empirical studies* but also publishes theoretical papers, reviews of the literature, and other forms of scholarship.

Computers in the Schools tends to publish more *professional practice papers* that are based on the experiences of practicing educators and educational technologists but also publishes many other types of scholarship including policy papers and overviews of new technologies and teaching methods.

Computers & Education publishes an eclectic mix of papers that include experimental studies of the implementation and impact of computer-supported instructional components and packages. Papers describing computer-based instructional tools are also published, with and without empirical data, as well as case studies of instructional design projects and case studies of the use of innovative instructional design procedures. Few qualitative or purely theoretical papers are published in this journal.

Journal of Computer Assisted Learning is a source of scholarship on instructional development, particularly papers that include data related to the design process or the evaluation of the instructional product created. Papers on how to use specific procedures, techniques, and methods in the creation of computer assisted learning are also regularly published (e.g., using semantic web technology or guided interaction with pre-school children) as well as papers reporting the effectiveness of components of computer assisted learning materials and computer assisted packages and systems. Many of the papers include quantitative or qualitative data, but a substantial number are also sophisticated discussions of concepts, issues, and problems related to computer assisted learning.

Leading and Learning with Technology is primarily a practitioner journal that publishes papers of interest to professionals working in K–12 settings such as teachers or computer coordinators. A secondary audience is teacher educators interested in the integration of technology into teacher education. Many of the papers in this journal are overviews and introductions to new pedagogies, new technologies, and new ways of integrating technology into K–12 education. Other papers discuss procedures for training teachers, developing technology plans for schools, integrating technology into different levels of education, and the teaching of a particular subject matter. Many of the papers are based on the experiences of the authors and present professional practice knowledge. *Leading and Learning with Technology* also publishes a number of papers on how to do things like video capture or start a programming club.

Techné: Research in Philosophy and Technology publishes, as you might expect from the subtitle, philosophical papers on the uses and issues of technology in contemporary society. Most of the papers begin by establishing the background of an issue or idea, then proceed to a review of the major positions on the issue, and then a major portion of the paper is devoted to the author's analysis and explication of the issue.

The *Journal of Computer Mediated Communication* tends to publish papers based on data gathered from systematic studies but the journal accepts a range of methodologies. The October, 2006 issue, for example, contained studies using

- Simple statistics and graphical representations of the time between receiving an email and responding in three groups of email users.
- An experimental study in which the impact of moderation on the response rate and interactivity in several online discussion groups was studied.
- A quantitative study of the factors males and females used to guess the age, sex, and work patterns of two fictional participants in an online discussion group.
- A qualitative study using hermeneutic analysis the learn how a distributed workgroup developed shared understanding of job issues and concepts through online communication.
- A qualitative study using content analysis methods to look for differences in the way French, German, Japanese, and Dutch volunteer authors make contributions to an online information site (a Wikipedia).
- A another study using content analysis methods looked at ways universities portray racial and ethnic diversity on their campus and concluded they tend to do it visually rather than with text.
- A study using diffusion of innovation theory and qualitative methods, looked at factors that influence the adoption of wireless (Wi-Fi) in the workplace. Participants at a university that had recently installed Wi-Fi were interviewed and their responses analyzed to determine what factors influenced them to begin using the system. The results were compared to what popular theories of diffusion of innovation predict.
- In a special-topic section of the issue on "war coverage in cyberspace" one paper studied the coverage characteristics of 26 international newspaper sites. The study looked at the use of characteristics such as use hyperlinks, animations, multimedia content, and interactive elements. The authors drew general conclusions about the maturity of online journalism and also compared coverage on U.S. and international websites.

There were other articles in this issue of the journal but the sample above illustrates the preferences of this journal—papers based on data analysis but not limited to any particular type of analysis such as experimental, co-relational, or qualitative. Most methods seem to be acceptable.

In my view, the field of educational technology is advanced by maintaining a lively, active, and diverse set of scholarly traditions that encompass work within the traditions of Aristotle (e.g., "evidenced-based research") as well as the rational tradition of Plato (e.g., more reflective, qualitative, and philosophical work). *Any* group that tries to restrict the field to a certain type of scholarship makes a mistake and inhibits the progress of the field.

Educational Technology and Boyer's Types

Remember Boyer's four types of scholarship? They are:

- Scholarship of Discovery
- Scholarship of Integration
- Scholarship of Application
- Scholarship of Teaching

Do these broad categories reflect what is published in the journals on educational technology? Yes and No. Because the focus of educational technology is teaching, the last two types of scholarship, Application and Teaching, are basically merged for educational technology. The application area for the discipline is teaching and learning. The Scholarship of Integration is also a natural fit for educational technology. The discipline is less like history or chemistry than it is other professional fields like social work, clinical psychology, business, and medicine.

Professional fields tend to be intersections where knowledge, skills, and theories from many basic and applied disciplines meet and are integrated to improve the quality of service provided by the profession. Figure 3.1 illustrates this pattern. Educational technologists use the scholarship from all the disciplines shown in the figure as well as many others. For example, many educational technologists have responsibilities to help develop or guide the development of policies about educational technology and how it is supported, deployed and evaluated. That work may draw from fields like political science, economics, and the diffusion of innovation literature of business and social science. Many of the scholarly papers in the literature of educational technology are efforts to integrate and apply knowledge from several different disciplines.

The "fit" for the *Scholarship of Discovery* is not quite as clean and tight for educational technology as the fit for Teaching, Application, and Integration. The Scholarship of Discovery is generally thought of as an effort to uncover new knowledge. Educational technology is an applied field, how-

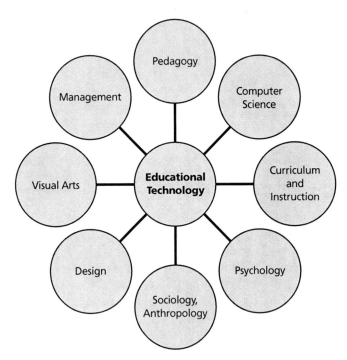

Figure 3.1 Educational Technology is a professional field where knowledge and expertise from many disciplines are used to design, produce, and deploy learning materials, systems, and procedures.

ever. As more basic fields, like the study of how humans learn, generate new knowledge and theories, those discoveries may be used by educational technologists to design and implement new computer-supported forms of learning, new pedagogies, new uses of information technologies, or new ways of encouraging and supporting the organizational and individual adoption of educational technology innovations. I would consider this type of scholarship as Discovery for educational technology.

Educational technology is, indeed, a very broad field and the diversity of scholarship that is useful to it is also very broad!

TYPOLOGIES OF QUALITATIVE SCHOLARSHIP

Most readers will already have some knowledge of the methods of quantitative research. Methods such as control-experimental group research and correlational studies are taught in virtually all introductory educational research courses. Less common are the methodologies used in qualitative research. In the list of articles in the *Journal of Computer-Mediated Communica-*

tion presented earlier in this chapter, qualitative research methods such as content analysis and hermeneutic analysis were mentioned. Do you know what these methods are and when they are appropriate to use? Many educational technologists are not because qualitative methods are not taught as often in graduate school as quantitative methods are. Below is a simple typology of qualitative research in educational technology that is based on the type of data collected. It will be followed by a typology based on the theoretical foundations used to guide research. Both typologies are helpful in organizing your thinking about qualitative research. The first typology, based on sources of data, includes the most common and traditional types of qualitative data (adapted from Willis, 2007, Chapter 7).

A Typology of Qualitative Scholarship Based on Sources of Data

Quantitative research tends to focus, naturally, on numeric data like test scores or the number of lessons completed in a given time. A large and ever growing set of procedures have been developed to analyze quantitative data. There are so many, in fact, that no one can keep up with all the ways of analyzing quantitative data these days. The best we can do is learn to competently use a few procedures that are most relevant to our scholarship and then try to "know someone" who can help when we get into uncharted territory and need help. The types of qualitative data are also very diverse, and each year new methods, as well as new versions of old methods, emerge to help us make sense of our qualitative data. The list below illustrates the range of possibilities for qualitative data in educational technology. Keep in mind, however, that most qualitative researchers do not necessarily limit themselves to one source of data. They may gather data from several sources.

Ethnography—Observation in the Real World. Observation in the context of interest is the hallmark of anthropological research, and it is also a commonly used source of data in educational technology. In her pioneering study of the way children and adults interact with computers Sherry Turkle (1983) observed children and adults working and playing on early computers. Her conclusions, published in *The Second Self: Computers and the Human Spirit,* helped us better understand how we define what is "human" and what is not.

Interview Studies: Asking Questions. There are many forms of interviews, from tightly structured sessions that ask for yes or no answers to open, flexible interviews that allow a person to answer freely and fully. Individual interviews are the most common form in research, but there are many types of group interview strategies including Focus Groups and Delphi techniques.

Thousands of educational technology studies have been conducted by gathering individual and group answers to questions.

Historiography. When an educational technologist studies how computers came to be integrated into American schools over the past six decades, that scholar is doing historical research. Historiography is the term for the methods of research used by historians. While historical research is not very common in the educational technology, there are some historical studies and the field would benefit from more.

Archaeology and Artifacts. A discussion of scholarship based on the study of artifacts tends to bring up images of kaki-clad scholars sweating while they brush the dirt off a pot shard or piece of bronze found in an excavation trench at some remote site that was once the center of an ancient civilization. That need not be the case. An artifact can be anything produced by humans, including the portfolios developed by a group of educational technology graduate students, the stories a group of children have collaboratively written using special software, or the fly-through animations architectural students have created for a class on the design of energy efficient buildings. Artifacts need not even be physical objects made by humans. They may be ideas, attitudes, or actions that are the result of human traditions, viewpoints or actions. For example, suppose a study that found males in mixed groups of high school students working on computers tended to expect the female students to play support roles while the males took charge of the computers. The males' actions that attempted to relegate females to secondary roles could be thought of as an artifact of the sexism in their society.

One study I have wanted to do for years but will probably never do is an analysis of the ways computers have been portrayed in popular movies since the 1950s. Movies are artifacts that reflect cultural concerns and interests, and my guess is that in the early years computers were most often presented as dangerous threats. However, with the arrival of personal computers they became friends and helpers in movies. Recall the computer named Hall in the movie *2001: A Space Odyssey,* and compare Hall to R2D2 in the more recent series of *Star Wars* movies.

Products and Characteristics of Products. Another scholarly tradition looks at artifacts in a different way—as *products* of an activity or process. Suppose you are interested in how the use of computers in a college writing course influences the process of writing. You might do observations in several college classes as part of your research. However, you might also look at the products of the writing courses at various points such as initial attempt, revised version, and final version. Information as well as educational technologies now permeates our society at work, in school, and at home. The products of that permeation may be excellent data in many types of studies. What depth of understanding of basic algebra concepts, for example, is exhibited in the visual representations of algebra problems produced by students in a high school Algebra I class? In an English composition class that includes written as well as visual essays (e.g., digital video for example), what are the differences in process and topics as well as emotional tone and range of expression? These are questions that qualitative research can address when products are available.

Text. The word text has multiple meanings in qualitative research. It can simply mean what it means in everyday use—a document that contains letters and symbols that contain meaning for readers who understand the language used to write the document. Using this meaning of "text" a researcher might simply be trying to get the "real meaning" of whatever text is being studied. There is even a typology of types of text:

- Narrative text tells about an event or "tells a story"
- Procedural text tells how to do something
- Horatory, Persuasive or Argumentative text is an effort to convince the reader of something
- Expository text explains something
- Descriptive text, naturally, describes something

Examples of all five types of text are easily found in the scholarly literature of educational technology. There is, however, more to text.

Today the simple but comforting meanings of the term text have been joined by several more complex meanings. Several movements that are often lumped together under the term *postmodernism* have questioned the simple idea that writers put meaning in the texts they write so that readers can understand what they want to communicate. Critics propose that such as idea is woefully inadequate. The *deconstructionist* movement has tried to demonstrate that texts (defined broadly to mean efforts to communicate meaning to others) often have in them multiple, and contrary, "messages." The text of a white writer discussing the need for social justice might, for example, be examined to show how the text both supports and opposes the concept of social justice. *Reader-response theory* sometimes argues that it is the reader, not the writer, who creates meaning from text. Some approaches have also extended the term text to mean things like styles of dress that represent a particular meaning or message, and movements in art that convey an attitude and set of beliefs through the artistic format and style. This is all part of "the linguistic turn" in philosophy, literature, and the arts that emphasizes the situational and fuzzy nature of meaning as well as the contextual nature of truths and meanings. *Semiotics* is a field that studies signs, including text, and their meaning. *Discourse analysis* is a large and growing field of theory and research methods that focus on understanding the meaning(s) in text and how it can be analyzed. In educational technology, semiotic and discourse analysis methods have been used to study topics like gender stereotypes in computer games and educational software. *Conversational analysis* is a related method that is often used to analyze social interactions.

While the type of data used is one important way to think about qualitative scholarship there are others. One is by the theoretical framework you adopt.

A Typology of Qualitative Scholarship Based on Theoretical Paradigm

Qualitative scholars generally agree that you cannot collect and analyze data without having a theoretical framework that guides your work. The question is not whether you use a theoretical framework or not, it is whether you are aware of it or not, and whether you make your readers aware of the framework or not. Although different authors have widely varying views on the number and type of paradigms actively used in qualitative research today, I will re-present three different major frameworks here that have also been discussed in earlier chapters. This list is based primarily on Willis (2007) and Anderson, Hughes and Sharrock (1986).

Positivism/Postpositivism: The Scientific Method, Evidence Based Research and Practice. This theoretical framework has already been discussed in some detail. Basically, it asserts that the best source of knowledge, knowledge you can be *positive* about, is the careful use of the experimental method to quantitatively study topics of interest. While there are many variations of this approach, the basic idea is that you develop a theory about the world, derive implications of that theory that can be systematically tested in experimental research (or other forms of quantitative research), and then conduct research to test whether the implications are true or not. Postpositivism is the current version of this family of paradigms and the main difference between postpositivism and traditional positivism is that postpositivism does not assert that you can ever do enough research to be absolutely sure your theory is correct. There is always the possibility that you have been mislead in some way and that further research will show you the error of your ways. However, even with that caveat, proponents argue that the scientific approach is still by far the best method to search for knowledge.

Critical Theory. A second active theoretical framework today is critical theory which is sometimes called NeoMarxism or the socio-cultural perspective. The focus of this paradigm is on power relationships that oppresses some groups and allows others to maintain their power over their lives and the lives of others. Some versions of feminist theory are also part of the critical theory family of paradigms as are some approaches to media literacy. Authors who address questions about educational technology from a critical theory perspective include Michael Apple, C. A. Bowers, Suzanne Damarin, Ann DeVaney, Robert Muffoletto, Michael Streibel, Nancy Nelson Knupfer, Neil Postman, Andrew Feenberg, and Andrew Yeaman (who prefers the term postmodernist). Studies in this tradition tend to be of two types. There are many critiques of current practices in education and educational technology that critical theorists point out as examples of oppression (such as attempts to use technology in ways that "deskill" teachers and make them technicians rather than professionals). Many of these critiques are essays, philosophical or theoretical analyses, or manifestos. Another type of research in this tradition is called *emancipatory* research. The goal is to help individuals or groups identify the beliefs they have accepted as true that dis-empower them and maintain the power of others. At the same time emancipatory research helps the disempowered develop strategies for taking control of their lives and build a society based on social equity and democracy.

Interpetivism. One of the core beliefs of interpretivism is that the search for absolute truths has been more of a problem than a benefit. Thus, we should adopt methods of scholarship that help us develop a better understanding of local contexts and situations rather than seek laws of behavior. Truth is socially agreed upon rather than discovered through special forms of research. Another characteristic of interpretivist scholarship is that it tends to shift the responsibility for generalization to the reader rather than making it the responsibility of the writer/scholar. An educational technologist, for example, who is reading an interpretivist paper has the responsibility to decide what in the paper seems worthy of tentative adoption or adaptation in the reader's work context. The reason for this shift of responsibility is that interpretivists do not believe there are very many, if any, "laws of human behavior." What happens when, for example, a new use of instructional technology is adopted in a school will not depend so much on dependable patterns that are the same across many different situations. Instead, what happens is heavily dependent on the local context. Papers in this tradition tend to be based on "thick" data sets such as hundreds of hours of observation in a classroom or computer lab, and the papers themselves tend to provide much more detail and context than is typical of papers written from a postpositivist perspective.

The characteristics of interpretivism already discussed apply more or less to a number of movements that guide qualitative researchers today. A few of them will be introduced next.

Hermeneutics. One approach to scholarship that is used by both interpetivists and critical theorists is hermeneutics. The term originally meant the study of ancient and often holy texts to more fully understand their meaning. Anderson, Hughes and Sharrock (1986) introduce hermeneutics by discussing how it was used to understand the Dead Sea Scrolls (Nag Hammadi manuscripts) that were found by an Egyptian farmer in 1945.

> The texts proved to be translations of Greek materials written 150 years or so earlier. The texts presented a very different picture of the Christian church to that usually given. They showed it to be deeply divided doctrinally and organizationally. They also reported very different facts about Jesus' life to the traditional account. So, making semantic, archaeological and historical sense of these texts involved not only linguistic matters, important thought these were, but also required them to be related to the wider social context in which they were originally produced. Who wrote them? For what readership? Why were they concealed? Could their meaning be taken at face value, or were other issues at stake? These are just some of the questions that had to be answered. (p. 64)

Anderson and his coauthors trace the migration of hermeneutic methods from the study of ancient texts to the social sciences. They point to several reactions against the use of research methods from the natural sciences in the social sciences and humanities. One was the Romantic revolt.

> What the romantics objected to was that the use of the natural science model of knowledge, with its 'empiricist' and 'positivist' overtones, left no room for the idea that history and social life were human creations, and that the essence of all social forms was that they expressed human creativity. In their eyes, the study of human history had to be based on the fact that humans are free, intentional and purposive creators whose lives are bounded by a reality which has meaning for them. They act towards the world and each other on the basis of these meanings. (p. 64)

And, because those meanings are subjective the Romantics did not believe the methods of natural science could be used to understand the true essence of humans and their interactions.

> Understanding the actions, events and artifacts that are the expression of human spirituality and creativity requires grasping the place, the significance that they have within human life. This task is very different to the observation of an external reality felt to be typical of science. The general line that was adopted to provide such a method was to treat human action and its artifacts as analogous to texts. Deciphering the meaning of history was similar to deciphering the meaning of a long lost text. In this way, Hermeneutics came to refer not just to the study of historical texts and the problems of translation, comprehension and contextualizing associated with them, but to a broader endeavor: that of discovering or uncovering the meanings of all human artifacts and action. The way that these meanings were grasped was through a process of interpretation through which the action, event, artifact or text was located as the expression of a deeper, underlying, unifying spirituality.

Hermeneutics was, then, determined to show that the generalizing of the natural science model of knowledge to all spheres of knowledge was unacceptable. (p. 65)

This extended quote gives you a flavor of the hermeneutic approach. It puts considerable emphasis on understanding in context. "Meaning does not exist separate from other meanings. It is caught up with them and interconnected to them. The phrases that recur again and again are 'a web of meaning' and 'a field meaning' (p. 66). Today the hermeneutic approach is a major thread in both interpretive and critical qualitative research. The basic goal of hermeneutic scholarship is *understanding* (*verstehen* in German). This is a very important shift in the purpose of research and scholarship but it is a goal that many scholars who adopt a paradigm other can postpositivism can accept. It treats a group of human experiences like the first hermeneutic scholars treated ancient texts and tries to develop an *understanding* of that "text."

Phenomenology. The emergence of the natural sciences as disciplines separate from philosophy during the Enlightenment period, and the adoption of the scientific method as the sole source of real or "scientific" truths, put pressure on the emerging social sciences. Many felt they should adopt the same scientific methods. However, that meant they would also be searching for objective laws of behavior. I have already mentioned the Romantics who rejected this notion of human behavior. Phenomenology not only rejected objectivity for human behavior, it rejected it for the natural sciences as well. "Phenomenology resisted this 'scientism' and the fawning upon science which often accompanied it. Phenomenology did not reject the achievements of science nor deny its power. What it did question was the claim that scientific knowledge had somehow wrenched itself free from subjectivity. The argument was deceptively simple. All knowledge begins in consciousness, in subjectivity, even science. The 'impersonal', 'objective' rules of scientific procedures and arguments are just as rooted in consciousness as any other form of knowledge" (pp. 83–84).

From the philosophies of Husserl and Sartre, among others, a phenomenological approach to qualitative research has emerged. It emphasizes that perception is not simply the passive reception of information from the external world. It is an active process in which human consciousness controls that process and helps determine what "reality" is perceived. "Although the term 'construction' came into fashion much later, we might say that consciousness constructs as much as it perceives the world" (Holdstein & Gubrium, 2005, p. 485). Phenomenological research often uses extended interviews to get an in depth understanding of the "lived experience" of humans. It often involves the subjective study of ordinary people and the ordinary activities of life. The focus is on understanding the subjective perspectives of individuals.

The Center for Advanced Research in Phenemonology (http://www.phenomenologycenter.org/index.html) proposes seven characteristics of the approach. Phenomenologists conduct research in ways that share most of the following positive and negative features.

1. Phenomenologists tend to oppose the acceptance of unobservable matters and grand systems erected in speculative thinking;
2. Phenomenologists tend to oppose naturalism (also called objectivism and positivism), which is the worldview growing from modern natural science and technology that has been spreading from Northern Europe since the Renaissance;
3. Positively speaking, phenomenologists tend to justify cognition (and some also evaluation and action) with reference to what Edmund Husserl called Evidenz, which is awareness of a matter itself as disclosed in the most clear, distinct, and adequate way for something of its kind;
4. Phenomenologists tend to believe that not only objects in the natural and cultural worlds, but also ideal objects, such as numbers, and even conscious life itself can be made evident and thus known;
5. Phenomenologists tend to hold that inquiry ought to focus upon what might be called "encountering" as it is directed at objects and, correlatively, upon "objects as they are encountered" (this terminology is not widely shared, but the emphasis on a dual problematics and the reflective approach it requires is);
6. Phenomenologists tend to recognize the role of description in universal, a priori, or "eidetic" terms as prior to explanation by means of causes, purposes, or grounds; and
7. Phenomenologists tend to debate whether or not what Husserl calls the transcendental phenomenological epochê and reduction is useful or even possible.

Keep these seven characteristics in mind when you read the paper at the end of this chapter about the development of web-based information systems by Pradip Sarkar and Jacob Cybulski from Deakin University in Australia. The paper introduces the phemenological approach and then reports the authors' phenomenological study.

Structuralism and Post-Structuralism. When I created the previously discussed typology of qualitative research based on types of data collected I was doing either structuralist or post-structuralist research. It was structuralist if I was looking for the natural and real structure of qualitative research. This is sometimes called *elementism*, the search for the basic elements and structure of things. The scientific or biological classification of living things into King-doms, Phylum, Class, Order, Family, Genus, Specie (which school children for generations have learned to remember by mneumonics such as "King Phillip can only find Girl Scouts") is an example of an effort in the biological sciences to discover the organizational structure of living things. Another ex-ample of structuralism is the development of the periodic table of elements.

In psychology, structuralism was the first "school" or theoretical frame-work, and it was used by the founder, Wilhelm Wundt, of the first psycho-logical laboratory in Leipzig, Germany. For Wundt and other structuralists, the task was to discover the basic elements of human consciousness. Wundt used a method called introspection which consisted essentially of asking subjects to focus on their mental processes and to describe them in detail to the researcher. Instrospection was discredited in the early 20th century by behaviorists who considered the method too subjective. The behavior-ists accepted only observable behavior as data for research. However, the instrospective method is alive and well in 21st century educational tech-nology as the *think aloud* method for gathering information from users in the instructional design process. The think-aloud protocol asks students to engage in an activity such as user testing a draft version of an instruction-al package or piece of computer software and to "think aloud" while they are working. The instructional designer may record or videotape the think aloud session and analyze it later, or observe and take notes as the student works and makes his or her thought processes public by verbalizing them. The process generally involves describing thoughts as well as explaining the reasons for actions. The think-aloud protocol was developed by Clayton Lewis while working at IBM. A paper describing how to use think-aloud protocols (written by Lewis and John Rieman, 1994) is available online at http://grouplab.cpsc.ucalgary.ca/saul/hci_topics/tcsd-book/chap–1_v–1. html. The title of the paper is *Task-Centered User Interface Design: A Practical Introduction,* and it is an excellent guide to using this introspective method of data collection.

When psychology was emerging as a separate discipline in the late 1800s, some of the pioneers wanted to do things like "map" the mind—to discover its basic structure and organization. Mind was one of many psychological, sociological, and anthropological concepts that became the focus of struc-turalist research. Researchers used a variety of methods, but the goal was to understand the real and true structure of a phenomenon and communicate that information to others. Structuralists wanted to get beyond the surface ap-pearance of things and look at the deeper, often hidden, reality that revealed its parts and how they were related to each other. This approach was used to study everything from the mind to social groups, nations, and cultures.

Post-structuralism is a newer variant of structuralism. While there are a number of ways of explaining the difference between structuralism and post-structuralism, I think the core difference is that while structuralism was looking for structures and elements that are enduring and stable, post-structuralists question how "real" and stable they are. Post-structuralists tend to see the conclusions of research on consciousness as efforts to create useful concepts that also reflect the culture and context of the research instead of the discovery of real elements. For example, when Freud organized the mind into conscious and unconscious compartments and developed the idea of the Id (completely unconscious), Ego (mostly conscious), and Superego (partly conscious) to explain the mental functioning of humans, he was a structuralist who believed he had discovered some universal characteristics of the human psyche. On the other hand, a scholar who concludes her research shows that Freud's structure of the mind is useful but has its roots in the turn of the century culture of Europe, especially Vienna, is a post-structuralist. (Note: Freud's tripartite mind is very similar to Plato's division of the mind, or soul, into three different spheres—the "impulsive/instinctive" element, the intellectual/reasoning element, and the emotional/spiritual element.)

An example of structuralist (actually poststructuralist) scholarship in educational technology is the work of Judi Harris on "activity structures." (See the website http://www.2learn.ca/Projects/Together/structures.html for more information.) One of Harris' major scholarly interests is the integration of internet activities in instruction. She developed a two-tiered structural model of the types of activities a teacher can consider. The first tier (see Figure 3.2) organizes activities into three broad categories.

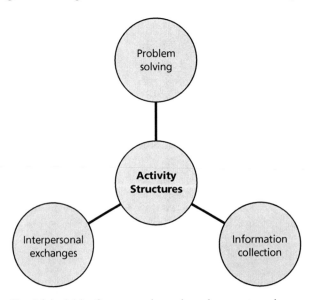

Figure 3.2 Harris' Activities Structures have three large categories.

Within each of her three broad categories there are more specific types. They are shown in Figures 3.3a, b, c.

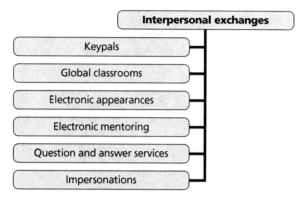

Figure 3.2a   The elements in the Interpersonal Exchanges category.

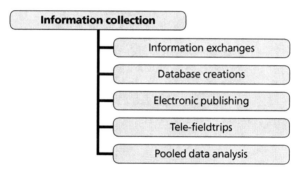

Figure 3.2b   The elements in the Information Collection category.

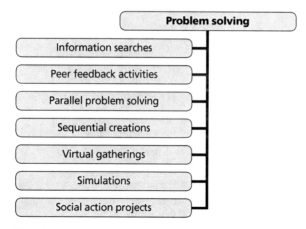

Figure 3.2c   The elements in the Problem Solving category.

Harris' structure is very helpful when considering how to use Internet access in a classroom. Her work, however, is more poststructuralist than structuralist because she does not claim to have discovered the *only* correct and true way to think about the Internet and learning. In fact, as scholarship in the areas of information technology and pedagogy progress she may well make significant changes to the structures she has created.

In the next chapter the framework for thinking about research will be expanded to include a much broader range of knowledge sources. The arts and the humanities as well as philosophy will be added to the sources of data, methodologies, and ways of communicating scholarship.

SUMMARY

Organizing approaches to research into a set of neat categories is not an easy task. It may not even be possible because our beliefs, theories, and ideologies influence how we divide up the different approaches. One broad categorization that may help orient us is the relative emphasis Plato and Aristotle places on thinking versus sense data. For Plato, thinking was the most important activity. Today's rationalists owe a considerable debt to him. On the other hand, Aristotle believed you must observe and study the physical world in order to know more about it. His empiricism can still be seen in much of contemporary research in education and the social sciences. Educational technology has been a particular stronghold of empiricism.

Boyer's four types of scholarship (discovery, integration, application, and teaching) represent an effort to organize scholarship according to purpose rather than method. This may be a more fruitful way of thinking about scholarship in fields like education and educational technology which are really fields of professional practice that draw on the scholarship of many different disciplines. However, the traditional way of organizing traditional qualitative scholarship is by the sources of data. They include ethnography (observation), asking questions (interviewing), historiography, artifacts (archaeology), products, and text (in the broad sense of that term).

Another way of organizing our thinking about research and scholarship is by the theoretical foundation that guides it. Today there are three major theoretical paradigms or ideological traditions—positivism/postpositivism, critical theory, and interpretivism. Each of these has developed its own set of research methods but many methods are shared across all three of the paradigms. However, structuralism is more associated with positivism while versions of hermeneutics, phenomenology, and post-structuralism are used by interpretivists and critical theorists.

REFERENCES

Anderson, R., Hughes J. & Sharrock, W. (1986). *Philosophy and the human sciences.* London: Routledge.

Gadamer, H. (1989). *Truth and method* (2nd revised ed.). New York: Continuum.

Holstein, J. & Gubrium, J. (2005). Interpretive practice and social action. In N. Denzin & Y Lincoln (Eds.), *Handbook of qualitative research* (3rd ed., pp. 483–505). Thousand Oaks, CA: Sage.

Holton, G. (1992). How to think about the "anti-science" phenomenon. *Pubic Understanding of Science, 1,* 103–128.

Huck, S. (2000). *Reading statistics and research.* New York: Longman.

Jonassen, D. & Harris, P. (2003). *Handbook of research on educational communications and technology* (2nd ed.) Mahwah, NJ: Lawrence Erlbaum.

Murphy, J., Katula, R., Hill, F., & Ochs, D. (2003). *A synoptic history of classical rhetoric.* Manwah, NJ: Lawrence Erlbaum.

Turkle, S. (1983). *The Second Self: Computers and the human spirit.* NY: Simon and Schuster.

Willis, J. (2007). *Foundations of qualitative research.* Thousand Oaks: Sage.

READINGS FOR CHAPTER 3

Reading 3.1

Solomon, D. (2000). *Philosophical Inquiry in Instructional Technology: The Forgotten Pathway to Learning.* Paper presented at the Association of Educational Communication and Technology 2000 International Convention (Long Beach, Ca. February 16–20, 2000). Available: http://www.learndev.org/dl/SolomonPhilosophy.PDF

One of the "types" of scholarship introduced in Chapter 3 is philosophical inquiry which is rarely discussed as a "research method" in educational technology even though many influential papers and books in the field are precisely that. The first reading for this chapter is on that exact topic, and is titled *Philosophical Inquiry in Instructional Technology: The Forgotten Pathway to Learning.* The author, David Solomon at Wayne State University, uses the term Instructional Technology to indicate basically the same field I refer to using the term Educational Technology. In the paper he traces the general development of philosophy and instructional technology (which has a much shorter official history than philosophy).

Does Dr. Solomon define philosophy in essentially the same way as I do in Chapter 3? Do you see differences in emphasis or focus? How does he link philosophy to instructional technology? That is, how does philosophical thinking come to influence what an instructional technologist does or thinks? Do you agree with the pattern of influence he proposes?

Rationalism and empiricism were discussed in Chapter 3 but pragmatism was not. Are you familiar with this American philosophy that was developed by one of the first American psychologists, William James? If you are not, how could you go about finding a paper or tutorial on the Internet that introduces you to pragmatism?

Solomon says philosophical inquiry is criticism and criticism is critical thinking. He says that at its best, criticism in instructional technology is "like art or literary criticism." How could you see that working? How would you approach a topic or question or position in educational technology that would be similar to the way someone would evaluate a novel or painting (or a genre of art)?

Solomon explains the philosophical analysis of learning as beginning with breaking things down. "One must first break it down into individually necessary and jointly sufficient conditions." Does that seem reasonable to you? Some have argued that philosophical analysis actually involves "moving up" to higher, more holistic, approaches to thinking about a topic. What is your opinion? Solomon's example of doing a philosophical analysis of learning actually reflects the way someone who has already adopted a particular theory of learning might do it. Would someone who takes a constructivist or a cognitive science view of learning be comfortable with the approach proposed by Solomon? Why?

What do you think about the four *trancendentals* proposed by Morris? Is philosophical analysis a way of bringing aspects of human existence such as beauty, morality, and spirituality into the discipline of instructional technology? Is that good or bad? Why? Can you think of two or three things that would change in the way you approach educational technology if you adopted this framework? What are they?

Reading 3.2

Feenberg, A. (Summer, 1999). Whither educational technology. *Peer Review, 1*(1)

The second reading for this chapter is a paper by Andrew Feenberg who is the Canada Research Chair in the Philosophy of Technology at Simon Fraser University in Vancouver. Professor Feenberg has a long history of contributing to the scholarship of both philosophy and the broad field of technology theory and the foundations of educational technology. This paper is an example of the type of philosophical analysis that was introduced in this chapter. The paper is written from a critical theory perspective, which was also introduced in this chapter.

Professor Feenberg points out that at least since Plato, new technologies (such as writing) have been denounced and criticized. Some Greeks were unhappy with writing because it tended to replace spoken discourse and they felt the give and take of a conversation, a dialog, was critical to the pursuit of knowledge. Someone listening to a speaker deliver a talk could ask questions, raise critical issues, and involve themselves in the conversation in many other ways. A reader, however, became the passive recipient of whatever the writer had written, with no opportunity to ask questions or otherwise interact with the speaker. And, of course, the speaker was deprived of the opportunity to hear what the listeners wanted to contribute to the conversation.

The idea that the search for knowledge can take the form of a conversation was revived over 2000 years later when 20th century hermeneutics began to influence the social sciences as well as philosophy and literary criticism. Hans-Goerg Gadamer, in his book, *Truth and Method,* proposed the idea that the hermeneutic method of understanding humans is at its core a *conversation.*

Feenberg takes a critical view of new technologies. New technologies can be detrimental, but it depends on "how it is designed and used." However, Feenberg does bring up a common criticism of current educational technologies—that they are often designed and deployed in a way that "deskills" teachers. What is your opinion of this perspective?

Feenberg is much more optimistic about the future uses of technology in education than many critical theorists, but he too is concerned about the crucial questions of design and use. Is his "third way" a viable alternative that could, and should, replace guiding paradigms like technological determinism? What do you think, and how would the field of educational technology change if Zuboff's "informating" became the dominant paradigm?

Feenberg is positive about distance education but is concerned that a model based on a very inexpensive way of disseminating higher education to many students will triumph over one that supports "human contact" with sophisticated communication technologies. What do you think? Is distance education as promising as Feenberg seems to think? Why? And, what factors are likely to determine which of the two models he discusses becomes the dominant model? Is it possible or likely that "economic and political realities" and the adoption of the "corporate" profit model in higher education will be the determining factors?

Reading 3.3

Gallagher, S. 2002. Conversations in postmodern hermeneutics. In H. Silverman (Ed.), *Lyotard: Philosophy, Politics and the Sublime* (pp. 49–60). London: Routledge. A previous version of this paper was presented at the Collegium Phaenomenologicum, Perugia, Italy (August 1992)

Shaun Gallagher is a cognitive scientists and a philosopher at the University of Central Florida. His paper, *Conversations in Postmodern Hermeneutics*, takes us beyond the introduction to hermeneutics in Chapter 3. The term "postmodern" in his title requires an introduction before proceeding to the focus of the paper, which is conversation as a metaphor, and more, for hermeneutic study. Postmodernism is a broad term with a multitude of meanings, but I think its core meaning (outside art criticism where other meanings apply), is a loss of faith in the inevitability of progress through modern scientific research and advancing technology. Modernism is the reverse, a tendency to believe in progress as almost preordained. Many events in the 20th century conspired to support a shift from a modernist view of the world to a postmodernist view—two world wars, the continuing and pervasive poverty a high percentage of the world's population experiences, the many "small" wars and conflicts that have killed millions, the development of atomic weapons, the holocaust and the many similar events that occurred after the world declared "never again," and the failure of modern civilization to deal with disparities in economic, social, and educational opportunities that are blatantly apparent even in the richest of nations.

Gallagher's focus is not on postmodernism per se, however. It is on the role of conversations in hermeneutic theory. Gallagher's view is not the only one and I disagree with some of his viewpoints. He does present several sides of the issues, however, and true to his topic, he uses forms of conversation in his article.

One final introductory remark should be made before exploring the paper. Gadamer saw a relationship between his idea of conversation and Plato's dialogs. Many of Plato's papers about Socrates were in the form of a dialog. They are presented as a conversation between Socrates and other people. They begin with a question, such as "What is virtue?" or "What is truth?" One person is confident of the correct answer to the question and gives it enthusiastically. Socrates responds by asking questions that highlight contradictions, implausible or undesirable implications, or thoroughly dishonorable meanings of the "correct answer." As the conversation progresses, the confident knower becomes less and less confident. The end result may be a conversion to Socrates' views, a confession by the confident knower that they do not really know anything, or an abrupt end to the conversation when the knower decides other things must be attended to. The Socratic dialogs are a means of convincing others to think the way Plato/Socrates does, but they are not "real" conversations that were recorded as they happened. They are, though Plato would not necessarily agree, a form of rhetoric—a means of convincing others.

The paper you will read has three major parts. In the introduction Gallagher introduces Gadamer's understanding of conversation and says that it is infiltrated with "Romantic and metaphysical conceptions" that need to be removed to make it "more postmetaphysical, postmodern." To do this he uses the famous disagreement between Gadamer and Derrida. Gallagher characterizes Gadamer's approach as an effort to get at truth through conversation while he characterizes Derrida as rejecting the idea of finding any form of absolutist truth through conversation, or perhaps any other way ("radical suspicion"). How do you, personally, see these two positions?

A second issue for Gallagher is the idea of the "conversation of mankind" supported by the postmodern philosopher, (I would actually characterize him as a postmodern, interpretivist, and democratic pragmatist), Richard Rorty. Here Gallagher also focuses on the question of universality and questions whether there is any room for it in a postmodern perspective that emphasizes the subjective nature of knowing. As you read this section of the reading, I suggest you think about the question of universality as having two components. One has to do with whether the end result of a conversation can be truth in any dependable and general sense. Or, will the result be, as Rorty has argued, more like a consensus among the group participating in the conversation. Rorty calls this *consensus truth* but the term truth means there is agreement within the group. That is different from a definition of truth that compares what is said to what is "out there in the real world." Which of these perspectives would you support as a framework for thinking about educational technology research and why?

The second aspect of the universality question is method. Is "conversation" as conceived by the various participants in the conversations about it, a universal method for getting at "the truth," however that is defined? One side argues for conversation as universal because it is an open and democratic way of encouraging wide participation in the building of truth. Does that make sense in terms of research and scholarship? Or is it simply one of many ways of getting at "truth"? Or is it a blind alley that is not really research or scholarship in any sense of those terms?

Another issue discussed in this section is the necessity of knowing the history and cultural context in which a conversation occurs before you can fully participate and understand. Rorty's support of E. D. Hirsch's idea of cultural literacy is the focus of this section. When considering the scholarly conversations in the field of educational technology, do you think it is important that participants be well aware of the history and context of the field, and of education in America, before they can participate fully? Why?

Gallagher uses some of the techniques of deconstruction to try and show that some of the positions of Rorty, Gadamer, and Caputo are not what they are presented to be. "The conversation of mankind fails as a model of postmodern hermeneutics not only because it is a metadiscourse and worthy of our incredulity, but because it hides exclusionary rules beneath a rhetoric of inclusion." Do you agree? Is there within the idea of an open and democratic discourse a set of exclusionary rules that go against what the authors' propose? Also, what is your view of the idea of incommensurability—the idea that it is difficult if not impossible for people who support different paradigms or worldviews to understand each other and then come to consensus? What implications do your views have for how debates about paradigms and perspectives within educational technology research should proceed?

Gallagher opposes the first two understandings of conversation, but he supports the third, "a stripped-down, transformed Gadamerian model of conversation" that combines Gadamer's theory with the work of Lyotard. "I want to develop and defend a Gadamerian-Lyotardian conception of conversation(s) as a model of postmodern hermeneutics." A core idea in this third understanding of conversation is this: "The postmodern situation is nothing other than a paralogical multiplicity of conversations." From this idea of several conversations, Gallagher removes the idea of meta or universal narratives, the ability of conversation to adjudicate between different paradigms, and the idea that conversation is not a required means of coming to know. Instead conversation is universal because "we cannot avoid conversing," thus "wherever we find ourselves we are always in a hermeneutical situation, in a conversation." There is thus no one universal conversation but many that may or may not lead to agreement. As you consider how Gallagher blends Lyotard's ideas, such as "the different" with a humbled and less powerful version of Gadamer's conversation, what is your view of the result? By eliminating universality, the Romantic underpinnings, and the view that conversation is a useful, if not unique, means of striving toward truth, has Gallagher developed a better, or a worse, concept of conversation? Why? What are the implications of your view for educational technology research? And finally, what do you think of the revised versions of phronesis presented in the paper? Is it better, worse, or simply different?

Reading 3.4

Sarkar P., & Cybulski, J. (2004). Evaluation of phenomenological findings in IS research: A study in developing web-based IS. In T. Leino, T. Saarinen, & S. Klein (Eds.), *Proceedings of the Twelfth European Conference on Information Systems.* Turku, Finland: Turku School of Economics and Business Administration.

The final reading for Chapter 3 is a paper from Deakin University in Australia by Pradip Sarkar and Jacob Cybulski in the School of Information Systems. Their paper serves two purposes. It introduces phenomenological research and it is also an example of how this methodology is used in Information Systems research.

As you read the introduction, do you believe it is possible to, as Husserl suggests, to peel off the "layers of presuppositions" to get at the true nature of a phenomenon or are the more modest approaches of Heidegger and Gadamer more to your tastes? Why?

As you read this paper, do you see the basic purpose of "the investigation of individuals' lived experience of events" more appropriate for some types of educational technology research than others? Why? What is your position based on? Purpose? Topic of study? Type of data available? Something else?

After reading the paper, consider both the general framework for phenomenological research proposed by Moustakas and the specific steps used by the authors in their study of Web-based Information Systems (WBIS). Can these general and specific procedures be applied to educational technology research? If they can, how? Why would you use them? Under what circumstances? Would you make any changes in them so that they more usefully serve your purposes in the areas of educational technology research that interest you the most?

CHAPTER 4

MORE GREEKS

Homer and the Sophists

Previous chapters have traced the links between current research traditions in educational technology and two Greek philosophers—Plato and Aristotle. In the social sciences the Empiricist paradigm that began with Aristotle and the Rationalist paradigm that began with Plato (and Socrates) have been influential from the beginning. However, in the last twenty years, two additional paradigms that began with the Greeks have also become influential in the social sciences and in education. They are the humanistic traditions that are exemplified by Homer and the rhetorical traditions begun by the Sophists.

Neither of these approaches has had much influence on the scholarship of educational technology, but there are good reasons to think they will become more influential over the next decade or two. Educational technology research and scholarship emerged as a distinct field of study between the end of World War II and the 1970s. Almost all of the journals in the field were founded after World War II, and the great majority began publication after the development of the personal computer in the 1970s. In that period, from 1950 to 1975, the dominant theoretical perspectives in American psychology were behaviorism and information processing theory. Both took the scientific method as the bedrock requirement for scholarship. The tra-

Qualitative Research Methods in Education and Educational Technology, pages 83–117

dition of preferring empirical sources of knowledge based on quantitative research methods is still the dominant paradigm in educational technology. As a field it has been much slower to embrace trends that have taken hold in the social sciences and in education. For example, both critical theory and interpretivism have been strong forces in education and the social sciences for at least twenty or thirty years. That is not the case in educational technology. However, one indication that educational technology is becoming more open to alternative forms of scholarship is the first edition of the *Handbook of Research on Educational Communications and Technology* (Jonassen, 1996). It was sponsored by the Association for Educational Communications and Technology (AECT) and contained a section titled *Foundations for Research in Educational Communications and Technology* that was edited by John Belland. That section contained chapters on several paradigms:

- Behaviorism
- Systems Theory
- Communication Theory
- Cognitive Theory
- Sociological Theories
- Constructivism (the theoretical foundation is interpretivism)
- Phenomenological psychology ("Media as Lived Environments")
- Critical Theory
- Postmodern and Poststructuralist Theory

These chapters present a broad range of theoretical perspectives and several chapters cover theories and perspectives similar to the three outlined in Chapter 3 of this book (Empiricism/postpositivism, Interpretivism, and Critical Theory). In addition, a chapter by Ann De Vaney and Rebecca Butler (1996) introduces and uses textual analysis methods and rhetorical analysis—two approaches more at home in the humanities and literary criticism than in educational technology. Had the *Handbook* been produced fifteen years earlier, the range of theoretical perspectives represented would not have been nearly as broad.

Compared to the social sciences and education, the field of educational technology seems to be inherently more innovative when it comes to the acceptance and use of new hardware and software technologies and inherently more conservative when it comes to adopting new "cognitive technologies" such as the paradigms most often used in qualitative research. However, being more conservative does not mean that new cognitive technologies are never adopted. Rather, they seem to be accepted and used a bit later in educational technology. If that assumption is correct, the next twenty years will be interesting because we can expect some of the changes that have occurred in other fields to finally begin to have a major impact in educational technology.

HOMER, THE POETS, AND THE LITERARY TRADITION
OF GREECE

Several hundred years before Plato and Aristotle, there was Homer. In Greek tradition Homer was a blind poet from Ionia who composed two great epic poems, the Illiad and the Odyssey. Actually, Homer may not have been a real person even though there is a bust of him in the British Museum. He may have been a composite that represented the ideal of a Greek poet during that era. However, to say that the Illiad and the Odyssey are epic poems does little to convey their role in Greek society. They emerged before the Greeks had a written language and were probably passed on from one generation to another through an oral tradition of storytellers for hundreds of years before they were finally codified in written form. The Illiad is the story of the last years of the war against Troy. Agamemnon has taken Brisēís, a Trojan widow who was captured by Achilles during the war. When Agamemnon is forced by an oracle to give up another woman he had captured, he takes Brisēís from Achilles. Achilles withdraws from the war because he thinks this was unfair and the rest of the story is about what happens, including the death of Achilles friend because Achilles was not in the battle to support him.

The *Iliad* is not, however, a simple story of adventure told to children. It is, instead, a vehicle by which Greeks transmitted their history, their beliefs, and their way of life from one generation to another. When the gods on Mount Olympus debate whether to support the Greeks in their war with Troy, this was not part of an adventuresome myth filled with fantasy and cliff hanger events. For the Greeks it was the true history of the Greek peoples and embedded within it were the values, religious beliefs, historical events, and cultural traditions of the Greeks. Greek poets like Homer thus did not have the role that poets do today. Instead they were at the center of the education process that taught every Greek what it was to be Greek. The poet was educator, priest, historian, and more.

Greek drama also played an important, and quite different, role in society than contemporary drama does today. Greek drama was of three types. The first was tragedy. By the time city states like Athens were powers to be reckoned with, tragedies were plays about extraordinary people (or gods) and a struggle with adversity. Although a bad ending is typically part of the definition of a tragedy, that is not always the case, nor was the idea that a "fatal flaw" in the hero could always be identified as the reason for the downfall. Tragedies were typically a part of Dionysian religious festivals and they generally illustrated what happens when one or more of the Greek values are violated. Over a three day period during a religious festival, an author would present three different plays—often organized around a theme. Several trilogies would be presented during the festival by different authors, and judges would award a prize to the author with the best trilogy. Audiences could be very large for these plays because attendance was part of the religious obligations of the Greeks and quite a few strongly believed that worship and respect for the gods influenced whether they intervened in human affairs to help the Greek city–state sponsoring the festival.

The author of the trilogy of plays also presented a second type of play, the *satyr play*. These were less serious performances that employed elements of both tragedy and comedy. They were generally based on Greek mythology and the themes were often overtly and crudely sexual activities (with huge phallic props prominently displayed on stage), drinking, or the tricks that could be played on unsuspecting gods and humans. Burlesque is in many ways similar to the satyr plays. These plays provided some relief to the tragedies they accompanied.

A third type of drama is comedy and unlike tragedy, the main characters of Greek comedy were not extraordinary people. They were, instead, average, or worse, people who lacked the expected level of virtues that should characterize a Greek citizen. Typically the main characters experience an improvement in circumstances in the play and they speak in everyday language (tragic characters speak in an elevated language). Comedies are less sophisticated than tragedies and many would be considered coarse today. They often used humor to satirize contemporary social or political traditions or behaviors, but not all of them were funny. Many, particularly at the beginning of the comedic tradition, relied heavily on obscene humor. More than one high official or well known citizen was the target of very funny, and very biting, comedies. (Today the slander and libel laws would prevent contemporary versions of many comedies from being written or performed.)

Plato and The Humanities

The Greeks did not create such a chasm between what was scientific, what was philosophical, and what was poetry (a term which, in Greek, covers literature, poetry, and drama). In fact, the sciences did not emerge as disciplines distinct from philosophy for well over a thousand years. During the classical Greek period a chemist or a physicist would simply have been another philosopher—or "lover of wisdom." Later, much later, an intermediate phrase developed that bridged the centuries between the Greeks' very broad meaning of the term philosophy and the separation of the sciences into different and distinct disciplines. That intermediate phase was natural philosophy, and for hundreds of years the term "natural philosopher" signified someone who was studying the characteristics of the physical world.

There are still some ancient universities that have a Chair of Natural Philosophy. Today they are typically occupied by physicists.

During the classical Greek period, there was, however, a separation between the humanities and philosophy. The prevailing attitude of contemporary 21st century scientists (who would have been philosophers in Plato's time) is basically negative insofar as any suggestion that the humanities can be a source of knowledge and understanding in the same way as the methods of science can. This is a continuation of Plato's attitude toward the humanities. In the *Republic*, Plato comments that "there is an old quarrel between philosophy and poetry" (*Republic*, 607b5–6). For reasons that made sense in Plato's theory of what is real and what is not, he believed poets were liars who misled people and convinced them that what was clearly untrue (at least to Plato) was true. In the *Republic* Plato tried to lay out the criteria for a perfect city–state, including the proper forms of education for various classes of citizens, the best type of government, and the correct economic system. He felt poets were such a danger to his perfect state that he proposed all but the most austere be banished, and they would be forbidden to practice the entire range of poetic skills. In the *Republic* Plato often compared poetry to painting and that has led some to believe Plato meant his severe criticism of poetry to apply to the visual arts as well. One of the reasons Plato was so negative about poetry (in all its forms including epic poetry, Greek drama, and perhaps even painting) is that he considered the poets to be creating or making something while the goal of philosophy was to understand what is already there in the world. The Greek word for poetry comes from the Greek word *poiein* which means "to make." Plato does not want anyone to create something and then present it as real. That takes us in the wrong direction; the responsibility of a philosopher is not to create, it is to uncover what already exists but of which humans are still unaware. This is a classic issue that is part of contemporary social science, education, and educational technology. Postpositivists have a view that is very close to Plato's (yet, they have adopted the scientific methods that come from Aristotle via the Enlightenment). On the other hand, interpretivists and constructivists argue that what is "real" to us, that is, what we call reality, is socially negotiated and thus very dependent on the context. They have no trouble accepting the work of poets as a source of knowledge and understanding because they consider all our knowledge to be made or "constructed" by humans.

In a later section of this chapter I will discuss another method of "making" reality—rhetoric. It also as roots deep in classical Greece. Plato's opinion of rhetoric was about as negative as his view of poetry. That is ironic because Plato's own writing is often considered some of the best from a rhetorical point of view.

Aristotle and Literary Criticism

In contrast to Plato, Aristotle was always a strong supporter of poetry. In fact, one of Aristotle's works, *Poetics,* is considered the first piece of literary criticism. Here is now it starts:

> I PROPOSE to treat of Poetry in itself and of its various kinds, noting the essential quality of each, to inquire into the structure of the plot as requisite to a good poem; into the number and nature of the parts of which a poem is composed; and similarly into whatever else falls within the same inquiry. Following, then, the order of nature, let us begin with the principles which come first.
>
> Epic poetry and Tragedy, Comedy also and Dithyrambic poetry, and the music of the flute and of the lyre in most of their forms, are all in their general conception modes of imitation. They differ, however, from one another in three respects- the medium, the objects, the manner or mode of imitation, being in each case distinct.
>
> For as there are persons who, by conscious art or mere habit, imitate and represent various objects through the medium of color and form, or again by the voice; so in the arts above mentioned, taken as a whole, the imitation is produced by rhythm, language, or "harmony," either singly or combined.
>
> Thus in the music of the flute and of the lyre, "harmony" and rhythm alone are employed; also in other arts, such as that of the shepherd's pipe, which are essentially similar to these. In dancing, rhythm alone is used without "harmony"; for even dancing imitates character, emotion, and action, by rhythmical movement.
>
> There is another art which imitates by means of language alone, and that either in prose or verse—which verse, again, may either combine different meters or consist of but one kind—but this has hitherto been without a name. For there is no common term we could apply to the mimes of Sophron and Xenarchus and the Socratic dialogues on the one hand; and, on the other, to poetic imitations in iambic, elegiac, or any similar meter. People do, indeed, add the word "maker" or "poet" to the name of the meter, and speak of elegiac poets, or epic (that is, hexameter) poets, as if it were not the imitation that makes the poet, but the verse that entitles them all to the name. Even when a treatise on medicine or natural science is brought out in verse, the name of poet is by custom given to the author; and yet Homer and Empedocles have nothing in common but the meter, so that it would be right to call the one poet, the other physicist rather than poet. On the same principle, even if a writer in his poetic imitation were to combine all meters, as Chaeremon did in his Centaur, which is a medley composed of meters of all kinds, we should bring him too under the general term poet. (written about 350 BCE, translated by S. H. Butcher and available at http://libertyonline.hypermall.com/ Aristotle/Poetics.html)

Although still read and cited in the humanities, Aristotle's discussion of the desirable characteristics of poetry in *Poetics* is strongly criticized because of the author's own clumsy writing:

> Aristotle's *Poetics* is a much-disdained book. So unpoetic a soul as Aristotle's has no business speaking about such a topic, much less telling poets how to go about their business. He reduces the drama to its language, people say, and the language itself to its least poetic element, the story, and then he encourages insensitive readers like himself to subject stories to crudely moralistic readings, that reduce tragedies to the childish proportions of Aesop-fables. Strangely, though, the *Poetics* itself is rarely read with the kind of sensitivity its critics claim to possess, and the thing criticized is not the book Aristotle wrote but a caricature of it. Aristotle himself respected Homer so much that he personally corrected a copy of the *Iliad* for his student Alexander, who carried it all over the world. In his Rhetoric (III, xvi, 9), Aristotle criticizes orators who write exclusively from the intellect, rather than from the heart, in the way Sophocles makes Antigone speak. Aristotle is often thought of as a logician, but he regularly uses the adverb *logikôs*, logically, as a term of reproach contrasted with *phusikôs*, naturally or appropriately, to describe arguments made by others, or preliminary and inadequate arguments of his own. Those who take the trouble to look at the *Poetics* closely will find, I think, a book that treats its topic appropriately and naturally, and contains the reflections of a good reader and characteristically powerful thinker.

This comment, from a paper by Joe Sachs published in *The Internet Encyclopedia of Philosophy* (http://www.iep.utm.edu/a/aris-poe.htm) highlights both Aristotle's shortcomings and his strong belief in the value of poetry. I will return to this topic later but the point to be made here is that in the modern Western intellectual tradition, the role of the poets as sources of knowledge has been gradually reduced to the vanishing point by proponents of the scientific method. The early Plato would be pleased with that treatment of poets but very unhappy that philosophers have also been squeezed out as well—leaving the field to the empiricist supporters of the scientific method. A similar thing has happened to another group that was the target of some of Plato's harshest criticisms.

PLATO, THE SOPHISTS, AND RHETORIC

Rhetoric is "the systematic analysis of human discourse for the purpose of adducing useful precepts for future discourse" (Murphy, 1983, p. 3). It "is one of the oldest disciplines in the Western world. Long before 700 B.C., the Greeks learned to arrange speeches in ways that were calculated to achieve a desired effect. The carefully organized "orations" found scattered throughout Homer's Iliad testify that this development took place at an early date" (p. 3).

Before the invention of movable type, film and video, multimedia, hypertext, and the Internet, the focus of rhetoric was public speaking because that was the primary means of persuasion. Today, modern versions of rhetoric deal with everything from electronic journalism to the creation of documentaries that are shot with high definition digital cameras and edited on relatively well-equipped personal computers. Knowledge of rhetoric and the practiced ability to convince people to accept, or at least consider, your view of the world, is a critical skill for many professionals today—including educational technologists. A well-written paper, regardless of whether its content is "true" or not, is more likely to be published in an educational technology journal than a poorly written paper. And, the lack of any systematic training in rhetoric in most educational technology programs is painfully obvious to many editors and reviewers of scholarly journals. Rhetoric was once one of the pillars of a university education. In fact, today's virtually universal requirement that a Ph.D. candidate make an oral defense of the dissertation goes all the way back to the Middle Ages when there might not even have been a written dissertation. The oral defense itself was the dissertation and it was an opportunity for the university professors to examine the rhetorical skills of the candidate.

Our current attitudes toward rhetoric, however, goes back to Plato and his attitude toward a group of intellectuals in Athens, the Sophists. A literal translation of Sophist is "wisdom-bearer" but that is not what Sophists were, at least in Plato's option. In 5th century B.C.E. Greece, Sophists were itinerant teachers who accepted money to teach their students. Murphy (1983) distinguishes three types of teachers: "Certain teachers set themselves up to give their students either wisdom itself (like Socrates), merely eloquence (like Gorgias), or a usable combination of both (like Isocrates). Only through the excesses of such eloquence-teachers as Protagoras and Gorgias has the term "sophist" acquired a pejorative meaning" (p. 8). Protagoras was lampooned by Aristophanes in a play named *The Clouds* and also in one of Plato's dialogues named after the Protagoras. Murphy (1998) comments that:

> In practice Protagoras seems to have believed that since no man can be certain of the truth in a given situation, each man has the right to express his own personal view as strongly as possible. His most famous statement is "Man is the measure of all things," and he is credited with the statement, "On every question there are two speeches that oppose each other." He encouraged his students to debate both sides of a question in order to train them to understand the nature of controversy and to defend themselves better. His critics, however, declared that such exercises essentially taught the students how "to make the worse appear the better cause." (p. 9)

One of the strongest critics of the sophists and rhetoric was Plato but he was not as consistent in his criticism of sophists as he was of poets. In early dialogues, including *Protagoras* and *Gorgias,* he was very critical because it was nothing more than the ability to "produce pleasure and gratification in an audience," it was just a type of flattery, it gave people the power to influence others for evil because it took advantage of the ignorance of the audience, and rhetoric teachers claimed knowing rhetoric made a person virtuous when that came from wisdom, not rhetoric (Murphy, 1983). "In a later dialogue, *Phaedrus,* however, Plato praises rhetoric (the art of winning [enchanting] the soul by discourse") and even proposes certain principles to be followed" (p. 18). Some of those principles are (from Murphy, 1983, p. 18):

- Disgrace lies in speaking badly, not in the act of speaking itself.
- Knowledge of the matter is essential to the speaker
- Rhetoric is most useful in doubtful matters (that is, where the outcome is still in doubt)
- Rhetoric is a difficult art, but worth practicing.

Aristotle and Rhetoric

Aristotle seems to have valued a much wider range of knowledge sources than Plato and his relationship to the Sophists illustrates that breadth of appreciation. Sophists tended to teach their students how to improve their orations and become more convincing. This emphasis on the techniques for convincing rather than how to find truths was what bothered Plato. With too little wisdom and too much skill at convincing others, a person could do a great deal of harm.

There is also a bit more to the Sophist than just the focus on teaching people how to make more convincing speeches. As noted earlier a famous quote from Protagoras is "Man is the measure of all things." Gorgias is famous for a line of logic that comes to the conclusion that "Therefore, nothing exists" and continues to conclude that if anything does exist it cannot be understood, and if it can be understood that understanding cannot be communicated to others. Plato's hostility toward Protagoras was, at least in part, because of Plato's view that Protagoras advocated as *relativism* which was certainly not acceptable to Plato who felt he not only understood the methods required to search for Truth but had used them to discover many Truths. Sophists did not automatically adopt established truths and because they were more flexible they were more likely to consider more than one position on an issue. That led some to claim that being flexible on questions of what was good made Sophists immoral. This has a familiar and very modern ring in America today. Consider how many times you have heard a proponent of one view on abortion or global warming, or the war in Iraq call a proponent of an opposing view immoral, unpatriotic, or even a traitor.

Another strike against the sophists in general relates to the class system in Greece.

> Protagoras was the first of those traveling teachers of philosophy and rhetoric who became known as "Sophists." Sophists were not as interested in metaphysical theories as they were in the skill of arete, or "excellence," in the sense of bettering oneself. Many conservative Greeks, such as Aristophanes, considered proper speech and good manners the inherited characteristics of the upper classes. The Sophists, however, taught such skills for a fee–to the consternation of the aristocracy. (quoted from http://www.whitworth.edu/Core/Classes/CO250/Greece/Data/d_sophi.htm)

A willingness to teach those who were not from the higher classes anticipates some of the issues and questions raised by critical theorists today, and a tendency to doubt the Truths distributed so confidently by some, is a characteristic of contemporary interpretivism and constructivism. Sophists thus represent one of the threads of thought that led us to these alternative paradigms. Further, the critical theorists' focus on power fits with the Sophists' emphasis on teaching the methods that enhanced the power and persuasiveness of those who were not born with power. That anticipates the emancipatory scholarship of critical theorists.

Despite his broader acceptance of ways of knowing Aristotle was also critical of the Sophists. In Book 1, Chapter 1 of *Rhetoric* he makes this comment:

> It is clear, then, that rhetoric is not bound up with a single definite class of subjects, but is as universal as dialectic; it is clear, also, that it is useful. It is clear, further, that its function is not simply to succeed in persuading, but rather to discover the means of coming as near such success as the circumstances of each particular case allow. In this it resembles all other arts. For example, it is not the function of medicine simply to make a man quite healthy, but to put him as far as may be on the road to health; it is possible to give excellent treatment even to those who can never enjoy sound health. Furthermore, it is plain that it is the function of one and the same art to discern the real and the apparent means of persuasion, just as it is the function of dialectic to discern the real and the apparent syllogism. What makes a man a "sophist" is not his faculty, but his moral purpose. In rhetoric, however, the term "rhetorician" may describe either the speaker's knowledge of the art, or his moral purpose. In dialectic it is different: a man is a "sophist" because he has a certain kind of moral purpose, a "dialectician" in respect, not of his moral purpose, but of his faculty.

Here Aristotle distinguishes sophists from practitioners of rhetoric on the basis not of their method but their purpose. They were willing to use their skills to persuade someone to believe something that was not true and that was not a moral thing to do. Aristotle generally ignores sophists or treats them with considerable scorn when he does mention them. However, in *Rhetoric* he is yet again credited with the founding of a discipline that still exists today. Rhetoric deals with how you convince someone of the truthfulness or validity of your position. Both Aristotle and Plato have been interpreted as dismissing the sophists out of hand, and since virtually nothing remains of the sophists' original writing we can only understand them through what others have said. One shudders to think how the proponents of constructivist instructional design and those who propose the use of constructivist teaching strategies will be considered if, 100 years from now, the only evidence they existed will be from the writing of David Merrill. His "Reclaiming Instructional Design" (Merrill et al, 1996), with its "sinners in the hands of an angry god" tone, is about as scathing of the constructivists as it can be:

> Too much of the structure of educational technology is built upon the sand of relativism, rather than the rock of science. When winds of new paradigms blow and the sands of old paradigms shift; then the structure of educational technology slides toward the sea of pseudo-science and mythology. We stand firm against the shifting sands of new paradigms and "realities." We have drawn a line in the sand. We boldly reclaim the technology of instructional design that is built upon the rock of instructional science.
>
> . . .
>
> We still have a long way to go, but abandoning the path of scientific method and following the uncertain wilderness of philosophical relativism will distract us from our goal and unnecessarily delay our journey. (p. 3)

Had Merrill, who has made many significant contributions to the field of educational technology, been a Greek in the 5th century BCE, the sophists would have fared no better than contemporary constructivists do.

However, a strange thing is happening in philosophy today. Some are proposing that we take another look at what Aristotle said about the sophists and about rhetoric. It has been generally accepted that while Aristotle considered rhetoric very important he rejected the sophists. Jacob (1996) is one of several philosophers who argue that we need to take another look at what Aristotle wrote about the sophists. In doing so, he believes we will discover more respect and attention than previously thought. Sophists might profitably be considered one thread of the tradition of rhetoric.

However, in the contemporary environment rhetoric sometimes is treated as badly as the sophists were when Athens was one of the most powerful cities in the world. In a paper titled *The Rhetoric and Reality of Aid: Promoting Educatonal Technology in Egypt,* Mark Warschauer (2004) uses the term *rhetoric* to mean the contrast between the stated aim of a U. S. aid program and the way it was really carried out. As he put it,

> The contradiction between the rhetoric of educational technology campaigns and the actual ways that new technologies are used in the classroom has been an important theme in educational research over the last two decades. (p. 22)
>
> . . .
>
> In developing nations, the rhetoric behind educational technology may even be loftier, as technology holds the allure not only of improving education and economic competitiveness, but also of allowing a nation to leapfrog to modernity. (p. 24)

Warschauer goes on to make the case that the integration of technology into Egyptian schools was actually hindered by many of the project's actions because those actions were really attempts to support the Westernization and Americanization of Egypt rather than finds ways of effectively integrating modern educational technologies into Egyptian schools. To make his case Warschauer did not, however, use the scientific method to conduct his study. Instead he used

> a critical theory of technology [that] distinguishes itself from both determinist approaches (which view technology as of necessity having a positive or negative impact) and instrumental approaches (which view technology as a valueless tool which can be deployed toward any end) . . . Both determinist and instrumental approaches are seen as downplaying the embeddedness of social, political, economic, and culture factors in technologies, which shape (but do not determine) how technologies are deployed. In a critical approach, technology is viewed as a site of struggle, and investigations of technology implementation seek to uncover underlying power relations that shape how technology is used, similarly, for example, to how critical literacy studies seek to uncover the underlying power relations framing literacy practices . . .

The overall research methodology is that of an interpretive qualitative study. Sources of data for the study include (a) participant-observation of efforts to plan, implement, and evaluate technology-based interventions in Egyptian schools and inservice and pre-service teacher education programs, including attendance at meetings of Ministry of Education bodies, international donor and implementation agencies, and Egyptian non-governmental oganizations, attendance at and participation in in-service and pre-service teacher training programs, and participation in online discussion forums of Egyptian educators related to technology use in education; (b) professional visits to 25 Egyptian primary preparatory (i.e., middle), and secondary schools located in rural and urban areas throughout the country and to colleges of education in 10 Egyptian universities; (c) individual and focus group interviews with Ministry of Education (MOE) officials, business leaders, school teachers, university faculty, and representatives of non-governmental organizations, parents, and students; and (d) analysis of print and electronic documents and reports issued by the Egyptian government and MOE, donor agencies, and non-governmental bodies related to technology in education.

Data was analyzed in an iterative fashion to search for overall patterns. Triangulation was used to confirm that possible patterns were found in various types of data. Efforts were even made to seek out disconfirming examples. Finally, results were discussed with Egyptian educators to confirm that interpretations were consistent with their own understandings of events (pp. 25–25).

This study used many of the sources of data mentioned in the previous chapter and it adopted one of the three major paradigms mentioned at the end of Chapter 3, critical theory. The author used the term interpretive in a broader way than used in this book. For him the term seems to imply a qualitative research method that takes a relatively broad and flexible approach to gathering and analyzing data. I use the term in this book to mean a form of qualitative research that is solidly in the relativist camp that acknowledges the findings of a study are heavily influenced by who does the study, what paradigm they used, and what values they hold. Warschauer is, in my view, clearly a critical theorist doing qualitative research because he looks for, and finds, inappropriate power relationships that influence the way the project was implemented:

> The three main...projects all were marked by an emphasis on Westernization, through bringing Egyptian teachers to the U.S. [at a cost of $5000], showcasing U.S. technology in Egypt, or building technology-enhanced communication between Egyptian and American institutions. In a broader sense, the devotion of such considerable resources exclusively to the teaching of English, while ignoring the broader subjects taught in Egyptian schools and universities, is further evidence of the central element of Westernization in the project....The larger concern here is when the focus on building of ties and influence becomes so predominate that it detracts from the educational value of the projects involved, as appeared to be the case in the programs described.

Warschauer's paper is an excellent one to illustrate a number of trends in educational technology scholarship. It shows how the preferred paradigm of a scholar can guide a study, it illustrates the way many types of qualitative data can be flexibly and somewhat informally used to develop findings that are communicated to readers and supported by excerpts and examples from the qualitative data. Finally, if you read the paper it illustrates how important the skills of rhetoric are to the communication of the author's findings. The paper tells the story of the project in a way that draws the attention of the reader to issues and events that support the points the author wishes to make. In this paper it is done in a skillful way and is one of the factors in convincing the reader that it is possible the author is correct in his conclusions. If you would like to read this paper in full it is available online as a preprint at http://www.gse.uci.edu/faculty/markw/rhetoric.pdf.

Using the Methods of the Humanities, Philosophy, and Rhetoric in Educational Technology Research

One of the reasons scientific research has been the focus of scholarship in educational technology for at least half a century is the postpositivist foundations of the field, particularly two postpositivist assumptions:

- That there is "an answer" for most important questions about educational technology, learning, and pedagogy. It can be found, and once found, can be used as the foundation for professional practice through the implications that naturally flow from it.
- That the answers are best found through the application of the scientific method.

These two assumptions point us toward two foundational assumptions about our field:

- That "good practice" can be identified by the degree to which a practitioner follows the conclusions and implications of sound empirical research.
- That sound empirical research is the sole reliable source of generalizable principles and knowledge.

If you feel I have stated these in terms that are too absolute, consider these quotes from David Merrill's declaration that was mentioned earlier:

- There is a scientific discipline of instruction and a technology of instructional design founded on this science.
- The technology of instructional design is founded on scientific principles verified by empirical data.
- Instructional science involves identifying the variables to consider (descriptive theory), identifying potential relationships between these variables (prescriptive theory), and then empirically testing these relationships in the laboratory and the field.
- Appropriate instructional strategies can be discovered, they are not arrived at by collaborative agreement among instructional designers

or learners. They are natural principles which do exist, and which nature will reveal as a result of careful scientific study.

Merrill and colleagues define the field as a postpositivist enclave and reject anyone who proposes a different foundation or guiding paradigm.

> Those persons who claim that knowledge is founded on collaboration rather than empirical science or who claim that all truth is relative, are not instructional designers. They have disassociated themselves from the technology of instructional design. We don't want to cast anyone out of the discipline of instructional science or the technology of instructional design; however, those who decry scientific method, and who deride instructional strategies, don't need to be cast off; they have exited on their own.

The field is thus not defined solely by its topic and focus, it is also, at least according to Merrill and his colleagues, defined by paradigm. If you don't accept the postpositivist paradigm you can not be in the same discipline as Merrill.

While there are still a large number of educational technologists who would agree with Merrill's position, there are more and more every year who take either a moderate ecumenical view (e.g., there is value and knowledge to be gained from scholarship and professional practice based in all the major paradigms) or a more radical view (that one of the emerging paradigms like critical theory or interpretivism is the best framework for educational technology scholarship and practice).

When it comes to being a consumer of scholarship, I take the middle, ecumenical, road that there is value in scholarship from many different, even conflicting paradigms. As a producing scholar, I am more likely to use an interpretivist or a critical theory framework for guidance. As a practicing educational technologist I am split about 50–50 between an interpretive/constructivist and a critical framework (although I will comfortably integrate teaching and learning methods developed within the behavioral, information processing, and cognitive science perspective, which are based on a postpositivist paradigm.)

Suppose the two assumptions of positivism mentioned earlier are not true. What if (1) "good educational technology practice" does not necessarily mean following the implications of empirical research? And, what if there are many paths to better understand the uses of technology in education? There are as many, if not more, reasons to reject the two assumptions of positivism than there are to accept them. Perhaps the most crucial reason to reject both these assumptions is that more than fifty years of empirical research in educational technology has not "settled" most of the issues that research addressed. If you look at research in the 1960s you will see that many of the issues that were the focus of research are still debated today. Very little of substance has been agreed upon. Instead, topics of research have changed primarily because our interests have shifted. Other topics are more interesting today and many that were "hot" then are not so interesting today. That does not, however, mean that empirical research is useless. It simply means that it has not achieved the positivist goal of finding the answers to the critical questions for educational technology. In my view that is not the fault of empirical research. Nothing will find those Universal answers. On the other hand, empirical research can provide us with useful information that helps us make decisions in our professional practice. Empirical research does not make those decisions for us, but it does help us make them.

Why don't we find more Universal answers? The main reason is that education is an applied social science and that means we are studying individual humans and groups of humans. How individuals behave and think, and how groups interact with the world depends on many different factors, not the influence of two or three laws of human behavior. Thus, the context in which individuals and groups operate is important to understanding how and why things happen. However, if understanding the context is critical to understanding, that means context is critical to generalizing from the context of the research to the context of application. If we make those assumptions, then it is incumbent upon the researchers and scholars to provide a great deal of information about the context in which their studies were conducted. Consumers of their work need it to make decisions about what is usable. This approach to thinking about generalization suggests that it is not so much the responsibility of the scholar or researcher to decide what the practical implications of a study are; it is the responsibility of the person reading the study to make decisions about how to use the information in the study.

AN EXAMPLE OF POSTPOSITIVIST EDUCATIONAL TECHNOLOGY RESEARCH AND THE ALTERNATIVE

Recently I served on a dissertation committee for a very capable student who proposed a study that is a good example of the type of postpositivist research often done in educational technology. The study was about distance education and it was concerned with the instructor's role in distance education programs that involve online collaborative learning. The student and her major professor were both familiar with traditional research design, and the dissertation study was well designed within that paradigm. For example, in keeping with the positivist concern about avoiding fuzzy terms that are poorly tied to observation, the student defined each of the dependent and independent variables operationally. That is, they were defined by the ways they would be measured. For example, the doctoral student had cited research on the importance of "instructor presence" and its influence on students' opinions of online learning. Instructor presence was defined operationally as, among other things, "the frequency and timing" of the instructor's communication (feedback) with students. This was further operationally defined: *Immediate feedback* was responding to a student's posted message before other students posted a response. Delayed feedback was defined as the instructor waiting to respond until other students responded to the post.

Operational definitions are one way of making it possible to do empirical, quantitative research. However, few would argue that in distance education the absolute most important aspect of an instructor's participation in the course is whether he or she responds to student posts before or after other students do. When we are taught that operational definitions are essential to "good research" it may force us to choose between variables that are important but difficult to measure quantitatively and variables that are quantifiable but not as important. Also, defining variables before starting the research means the insight that come as the study progresses do not have an impact on things like operational definitions, which were created before the study began. We thus may develop those definitions at the point when we know the least about the study we are about to conduct. It would be better if a more open and flexible approach were used—one that leaves some decisions until later and also allows for major revisions and changes in the direction and focus of the research.

Another requirement of positivist and postpositivist research is the statement of specific questions and hypotheses before the research is begun. The doctoral student posed several questions including "Does the frequency of instructor participation affect student perceived learning and satisfaction in the course?" and "Does the timing of instructor participation affect student perceived learning and satisfaction of the course?" and "What effect does the frequency at which the instructor provides feedback in online discussions have on the depth of dialogue and engagement in higher-order learning among students?" These are all very important questions and definitive answers to them would be a boon to the many thousands of instructional designers creating online courses and online learning environments. This is precisely the sorts of very specific questions that applied educational technology research attempts to answer when it is guided by the postpositivist paradigm.

The problem, in my view, is that it is virtually impossible to answer such questions in any way that produces a generalizable, law-like answer. That is because the learning environment is a complex setting in which hundreds, if not thousands, of factors can influence the outcomes. You cannot design a study of online learning, for example, that will represent *all* online learning. It does not exist. There are too many possible differences. Here is a list of the way the online course to be studied in this dissertation was different from some, most, or virtually all other online courses:

1. The students were in high school.
2. Many were taking the course because it was needed to qualify for college financial aid.
3. The course topic was computer science.
4. Students were at several schools and groups of students at each of the participating schools completed the course in a computer room at their school. Thus, they had the opportunity to talk face to face and discuss the course with the other students at their school who were taking the course. Many, in fact, knew each other before they began the course.
5. There was a certified teacher who facilitated the course and supervised the computer room while the course was being taught.
6. The research was conducted in a "high stakes testing" state.
7. Many students were taking their first online course.
8. The course was somewhat teacher-centered in that there were weekly assignments, readings, homework assignments, and required group discussions using threaded discussion software and email. Discussions were initiated by a question the teacher posed. However, there were also some student-centered activities including the requirement that students collaboratively create and carry out a group project.

How can we make law-like generalizations from this study to other online courses when so many things that may influence the outcome will be different? We can't. The positivist approach of looking for universal or general answers in studies that are done in either laboratories where everything can be controlled (but which are nothing like the applied context of a classroom) may be hopeless. However, the applied positivist approach of doing research in the real world—in this case the distance education classrooms of several high schools—is also problematic because there are too many potentially powerful influences in those classrooms that may not be present in other distance education courses. Would research done in rural Texas high schools, for example, produce conclusions and implications that we can confidently predict will be applicable in open university courses taught in Indonesia, or Siberia, or Westchester County, New York? Would we even have the confidence to apply them to a high school distance education course taught in the inner city schools of Los Angeles, or in the rural wheat lands of Saskatchewan, or the sunny classrooms of Bermuda?

Another potential threat to the validity of this study is the research design. It uses a sophisticated time series design in which half the students will experience "immediate feedback" from the instructor and half will have "delayed feedback." Thus, at any given time, half the students in each school will be getting immediate feedback while the other half will be receiving delayed feedback. Across the semester the two treatments will switch several times. Students receiving immediate feedback will be switched to delayed, and vice versa. This is an interrupted times series design and it has much to recommend it. However, there are two contraindications. One is that the treatment may have a permanent or long lasting effect. For example, if you are conducting a study of blood pressure medications, this type of research methodology would be fine if the effect of a medication on blood pressure stops immediately when the medication is discontinued. However, if a medication stays in the body for extended periods of time and continues to influence blood pressure (or causes a permanent change in the body's own control mechanisms) an interrupted time series analysis would not be appropriate because you could not tell if the data you are gathering reflects the impact of the current medication, or a medication the subject was taking weeks, or months ago. In an educational study, the response style of an instructor could, potentially, have extended effects which makes the time series design questionable. A second concern is that the switching back and forth between treatments may itself generate a response that affects the outcome of the study. Humans are not rocks. They respond not simply to what actually happens to them but to their interpretation of *why* it is happening. Some students, who do not get quick replies from the instructor, may develop their own reasons for why others get fast replies and they do not. Some may think their posts must not be very good, or that the instructor is biased against their school, gender, or race. Such reactions will not happen if you treat two sets of sedentary rocks differently and there is no need to consider the possibility if you are a geologist studying rocks. However, humans are not only capable, they are likely to make such responses and that must be taken into consideration in evaluating the usefulness of a particular research design.

For the first ten or so years after completing my doctoral work, I devoted myself to positivist research, looking for answers to important questions in my field. However, as I began to doubt the research model, I began to look for alternatives. One alternative is to conduct studies that provide detailed information on what happened in a particular context (and to describe that context in detail as well). Many forms of qualitative research fit that description. A further departure from postitivist models would be to leave the generalization to the reader. Your responsibility is to help the reader develop an understanding of what happened in a particular situation. You may even propose abstract explanations or theories of why things happened the way they did in your study. But you do not propose those as Laws or Theories that are universal. Instead, it is the reader's responsibility to decide what he or she can take from your work and use, or adapt, to their context of professional practice.

How would a study of the instructor's roles in an online course using collaborative learning be conducted using this alternative framework? First, there would probably not be two treatment conditions. Instead, the instructor might be asked to read the stories, narratives, and research studies relevant to instructor roles and then develop his or her own approach. Then the researcher might study the course through a combination of observation and an analysis of the discussion threads. Interviews of the instructor and students might focus on their views of the instructor's roles, and the patterns of interaction in the discussion threads could help the researcher come to some conclusions about instructor roles and online learning. These would be presented in an article that tells the story of that course and the understanding of how it worked that evolved from the researcher's analysis of the qualitative data such as interviews, artifacts such as projects, and observations.

If we give up the positivist perspective on how empirical research should be used to guide practice then sources of knowledge expand considerably. That is particularly true if we adopt a more context-sensitive form of generalization that assumes many aspects of the context of study are important. Some of the potentially useful forms of scholarship that are alternatives to traditional quantitative research are discussed in the next section.

ALTERNATIVE SOURCES OF UNDERSTANDING

Educational technologists who are either ecumenical or who prefer one of the newer paradigms of scholarship are likely to be open to new forms of scholarship. Several "new paradigms" of scholarship will be introduced here and most of them will be discussed in more detail in later chapters:

- **Professional Practice Knowledge**—developed by experienced and reflective practitioners who base their suggestions and ideas on thoughtfully considered experience.
- **Philosophical Inquiry**—papers and books based on the scholarly methods of philosophy and applied to important, even foundational, issues and topics in educational technology. In his paper, Philosophical Inquiry in Educational Technology: The Forgotten Pathway to Learning, David Solomon (2000) makes the case for expanding the use of philosophical inquiry in educational technology scholarship.
- **Narrative Knowing**. There are many ways of knowing something, and one of them is narrative knowing. That is, coming to know something by reading, listening to, or watching the story of an experience, event, or life. Some use the term "lived experience" to indicate what narrative forms of inquiry study and report. Narratives may be true or fictional, and they may be expressed in many different forms—from short stories to plays, films, and novels.
- **Autoethnography.** In this type of qualitative research the researcher is also the subject of the research. Nicholas Holt (2003) explained autoethnography this way:

  > Autoethnography is a genre of writing and research that connects the personal to the cultural, placing the self within a social context. . . . These texts are usually written in the first person and feature dialogue, emotion, and self-consciousness as relational and institutional stories affected by history, social structure, and culture . . . by writing themselves into their own work as major characters, autoethnographers have challenged accepted views about silent authorship, where the researcher's voice is not included in the presentation of findings. . . . This development may have liberated some researchers from the constraints of the dominant realist representations of empirical ethnography. (p. 2)

Holt's paper contains advice on how to write an autoethnography and while the focus is on anthropological and sociological issues, it is also a useful guide to writing authethnographies in educational technology. Suitable and informative applications of this type of research includes autoethnographies written by designers as they work through the process of leading instructional design projects, by teachers as they try to cope with new educational technologies in the classroom, and teacher education students trying to make the transition from user of consumer information technologies to professional educator considering the possible ways to integrate technology into the classroom.

- **Rhetorically superior books and papers.** Today there are outstanding books, workshops, and seminars on everything from how to write the great American novel to designing an outstanding Power-Point presentation or producing a compelling documentary. Writing, and the creation of multimedia materials, is a technical process at some level. But the creation of outstanding, superior papers, books, and multimedia are also artistic activities that depend both on innate potential, experience, and developed talents. Few of us received very much training once we were in graduate school in the arts of persuasion. In my own experience, I completed my doctorate in a psychology department where the ideal for writing papers was the terse, boring format of the psychology research paper. It took me years to unlearn that form and begin to write readable papers. While I believe it is important that scholars become better communicators, regardless of the paradigm they use, one of the most interesting books I have come across lately is by James Ladwig (1992) at the University of Newcastle in Australia. In his book, *Academic Distinctions: Theory and Methodology in the Sociology of School Knowledge*, Ladwig argues that many of the dichotomies such as qualitative-quantitative and the ism conflicts such as positivism versus critical theory boil down to rhetoric rather than foundational issue. In Chapter 6, Wherein Lies the Scientific Rhetoric?, Ladwig comments that his critique of older postpositivist paradigms and newer more relativistic paradigms will begin by

  > viewing science as a form of rhetoric. To question the modes of rhetoric in the discourses of RSSK [Radical Sociology of School Knowledge], I then present a distinction between two forms of rhetoric: what I heuristically call a philosophic rhetoric of demonstration and a scientific rhetoric of evidence. [While I have] chosen to emphasize the way in which these discourses have tended to rely mostly on philosophic discourse, and to question the structure of authority in their rhetorical mode, this distinction is admittedly and intentionally polemic... But this perspective on science is not only mine. The notion that scientific discourse is a form of rhetoric itself has origins in many disciplines, one of which is the study of rhetoric itself, and has been suggested partially as one way of relating competing knowledge claims. (p. 144)

If Ladwig is correct, being a successful scholar in education and educational technology will require us all to learn some of the basics of rhetoric, and to successfully convince others to consider our viewpoints, ideas, and research findings calls for us to use our own well-developed rhetorical talents.

- **Qualitative Case Studies.** Instead of collecting a small amount of information (e.g., a test score) from hundreds of subjects, qualitative case studies collect a huge and diverse amount of qualitative and quantitative data from only a few subjects. Case studies often focus on only one individual or one school, classroom, or group of children or teachers. If understanding the context is very important when considering the application of study findings to other settings, the rich and diverse range of data provided is an important and desirable feature of qualitative case studies.
- **Design As Research.** In their introduction to a research symposium (http://www.riba.org/go/RIBA/Member/Practice_4879.html) on design as research, the Royal Institute of British Architects introduced the topic this way.

> In recent years the architectural profession has seen the rise of new research-oriented activities that extend and challenge existing ideas of architectural practice. In a profession that has for many years focused design work and thinking on one-off or singular building and planning commissions, architecture is finding itself increasingly drawn towards ways of working and new kinds of projects that emphasize sustained, extended, forms of research. Areas of research include new digital and other design systems; new building materials and construction technologies; new forms of design related to the management of client spaces, facilities and other resources; new kinds of creative, multi-disciplinary and collaborative working environments; and the new ways in which traditional "built" forms of space and structure relate to today's expanded media, product, and design environment. At the same time new graduate and design programmes have been established whose interest is in pursuing these and other related topics; to the degree that professional and academic interests are now converging in many new and unexpected ways around the topic of design as research.

This description of design as research could easily be transported to educational technology with only a few revisions. A core activity of educational technologists is the design of instructional resources and there is a growing interest in scholarship that looks at the design process itself or the design process as a way of producing certain types of resources. The idea of considering instructional design and related activities as potential scholarship or research would probably have been considered humorous by many a decade or so ago. Today, "design as research" (DAR) and "research as design (RAD), or both together RADDAR, is a hot topic in education, educational technology, and in educational research.

For example, *The Handbook of Research Design in Mathematics and Science Education* that was published in 2000 by Lawrence Erlbaum Publishers devotes Part 6 of the handbook to "Curriculum Design as Research." Also, the AERA journal, *Educational Researcher,* published a special issue on design as research in January/February, 2003 (Issue 32, Number 1). While many of the papers use a postpositivist foundation, the special issue is well worth reading and it is available online at http://www.aera.net/publications/. One person who has been a spokesperson for design as an artistic and scholarly/research process is Brenda Laurel. She recently (2003) edited a book, *Design Research: Methods and Perspectives,* that is both an example of one form of design research and a valuable source of information about design as research. It contains the reflective comments and discussions of 49, mostly American, designers. Interest in design as research (DAR) has spread to many of the disciplines that focus on the creation of products. Popovic (no date), for example, teaches in the School of Design and Built Environment at Queensland University of Technology. His paper is a discussion of how "product design research should not function as a distraction from practice, but as a development of it" (p. 1). His work focuses on industrial design but it applies to instructional design as well. He is concerned to make doctoral research more relevant and more closely tied to professional practice. While he believes there is an important body of knowledge and expertise that supports the design process, he also notes that

> the most recent studies of human expertise demonstrated the importance of situation and context. They showed a much broader view toward human expertise and knowledge acquisition and utilization taking into account the importance of the social condition and the context in which the activity occurred. (p. 3)

He suggests that doctoral research "should be directed toward new or significant contributions to knowledge, where the knowledge sources are generated from people, context, activity and culture" (p. 3). His approach is very similar to the one proposed in this book because it acknowledges the importance of context and focuses on scholarship in the real world rather than in artificial or laboratory settings. Popovic even provides a list of data collection techniques and research methods, all of them qualitative approaches: checklists, focus groups, ethnographic methods, interviewing users, observation, protocol analysis, questionnaires, stories, scenarios and life-style explorations.

An approach related to DAR is "research for practice." One group of proponents (Shrader, et al., 2001) at The Center for Learning Technologies in Urban Schools believe that

> while educational researchers have much to offer schools in terms of improved practice, we have been largely ineffective in providing that help. In our view, this failure derives from reliance upon a "knowledge delivery" model of educational innovation in which researchers design solutions steeped in theory and research and deliver them to schools. Practitioners often see these solutions as too theoretical and impractical for real world classrooms. Learning to leverage the products of educational research toward improved schooling requires both researchers and practitioners to learn new practices. Research for practice bridges the divide by engaging researchers and practitioners in participatory design teams that value the knowledge, experience and expertise of all involved. In effect, participatory design becomes a mechanism for researchers and practitioners to learn through interaction with one another. (p. 1)

The paper, which is available online, is a thoughtful exploration of an approach to engaging academics and practicing teachers in a participatory process of designing and deploying innovations. The model they use is one attractive way of practicing design as research. Another interesting application of the design as research model is Andrew Stapleton's (2003) doctoral dissertation at Curtin University of Technology in Australia. The focus of the dissertation is the design of an interactive multimedia system, SR Voyager, for physics instruction. Stapleton's dissertation is an example of design as research but the software he developed also uses the idea of design as a means of learning. His format for the dissertation was also interesting and unusual:

> In writing the thesis, I adopted a *screenplay* metaphor that enabled me to present the stages of inquiry as three "acts" (the classic "beginning," "middle," and "end" structure) ... Within each act there exists a hierarchical structure that follows the format of Act, at the top of the hierarchy, then Scene, Shot, Frame and Focus (which can also be subdivided) at the bottom. ... In each act, the first scene provides a largely linear *narrative account* of my research journey. Narrative approaches in qualitative research ... are a representational means of binding researcher, researched and reader, through a written research story. By adopting this style, the reader enters an interpretive, descriptive, emotional, dramatic, fragmented and personal account of the research that aims to (insightfully, reflexively, dialogically) situate the reader in the lifeworld experiences of those involved. This style is quite

> unlike reports in the realist genre which, under the "myth of cold-reason"... of positivism, adopt a rationalistic worldview and offer an (illusionary) value-neutral, objective, and unemotional representation of the research which concentrates on the researched, with the voice of the researcher noticeably absent. (p. 4–5)

Stapleton's thesis is online at http://pctaylor.smec.curtin.edu.au/mentoring/Andrew%20St/Stapleton-Thesis_Excerpt.pdf .

- **Clinical Research.** This form of scholarship is most often associated with medical research. It involves the study of real patients with real problems in the context of professional practice. Miller and Crabtree (2005) describe clinical research this way:

> the clinical research space is created by focusing on the questions arising from the clinical experience and opens many possibilities for using the full range of qualitative data-gathering and analysis methods... The challenge is to preserve the integrity of the questions and to translate qualitative collection and analysis methods into clear and jargon-free language without sacrificing the methods' integrity rooted in the soil of disciplinary conversations.

The authors also suggest that clinical researchers have at least six different research styles available to them: experimental, survey, documentary-historical, qualitative field research, philosophical scholarship, and action/participatory research. These methods should be used by clinical researchers to accomplish two major goals: "to deepen and contextualize the practical and ethical questions, concerns, and emerging understanding for healers and their patients and policymakers" and to "trouble the waters and seek change within the clinical research world itself" (p. 609). As viewed by Miller and Crabtree clinical research has much in common with design as research scholarship and critical theory scholarship. However, clinical research has its own traditions, journals, and organizations and the field of clinical research may be a source of models and frameworks for research in educational technology. Miller and Crabtree, for example, believe clinical research has unique demands that call for a diversity of methods.

> Research designs in clinical research inherently require multimethod thinking and critical multiplism, with the particular combinations of data-gathering and analysis/interpretation approaches being driven by the research question and the clinical context. There are infinite possibilities for integrating qualitative and quantitative methods, with the design being created for each study and the qualitative aspects often evolving as a study progresses in response to the emerging questions. Participatory research approaches, in particular, usually involve a more emergent design process. (p. 621)

- **Participatory Action Research (PAR)**. PAR is a form of scholarship that focuses on the problems and issues of professional practice. It involves the identification of a significant issue, the development of a collaborative group of stakeholders who are interested in exploring solutions or answers, and a period of careful study that often involves the development and implementation of potential solutions to a problem. PAR is often a recursive process because a solution that is tried out often fails to achieve all that was hoped for it, and a new round of PAR begins with the development of a new solution (or the revision of an old one). Yoland Wadsorth (1998) has described how she sees PAR in relationship to traditional research.

> For me, participatory action research is not a different and separate matter from science at all, but constitutes a formulation of how I understand all science in the wake of the wave of thinking that is popularly being called the "new physics." This "new physics" or "new paradigm science" in the natural physical world seems to me to match a "new paradigm science" in the social world. I identify "participatory action research" not as an optional variant or specialist technique, but as one of the more inclusive descriptions of this new understanding of social science.

Her short paper is a good introduction to one method of PAR and it is available online.

- **Professional Discourse.** One of the often overlooked forms of scholarship and learning is the discussions professionals and scholars have in their day to day practice, at conferences and in workshops, through seminars, and via other settings where it is appropriate to "talk shop." While all these are considered rather informal ways to disseminate ideas and to learn about ideas, they are, nevertheless, very important sources of information. It is important to join or develop one or more professional/scholarly communities that are a source of professional and scholarly knowledge and expertise. Often, instructional technologists are members of one or more local or regional groups (plus as a group at the organization where they work) as well as members of two or more national/international groups.

Many educational technologists who are comfortable with non-postpositivist paradigms of practice and scholarship may also be comfortable with new formats for the presentation of scholarship such as:

- **Performance Ethnography.** This involves presenting results of scholarship in formats such as plays, music, video, and works of art. Barbara Tedlock (2005) justifies performance ethnography this way.

> Performance is everywhere in life: from simple gestures to melodramas and macrodramas. Because dramatic performance can communicate engaged political and theoretical analysis, together with nuanced emotional portraits of human beings, they have gained acceptance by a number of documentarians. Plays and other performances become vibrant forms of ethnography and combine political, critical, and expressive actions centering on lived experiences locally and globally. A number of ethnographers have served as producers, actors, and dramaturges...Because culture is emergent in human interaction rather than located deep inside individual brains or hearts, or loosely attached to external material objects or impersonal social structures, dramas are a powerful way to both shape and show cultural construction in action. Because of this subjective quality, plays create and enact moral texts that communicate vibrant emotional portraits of human beings, together with an empathic response and deeply engaged political analysis. (pp. 469–470)

Very little, if any, of the scholarship of educational technology uses performance ethnography but many applications come to mind.

- **Documentary Film.** This form of presentation is akin to performance ethnography, and it has not been extensively used in educational technology research. It has considerable potential, however. Spike Lee's recent documentary film, When the Levees Broke, is a very powerful way of telling the story of what happened to citizens of New Orleans when Hurricane Katrina hit. It does not replace the statistical analyses, empirical research, or newspaper reports, but the visual and personal nature of the documentary helps viewers develop new and different insights and understanding about what happened. Documentary film is one of many forms of visual representation. The term visual ethnography covers several forms of scholarship in which the topic of study or the medium of expression is video, still images, or audio. For example, the result of a study in visual ethnography or visual anthropology may be a photo essay or a documentary film. Jay Ruby, a professor of cultural anthropology at Temple University, conducted a study of diversity in Oak Park, Illinois. His report contains photos and video clips. The study, *Maintaining Diversity: An Ethnographic Study of Oak Park, Illinois*, was completed in December of 2006. You can read and view it online at http://astro.temple.edu/~ruby/opp/. It illustrates one way of presenting the results of a study using a format other than traditional text-based papers. If you are interested in making documentary films one useful resource is Barry Hampe's (2007) *Making Documentary Films and Videos: A Practical Guide to Planning, Filming, and Editing Documentaries*. Another is Sheila Curran Bernard's (2007) *Documentary Storytelling*.

- **Stories, Storytelling and Narrative Inquiry.** Sometimes it is more powerful to tell the story of one student, one class, or one community than it is to present an analyzed and synthesized generalization that is one or more levels of abstraction away from the reality that stories bring the reader. Traditional research papers, even when they are dealing with terrible things that happen to children and adults, often engage cognition but not emotion. But, a full understanding of many things calls for both a cognitive and an emotional connection. In their paper on how instructional designers deal with issues such as values and ethics as they serve as agents of social change, Katy Campbell, Richard Schwier and Richard Kenny (2005) used a combination of philosophical analysis and story telling. Many of their points were made through telling stories about the work of two instructional designers. The narrative they present is a primary means of making their points. This paper is one of the readings for this chapter and it illustrates the use of both story telling and philosophical inquiry.

  One of many forms of narrative or story telling is *testimonio—*

  > a novel or novella-length narrative, produced in the form of a printed text, told in the first person by a narrator who is also the real protagonist or witness of the events she or he recounts. Its unit of narration is usually a 'life' or a significant life experience. Because in many cases the direct narrator is someone who is either functionally illiterate or, if literate, not a professional writer, the production of a *testimonio* generally involves the tape recording and then the transcription and editing of an oral account by an interlocutor who is a journalist, ethnographer, or literary author. (Beverley, 2005, p. 547)

  Susan Chase (2005) also used narrative inquiry in her study of women school superintendents and she is positive about the developing interest in narrative. "These days, narrative inquiry in the social sciences is flourishing. Signs of this burgeoning interest include an interdisciplinary journal called *Narrative Inquiry,* a book series of The Narrative Study of Lives, and professional conferences specifically showcasing narrative work" (p. 651). However she sees narrative inquiry as still a work in progress.

  > Nonetheless, I still get the sense that narrative inquiry is a field in the making. Researchers new to this field will find a rich but diffuse tradition, multiple methodologies in various stages of development, and plenty of opportunities for exploring new ideas, methods, and questions. (p. 651)

  Many topics in educational technology are suited to narrative inquiry.

SUMMARY

Traditional research methods in the social sciences have typically been based on the foundations laid by Aristotle and Plato. Both Plato's rationalist and Aristotle's empiricist traditions are also alive and well in education and educational technology. Two other Greek traditions have been less influential over the last 100 years. They are the literary tradition of Homer and the rhetorical tradition of the Sophists. However, these traditions are potential contributors to both the scholarly methods of education and educational technology as well as the methods of communicating scholarly knowledge. The narrative and storytelling traditions of the Greeks, in fact all of the Greek humanities, were rejected by Plato as misleading and undesirable. Unfortunately, intellectual descendants of Plato have generally held sway in American social sciences, particularly psychology, and in education. The result is that only recently have the methods of the humanities begun to be considered by a few as part of the methodological resources of scholars. This shift, which is a shift away from Plato's view and toward Aristotle's opinions about the humanities, has opened the door to a wide variety of methods that were previously considered totally unacceptable. As a field, educational technology, has typically lagged behind other areas of education when it comes to considering these new options, but even educational technology is becoming more open to them.

The same is true of rhetoric which is really the art and craft of communicating effectively. Fields like advertising have always been aware of the importance of the quality of the message as well as the content. Scholars have not always understood that and, in fact, have often seemed to reject the idea that research and scholarship will have a greater impact if it is communicated well. Stroll through the periodical room of any university library and select a few hard core research journals. Then compare them to a few successful magazines that compete for market share with other for-profit magazines. The difference in design quality between the research journals and the mainstream magazines is striking. This may even be particularly true when it comes to the journals in our field—educational technology! Well written, well designed papers, conference presentations, and web resources are more effective in influencing others, but we do not seem to pay a great deal of attention to this truism. Also, despite its emphasis on the design of effective learning resources, educational technology rarely uses innovative methods to communicate scholarship such as performance ethnography, documentary film, narrative, or storytelling. There is a great deal of room for improvement!

REFERENCES

Beverley, J. (2005). Testimonio, subalternity, and narrative authority. In N. Denzin & Y. Lincoln (Eds.), *Handbook of qualitative research* (3rd ed., pp. 547–558). Thousand Oaks, CA: Sage.

Curran B. S. (2007). *Documentary storytelling* (2nd ed.). Burlington, MA: Focal Press/ Elsevier.

Hampe, B. (2007) *Making documentary films and videos: A practical guide to planning, filming, and editing documentaries* (2nd ed.). New York: Holt Paperback.

Hold, N. (2003). Representation, legitimatino, and authethnography: An autoethnographic writing story. *International Journal of Qualitative Methods, 2*(1), Article 2. Retrieved May 1, 2007 from http://www.ualberta.ca/!iiqm/backissues/2_1final/html/holt.html.

Miller, W. & Crabtree, B. (2005). Clinical research. In N. Denzin & Y. Lincoln (Eds) *Handbook of qualitative research* (2nd ed., pp. 605–639). Thousand Oaks, CA: Sage.

Jonassen, D. (Ed) (1996). *Handbook of research for educational communications and technology.* New York: Simon and Schuster.

Merrill, M. D., Drake, L., Lacy, M., Pratt, J., & the ID2 Research Group (1996). Reclaiming instructional design. *Educational Technology, 36*(5), 5–7.

Murphy, J. (1983). *A synoptic history of classical rhetoric.* Davis, CA: Hermaoras Press.

Jacob, B. (1996, Spring). What if Aristotle took sophists seriously? New readings in Aristotle's Rhetoric. *Rhetoric Review, 14*(2), 237–252.

Popovic, V. (no date). *An approach to knowledge generation by research and its utilization in practice—situating doctoral research around artifacts.* Retrieved May 1, 2007 from http://www.idemployee.id.tue.nl/g.w.m.rauterberg/conferences/CD_doNotOpen/DED/d_final_paper/d_14.pdf

Shrader, G., Williams, K., Lachance-Whitcomb, J. Finn, L., & Gomez, L. (2001). *Participatory design of science curricula: The case for research as practice.* Paper presented at the annual meeting of the American Educational Research Association, Seattle, Washington, April 11, 2001.

Stapleton, A. (2003). *A study of the design of interactive multimedia to improve learning of physics concepts.* Thesis presented for the Degree of Doctor of Science Education at Curtin University of Technology. Retrieved May 1, 2007 from http://pctaylor.smec.curtin.edu.au/mentoring/Andrew%20St/Stapleton-Thesis_Excerpt.pdf

Wadsworth, Y. (1998). What is participatory action research? *Action Research International,* Paper 2. Retrieved May 1, 2007 from http://www.scu.edu.au/schools/gcm/ar/ari/ari-papers.html

Warschauer, M. (2004). The rhetoric and reality of aid: Promoting educational technology in Egypt. *Globalization, Societies and Education, 2*(3), 22–39.

READINGS FOR CHAPTER 4

Reading 4.1

Stapleton, A. & Taylor, P. (2003). *Representing Research (&) Development.* Paper presented at the annual conference of the Australasian Science Education Research Association (ASERA), Melbourne, 9–12 July 2003. Available: http://www.andrewstapleton.com/?page_ID=21

Andrew Stapleton is a professor at Swinburn Univesity of Technology in Melborune, Australia and one of his specialties is game design. Peter Taylor is a professor at Curtin University of Technology in Sydney, Australia. Dr. Taylor is a specialist in science and mathematics education with a focus on preparing teachers to become critical reflective practitioners. Together, these two scholars have written a paper titled "Representing Research (&) Development." The paper focuses on interpretive research and deals specifically with the question of how research and development work should be "represented." That is, how should it be disseminated to others? The authors begin with a discussion of "the literary turn" which has brought to educational research and scholarship new alternatives for how to present the findings of scholarship and research.

Do you agree with the authors that adopting an alternative style of disseminating your scholarship must necessarily influence "our epistemology of inquiry? Why? Could you not remain a positivist and an empiricist and write a play or a Platonic dialog about your research? If not, why not?

The idea that "as one writes one inquires" is a common perspective in interpretivist research. How would adopting that stance change research and scholarship in educational technology? The more common format is to collect data, analyze it, and then write the results and discussion sections of your paper. It is a fairly linear process. Would you be comfortable writing as you were collecting data and revising, reformulating, and developing implications from the start of the study? Does blending writing with all the other actions of research and scholarship make sense? Why?

How comfortable were you with ideas in the paper like including confessional and impressionist voices, and many other subjective components? Why do you think your comfort zone is as it is? Do you think the university program you graduated from (or that you currently attend) would accept Andrew's dissertation which uses a screenplay metaphor? Why?

Which is most foreign to you in Andrew's dissertation—the screenplay metaphor, the heavy reliance on narrative, or the non-linear structure? Explain why you feel the way you do?

Take a traditional scholarly or research paper in educational technology that is based on an objectivist and positivist framework. Then decide what would change in the paper if it were written under the guidelines proposed by Stapleton and Taylor. Could it be the "same" study, or would the guidelines force it to become a "different study?"

A few electronic journals accept papers with hyperlinks, multimedia material, and other forms of advanced digital information. How do you see the future? Will most of the educational technology journals eventually do this too? Will it be because the editors change their views of what "good" research is, or because the technology is available and editors want to use it?

Reading 4.2

Craig, C. (2006). Why is dissemination so difficult? The nature of teacher knowledge and the spread of curriculum reform. *American Educational Research Journal, 43*(2), 257–293.

Cheryl Craig is a professor of curriculum and instruction and one of her research interests is dissemination. The beginning of her title expresses her concern precisely, "Why is dissemination so difficult?" To get at this issue she used narrative inquiry to look at a significant effort at curriculum reform. After reading this article, what is your understanding of narrative inquiry as a research method? Does Craig's use of it seem to be a typical "mainstream" approach or is it a specialized application?

When you read the entire paper develop two or three ideas for a narrative inquiry in educational technology. What topics would you study? How would you gather data, and how would you interpret it and write the papers based on your narrative study? Would your studies be based the same theoretical foundations Craig used or something different? Structuralist theory? Poststructuralist? Critical theory? Interpretivism? Hermeneutics?

Craig uses the theories of Dewey, Jackson, Schwab, Eisner, Schon, Lyons, as well as Clandinin and Connelly. Which of these seem to be theories about human behavior and which seem to focus on theories about how to study human behavior? Can you separate these two issues, or are they so interrelated that you cannot talk about one without talking about the other? Why?

Craig uses a number of phrases and terms in her paper that are important to an understanding of her approach to the issue she addresses. One of them is "teachers' professional knowledge landscapes." What does this mean and does the term effectively convey what Craig intends? Why? Are there other critical phrases or terms that are unusual but essential to understanding Craig's paper? What are they and how do they work?

Consider the stories Craig told in her paper. Is narrative inquiry really a research method and is telling stories a way of contributing to our understanding of education? Defend the position you take and anticipate the arguments that would likely be made against your position. How would you answer critics who make those arguments?

What is your opinion of the power of Craig's narrative inquiry to address the questions that concerned her? Would another method have been more effective? Why? Given that she used narrative inquiry, how confident are you of the knowledge you drew from reading the paper? Would you be more confident if another research method had been used? Why?

Finally, what issues in educational technology would, in your opinion, be profitably approached by narrative inquiry?

Reading 4.3

Coulter, D. (1999, May). The Epic and the Novel: Dialogism and Teacher Researcher. *Educational Researcher,* 4–13.

The research and scholarship of the social sciences has two "relatives" and one of them has been very close to the social sciences for over a hundred years while the other relative has often been ignored and rejected. The "close" relative is the research methods of the natural sciences and the rejected relative is the scholarly methods of the humanities. In Chapter 4 I suggested that we tear down the walls between the social sciences and the humanities so that we can use the knowledge of the humanities as well as learn the methods of inquiry of the humanities. This paper, by David Coulter at the University of British Columbia, is an exploration of the implications for dialog and education. His basic premise is that practicing teachers are an invaluable source of knowledge about education, and that the voices of teachers have been silenced or unheard for at least a century. For much of the 20th century the role of a teacher was to consume research (or at least the implications of research) done by others. Teachers, because they were practitioners, because they were invested in the success of their students and thus subjective, and because they worked in the real world where the precise and controlled conditions of experimentation could not be arranged, were not acceptable as sources of scholarship and research. Coulter points out that hermeneutic inquiry has become a foundation for a growing advocacy of the teacher as researcher. The best known result of this line of support is a set of methods for doing research and scholarship in the real world. The most popular of these today is action research or participatory action research, but there are a number of others.

Coulter proposes another way of bridging the gap between practitioners and researchers, and uniting them in the same person. He refers to it as *dialogic research.* The foundation of this approach is a bit off the beaten path for research in education. It is the literary theories of Mikhail Bakhtin, a Russian scholar who was born in Czarist Russia in 1895 and lived through the 1917 Revolution and through both Lenin's rule and Stalin's totalitarian rule. He died in 1975, just ten years before Mikhail Gorbachev became leader of the USSR and 16 years before the Soviet Union collapsed.

As you read the summary of Bakhtin's theories of dialogue, language, and literature (especially the novel) ask yourself these three questions: In traditional educational technology practice is this relevant or irrelevant? If it is relevant, how does the traditional epistemic or "natural science" view in our field deal with the same topic? Finally, what would be the implications of adopting Bakhtin's theories as both relevant and believable?

There are a number of odd terms in Bakhtin's theories. Keep a list of them and write a brief, one or two line explanation of what they mean to you. Include terms like langue, heteroglot, polyphony, chronotope, and carnival.

Do you think Bakhtin's idea of languages having built in support for particular viewpoints and perspectives is accurate? Is language a messy but useful way of communicating in a process that is simultaneously trying to create divergent languages that best represent particular positions and perspectives while at the same time trying to unify different languages into a universal One language? What implications does this have for educational technology scholarship? Are there groups within educational technology that engage in monologues? Who are they? Are there groups that engage in dialog? Who are they?

Are Foucault's concerns with monologism as a means of creating and supporting one dominant ideology realistic? Isn't that what a scientific approach tries to do—gradually bring us closer and closer to the Truth about what we are trying to do in a profession?

In educational technology, how could you apply the techniques Bakhtin used to study dialogic communication in the novels of Dostoevsky and Rabelais as well as uncover monologue/ideology? How would a teacher use the method? A scholar looking at the research literature of educational technology, or the papers produced by various organizations or think tanks? How would the concepts of chronotope and carnival be integrated into educational technology scholarship?

How do you think a paper about educational technology that is dialogic rather than monologic and that includes "a plurality of independent and unmerged voices and consequences, a polyphony of fully valid voices" would be treated by the reviewers of a journal in the field? Don't we expect papers to raise an issue and then provide a solution? Can research and scholarship be polyphonic? Can it be like one of Dostoevsky's novels?

Coulter applies the theories of Bakhtin to a problem he faced while working as an Assistant Superintendent in a school district. After he tells the story of the project to study the value of retention, he concludes that "the epic was supplanted by the novel." What does that mean? And is it a reasonable outcome for educational research and scholarship?

SECTION 2

PATHWAYS TO UNDERSTANDING

CHAPTER 5

PURPOSES, PHRONESIS, AND BENT FLYVBJERG

Earlier chapters have already discussed the goals of positivist and postpositivist models of research. The goal is to do research that helps us develop "universal laws of behavior," "dependable regularities," or some other form of relatively abstract and general statements that apply to many different local instances of the general law. Since the natural sciences developed laws like that (e.g., Boyles Law of Gasses, Newton's Law of Gravitation), some scholars in the social sciences have envied the successes of the older and more established natural sciences. They have attempted to build social sciences on the same foundation and for the same purpose—to find laws of human behavior.

In this approach, basic social science research begins with a theory and derives basic but testable conclusions that will be true if the theory is true (see Figure 5.1). When those conclusions are tested by well designed empirical research and supported by the data, they become potential laws of human behavior.

The product of basic positivist research is thus a set of laws or rules that tell us how humans will behave in certain circumstances. Basic researchers then derive implications for practice from those laws that can guide professionals in their day to day work. Those implications thus guide professional practice. This model is often referred to as the technical-rational model because it seems to reduce good professional practice to following the

Qualitative Research Methods in Education and Educational Technology, pages 121–147
Copyright © 2008 by Information Age Publishing
121

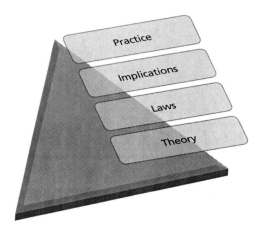

Figure 5.1 A hierarchical model of basic positivist social science.

guidelines (implications) for practice that naturally flow from the laws of human behavior developed from empirical research. This approach presents the research endeavor as a monolithic march toward more and more precision and accuracy in the laws developed, and thus better and better implications. Anyone familiar with the literature on teaching, educational technology, or education policy will know that this process is certainly not monolithic. The laws developed are generally embedded in a particular theory (e.g., cognitive science, Vygotskian social constructivism, Piagetian cognitive constructivism, Skinnerian behaviorism, Freudianism, or any of a dozen or more theories about human development and learning.

Applied social science research (and I include education and educational technology in this category) strives to show how models or theories of professional practice derived from the implication of laws embedded in theories can be shown to work.

Figure 5.2 illustrates the process. From the implications of laws an applied theory or a model for practice is developed. For example, many of the models for doing instructional design fit this linear pattern. Applied to instructional design, the general theory or model would be at the bottom of the pyramid. At that level you could, in a positivist research model, do several types of research. Does a particular ID model (e.g., Dick and Carey model, the generic ADDIE model (e.g., Analyze, Design, Develop, Implement, Evaluate), or one of the hundred or so other models) support the development of effective instructional resources? Does a behavioral, linear model work "better" than a non-linear, constructivist ID model? At the next level up, the focus is on strategies which are more specific. In instructional design models, there are generally a number of components. Research questions that can be asked at this level include "Is learner analysis a critical

Figure 5.2   A model of applied positivist social science research.

step in the process? Or, should learner analysis be done early in the process or spread across the design and development process? Or, does using a participatory team in ID enhance the quality of the materials developed? If so, at what cost in terms of time and effort?

In a positivist/postpositivist framework, the result of research on both ID models and ID strategies can be one or more recipes. These recipes are essentially prescriptions about how to perform professional tasks such as design instructional materials, teach a science lesson to middle grades students, or develop collaborative teams in high school history classes.

The basic and applied positivist research models represent one form of generalization that is based on the ability of the social sciences to find law-like rules that apply across many, diverse situations. I do not believe the social sciences have achieved that degree of accuracy and I am not sure they ever will. What is needed is a new form of generalization which was mentioned in an earlier chapter. It assumes that what can be generalized from social science scholarship is a local, not a universal phenomenon. And, if research is local and contextual, then the successful application of the findings, conclusions, implications, models, and strategies also depend on the local context of application. Thus, someone who knows the local context intimately is in the best position to make decisions about what to take and apply or adapt in a new context. There are thus no "recipes," only suggestions, guidelines, and hunches. This kinder and gentler form of generalization is supported by a theoretical perspective that began with Aristotle. It is to that perspective that we turn in the next section.

A further problem for the applied positivist research model is that it expects us to maintain doctrinal purity. That is, if you are creating and evaluating an instructional design model based on behavioral theory, the approach does not take kindly to designing a blended ID model that includes features from different theoretical frameworks. If excellent work on ID models has been done within a "foreign" theoretical framework, practitioners and scholars working in a different paradigm may not even know about it. And if they do, they may be very reluctant to consider incorporating it into their own ID model. This is an example of the type of theoretical fundamentalism that can become everyday practice in the positivist research model. This approach would be appropriate if the research and scholarship on ID were bringing us closer and closer to the Truth about how to design educational materials. Thus far, the opposite seems to be the case. Work on ID models over the last fifteen years has opened up the field to an increasing variety of ID models rather than helping us focus more and more tightly on the Right way to do it. Unlike the natural sciences, the social sciences in general have not been very successful at this—using positivist research to bracket the truth about an issue and then gradually narrowing the focus until the Truth is revealed. It is time to consider another model of research and scholarship.

ARISTOTLE'S TYPES OF KNOWLEDGE

Much of Greek philosophy was aimed at understanding the eternal truths of what constituted virtuous behavior and what humans should do to become more virtuous. One way of thinking about Plato's epistemology is to say that he divided ways of knowing into different types but he put philosophical knowledge, which might also be called rational knowledge acquired through reflection and contemplation, at the top of a hierarchy that included understanding (which comes from science and mathematics), beliefs, and conjectures. These types of knowledge were organized into the two broad categories of Knowledge (philosophical knowledge and understanding) and Opinion (beliefs and conjectures) (see Figure 5.3).

His view was, however, a hierarchical one with philosophical knowledge by far the most important. That is why Plato believed the ideal rulers of a Greek city state or *polis* should be *philosopher kings*. For Plato, only philosophical inquiry was capable of bringing us in touch with true reality. That true reality, for Plato, was not the changing physical world that Aristotle studied so carefully. It was a reality that could be best understood through mental effort. That mental world was where eternal truths resided. "Having access to such a world, philosophy can offer pertinent and definitive criticisms of received opinions about the nature of meaning, beauty, and goodness. And since it concerns itself with the relationship between eternal and unchanging entities and verities, philosophy can validate its claim to

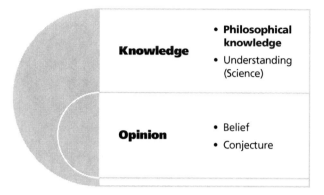

Figure 5.3   A rough representation of Plato's types of knowledge.

possess certain knowledge of what actually exists rather than what seems to exist" (*Science Encyclopedia*, 2007, p. 1–2).

   While the epistemologies of Plato and the positivists are very different on many, if not most, points, they do share one thing in common—both assume the most important type of knowledge, what must be sought over all other types, is absolute, eternal, and universally true knowledge. "The logical positivists had maintained that we can have knowledge only of empirical facts and abstractions, primarily mathematical abstractions, based on those facts. In this view all statements referring to metaphysics, religion, and ethics, if not utterly meaningless, were simply expressions of emotional feelings and preferences—hence the term emotivism to describe an ethics in which all ultimate goals and values are seen as having their roots in the unknowable and irrational" (Sloan, 1994, p. 123). The difference between Plato and positivism is whether that knowledge comes primarily from thought or observation, but the purpose is the same—universal knowledge.

   That was not the case with Aristotle. While he believed there were eternal truths he also accepted and valued a less definitive, less universal type of knowledge.

> Unlike Plato and Socrates, Aristotle did not demand certainty in everything. One cannot expect the same level of certainty in politics or ethics that one can demand in geometry or logic. In Ethics I.3, Aristotle defines the difference in the following way, "we must be satisfied to indicate the truth with a rough and general sketch: when the subject and the basis of a discussion consist of matters which hold good only as a general rule, but not always. . . . For a well-schooled man is one who searches for that degree of precision in each kind of study which the nature of the subject at hand admits: it is obviously just as foolish to accept arguments of probability from a mathematician as to demand strict demonstrations from an orator. (Hooker, 1996)

Thus, Aristotle, the person considered by some to be one of the founders of the modern empirical approach to knowledge, took an alternative view that is particularly appealing to applied disciplines like educational technology. In *Nichomachean Ethics*, Aristotle defined not one, but three types of knowledge:

- **Episteme**—epistemic knowledge or "scientific knowledge" is universal and independent of the context. This type of knowledge comes from the application of Aristotle's version of the scientific approach to studying the world (which some call "analytical rationality"). In Book 6 of *Nichomachean Ethics* Aristotle tells us that "science aims at knowledge of the eternal and is supposed to be teachable." Analytical rationality is a modern term that carries some of the same meaning as episteme. David Cooper (1965) describes it this way.

> By analytical rationality we mean a logic of exteriority according to which truth lies, according to certain criteria, in propositions formed outside the reality with which they are concerned. The epistemological model here is characterized by a dual passivity: the observed system is passive with respect to the observer . . . ; the observer is passive in relation to the system he observes. . . . This type of rationality has a valid field of application in, for example, classical physics, where the objects of science are inert totalities, but its transportation into the fields of psychology, sociology and history is another matter, for here its validity is severely restricted.

Cooper explains in some detail why analytical rationality is appropriate for the natural sciences but not appropriate to the study of humans.

> Experimental natural science is grounded in careful observation. Each investigation must proceed from observed facts. In physical and biological science these observed facts are usually inert facts, that is to say they are grasped from the exterior by an observer who is not disturbed by them and does not disturb them by his process of observation.

This is essentially the positivist/postpositivist tradition I have discussed in earlier chapters. Cooper goes on to critique the use of this approach when it is applied to the study of human behavior.

> In a science of personal interaction, on the other hand, mutual disturbance of the observer and the observed are not only inevitable in every case but it is this mutual disturbance which gives rise to the primary facts on which theory is based and not the disturbed or disturbing personal entities.

In other words, studying humans is not the same as studying chemicals because humans are self aware and that self awareness is part of the web of factors that influence their behavior. This applies to the humans studied as well as the human researcher. This self awareness disrupts the process of natural science styles of research which use carefully analyzed empirical data to develop theories which then guide decisions about professional practice. When this approach is used to study humans, the capability of the human subject,

> of altering his [or her] conduct from the expected, through reflective awareness of the factors that are conditioning him to a certain time, really constitutes a crucial difference. In short, while we are entitled to, and in any practical context must, have expectations (which we must expect to be disappointed) about a person's behavior, natural scientific prediction must be seen to be neither possible nor impossible in the sciences of persons but as inappropriate to the field of discourse.

While the majority of American social science today accepts analytical rationality, or positivism/postpositivism, as a legitimate way of studying human behavior, a growing number of social scientists, educational researchers, and educational technology scholars are rejecting this approach in favor of alternatives that are not based on the search for epistemic knowledge.

- **Techne**—This is Aristotle's "practical knowledge," "craft knowledge," "common sense," or "artistic skill." This is not universal knowledge; it is context dependent. The skills of an artist or a carpenter, are examples of techne. Technical or practical knowledge can involve the selective application of epistemic knowledge to an applied purpose. There are differences, however, between epistemic knowledge and techne. Epistemic knowledge alone is not sufficient for practical work. For example, a chemist may know a great deal of epistemic knowledge about petroleum, but, using only that epistemic knowledge, a chemist is not likely to be able to design and build a new oil refinery. On the other hand, some chemical engineers have both epistemic knowledge about chemistry and technical knowledge about the design and operation of chemical plants and refineries.

In Book 6 of *Nichomachean Ethics* Aristotle described techne this way,

> Art, or craft skill, is concerned with bringing something into existence, the cause of which is reasoned in the producer not the product. Since production is different to action, art is not concerned with action but has an element of chance, as Agathon says: Art loves chance, and chance loves art.

Thus technical knowledge is, in a general sense, about making or producing. Aristotle also gave some examples of craft knowledge and distinguished it from epistemic knowledge. "When we call Phidias a wise sculptor or Polyclitus a wise portraitist we mean that they have artistic [techne] wisdom."

The modern term *instrumental rationality* is similar to techne. One meaning is the skills, procedures, and knowledge you use to accomplish something practical (such as building a chemical plant). This is the *means* in the phrase *means to an end*. However, an important aspect of the term is that instrumental rationality does not involve value judgments or ethical decisions. The "how to" or technical knowledge to build a chemical plant could as well be used to build a factory to produce life saving medicines or deadly poison gasses. Thomas Kelly (2003) began his analysis of epistemic rationality and instrumental rationality with an effort to distinguish between the two.

> By epistemic rationality, I mean, roughly, the kind of rationality which one displays when one believes propositions that are strongly supported by one's evidence and refrains from believing propositions that are improbable given ones' evidence. . . . By instrumental rationality, I mean the rationality which one displays in taking the means to one's ends. Thus, if I have the goal of asking the speaker a question, and I know that I will only be able to ask the speaker a question if I raise my hand, then (all else being equal) it is instrumentally rational for me to raise my hand.

Perhaps a good and concise explanation of techne is that it is the *means* you use to make or produce something. In his discusson of techne Aristotle distinguished it from another type of knowledge, phronesis. "But some people are not wise 'at something' [techne] but wise without any qualification. Wisdom [phronesis], therefore, seems the most finished form of knowledge. Wisdom is scientific and intuitive knowledge of what is by nature most precious. That is why a wise person can often be more effective in action than one with specialist knowledge." Aristotle thus puts this last form of knowledge, phronesis, at the top of his hierarchy of knowledge when it comes to action. It is to phronesis that we turn to next.

- **Phronesis**—This third form of knowing has been translated into English several ways including prudence, wisdom, and "practical wisdom." I think the term practical wisdom may be the most appropriate translation for our purposes. Phronesis is the type of knowledge needed to make good decisions in a given context. It may involve the use of general principles, but it is not absolutist because phronesis involves careful consideration of the local situation, the context, as well what the practitioner of phronesis already knows. It is also general. It applies as well to a ruler making governmental decisions as to a parent deciding how to handle an unhappy child. In Aristotle's words

> To understand prudence, or practical wisdom, we may consider what type of person we call prudent. A prudent man [or woman] is able to deliberate rightly, not just about particular things like health, but about the good life generally. As prudence is not a fixed thing, then it cannot be a science. It does not aim at production, so it is not an art [techne]. Prudence, then, is a virtue, and one which is of the calculative, reasoning part of the soul. But it is not merely a rational state, for such can be forgotten while prudence cannot.

Aristotle's three forms of knowledge, or ways of knowing, are very relevant to the field of educational technology. Most knowledge that is treated as epistemic—the immutable laws and eternal truths—that educational technologists apply in their professional practice, comes from other, more basic, fields like psychology and sociology. If you, for example, believe that the theories of learning based on behaviorism (or constructivism, or instructivism, or information processing theory or cognitive science), can be counted on as generally applicable truths to be used in the development and application of educational technology, then you are treating those theories of learning as epistemic knowledge.

Both techne and phronesis are a bit more difficult to pin down and there is some debate about what is techne and what is phronesis. Following Aristotle, Carrie Birminghan (2004) points out that while the term episteme relates specifically to knowledge, phronesis is about action. It is about how to decide what to *do*. In the same vein, techne is about how to make things—from a clay pot or a painting to a multimedia instructional package. Rafael Capurro (2004) also noted that epistemic knowledge is about "perennial phenomena" while *techne* and *phronesis* are about "changing phenomena." "*Techne* is concerned with the production of material things (*poiesis*), while *phronesis* has to do with human actions (*praxis*). These different kinds of knowledge refer to different kinds of truth, namely theoretical, practical, and poietical" (p. 48). Birmingham also pointed out that Aristotle defined *phronesis* by contrasting it with other "mental states":

> The first of these is episteme, translated scientific knowledge, which Aristotle considers to be about things that are necessarily true and which "does not even admit to being otherwise." ... In contemporary work, episteme is considered to be a form of expert propositional knowledge, which is claimed to be true, provable, or at least consistent with a given theory, formulated in abstract terms, fully cognitive, and transmittable from one person to another. ... Episteme is the form of knowledge taken by educational theory.
>
> Second, Aristotle ... distinguishes phronesis from techne, translated craft or craft knowledge, "a state involving true reason concerned with produc-

tion."... In teaching, techne is the condition of possessing knowledge about the means to reach a given end—for example, how to increase students' test scores or how to maintain an orderly classroom. Techne does not deal with the nature of the goal, only with the most effective means to reach the goal. In fact, Aristotle does not even consider techne to be a virtue because 'there is virtue [or vice in the use] of craft." ... In other words, techne can be used to promote moral or immoral ends, so it has no intrinsic moral value itself.

One way of getting a handle on how these three forms of knowledge relate to educational technology is to look at the courses in a typical master's program (if there is such a thing as typical) and decide what type of knowledge is the focus of each course. I am very familiar with the particular graduate program represented in the list below and have used that familiarity to decide what type of knowledge is the focus of a particular course:

Name of Course	Primary Type of Knowledge
Computer Technology in Education	Techne/Phronesis
History of Education	Usually Epistemic
Educational Telecommunications and the Internet	Techne/Phronesis
Applied Statistics in Education OR	Techne
Understanding and Applying Research in Education	Techne
Technology and Educational Leadership	Techne/Phronesis
Instructional Design	Techne/Phronesis
Design & Development of Multimedia Instructional Units	Techne/Phronesis
Administration of Technology Programs	Techne/Phronesis
Implementing and Evaluating Technology-Supported Instruction	Techne/Phronesis
Professional Development for K–12 Technology Integration	Phronesis/Techne
Practicum in Educational Media	Techne/Phronesis
Education and Cognition	Epistemic/Phronesis

As you can see, this particular master's program deals with technical knowledge in all but two of the courses. It is heavily focused on technical or *means to an end* knowledge. Where techne is the first type of knowledge listed, it generally means the focus is on software and hardware or the process of creating or making something like educational resources. Where phronesis is the second type of knowledge listed, it usually means that what is being created or used is for humans (e.g. teachers, students). Since phronesis is the type of knowledge that involves interaction with humans (e.g., teaching, governing, and so on) phronetic knowledge is also needed in these courses.

The content of courses like Applied Statistics and Instructional Design (ID) are obviously techne because they focus on the means of producing something (a statistical analysis of data or the creation of instructional resources). However, ID involves the creation of learning resources for humans and that means phronetic knowledge is also important.

Thought it may be less obvious, techne knowledge is also an important part of courses like Administration of Technology Programs, Educational Telecommunications and the Internet, and Professional Development for K–12 Technology Integration. All of these courses focus on knowledge and skills that have to do with the means or "how to" to accomplish something. However, there is also an important element of phronetic knowledge in these courses because they deal with human interaction as well.

In this graduate program there are few places where epistemic knowledge is covered and only a few courses where phronetic or practical wisdom is a primary focus. I judged phronesis to be a secondary focus in Instructional Design because in this program it is not a how-to course that teaches students to use a particular design model such as Dick and Carey or Rapid Prototyping. Instead, it covers many different design models and their foundational assumptions; then students are expected to select or build their own model and show how they would use it in a simulated design project. Designing learning materials for a group of students involves understanding the context of the learning and the students, which is phronetic knowledge.

There are several ways to graphically depict Aristotle's theory of knowledge, Figure 5.4 may be helpful as a summary of our discussion to this point.

The visual in the figure is from Raphael's painting, *The School of Athens*, that depicts Aristotle and Plato in the middle of a large scene. Plato is pointing upward to indicate he finds truth in the "ideal forms" that reside in a

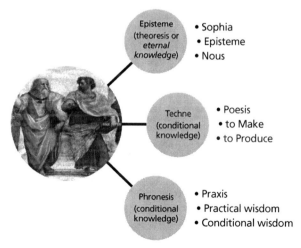

Figure 5.4 A version of Aristotle's organization of types of knowledge.

nonphysical world above. Aristotle is gesturing to indicate he finds truth in the physical world.

Aristotle's three forms of knowledge are theoresis (eternal knowledge), techne, and phronesis. However, these three forms are dealt with in different ways in the writings of Aristotle that have survived. Theoresis can be thought of as having nothing more than the intellectual and philosophical goal of knowing what is true. However, it may be used in the application of both techne and phronesis. Episteme is sometimes used with that same meaning, and sometimes as scientific knowledge. In Figure 5.1 it appears twice, once as a general term like theoresis and once as a term meaning "scientific knowledge" that comes from the observation of the physical world. It is not the only form of eternal knowledge, however. Nous and Sophia are also sources. Sophia can be thought of as knowledge developed through philosophical inquiry and Nous is knowledge developed by thinking about what the senses tell you. Nous is thus the intellectual work you perform on sense data. In a traditional research paper it is what you do with the data once it has been collected. It is important to note, however, that Aristotle considered Sophia or philosophical inquiry to be superior to the other sources of eternal knowledge. Nous and scientific knowledge are subservient to Sophia.

The second type of knowledge is techne which is needed when you make or produce something. The act of using that type of knowledge is Poeisis, which comes from the Greek word "to make." It is also the base for the English word poetry which is something poets "make." It could be argued that in a discipline named *Educational Technology* or, alternatively *Instructional Technology*, it is to be expected that much of the advanced training in the field will be technical. And, if epistemic knowledge is difficult if not impossible to obtain in the social sciences (perhaps especially in the applied social sciences) then there is justification for not emphasizing it in an educational technology graduate program. That leaves the third type of knowledge, phronesis, which like techne is also conditional rather than absolute knowledge. It is also knowledge that Aristotle considered essential to successful practice (praxis). It plays a secondary role in the graduate program courses listed earlier, and perhaps in most instructional technology graduate programs where techne is more often the focus. However, because phronesis is a more general type of knowledge that is essential to successful practice, I would argue that it deserves a much larger place in graduate programs, in what we elect to study, and in how we practice educational technology. In a moment I will introduce one framework for making phronetic knowledge the focus of research and practice in the social sciences and then look at the implications of that approach for educational technology. First, however, it is important to consider the implications of Aristotle's types of knowledge on why we do research.

ARISTOTLE AND THE PURPOSES OF RESEARCH

Recently I (Willis, 2007) suggested that in the social sciences there are six basic reasons for doing scholarship and research. Those reasons can be roughly organized under Aristotle's three types of knowledge as well as Boyer's (1990) four forms of scholarship.

Epistemic Knowledge and The Scholarship of Discovery. Three of the reasons people do research involve the search for epistemic knowledge and also fit Boyer's description of the scholarship of discovery. One is (1) *to test a general theory.* This is the core purpose of positivist quantitative research. Research is a quest for epistemic truths that apply across many contexts. A second reason to do research is (2) *to find local truth.* Many qualitative studies have local truth as their goal. The researcher acknowledges that a study set in a particular school or using a particular set of tutorial software cannot be expected to prove anything universal. However, the researcher still hopes to establish "the truth of the matter" so far as the specific context is concerned. One of the goals of this form of research is to abstract out of the detailed data collected some general explanations or theories of why things happened the way they did. This is a more modest version of positivism because it is still searching for some form of truth that can be depended upon. However, the purpose is the discovery of local truth rather than universal truth. An even more modest positivist goal for research is (3) *objective description.* "General and local theory research involves inference. You develop generalizations from the raw data and emphasize those generalizations in the research paper. A third approach, also based on the assumption that qualitative research can lead to the truth about a situation, focuses on accurate description of the situation under study. Description is at the basis of both general and local theory research, but it can be a goal in itself" (Willis, 2007, p. 292). This is still a positivist approach that both critical theorists and interpretivists may not accept. "Description is selective, it is the interpretation of the describer, and therefore it is subjective. [At least for interpretivists] there is no possibility of objective description" (p. 292).

Techne and the Scholarship of Application. My original list of six purposes for research included the three already mentioned and three more: *hermeneutic understanding (verstehen), storytelling,* and *narrative.* These three will be discussed in more detail in the section on phronesis. All three can also communicate techne, but they are equally capable of focusing on phronetic knowledge. However, after specifically thinking about the research and scholarship in educational technology, I would like to add a seventh category to my list of purposes for doing research. That is (7) *techne or "how to" knowledge.* When educational technology is the focus, much of what is published would be categorized as techne, and virtually all of that would also be Boyer's scholarship of application or scholarship of teaching.

Techne is knowledge of how to use "things" to accomplish a task. An example would be learning to use Dreamweaver or InDesign to create websites. For example, Lloyd Reiber's (2000) book on using the *Authorware* program to develop instructional simulations and games is an excellent example of techne as well as the scholarship of application, and of teaching (see http://www.nowhereroad.com/authorware/). So is his 2004 book, *Getting Up and Running With Dreamweaver By Building a Web-based Portfolio* (see http://www.nowhereroad.com/dreamweaver/). Many of the papers published in the major journals in the field also focus on techne.

Techne or "technical knowledge" is a major component of the knowledge base of educational technology. Technical knowledge is about our ability to create. It is also knowledge that links a practitioner to the resources needed to *create*. The techne knowledge a designer would use to create educational resources includes skill in using design and development software such as Dreatweaver, Flash, and Photoshop. In some interpretations of Aristotle, it would also include include the educational strategies or the user interface concepts that might be applied. That knowledge is less precise and context is more likely to be very important in determining what the "right" pedagogical strategies are and the "best" way to structure the user interface. For that reason I believe those decisions call for the application of phronesis or "wisdom." Thus, even ID which is clearly a "making" activity, uses phronesis as well as techne.

Phronesis and the Scholarship of Application, Teaching, and Integration. One of the less appreciated aspects of Aristotle's thought is his emphasis on the importance of the local context when it comes to decisions about actions. While Socrates tended to develop hard and fast rules when it came to actions such as designing and running a government, Aristotle thought the context of practice was too variable and too influential to permit the use of what today is called the "technical-rational approach." Technical rationality involves deriving rules from the eternal truths we have discovered and letting those rules precisely direct what we do in practice. This applies to "big decisions" such as basing foreign policy on an epistemic truth that the American form of democratic government is always the "best" form of government and then imposing that on a nation with a history and culture that is quite different from America's history and culture. It also applies to "small decisions" such as following a rule that every infraction of a classroom rule must be handled the same way regardless of who broke the rule and why. This approach essentially reduces professional practice to techne.

Aristotle rejects technical rationalism and proposes that a good leader or decision maker must use phronetic knowledge or *practical wisdom* that takes many things into consideration when deciding what action to take. Table 5.1 is a summary of Aristotle's three types of knowledge (actually he proposed other types but I will not deal with them here).

TABLE 5.1   Aristotle's Types of Knowledge and Their Relationship to Action

Type of knowledge	Related Virtue	Applicability	Use
Episteme	Eternal truth	Universal	Nature's laws, you can depend on them
Techne	Poiesis, "making"	Contextual, deals with things	Helpful, but must be considered in context
Phronesis	Praxis, "practical action"	Contextual, deals with people	Practical wisdom for working with people in context

In the next section phronesis will be explored in more detail as a foundation for the social sciences in general and educational technology in particular. However, to give you an idea of what scholarship based on a phronetic approach might look like, I will summarize a paper published in Issue 2 of the 2005 volume of *Educational Technology Research and Development* (Underwood et al., 2005).

AN EXAMPLE OF PHRONETIC RESEARCH IN EDUCATIONAL TECHNOLOGY

Underwood, J., Hoadley, C., Stohl Lee, H., Hollybrands, K., DiGiano, C., & Renninger, K. A. (June, 2005). IDEA: Identifying Design Principles in Educational Applets. *Educational Technology Research and Development*, 53(2), 99–112.

IDEA: Identifying Design Principles in Educational Applets. The NSF funded Educational Software Components of Tomorrow (ESCOT) project produced many small programs that help students learn various concepts in mathematics. These "applets" were designed by a team with experts from many areas, including teaching, instructional design, and educational technology. When they were released and made available online, some of them were very popular and widely used; others were not. This paper describes a study of 25 applets that were considered very successful. The authors were looking for "design principles" that might explain part of the appeal of the applets. They found 21 design principles and organized them into three groups: principles about motivation, presentation, and support for problem solving. However, the focus of the paper was not on the derived design principles, it was on the methodology the authors developed to discover the principles: "to operationalize a method for post hoc extraction of design principles from an existing library of educational software." From this statement the study appears to be an example of taking an epistemic approach to techne and phronetic knowledge. This is reinforced by comments such as "By identifying what worked and what did not work from the ESCOT experience, we are generating hypotheses about useful design principles that can be generalized beyond the specific context." This thus seems to be a search for epistemic knowledge as well as research in the tradition of the scholarship of discovery. It is also, because of the topic being studied, techne because the topic is about how to create products—in this case educational software. An epistemic approach does not, however, fit the techne tradition because Aristotle considered techne knowledge to be context specific rather than universal.

In my view, the paper is not epistemic in its approach, it is phronetic. While the authors came up with 21 design principles (such as *make the links between representations obvious and warranted* and *draw attention only to things that support the problem solving*) they do not present them as epistemic knowledge (e.g., "We do not believe that there is one optimal set of design principles that will completely specify what must be done to make an educational applet work. . . . We propose them not as universal rules to be followed slavishly, but instead as possible, not necessary, techniques to achieve a desired aim."). The authors view their work as the development of a way "to link craft and theoretical knowledge in educational software design." All or virtually all of the principles they present in the paper are examples of technical knowledge which, as they note, is context dependent. But, their focus is on the development of a method to learn technical knowledge from studying what has been done before. That is a phronetic goal—to develop ways of making good decisions in context. The authors present the approach to readers as a way they can use to develop their own principles and they urge readers to think in a phronetic way about design: "Principles should be grounded in both personal expertise and theory." They use Donald Schon's model of the reflective practitioner as an illustration of how this would work. It involves an instructional designer who enters "an interactive dialogue with the designed artifacts and their setting.

Phronesis and the Purposes of Research

Phronesis is a critical component of professional practice. Three forms of qualitative research seem particularly suited to developing this type of situated, contextual knowledge. One is hermeneutic understanding that was discussed in Chapter 2. *Hermeneutic* methods of scholarship results in papers, books, and monographs that provide very rich details about the history, cultural, and social context of a particular action or process. Hermeneutic scholarship tries to help the reader not only understand what happened or what intellectual ideas and concepts are being expressed. It helps us understand *why* they happened or were developed.

Another type of methodology that is increasingly used in educational technology studies is *narrative inquiry*. In the journal *Medical Education,* Bleakley (2005) defined narrative inquiry as:

> A form of qualitative research that takes story as either its raw data or its product. Science and narrative can be seen as two kinds of knowing, reflected in the distinction between evidence-based medicine derived from population studies and narrative-based medicine focused upon the single case. A similar tension exists in the field of narrative inquiry between cognitive-orientated analytical methods and affective-orientated methods of synthesis.

As Bleakley points out narrative inquiry typically tells the story of a single case, event, or situation and it may focus on the emotional or cognitive aspects, or both. In healthcare it also represents an alternative to "evidence-based medicine" which is based on positivist/postpositivist models of both research and practice. Bleakley supports the use of narrative inquiry because the analytical rationalism of positivist research tends

> to lose the concrete story and its emotional impact to abstract categorizations, which may claim explanatory value but often remain descriptive. Stemming from discomfort with more integrative methods derived from the humanities, a science-orientated medical education may privilege analytical methods over approaches of synthesis. Medical education can redress this imbalance through attention to "thinking with stories" to gain empathy for a patient's experience of illness. Such an approach can complement understanding of story as discourse—how narratives may be used rhetorically to manage both social interactions and identity. (p. 534)

In their article, *Stories of Experience and Narrative Inquiry,* Connelly and Clandinin (1990) introduced narrative inquiry this way:

> Although narrative has a long intellectual history both in and out of education, it is increasingly used in studies of educational experience. One theory in educational research holds that humans are storytelling organisms, who, individually and socially, lead storied lives. Thus, the study of narrative is the study of the ways humans experience the world. This general concept is refined into the view that education and educational research is the construction and reconstruction of personal and social stories; learners, teachers, and

researchers are storytellers and characters in their own and other's stories. (p. 2)

If you find narrative inquiry interesting, a Colorado State University guide (http://writing.colostate.edu/guides/research/observe/com3a2.cfm) to different forms of qualitative research includes information on this type of qualitative research as well as many others. The data for narrative inquiries often includes:

> Field notes, interviews, journals, letters, autobiographies, and orally told stories. . . . For example, a researcher might do a study on the way in which fourth grade girls define their social roles in school. A researcher might look at such things as notes and journal entries, and might also interview the girls and spend time observing them. After this, the researcher would then construct her own narrative of the study, using such conventions as scene and plot. As Connelly and Clandinin [1990] also note, "Research is a collaborative document, a mutually constructed story out of the lives of both researcher and participant."

Narrative inquiry which is sometimes simply referred to as "storytelling" is a distinct way of both gathering (narrative inquiry) and communicating (storytelling) knowledge that is deeply embedded in the context of the story being told. This form of scholarship fits phronetic knowledge very well because phronetic knowledge cannot be distilled from the context and then communicated in abstract form to others. It is not epistemic, it is phronetic and if readers are to best use the knowledge it must be presented to them in a format that maintains the rich texture of the situation in which it was used. For an applied social science like educational technology, phronetic knowledge is at heart of many daily decisions and issues, and narrative inquiry as well as storytelling is a very useful form of scholarship.

In the next section I will introduce a theoretical framework that makes phronetic knowledge the core of social science research. It is a framework that has much to offer educational technology.

BENT FLYVBJERG
AND *MAKING SOCIAL SCIENCE MATTER*

In 2001 Cambridge University Press published the English language version of a book written by an urban planner who is a professor of planning at Aalborg University in Denmark. Originally published in Danish a few years earlier, the book probably aroused many people's curiosity because of the provocative title, *Making Social Science Matter. Why Social Inquiry Fails and How*

It Can Succeed Again. Whatever the initial reason for paying attention to the book, it has become a very influential statement of both why social science has failed to achieve its goals and also how it should be changed so that it becomes a successful, contributing source of scholarship that is helpful to society.

Why Social Science Has Failed

Flyvbjerg (2005) succinctly summarized his explanation of why social science has failed this way:

> We should avoid social sciences that pretend to emulate natural science by producing cumulative and predictive theory. The natural science approach simply does not work in the social sciences. No predictive theories have been arrived at in social science, despite centuries of trying. This approach is a wasteful dead-end. (p. 38)

He rejects the scientific or "epistemic model" at several levels and for several reasons:

> The epistemic model finds its ideal in the natural science model for doing science. Here the objective of the social scientist is to discover the theories and laws which govern social action, just as the objective of the natural scientist is to discover the theories and laws which govern natural phenomena. Praxis, according to the natural science model of social science, is social engineering which applies social theories and laws to solve social problems.
>
> . . .
>
> The epistemic or natural science model sees social scientists and social science professionals as technocrats who through their insight into social theories and laws—may provide society with solutions to its social ills. (p. 39)

Many other scholars have come to similar conclusions. For example, Lonner (2003) feels the search for absolute laws has weakened rather than strengthened social sciences like psychology.

> Another factor that is particularly dampening to the growth of psychology, and which can be perniciously ethnocentric, is the absolutistic map of the world–the belief that laws of human behavior, wherever they may be established, transcend cultures. In its extreme form absolutism would contend that human "cultures" constitute nothing more than a thin veneer that just barely mask a broad spectrum of universal laws governing thought and behavior. (p. 22)

Lonner, a professor of cross-cultural psychology, does not believe there are many laws of human behavior that apply everywhere, in every culture. To be fair in quoting him, Lonner sees the opposite view as equally unsatisfactory:

> The obverse of this view is the doctrine of radical relativism. Relativists believe that behavior and thought can only be understood in the intricate context of specific ecocultural systems. Radical relativists hold the view that everything about the human condition is based on the social constructionist argument that mind and culture make each other up, and that the pattern is never re-peated. Consequently, they would argue, it is impossible to make comparisons across cultures. The view that culture and mind are co-constructed is held by a growing number of psychologists who identify with the closely related per-spective known as cultural psychology. . . . Not surprisingly, most cross-cultural psychologists tend to find comfort in the middle or compromise position of universalism—the a priori belief that there is considerable continuity in all human thought and behavior, and also the conviction that culture plays an enormously important moderating or mediating role in most domains of psy-chology. Indeed, it could be argued that culture is antecedent to all thought and behavior. (p. 22)

Flyvbjerg would probably find Lonner's universalism acceptable because it requires the humans involved in a situation to make decisions about what is universal and what is contextually or culturally-based. In his 2001 book Flyvbjerg takes several chapters to lay out his view and offer supporting evidence, but the main points are summarized in the previous quotes. He believes the subject matter of social science is not like the subject matter of natural science and any attempt to import the methods, purposes, and paradigms of natural science into social science is destined to failure. A major reason for his position is that humans are different from the things natural science studies.

> Ultimately, the human skills that determine the social context are based on judgments that cannot be understood in terms of concrete features and rules. Therefore a "hard" theory of context in the social sciences is seemingly im-possible. But if context decides what counts as relevant objects and events, and if the social context cannot be formalized in terms of features and rules, then social theory cannot be complete and predictive in the manner of much natural science theory, which does not have the problem of self-interpretive objects of study. (p. 39)

Flyvbjerg's approach to critiquing the current status of social science shares many perspectives with other active movements today. Postmodern critiques also reject the positivist and postpositivist methods of the natural sciences and the goal of discovering absolute truths or laws about human behavior. Similarly, the hermeneutic approach to psychology advocated by

Rom Harre (2002, see also the *Journal of the Theory of Social Behavior*) at Oxford University overlaps considerably with what Flyvbjerg calls a "praxis-oriented social science" and "phronetic social science." Also, the interpretive or constructivist paradigm is very compatible with phronetic social science.

What is a Phronetic Social Science?

Flyvbjerg is very clear in his advice about what to get rid of in social science. It is the foundation of "scientism" that has been borrowed from the natural sciences:

> Two scenarios may be outlined for the future of social science. In the first—and today, dominant—scenario, it is scientism, the belief that science holds a reliable method of researching the truth about the nature of things, which continues to dominate the social sciences. But scientism in social science will continue to fail, because the reality of social science does no and cannot live up to the ideals of natural science. Consequently, social science will increasingly degenerate as a scholarly activity, and will find it more and more difficult to gain public support and funding for its activities. (Flyvbjerg, 2005, p. 42)

His alternative is a social science based on phronesis and he has made considerable progress outlining what that could look like (although he expects his views to evolve and he invites others to enter into a dialog about the nature of this new form of social science):

> The second scenario replaces scientism with phronesis. Here the purpose of social science is not to develop epistemic theory, but to contribute to society's practical rationality by elucidating where we are, where we want to go, and what is desirable according to different sets of values and interests. The goal of the phronetic approach becomes contributing to society's capacity for value-rational deliberation and action. The contribution may be a combination of concrete empirical analyses and practical philosophical-ethical considerations—"fieldwork in philosophy," as Pierre Bourdieu called his own version of phronetic social science. In this scenario social scientists actively ensure that their work is relevant to praxis. The aim is to make the line between research and the world direct and consequential

He presents two general guidelines for phronetic social science. The first is:

> We should promote social sciences that are strong where natural science is weak—that is, in reflective analysis and deliberation about the values and interests aimed at praxis, which are essential to social and economic development in society. We should promote value rationality over epistemic rationality, in order to arrive at social science that matters. (2005, p. 38)

As an applied social science, educational technology seems ideally suited to this way of thinking about its purpose. It is an applied field that is intensely focused on praxis, and educational technologists are often already integrated into a context of practice such as schools, organizations, businesses, agencies, or institutions that prepare practitioners such as colleges of education. Flyvbjerg's strong advocacy of a shift from epistemic rationality (do what the laws of human behavior tell you is Correct) to "value rationality" may be hard to accomplish because as a field we have deeply invested in epistemic rationality virtually since the founding of the discipline. It would mean that educational technologists must give up some degree of Certainty as well as the authoritative role of the expert "who knows." In its place would be a messier and more complicated process in which the educational technologist works with others, each with expertise and investment in the issue being explored, to decide collaboratively what is "best" to do. I would argue that this latter model is what many educational technologists do already. In addition, Flyvbjerg's explanation of what value rationality means is tempting:

> The phronetic model is named after the Aristotelian concept phronesis, which is the intellectual virtue used to deliberate about which social actions are good or bad for humans. The basis of deliberation is value rationality instead of epistemic rationality.
>
> At the core of phronetic social science stands the Aristotelian maxim that social issues are best decided by means of the public sphere, not by science. Though imperfect, no better device than public deliberation following the rules of constitutional democracy has been arrived at for settling social issues, so far as human history can show. Social science must therefore play into this device if it is to be useful. (p. 39)

Phronetic social science should focus on answering four questions:

> The principal objective for phronetic social science is to understand values and interests and how they relate to praxis. The point of departure for this type of social science can be summarized in the following four value-rational questions, which must all be answered for a specific, substantive problematic, for instance in management:
>
> 1. Where are we going?
> 2. Who gains and who loses, and by which mechanisms of power?
> 3. Is this development desirable?
> 4. What, if anything, should we do about it? (p. 40)

Flyvbjerg points out that there is no universal "we" that will deliberate and decide these matters. Often the group may be made up of social scientists but more often it will be "a group including other actors as well.

Phronetic social scientists are well aware that different groups typically have different world views and different interests, and that there exists no general principle by which all differences can be resolved" (p. 40).

Flyvbjerg's praxis-focused social science is to be "problem-driven, not methodology-driven." Thus, he does not reject the use of many forms of quantitative data and data analysis procedures. He does, however, reject the paradigm of the natural sciences that guides the analysis and interpretation of much of the quantitative data gathered in the social sciences.

Finally, a second general guideline for phronetic social science seems particularly important for educational technology:

> [We should be] making sure that such analyses [reflexive analyses] are fed into the process of public deliberation and decision making, in order to guarantee that legitimate parties to this process, i.e., citizens and stakeholders, receive due diligence in the process.

In my view, educational technology scholarship is often conducted by and written for a narrow audience of specialists. Very little of our work is in a form that would even be readable, much less helpful, to audiences such as school board members, policy makers, parents, teachers, and students. In fact, the cultural values of the field seem to assign much higher value to a paper written for a small group of fellow specialists than one written for teachers, school board members, or policy makers. The values that lead to such preferences are probably based on an assumption that papers written for a small group of specialists are probably epistemic in nature, and epistemic work is more valuable than research that focuses on knowledge in the techne or phronesis categories. A shift to a phronetic paradigm would virtually reverse those values.

SUMMARY

When Positivism, or its kinder, gentler contemporary variant, postpositivism, is the foundation for research in the social sciences and education, it imposes a very strong value system on the research endeavor that specifies what is to be valued in both basic and applied research. Those values dominated American social science and education for most of the 20th century. However, Brent Flyvbjerg's blending of something old—Aristotle's three types of knowledge—and something new—Flyvbjerg's redefinition of the purpose of social science, is appealing on two levels. First, he offers a plausible explanation of why the social sciences (and education as well as educational technology) have failed to make a major difference in society. It is because we have assumed all these disciplines are like the natural sciences and should, therefore, have similar goals and use similar methods. Second, he proposes a sweeping solution that, if he is correct, would make us more successful by changing both our goals and our methods. The solution, a phronetic social science, that eschews "scientism" and instead focus on contributing to practical knowledge (he sometimes uses the term "practical rationality"). Flyvbjerg's approach is flexible, focused on practical issues and action, respectful of many sources of knowledge including philosophy, and also respectful of diverse viewpoints. Would it make a difference as a framework for thinking about scholarship in educational technology?

REFERENCES

Birmingham, C. (2004), Phronesis: A model for pedagogical reflection. *Journal of Teacher Education, 55*(4), 313–324.

Flyvbjerg, B. (2005, October–March, 2006). Social science that matters. *Foresight Europe, 2,* 8–42.

Flyvbjerg, B. (S. Sampson, Trans). (2001). *Making social science matter: Why social inquiry fails and how it can succeed again.* Cambridge: Cambridge University Press.

Bleakley, A. (2005, May). Stories as data, data as stories: Making sense of narrative inquiry in clinical education. *Medical Education, 39*(5), 534–540.

Boyer, E. (1990). *Scholarship reconsidered: Priorities for the professoriate.* Princeton, NJ: The Carnegie Foundation for the Advancement of Teaching.

Capurro, R. (2004). Skeptical knowledge management. In H.-C. Hobohm (Ed.), *Knowledge management: Libraries and librarians taking up the challenge.* IFLA (International Federation of Library Associations and Institutions) Publication 108, 47–67. Munich: Saur. Retrieved May 16, 2007 from http://www.capurro. de/skepsis.html.

Connelly, F. M., & Clandinin, D. J. (1990). Stories of experience and narrative inquiry. *Educational Researcher, 19*(5), 2–14.

Cooper, D. (1965, January–February). Two types of rationality: *New Left Review, I/29.* Retrieved May 16, 2007 from http://newleftreview.org/?view=313

Harre, R. (2002). *Cognitive science: A philosophical introduction.* Thousand Oaks, CA: Sage.

Kelly, T. (2003, May). Epistemic rationality. *Philosophy and Phenomenologial Research, 66*(3).

Lonner, W. (2003). On the growth and continuing importance of cross-cultural psychology. *Eye on Psi Chi, 4*(3). Retrieved May 17, 2007 from http://www.psichi. org/pubs/articles/article_82.asp .

Science Encyclopedia. (2007). Philosophy—Relations to other intellectual realms— After Plato, medieval and renaissance, early modern, modern times, bibliography. *Science encyclopedia: The history of ideas, Vol. 4.* Retrieved May 10, 2007 from http://science.jrank.org/pages/7965/Philosophy-Relations-other-Intellectual- Realms.html

Sloan, D. (1994). *Faith and knowledge.* Louisville, KY: Westminster John Knox Press.

Hooker, R. (1996). *Greek philosophy: Aristotle.* Retrieved May 16, 2007 from http://www.wsu.edu/~dee/GREECE/ARIST.HTM .

Willis, J. (2007). *Foundations of qualitative research: Interpretive and critical approaches.* Thousand Oaks, CA: Sage.

Underwood, J. , Hoadley, C., Lee, H., Hollebrands, K., DiGiano, G., & Renninger, K. (2005). IDEA: Identifying design principles in educational applets. *Educational Technology Research & Development, 53*(2), 99–112.

READINGS FOR CHAPTER 5

Reading 5.1

Flyvbjerg, B. (2005). Social science that matters. *Foresight Europe,* 38–42. Retrieved 05/16/2007 from http://flyvbjerg.plan.aau.dk/Publications2006/ForesightNo2PRINT.pdf

The article "Social Science That Matters" was written by Bent Flyvbjerg in 2005. It is, in some ways, a summary and an update of his book on phronetic social science that was published in 2001. You probably have not read the book, but you have read the summary of his position in Chapter 5. Of course, a summary rarely does justice to the full paper and to the way the original author organized his points. As you read this paper, make a list of the ideas and points that you do not remember from the summary in Chapter 5. Some material may not have been in Chapter 5 at all and some may not have been memorable enough to stick in your memory.

After reading the entire paper, look back over your list and ask how these "new" points and issues would influence educational technology if they were part of a phronetic model of educational technology research and scholarship? And, what impact would they have on practice in the field?

Finally, in the conclusions Flyvbjerg suggests three actions that need to be taken to increase the role of phronesis in social science. Why? Which of those would be the easiest for the current generation of educational technologists to adopt? Is the same true for the next generation of educational technologists? Which of the three recommendations would be the least likely for the current generation? The next generation? Why?

Reading 5.2

Inouye, D. K., Merrill, P. F., & Swan, R. H. (2005). Help: Toward a new ethics-centered paradigm for instructional design and technology. *IDT Record.* Retrieved 05/17/2007 from http://www.indiana.edu/~idt/articles/documents/ethics.htm

The second reading for Chapter 5 is an unusual one. It was published on a web site, IDT Record, that is maintained by the instructional design and technology program at Indiana University, one of the most successful and most prestigious programs in the country. Quite a few of the graduate programs in instructional and educational technology maintain useful web sites that host resources of interest to people outside the sponsoring program. The IDT Record at Indiana University in Bloomington is one of the most interesting. The IDT Record site is at http://www.indiana.edu/Eidt/index.html .

(Another very useful and high quality resource from a ET or IT program is maintained at the University of Georgia. UGa's IT Forum [http://itech1.coe.uga.edu/itforum/] is even larger than the IDT Record site and a major activity is discussion of papers submitted to the forum for that purpose.)

This reading from IDT Record was written by three instructional design and technology specialists at Brigham Young University. Dillon K. Inouye and Paul F. Merrill are professors in the Instructional Psychology and Technology program at BYU and Richard Swan is a Teaching and Learning Consultant for the Center of Instructional Design at Brigham Young University.

The second author, Paul Merrill, has been a major figure in the field for decades and has an established role as a defender of what I term a postpositivist approach to research in educational technology. It thus came as a considerable surprise when I ran across this paper while looking for suitable readings for this chapter. The paper is a sophisticated proposal for redefining the field I refer to as educational technology and the authors refer to as Instructional Design and Technology.

The authors begin by looking at four possible "centers" for IDT: Three of the centers or cores are traditional ones that are already accepted by many people in the field. They are (1) the scientific paradigm, (2) the design paradigm, and (3) the technology paradigm. The authors introduce these centers around which the field of IDT can be developed by linking them to one or more of Aristotle's types of knowledge:

Guiding Framework	Aristotle's Types of Knowledge
The Scientific Paradigm	Theoresis, Sophia, Nous, and Episteme
The Design Paradigm	poesis (to make)
The Technology Paradigm	techne, but modern technology also uses knowledge considered episteme and poesis as well

After identifying the "three traditional views of central concern to IDT" the authors offer a fourth which they refer to as an "ethics-centered paradigm." They justify that description by defining the focus of IDT as action—

praxis to use Aristotle's term. More specifically they propose that IDT's main responsibility is to help, particularly to help learners learn. As the authors note, for Aristotle the term praxis meant "the realm of political and ethical concerns for citizens in the *polis,* or city." As Aristotle did, Inouye and his coauthors include teaching in the realm of praxis and that makes IDT another realm in which pronesis is a very important type of knowledge.

As you read this paper note that the authors take us on a philosophical inquiry and that they even use elements of what might be called Platonic dialog in the paper. They also ask us to use the original meanings of words that have changed their meaning since the Greeks used them to build grand theories of how we should live virtuous lives. Ethics, for example, has a narrower meaning today. Are you comfortable with the meaning of the term used in this paper? Does it make sense to consider IDT an ethics-centered profession? How do you defend your viewpoint?

Does this paper convince you that using Aristotle's types of knowledge such as episteme, techne, and phronesis to refocus IDT and make it a quite different profession is a good idea. Why? Why not?

Do you agree with the history presented in this paper—that poiesis and praxis knowledge were not honored for several centuries unless it was reduced to epistemic knowledge? Is this one possible reason why much of the history of IDT has emphasized epistemic knowledge? If you agree, do you think that scholarship that leads to poiesis and praxis knowledge can be elevated to a high status? How would that happen?

Do you completely agree with the organization of Table 5.1 in the paper? Are there any parts you question or disagree with? Why?

What about the "General Implications for the Discipline" and the "General Implications for the Profession"? Do you agree with all the implications? Why or Why not" What do you think are the most likely implications to be taken up by the discipline/profession in the next 20 years? The least likely?

CHAPTER 6

BUILDING YOUR RELATIONSHIPS WITH RESEARCH

In this short chapter we will explore qualitative research in educational technology from a more personal perspective—the relationship between you and the research and scholarship of educational technology. That relationship can take many forms—from estrangement to lifelong engagement and interaction. Whatever that relationship is, however, it will be based on a number of factors that vary considerably from one person to another. The first part of this chapter will look at one of the major factors, the purposes of research. Once that issue, and some of the paradigms for thinking about it, have been addressed, the rest of the chapter will explore other aspects of the personal relationship between educational technologists and qualitative research/scholarship.

Research and scholarship tends to be handled in one of two different ways in graduate programs. In the sciences and engineering fields graduate research professors typically have a research program that includes studies they will conduct over the next three to ten years. They write grants to fund their work and then select students from the pool of applicants each year who will join their research team and receive assistantships. This pattern of graduate work generally means that if you are accepted into a program and assigned to a professor, that professor already has a general idea of

Qualitative Research Methods in Education and Educational Technology, pages 149–166
Copyright © 2008 by Information Age Publishing
All rights of reproduction in any form reserved.

what your dissertation topic will be. You will fit into the already established program of research of that professor (or group of professors). That means many decisions will be made for you, including which journals to read, which conferences to attend, and what research methods to learn.

In the social sciences and education, including educational technology, a few students will come into programs that use the science and engineering model, but the great majority will follow another pattern. In most educational technology graduate programs, professors pursue their own research and scholarly agendas, but grant funding is neither so dependable nor so predictable that they can regularly plan multi-year agendas. Often research plays a much smaller role in the life of educational technology professors and many graduate students come to their dissertation without ever having been a member of a research team. This often means there has been little mentoring, very little, if any, immersion in the research process, and little or no guidance in terms of topics that might be suitable for a dissertation. While this may sound rather bleak, it also means students have a great deal of freedom when it comes to things like deciding what literature to read, what topics to explore, what methods to consider, and what dissertation study to pursue. These same decisions come up over and over as a graduate pursues his or her career as an academic, a professional, a policy maker, or as a manager or director. In this chapter I will offer some advice on how to think about decisions related to research and scholarship.

The first step is to divide the decisions into two broad groups. One group is consumer related and another group involves decisions you must make as a producer of scholarship and research.

WHAT TYPE OF CONSUMER SHOULD YOU BECOME?

In his book, *Reading Statistics and Research*, Schuyler Huck (2000) explains the purpose of his book this way:

> This book is designed to help people decipher what researchers are trying to communicate in the written or oral summaries of their investigations. Here, the goal is simply to distill meaning from the words, symbols, tables, and figures included in the research report.... Beyond being able to decipher what is presented, readers of this book will improve their ability to critique such research reports. This is important because research claims are sometimes completely unjustified due to problems associated with the way studies are planned or implemented, or because of problems in the way data are collected, analyzed, summarized, or interpreted. (p. xv)

In my personal estimate, most doctoral and master's graduates from instructional technology programs do not graduate with the ability to independently distil and critique much of the existing research in our field. At best, they are comfortable with a small range of the research published. The rest they either ignore or simply "take the word" of the researchers about what the investigations mean and what the implications for practice are. Huck's 688-page book does a good job of preparing readers to consume one type of research—traditional experimental studies—and does an adequate job of introducing simple correlational and regression research. He does not even discuss some types of quantitative research such as surveys or program evaluations, and there is no coverage of many advanced quantitative methods such as factor analysis, and path analysis or structural equation modeling. Also omitted are topics like meta-analysis and how to assess the quality of reviews of the literature. While good, Huck's text is very, very limited in its coverage. There is no help in distilling and critiquing any of the many forms of qualitative research, humanities and arts-based studies, or philosophical investigations.

My comments about Schuyler Huck's book are not criticisms of him or the book. The book is very good and is a valuable tool for anyone interested in becoming an informed consumer of quantitative research in the experimental tradition. A similar comment could be made of the book you are reading. It focuses on qualitative research methods and procedures and thus is of little help in preparing you to consume quantitative research. However, when Huck's text, or others like it, are the only content students encounter in their graduate program that prepares them to become informed consumers of educational technology research and scholarship, students will graduate without the technical and conceptual knowledge and skills needed to become strong consumers of the broad range of scholarship in our field. The majority of past and current graduates of educational technology programs have not been prepared to effectively use the broad range of educational technology research and scholarship available today, and that situation is not likely to change anytime soon. Thus, it may be up to you to prepare yourself to become a competent consumer. There are, fortunately, many useful resources including the *Handbook of Research on Educational Communication and Technology* (Jonassen and Harris, 2003) which has chapters on some, but not all, the research and scholarship traditions in educational technology. There are also many free, online resources that cover different methods of scholarship and research. For example, Qual-Page (http://www.qualitativeresearch.uga.edu/QualPage/), a web site begun by Judi Norris and now managed by Judith Preissle, is an excellent source of information on many types of qualitative research methods and theories.

Educational technology is a field that generates and uses research and scholarship from a wide range of disciplines. That literature uses an amazingly diverse range of methods and paradigms, and it is produced for many different purposes. Given that this is the status of our literature, it is important that professionals, academics, and researchers in our field *become informed users and critics of a wide range of research and scholarship*. And, because most of us were not prepared to do that in our graduate programs, the responsibility to become informed users and critics falls on us as individuals. There are many ways to prepare yourself—from reading appropriate literature and attending conferences to participating in workshops and working with mentors and scholars who already have the expertise you need.

WHAT TYPE OF RESEARCHER SHOULD YOU BECOME?

The great majority of educational technologists are primarily or exclusively consumers of research. Their jobs, and their roles, do not include the responsibility (or the time) for producing research and scholarship. This is unfortunate because a great deal of knowledge and expertise is never disseminated to the field because those who develop it are not charged with sharing it with others. I am tempted to lecture those who don't share their innovations and expertise, but I would be doing that from the privileged position of a tenured professor at a research university where I teach six hours a week and have the opportunity and time available to do research and scholarship. What I will say is that if you have a job where you are expected to do research and scholarship, or you are personally interested in it even if it is not a formal part of your job, there are a number of decisions to be made.

What Do I study? There are many ways to answer this question. Three factors have generally guided my decisions about what to study. A major one is *what interests me*. Doing research and scholarship (R&S) requires the ability to delay gratification for a long time. For example, a simple study may take a year or more before you have the results in your hand. And, as is often the case, those initial results may tell you nothing other than you have to do the study again, and better, before you have the understanding you were seeking. Similarly, it takes an average of about two years to go from writing a proposal for a book and getting a contract from a publisher to having the printed book in your hands. One of my recent books took eight years from idea to publication and that is not so unusual! You must have a strong interest in a topic if you are going to work hard for that long before you reach your goal. Another factor I consider is *what, in my opinion, is currently important to the field*. For example, about 15 years ago I established a publication, the *Journal of Technology and Teacher Education*, because it seemed to be needed by the field. Many of my other books and research projects were initiated because I saw a need that was not being met. A third factor is *funding*. Some activities, like writing a book, are more personal and do not require external funding (but it does help if available). Other work, particularly large studies or development projects, often require funding to be done well. There have been times when I was interested in several projects I felt were important to the field and I selected the project that was fundable. Funds allowed me to do the work and also to do other important things like support doctoral students with assistantships and cover some of the costs of ordinary activities like attending conferences. Personal interest, importance to the field, and funding possibilities are my major criteria but they need not be yours. Each person must develop their own criteria and be prepared for the criteria to change across different stages of her or his career. There are many good online resources that can help you. For example, several web sites offer help and suggestions about how to select a dissertation topic:

http://www.dissertation-writing.net/dissertation_topic.html
http://www.dissertationdoctor.com/advice/topic.html
http://www.psychologicalscience.org/observer/getArticle.cfm?id=1502
http://www.gse.upenn.edu/student_life/advisor.pdf
http://www.uk-student.net/modules/wfsection/article.php?articleid=159

Many of these sites are also helpful for the beginning scholar who is trying to decide what investigations to undertake. With my own doctoral students I also suggest a final criteria when selecting a dissertation topic. Think of the ideal job you could realistically get when you graduate and then ask yourself what impact the dissertation you are considering will have on the search committee for your ideal job. Will it peak their interest and lead to extended discussions because the topic is important to them? Will it make them more interested in hiring you?

What Methodologies Should I Use? I am writing this book using Microsoft Word even though I am trying to wean myself from it and use one of the open source programs like *OpenOffice* or *AbiWord* that will work on both Windows and Linux systems (I'm also trying to wean myself from Windows). The main problem is that when new versions of my first word processing program, *Electric Pencil,* were no longer available, I started using *Microsoft Word.* Over 15 years or so I have learned its quirks, taken advantage of its strengths, and become familiar and somewhat comfortable with it (though the relationship has always been the love/hate sort). Making a change is a big step and I have not yet been able to do it cold turkey. I have the latest versions of both *Word 2* and *OpenOffice* on my computers, but I still use Word 90% of the time.

I think most of us tend to do the same with methodologies. If we learned how to do control-experimental group studies and gather quantitative data and analyze it with analysis of variance procedures, it will be harder to decide that a particular study calls for a case study that involves gathering and analyzing a lot of qualitative interview data. My advice is to make it a point to become proficient in two or three methodologies that seem to you to be particularly suited to the type of investigations you want to conduct. You will, of course, also be a consumer of research and scholarship based on your favored methodologies. You should also be a competent consumer of research and scholarship that uses different paradigms and methodologies. If not, that is the place to begin expanding your expertise as a scholar. Learn to critically consume research and scholarship from most of the relevant sources of knowledge on the topics that interest you. Then, from that base, begin to consider using some of those methods and procedures in your own research.

An emerging trend in education is the idea of "mixed method research" that combines methods from different theoretical and ideological camps (such as quantitative and qualitative). There are several excellent resources on how to conduct mixed research studies:

Tashakkori, A., & Teddlie, C. B. (2002). *Handbook of Mixed Methods Social and Behavioral Research.* Thousand Oaks, CA: Sage.

Tashakkori, A., & Teddlie, C. B. (1998). *Mixed Methodology: Combining Qualitative and Quantitative Approaches.* Thousand Oaks: Sage.

Creswell, J. W., & Plano Clark, V. L. (2006). *Designing and Conducting Mixed Methods Research.* Thousand Oaks, CA: Sage.

Johnson, B., & Christensen, L. (2007). *Educational Research: Quantitative, Qualitative, and Mixed Methods.* Thousand Oaks, CA: Sage.

There are also several good introductions to mixed method research in education and the social sciences on the web:

http://www.southalabama.edu/coe/bset/johnson/lectures/lec2.htm
http://www.southalabama.edu/coe/bset/johnson/lectures/lec14.htm
http://www.aera.net/uploadedFiles/Journals_and_Publications/Journals/Educational_Researcher/Volume_33_No_7/03ERv33n7_Johnson.pdf

The website on mixed methods at Florida International University also has several useful resources. *Bridges: Mixed Method Network for Behavioral, Social, and Health Sciences* is available at http://www.fiu.edu/~bridges/

Finally, the *User Friendly Handbook for Mixed Method Evaluation* from the National Science Foundation is available online at http://www.ehr.nsf.gov/EHR/REC/pubs/NSF97–153/START.HTM#TOC

The rapidly increasing popularity of mixed method research in education is one reflection of the growing conviction that using more than one method in investigations often strengthens the study and broadens its impact. Designing mixed method studies is one way to integrate several methodologies. Another way is to work with an interdisciplinary team. For example, a study of the implementation of distance education services at a university might benefit from the expertise of a computer scientist, an educational technologist, a leadership scholar, and a sociologist. Each scholar would bring unique understanding and methods of study to the project, and when the group members collaborate, the picture of the implementation process will be richer and more complete because of the interdisciplinary team. Interdisciplinary teams are an excellent way to conduct mixed method studies because there is expertise for each method on the team. Such teams, however, require the ability to build the group into a collaborative team, and skill in coordinating and integrating the contributions of individual members of the team.

Where Do I Publish? There are well over 150,000 journals in print or online today. Of those there are thousands on topics in education and hundreds related to educational technology. In addition, there are thousands of journals that occasionally publish papers on educational technology or publish papers on topics relevant to the field. Add to these established journals the hundreds of new journals that begin publication each year and you can hardly think of a topic related to educational technology that is not welcomed by at least one, if not many, journals. When deciding which journal to submit a paper to, there are a number of factors to consider.

Reputation and Distribution of the Journal. In every field there are journals that have very strong reputations and wide distribution. Publishing in those journals gets your work in front of more subscribers, and because libraries are more likely to subscribe to them than "second tier" journals, more potential readers will have access to your work. On the other hand, if you are doing particularly innovative work, or using new methods that are unfamiliar to reviewers at a particular journal, your paper may be rejected even if it is worthy of publication. New journals and journals that encourage work on emerging topics may be the better options.

Refereed or Not. The foundation of the scholarly publication process is peer review. A paper submitted to a refereed journal is sent to three peer reviewers who are competent to make judgments about whether the paper is worthy of publication. This peer review process typically results in one of three decisions: publish as submitted, reject, or publish after making revisions. Virtually all journals use the peer review process but some publications do not. Unless the publication has a very strong reputation or reaches precisely the audience you have targeted, journals that use the peer review process to make publication decisions should be preferred. An important factor for academics is that many universities do not count publications in non-peer review journals the same as they do peer-reviewed publications.

Preferred Topics, Paradigms, and Methods. Every journal has a personality that includes the types of topics it prefers, the theories and paradigms that are accepted and the methodologies that are welcomed. Some journals are very eclectic while others are quite narrow and focused. Make sure you are submitting your work to a journal that is appropriate in terms of topic, theoretical framework, and methodology.

Target Audience. Who reads the journal? A particular paper can be crafted to address the interests of many different groups. Educational technology journals tend to focus on the interests and needs of particular groups:

- Teachers and K–12 Technology Coordinators
  - Computers in the Schools
  - Leading and Learning With Technology
  - Technology and Learning
- Instructional Technology Specialists and Designers
  - Educational Technology
  - Educational Technology, Research & Development
  - Journal of Instructional Technology Systems
  - Computers and Education
- Administrators and Leaders
  - Educational Technology—The Magazine for Managers of Change in Education
  - TQ: Technos Quarterly
- Teacher Educators
  - Journal of Technology and Teacher Education
  - Contemporary Issues in Technology and Teacher Education
  - Journal of Computers and Teacher Education
  - Technology, Pedagogy and Education
- Readers With Discipline/Area Specific Interests
  - American Journal of Distance Education
  - EduCause (higher education)
  - Journal of Interactive Instruction Development
  - Journal of Computing in Higher Education
- Researchers, Psychologists, and Theorists
  - Instructional Science: An International Journal of Learning and Cognition
  - Journal of Technology, Learning, and Assessment
  - Journal of Educational Computing Research
  - Journal of Research on Technology in Education
- Policy Makers, Legislators, and Advocates
  - Most publications that address these audiences are not educational technology publications. Instead, they are aimed at the broad interests of these groups

- These groups also tend to respond to special studies, reports, and evaluations that are disseminated through channels other than scholarly journals

This list is subjective and does not reflect the exclusive interests of the sampling of journals included. Many of the journals listed also publish papers for audiences outside the groups indicated in the list. However, it does give you an idea of the range of audiences served by some of the journals in the field. There are also hundreds of other journals that also publish papers on educational technology.

Opportunity to Join a Scholarly Community. Some journals are stand-alone projects that stand apart from any organization or group of practitioners or scholars. Others are part of an active organization that invites newcomers to become participants in the activities of the journal as well as other activities of the sponsoring organization. Three groups of journals have especially active organizations behind them. The International Society for Technology in Education (ISTE) publishes several journals, including *Leading and Learning with Technology* and the *Journal of Computing and Teacher Education.* ISTE is a large and active organization devoted exclusively to the promotion of high quality integration of technology into education. Its conferences are well attended and it offers many opportunities for participation in the scholarly and professional aspects of the organization. ISTE's web site is at http://www.iste.org.

Another organization that publishes several journals is the Association for the Advancement of Computing in Education (http://www.aace.org). Founded by Gary Marks while he was a graduate student at the University of Texas, it began with the *Journal of Computers in Mathematics and Science Teaching.* Over the years AACE has added a number of other journals including the *Journal of Interactive Learning Research,* and the *Journal of Technology and Teacher Education* (in collaboration with an AACE affiliate—the Society for Information Technology and Teacher Education). AACE also holds annual conferences on Ed Media, teacher education, and E-learning. The Society for Information Technology and Teacher Education has regular meetings at its annual conference related to the publication of its proceedings and the two journals published by AACE for the society.

A third organization that continues to play a very important role in the field of educational technology is the Association for Educational Communication and Technology (AECT). It publishes several journals and newsletters, holds a well attended annual conference, and, like ISTE and SITE, supports a wide range of active Special Interest Groups (SIGS) and committees. Major journals and newsletters supported by AECT include *Educational Technology Research & Development, TechTrends, Instructional Science,* and *Journal of Instructional Development.* Although AECT's book publishing program is not as active as ISTE's, the organization does publish a number of important books and monographs. The organization's web site is at http://www.aect.org.

Open Access, For Profit, or Association? Although the problem is more serious in the natural sciences, the cost of journals has risen so high over the past 20 years that even a large, well financed library at a research university has problems paying the bill for journals. Until recently, there were two types of journals—those published by associations and scholarly organizations such as the International Reading Association (IRA) and the Association of Computing Machinery (ACM) and those from commercial, for-profit publishers such as Blackwell, Elsevier, Sage, Kluwer, and Taylor and Francis. While librarians have been more critical of some commercial publishers, the cost of journals, especially from for-profit publishers, has risen to such high levels that the price of subscriptions restrict access because so few individuals and libraries can afford to subscribe. Journals published by associations such as IRA and ACM tend to be less expensive but many associations use the earnings from journals to fund other activities, which raises the price of their journals.

One important response to the high cost of journals today is the Open Access movement. Open Access journals are generally published on the web and are available to anyone with access to the web without charge or fees. Open Access journals are different from the online journals published by commercial publishers that require a paid subscription to the journal for access, or charge a fee for access to an individual article. My most recent effort to access a online journal article from a for-profit publisher led to a screen that informed me the cost was $38 for a 15-page paper. In contrast, a paper in an Open Access journal is free to everyone. Blackwell, for example, publishes the *British Journal of Educational Technology* for the British Educational Communications and Technology Agency. To read Qiyun Wang and Huay Lit Woo's paper, *Comparing asynchronous online discussions and face-to-face discussions in a classroom setting,* that was published in the March, 2007 issue, I could purchase 30 days of access to the 15-page paper for $29. On the other hand, if I want access to Michael Lebec and Julie Luft's paper on *A Mixed Methods Analysis of Learning in Online Teacher Professional Development: A Case Report,* all I need to do is go the journal web site and either read the paper online or print it for use later. Lebec and Luft's paper is published in issue 7, number 1 (2007) of the Open Access journal, *Contemporary Issues in Technology and Teacher Education.* This online journal, which I helped found, is freely available which means you can read it yourself, print out copies of papers and distribute them to students, or put links to the articles in your online course syllabus without paying any sort of subscription or permission fee.

A number of scholarly organizations and universities have responded to the journal price crisis by urging researchers and scholars to publish in Open Access journals whenever possible, and to consider founding an Open Access journal where one does not exist and the comparable for-profit journal is exorbitantly priced. I second those recommendations. There is a growing list of Open Access journals in the field of educational technology. The list of Open Access journals that publish papers on topics of interest to educational technologists is growing quickly. Thus, any effort to provide an up-to-date list in print form is probably impossible. There are, however, several sources of online information that are updated regularly.

- For a list of Open Access journals see the Directory of Open Access Journals at http://www.doaj.org/
- the list of Open Access Journals in Education maintained by AERA at http://aera-cr.asu.edu/ejournals/
- the list of online psychology journals maintained by John Krantz at http://psych.hanover.edu/Krantz/journal.html
- or the massive list of online journals (not all are Open Access), newsletters and so forth at http://www.publist.com/

Also, Adrian Ho and Charles Bailey at the University of Houston maintain a sort "list of lists" that has links to many different sources of information about online and Open Access journals. It is located at http://www.escholarlypub.com/cwb/oaw.htm.

A few of the Open Access journals in educational technology that were online in the Spring of 2008 are listed below with their web addresses:

- *Australian Educational Researcher*
  http://www.aare.edu.au/aer/aer.htm
- *Brains, Mind, and Media*
  http://www.brains-minds-media.org/
- *Canadian Journal of Learning and Technology*
  http://www.cjlt.ca/index.html
- *Complexity: An International Journal of Complexity in Education*
  http://www.complexityandeducation.ualberta.ca/journal.htm
- *Computers in Higher Education Economics Review*
  http://www.economicsnetwork.ac.uk/cheer/
- *Contemporary Issues in Technology and Teacher Education*
  http://www.citejournal.org
- *Current Issues in Education*
  http://cie.asu.edu/
- *E-journal of Instructional Science and Technology*
  http://www.usq.edu.au/e-jist/
- *E-learning and Education*
  http://eleed.campussource.de/

- *Education Policy Analysis Archives*
  http://epaa.asu.edu/epaa/
- *Education Reviews* (publishes only book reviews)
  http://edrev.asu.edu/index.html
- *Educause Quarterly*
  http://www.educause.edu
- *Educause Review*
  http://www.educause.edu
- *Edutec: Revista Electrónica de Technología Educativa*
  http://edutec.rediris.es/Revelec2/revelec.htm
- *Electronic Journal for the Integration of Technology in Education*
  http://ejite.isu.edu/
- *Electronic Journal of E-learning*
  http://www.ejel.org/index.htm
- *Essays in Education*
  http://www.usca.edu/essays/
- *European Journal of Open, Distance and E-learning*
  http://www.eurodl.org/index.html
- *Forum: Qualitative Social Research*
  http://qualitative-research.net/fqs/fqs-eng.htm
- *Higher Education Perspectives*
  http://aries.oise.utoronto.ca/highered/index.php
- *Innovate: Journal of Online Education*
  http://innovateonline.info/index.php
- *Interactions: UCLA Journal of Education and Information Studies*
  http://repositories.cdlib.org/gseis/interactions/
- *International Education Journal*
  http://iej.cjb.net/
- *International Electronic Journal of Leadership in Learning*
  http://www.ucalgary.ca/~iejll/
- *International Electronic Journal of Mathematics Education*
  http://www.iejme.com/
- *International Journal of Educational Integrity*
  http://www.ojs.unisa.edu.au/journals/index.php/IJEI
- *International Journal of Mathematics Teaching and Learning*
  http://www.cimt.plymouth.ac.uk/journal/default.htm
- *International Journal for the Scholarship of Teaching and Learning*
  http://www.georgiasouthern.edu/ijsotl/
- *International Journal of Education and Development*
  http://ijedict.dec.uwi.edu//index.php
- *International Journal of Education and the Arts*
  http://ijea.asu.edu/

- *International Journal of Education Policy and Leadership*
  http://journals.sfu.ca/ijepl/index.php/ijepl
- *International Journal of Emerging Technologies in Learning*
  http://www.online-journals.org/index.php/i-jet
- *International Journal of Progressive Education*
  http://www.inased.org/ijpe.htm
- *International Journal of Special Education*
  http://www.internationaljournalofspecialeducation.com/
- *International Journal of Teaching and Learning in Higher Education*
  http://www.isetl.org/ijtlhe/
- *International Journal of Whole Schooling*
  http://www.wholeschooling.net/Journal_of_Whole_Schooling/
  IJWSIndex.html
- *International Review of Research on Open and Distance Learning*
  http://www.irrodl.org/index.php/irrodl
- *Issues in Educational Research*
  http://www.iier.org.au/iier.html
- *Journal of Critical Education Policy Studies*
  http://www.jceps.com/
- *Journal of Distance Education*
  http://cade.athabascau.ca/
- *Journal of Educational Technology & Society*
  http://www.ifets.info/
- *Journal of Information Technology Education*
  http://jite.org/index.html
- *Journal of Institutional Research*
  http://www.seaair.info/
- *Journal of Interactive Media in Education*
  http://www-jime.open.ac.uk/
- *Journal of Interactive Online Learning*
  http://www.ncolr.org/jiol/
- *Journal of Language and Learning*
  http://www.shakespeare.uk.net/journal/jllearn_home.htm
- *Journal of Learning Design*
  http://www.jld.qut.edu.au/
- *The Journal of Literacy and Technology*
  http://www.literacyandtechnology.org/
- *Journal of Online Learning*
  http://jolt.merlot.org/
- *Journal of Research in Rural Education*
  http://www.umaine.edu/jrre/
- *Journal of Research Practice*
  http://jrp.icaap.org/index.php/jrp

- *Journal of Scholarship of Teaching and Learning*
  http://www.iupui.edu/~josotl/
- *Journal of Special Education Technology*
  http://jset.unlv.edu/
- *Journal of Statistics Education*
  http://www.amstat.org/publications/jse/
- *Journal of Technology, Learning, and Assessment*
  http://escholarship.bc.edu/jtla/
- *Journal of Theory and Practice in Education*
  http://eku.comu.edu.tr/
- *Journal of Turkish Science Education*
  http://www.tused.org/internet/tufed/tufedmain.htm
- *Journal of University Teaching and Learning Practice*
  http://jutlp.uow.edu.au/
- *Kairos: Rhetoric, Technology, Pedagogy*
  http://english.ttu.edu/kairos/
- *Language Learning & Technology*
  http://llt.msu.edu/
- *Revista Latinoamericana de Tecnología Educativa*
  http://www.unex.es/didactica/RELATEC/
- *The Mathematics Educator*
  http://math.coe.uga.edu/tme/tmeonline.html
- *Meridian: A Middle School Computer Technologies Journal*
  http://www.ncsu.edu/meridian/index.html
- *MountainRise*
  http://mountainrise.wcu.edu/
- *New Horizons in Adult Education and Human Resource Development*
  http://education.fiu.edu/newhorizons/
- *Online Journal of Distance Education Administration*
  http://www.westga.edu/~distance/ojdla/
- *Practical Assessment, Research, and Evaluation*
  http://pareonline.net/
- *Radical Pedagogy*
  http://radicalpedagogy.icaap.org/
- *Reading Online*
  http://www.readingonline.org/
- *Reflecting Education*
  http://www.reflectingeducation.net/index.php/reflecting
- *Studies in Learning, Evaluation, and Development*
  http://www.sleid.cqu.edu.au/index.php
- *TESL-EJ: Teaching English as a Second or Foreign Language*
  http://www-writing.berkeley.edu/TESL-EJ/

- *Teaching English with Technology*
  http://www.iatefl.org.pl/call/callnl.htm
- *Teaching Exceptional Children Plus*
  http://escholarship.bc.edu/education/tecplus/
- *Transformations: Liberal Arts in the Digital Age*
  http://apps.nitle.org/transformations/
- *The Asia-Pacific Forum on Science Learning and Teaching*
  http://www.ied.edu.hk/apfslt/
- *Teaching English with Technology*
  http://www.iatefl.org.pl/call/callnl.htm
- *TOJET—Turkish Online Journal of Educational Technology*
  http://www.tojet.net/

Consider Open Source publications both as a source of information and as outlets for your own scholarship.

Note: If you are a member of a group interested in starting your own Open Access journal the Public Knowledge Project (www.pkp.sfu.ca) at Simon Fraser University in Canada has developed software for managing and publishing journals that is free to anyone. Founded by John Willinsky, the Public Knowledge Project is now a collaborative effort of the University of British Columbia, Simon Fraser University, and Stanford University. It designs and distributes software for publishing journals, managing conferences, and publishing monograph series, all freely available without charge.

SUMMARY

Your relationship to research and scholarship involves both consuming and producing research and scholarship. For most of us the consumer role is the larger, and often more important, role. Preparing for that role calls for a somewhat different approach than preparing to be a full time researcher. A good consumer of research and scholarship knows enough about both the theories and the methods used by a range of scholars to intelligently read and critique work done in many theoretical frameworks using a variety of methods.

The other part of your relationship to research and scholarship is the role of producer. There are very few full-time researchers in education and educational technology today, but many more have scholarly and research responsibilities as part of their workload. Your role as a researcher involves making many decisions, from what to study and what methodologies to use, to deciding where to publish. Being a scholar also involves becoming involved with organizations that support and advance the type of scholarship that interests you. A major issue that both consumers and producers of scholarship in education and educational technology need to pay attention today is the high cost of many journals and the Open Access alternative.

REFERENCES

Birmingham, C. (September, 2004). Phronesis: A model for pedagogical reflection. *Journal of Teacher Education, 55*(4), 313–324.

Capurro, R. (2004). Skeptical knowledge management. In H.-C. Hobohm (Ed.), *Knowledge management: Libraries and librarians taking up the challenge* (pp. 47–57). Munich: Saur.

Cooper, D. (1965, January–February). Two types of rationality. *New Left Review, 1*(29).

Hooker, R. (1996). *Greek philosophy: Aristotle*. Retrieved May 6, 2007 from http://www.wsu.edu/~dee/GREECE/ARIST.HTM .

Kelly, T. (2003, May). Epistemic rationality as instrumental rationality: A critique. *Philosophy and Phenomenological Research, 66*(3).

Lonner, W. (Spring 2000). On the growth and continuing importance of cross-cultural psychology. *Eye on Psi Chi, 4*(3), 22–26.

Rieber, L. (2004). *Getting up and running with Dreamweaver by building a web-based portfolio*. Retrieved May 4, 2007 from http://www.nowhereroad.com/dreamweaver/

Rieber, L. (2000). *Getting interactive with Authorware: Building simulations and games*. Madison, WI: Brown and Benchmark.

Science Encyclopedia. (2007). Philolsophy—Relations to other intellectual realms—After Plato, Medieval and Renaissance, Early Modern, Modern Times. *History of Ideas, V4*. Retrieved May 4, 2007 from http://science.jrank.org/pages/7965/Philosophy-Relations-other-Intellectual-Realms.html

Sloan, D. (1994). *Faith and knowledge: mainline Protestantism and American higher education*. Louisville, KY: Westminster John Knox Press.

Underwood, J., Hoadley, C., Lee, H., Hollebrands, K., Digiano, C., & Renninger, K. (2005). IDEA: Identifying design principles in educational applets. *Educational Technology Research and Development, 53*(2), 99–112.

Znaniecki, F. (1934). *The method of sociology*. New York: Farrar & Rinehart.

READINGS FOR CHAPTER 6

Reading 6.1

The Budapest Open Access Initiative Statement. Available at http://www.soros.org/openaccess/

The Budapest Open Access Initiative is a brief statement of justification for changing the way scholarly publishing happens. It is one of the many initiatives of George Soros, who was born in Hungary but became a very successful, and very rich financier in America. Soros lived through the Nazi occupation of Hungary and was probably saved from death when the Nazis began deporting Jews to concentration camps because his father sent him to stay with a non-Jewish family. After the Soviets took over Hungary Soros was able to escape to England in 1947 and he graduated from the prestigious London School of Economics where the best known 20th century philosopher of science, Sir Karl Popper, taught. Popper, a Jewish émigré from Austria, has been a major influence on Soros. Popper's book, *The Open Society and Its Enemies,* has been a foundation for Soros' humanitarian work. After moving to the USA in 1956 he amassed a fortune by understanding the financial markets in ways others did not. He has used his considerable fortune to support movements toward open, democratic societies all over the world, but especially in Eastern and Central Europe. Through the Soros Foundation and The Open Society Institute as well as other organizations funded by him, grants to support democratic projects have been made in many nations. He also helped create and continues to support the Central European University in Budapest.

Our particular interest here is on the Budapest Open Access Initiative (BOAI) which does three things. It highlights how the commercialization of the dissemination of scholarship has limited access to that scholarship because the high prices of subscriptions to journals keeps many university libraries and individuals from subscribing to them. Without personal subscriptions or subscriptions by nearby libraries, many scholars and practitioners are effectively excluded from the communities of scholarship that exchange ideas and research through journals. One solution to this delimma is the creation of Open Access journals that are published on the web and made available to anyone with access to the Internet.

The BOAI proposes several solutions to the problem and suggests how individuals and organizations can support the movement. Research libraries, scholarly organizations, the professional organizations of librarians, some government commissions and agencies, individual scholars, and many universities are backing the proposals in BOAI. However, in each of the potential groups of supporters there has been far more verbal support and encouragement than action. For example, only a small percentage of university libraries have begun to collaborate with scholars on their campuses to develop and support open access journals, and only a small number of the scholarly and professional organizations that earn part of their income from publishing journals have made their publications open access. Also, there has been a strong response from many for-profit journal publishers to the effect that open access is not a good idea. Some say, for example, that open access supporters underestimate the "true" cost of publishing a journal and that their model is thus unrealistic. Since the great majority of work done on most journals is "donated" by the volunteer scholars who edit and review papers, this does not seem to be a valid argument. However, anyone thinking about establishing a new online, open access journal should realize that there is a considerable and ongoing demand for quality time and attention to the journal. Fortunately, there are a number of free or inexpensive programs that automate much of the process of editing and publishing online journals that greatly reduce the time investment required to go from submitted paper to a new issue of a journal. Another criticism is that online, open access journals are unstable, they may be here this year and disappear the next. This means scholarship published in an open access journal may not be available for decades and centuries as print scholarship is. It is true that not all open access journals last past their first year or two of publication, but that has always applied to print journals as well. What saves print journals is that when libraries subscribe to them they are on the shelves of the libraries even if the publisher disappears. There are a number of efforts, including a major one at Virginia Tech University in Blacksburgh, Virginia to develop electronic repositories for online journals that ensures they will be available for centuries.

After you read the Budapest Open Access Initiative ask youself whether this seems to be a good idea or not. What makes you believe the way you do? And, regardless of whether you support the traditional system or open access, what specific actions could you take to ensure wider distribution of research and scholarship?

SECTION 3

PATHWAYS TO UNDERSTANDING:
THE METHODS OF RESEARCH AND SCHOLARSHIP

CHAPTER 7

MAKING SENSE OF THE FORMS OF SCHOLARSHIP

Thus far in this book we have looked at many frameworks for doing research, several research methods, three or four general paradigms (depending on whether you consider positivism and postpositivism to be one or two paradigms), and more than a few reasons for doing educational technology research and scholarship. At this point we have a large, unorganized wad of strings that are the paradigms, frameworks, methods, and purposes of educational technology research. It is time to organize all the strings we have into some reasonable framework that helps us think about how to do research and scholarship in our field.

RESEARCH VERSUS SCHOLARSHIP

Just what is the difference between the terms, research and scholarship, which have been used rather interchangeably in the previous six chapters? One popular way of thinking about the difference is to define research as what Boyer (1990) called the Scholarship of Discovery and to call everything else Scholarship (e.g., in Boyer's terms the Scholarship of Integration, the Scholarship of Application, and the Scholarship of Teaching). One professor of accounting, who put his course outline on the web, expressed this view in his syllabus:

Qualitative Research Methods in Education and Educational Technology, pages 169–197
Copyright © 2008 by Information Age Publishing
All rights of reproduction in any form reserved.

> Please remember the difference between research versus scholarship. Research, the extension of new knowledge, is never as easy as scholarship focused upon existing knowledge. Research is a flicker of light where the leading edge of literature drops off into a black unknown. A clever idea is far more enlightening than an encyclopedic mind at the dark edge. My hope is that some of you will have a clever idea. Without a clever idea, you will have to resort to only scholarship. I can't tell you where to find clever ideas. All I can do is help set the stage for your fertile imagination. (Jensen, 2000)

I do not find that approach to distinguishing between research and scholarship very enlightening. It simply serves to privilege in the social sciences and education the positivist perspectives of the natural sciences. Using this definition, the humanities never do research because the original work, such as writing a novel, is not "research" and writing about novels is also not research because it focuses on "existing knowledge" (e.g., the novel, play or some other expression of humanity) rather than jumping off "into a black unknown."

You will probably not be surprised that distinguishing between research and scholarship has occupied the minds of many commissions, study groups, and scholarly organizations. One such group is The Commission on Research at Emory University which was headed by Claire Sterk (2007), a professor and department chair in the School of Public Health. Emory is a "research university" with very strong work in many fields—from basic science to work in the social sciences, the humanities and the arts, and professional schools such as public health and medicine. After considerable discussion and debate about the terms research and scholarship, Emory's Commission came to this conclusion, "We debated the use of the term research versus scholarship and agreed that the Commission will apply a broad definition of research, including all scholarly activities that result in the creation and production of knowledge. Research may take place in a laboratory or a library; it may be funded or not; or it may focus on the natural world or on cultural production." The Emory commission took two years to produce a report, *Research at Emory*, which is available online at: http://www.emory.edu/ACAD_EXCHANGE/2002/febmar/sterk.html.

This is an extensive report, but if you are interested in questions such as how research and scholarship are defined, how to create an academic environment that supports a wide range of scholarship on campus, and how the tenure and promotion process should deal with teaching, research/scholarship, and practice, this report from Emory University is well worth reading.

The report further defines Emory's view of research and scholarship:

> Throughout this report, research and scholarship are used interchangeably. Some scholars refer to research as those activities funded by external sources, whereas others use the term to refer to a phase in the overall effort of scholarship. (Introduction, p. 6)

Emory did not simply leave the matter at this level—using the terms research and scholarship interchangeably and acknowledging that different professors use the terms in different ways. They also decided not to use departments as a means of differentiation—physicists and chemists do research while English and theater professors do scholarship. Instead, they decided to recommend that support be provided to several "cultures of research" within the university." They did this because "Cultures of research take into account the varying modes of inquiry, collaborative methods, scholarly products, and funding needs" (Introducton, p. 6).

The commission identified "distinct cultures of research in the humanities, social sciences, sciences, health sciences, business, law, and theology." These were distinguished by four factors:

- Mode of inquiry
- The nature and extent of collaboration among scholars
- The scholarly products produced in the culture of research
- The economies of research (such as the availability of grants, the expenses of research)

As they studied the different cultures of research they found that "Despite institution-wide tenure policies, each culture of research has its own norms and values for assessing scholarship" (Sterk, 2004). And the group was concerned with some of the current practices on campus. For example, while different cultures considered a wide range of output as scholarly products (e.g., "A book, article, play or discovery") they were bothered that a tendency to put a higher value on products that were supported by external funding, because funding is not available for all forms of scholarship. The Commission made many recommendations to improve the research and scholarly climate of Emory and to develop support systems for different cultures of research.

One of the most interesting aspects of the Commission's activities was the identification of cultures of research. Because these different cultures need different types of support, the recommendations for action were also linked to those cultures. Of interest to the field of educational technology is the description of the Health Sciences at Emory:

> The culture of research in the health sciences is the most complex, containing components of the three previously described cultures (humanities, social sciences, and sciences)....Clinical responsibilities...are unique to the culture of research in the health sciences....One clinical researcher relates the pressures associated with patient care as follows: "This is a completely different kind of pressure than you will find anywhere else in the university. (Cultures of Research, p. 41–42)

It strikes me that educational technology can have similar characteristics—it is an applied field in which "clinical research" is very important. Further, our field can, and should, draw on the methods, theories, and knowledge of the humanities, the social sciences, and the sciences. We might also think seriously about another topic discussed in the Commission report—intellectual neighborhoods. These are informal and formal groups that tend to cross disciplinary lines and collaborate to accomplish a common goal. For example, an educational technologist studying the patterns of schooling, and deployment of technology, in a failing urban school district might pull together a group that includes scholars from the humanities, the social sciences, and professional fields like social work, public health, and business. This group would become an intellectual neighborhood that might end up completing several studies over a period of years.

I believe the general approach of the Commission on Research at Emory is an excellent one because it does not try to elevate one form of scholarship over another. It acknowledges that there are many cultures of research and that the values and methods of deciding what is worth studying, and how it should be studied, varies across groups. I do not have a problem with calling a broad range of intellectual work either research or scholarship.

METHODS AND CULTURES OF SCHOLARSHIP

In this section I would like to focus relatively specifically on the types of research methods that come to educational technology from various cultures of scholarship. I see six different cultures of scholarship that are most relevant to our field. They are illustrated in Figure 7.1.

This list is not completely logical because it includes the name of a rather large discipline—the humanities, and also includes a specialized set of re-

Figure 7.1 The six cultures of scholarship that are most relevant to educational technology.

search methods (single subject designs) that are used by a subgroup of applied behaviorists, mostly psychologists and educators. Where is social science, education, and the field of educational technology itself? They are there in multiple locations. Education and the social sciences in general use methods of scholarship from all six of these cultures. The same is true of educational technology. While there are real differences between educational technology and the broader field of education (and the yet broader field of applied social science) those differences are not characterized by differences in research methods. One eminent scholar in education may, for example, use almost exclusively the methods of philosophical inquiry while another may do only quantitative research. Thus, while there are groups of methodological purists in education, educational technology, and the social sciences, all these fields are omnivorous as a group—they use methods from different cultures of scholarship.

QUANTITATIVE METHODS

In this section I would like to explore the various research methods used in these six cultures. I will begin with the two that will not be dealt with further in this book: quantitative methods and single subject designs. Figure 7.2 is

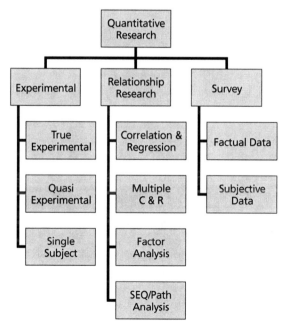

Figure 7.2 The main methods of Quantitative Research.

a simplified structure of the most common methods/designs used in quantitative research. Most quantitative research is some form of experimental research, survey research, or relationship research (e.g., uses correlational or regression statistics).

SURVEY RESEARCH

Most quantitative research falls into three broad categories: experimental, relationship research, and survey research. Of those three broad types, survey research is probably the most often used, although it is not always the most needed. Every year hundreds of educational technology surveys ask teachers, preservice teachers, and students what their opinions are about everything from the components of computer literacy to the quality of technology training in preservice teacher education. Many surveys collect subjective data such as opinions or preferences, but surveys are also used to collect factual data such as the level of education, age, prior technology training or experience, and so on.

Survey research is probably more common than can be justified by meaningfulness and appropriateness because a survey research study is relatively easy to plan and conduct. Unfortunately, ease of use is not always associated with value nor is it consistently associated with high quality survey research. Too many surveys in education are developed and used by researchers who pay very little attention to the formidable amount of knowledge available on how to design good surveys and how to appropriately use them in research studies. And, even when a survey is designed appropriately, it is not always a worthwhile way to spend your research time. For example, a survey that asks teachers with little expertise or experience with the classroom integration of technology to tell you what the content of technology professional development should be is not likely to provide worthwhile information. A better approach might be to conduct in-depth interviews with very successful technology-using teachers. Also, surveys that confirm what fifty other surveys have concluded do not contribute much to our knowledge base.

Despite my tendency to be suspicious of the value of survey research, there are times when surveys do provide precisely the type of information you need. They can be, for example, a useful way of taking an inventory of ways teachers are using technology in a school; they are also helpful when you want to know more about the general views of a particular group (or groups) on a topic (e.g., do computer coordinators and professors who teach preservice teacher education courses on technology agree on what new teachers should know and how they should be taught?). If you are interested in doing survey research online, the Balch Internet Research and Analysis Toolkit (BIRAT) is a sophisticated system for conducting Internet-based survey research. It is free and available online at http://birat.net/br. It was developed by Dr. Charles Balch. You will also find many examples of survey research in the education and educational technology literature, and there are a great many books and online resources to help you create and use a good survey.

Surveys can also be an efficient way of collecting needed factual information, as well as attitudinal and affective data, from a group. Several of the studies mentioned in the following section, on relationship research, used surveys for that purpose. An example of a specialized survey is the Mathematics and Technology Attitudes Scale (Pierce, Stacey, & Barkatsas (2007). The developers created this survey instrument to collect data from middle school students on their mathematics confidence, their confidence with technology, and two ways of becoming involved in mathematics learning. In their first use of the survey instrument, the authors found that boys who had more positive attitudes toward learning mathematics using technology also tended to be confident of their ability to use technology. For girls, there was no such correlation. Instead, girls who tended to be less confident of their math abilities tended to have negative attitudes toward using technology in mathematics classes. Both these findings are about the relationships between different variables being studied. In this case, the researchers used correlational statistics to study relationships. It is to that type of research, relationship studies, and to the different ways relationships can be studied, including correlational statistics, that we turn next.

RELATIONSHIP RESEARCH

Less common than survey research, but still very popular, is relationship research. Studies may look at correlations between variables like attitudes toward computers and the likelihood teachers will use technology in their classrooms. Simple correlational research typically involves looking at the relationship between a few, often two, variables. Correlations range from +1.0 to −1.0. A "high" correlation of .70 or higher means that a person who is high on one variable (e.g. positive attitudes toward educational technology) will likely be high on the other variable (e.g., tendency to use technology in the classroom). A high negative correlation of −.70 or lower means that a person who is high on one variable (e.g., a measure of computer anxiety) will be low on the second variable (e.g., tendency to use technology in the classroom). If the goal is to predict something like admission to a college, essentially the same basic statistical procedures can be use to decide whether scores on certain tests (or other types of quantitative data) predict things like maintaining a B average, or graduating from college within 5 years. This type of research is called regression analysis. More complicated relational research looks for relationships between, for example, multiple predictors and one or more factors the researcher wants to predict. For example, a study might take 15 different variables, each of which predicts college success, and calculate how well these variables, taken as a whole, predict success. This involves the use of multiple regression and multiple correlation procedures and they are widely used in the health sciences but have not been widely applied in educational technology.

Hewet and Brett (2007) used correlational statistics to address the question of how class size influences the patterns of student online interaction in graduate courses. They collected data from 28 different graduate courses and looked at the correlations between the number of students in the class and student participation in online conferencing/discussions associated with the course. They collected data on:

- Number of notes (posts) written
- Average size of the note
- Percentage of notes written by others that a student opened and read

The authors found that the larger the class the more notes written. However, there was a negative correlation between class size and length of note as well as percentage of notes opened. That is, students in larger classes tended to write shorter notes and they opened a smaller percentage of the notes written for that class by other students. In addition, the authors found that students in larger classes seemed to be more likely to scan long notes rather than read them in depth.

An example of a more complex piece of research that used correlational statistics is a study done by Margaret Ropp (1999) at the University of New Mexico. She looked at the relationship between certain characteristics of preservice teacher education students and changes that occurred across a semester-long educational computing course. She used several surveys to gather data on a number of variables:

- Attitudes toward computers (Attitudes Toward Technology scale and a Computer Attitude Scale)
- Technology proficiency (Technology Proficiency Self-Assessment scale and a measure of "previous and current contexts of computer use")
- Computer anxiety (Computer Anxiety Scale)
- Computer self-efficacy (Computer Self-Efficacy Scale)
- Computer coping strategies (Computer Coping Strategies measure)

Ropp gathered data at the beginning and end of an educational computing course that included both classroom discussions of technology and hands-on practice. She then calculated two sets of Pearson correlation coefficients

- One set was on all the pre-course data. For example, measures of attitudes toward computers were correlated with measures of technology proficiency, computers anxiety, and so on. Dr. Ropp also ran correlations between the data from her six survey instruments and background variables such as age, gender, computer ownership, and so on.
- Another set of correlations were calculated on the data gathered at the end of the course.

Ropp found that the measures of attitudes toward computers, technology proficiency, computer anxiety, and so on were highly interrelated. For example, a high (positive) attitude toward computers was correlated with a high level of proficiency and a low level of computer anxiety. Ropp noted that the correlations indicated "students who are less competent and have the most to learn apparently also are the most anxious about learning to use computers." Fortunately, the confidence of students increased over the course along with most other measures of student abilities to use technology. In addition, improvement was more substantial among students who were the least confident when the course began. However, while measures of "action-oriented characteristics showed significant growth" the results from "more affectively focused instruments showed no significant change."

Ropp's study is an example of how correlational research methods can be applied in ordinary professional settings such as teaching a course on educational computing. It is also an illustration of some of the problems of doing correlational research in applied settings. The study was based on the data from 53 students completing a course at one university. For correlational research like this, we could have much more confidence in the validity of the results if the statistical analysis had been based on more students—perhaps 100 or more in an ideal situation. And, of course, the educational computing course the students completed is one example of that type of course. There are many different ways of approaching the "educational computing" course and it is difficult to know how the content and methods of the course influenced the results of the study.

Some of the problems and difficulties of doing correlational research were highlighted in an interesting article written by three Australian scholars at Griffith University. Proctor, Watson, and Finger (2003) question the meaningfulness of simple correlations, especially in research about whether computers in the classroom have an impact on student achievement. Their paper is a response to some earlier research that made newspaper headlines because it reported that the more computers there were in a classroom the lower students scored on standardized tests of basic literacy and numeracy. These studies based their conclusions on simple correlations between number of computers in different classrooms and the average achievement scores of students in those classrooms. Proctor and her colleagues argued that correlational research like that is not very helpful. Too many factors are ignored in such simplistic studies. For example, a set of six computers in a classroom may be used in many different ways—and some of those different uses may not be effective at all while others may be very powerful. Or, the computers may be used as rewards—students get to play games on them when they finish their drill exercises on time. Or, they are not used at all; they are there but may even be stored in a closet. These authors argue that if you are going to look at the relationship between computers and achievement you must do it in a much more sophisticated way. They present in their paper a way of thinking about and assessing technology "curriculum integration" that considers many more factors than the simple presence of computers in the classroom.

Another type of relationship research is path analysis or structured equation modeling (SEQ). There are differences between these two procedures but they are essentially expansions of multiple regression and correlation techniques that give you much more sophisticated answers. Kadijevich (2006) used path analysis to study whether different types of support for students preparing to be teachers had any influence on the students' interest in using technology. One interesting finding of this study was that some factors being studied did not have a direct impact on the target attitudes but they did have an indirect positive impact. That is, they influenced other factors and those intermediate factors influenced the target attitudes. This type of information is one of the particularly useful results of path analysis.

The last type of relationship research is factor analysis. A typical use of factor analysis is to organize a survey or test with many items into clusters of items that seem to assess the same thing (e.g., the same *factor*). For example, Stuve and Cassady (2005) did a factor analysis on the NETS profiles of 956 teacher education students. NETS is short for the National Educational Technology Standards. These standards are widely used to evaluate how well a teacher is prepared to use technology in the classroom. The individual standards were organized into six groups by the developers. Those groups are:

- Technology Operations and Concepts
- Planning and Designing Learning Environments and Experiences
- Teaching, Learning, and the Curriculum
- Assessment and Evaluation
- Productivity and Professional Practice
- Social, Ethical, Legal, and Human Issues

Indicators of accomplishment in each of the six areas were identified, and in many teacher education programs, every student has a profile that indicates their success at achieving each of the indicators in the six areas. The scores on the indicators for each factor are combined to produce a score for that group or factor. If the NETS standards were organized into a meaningful structure by the developers, the authors of this study reasoned that a factor analysis should empirically demonstrate that there are six separate factors in the profiles of teachers, and that those factors roughly correspond to the six groups created by the developers. In addition, the authors assumed that an indicator the developers assigned to "Technology Operations and Concepts" or to "Assessment and Evaluation," should be strongly associated with that factor and not with other factors. The factor analysis did not confirm any of those expectations. Instead, it found only two factors which the authors named *Technology Self Concept* and *Policy and Professionalism*. This does not, however, mean the NETS groupings are wrong or that the teacher profiles are inaccurate. Factor analysis does not necessarily tell us "the truth of the matter" when it comes to how items on a test should be grouped. However, findings such as those of Stuve and Cassady do suggest additional attention might be profitably paid to the standards, how they are assessed, and how they are organized. The way Stuve and Cassady used factor analysis is called "confirmatory factor analysis" because it was an attempt to confirm that a particular way of organizing data made sense and reflected the underlying mathematical structure of that data. Other forms include "exploratory factor analysis" which involves using the procedure to try to organize a collection of data that has not yet been organized using other methods or procedures.

Experimental Research. The last type of general quantitative research to be discussed is experimental. This approach, which is at the heart of the positivist, natural science model of research, involves dividing subjects into one or more control groups and one or more experimental groups. After treatments are administered to the experimental groups, a statistical analysis tells the researcher whether there are differences in the average scores of students in the experimental and control groups. In an ideal world, if the treatment group or groups do better on the assessment, we should be able to conclude the treatment is effective. However, experimental studies must meet a host of requirements to be considered "true experimental" research. Most studies in education and educational technology do not meet all the requirements. The criteria most often not met is random assignment to groups. To be truly random, every student participating in the study must have the same chance of being assigned to the experimental and control group. This is often impossible to do in educational research and a popular alternative is a "quasi-experimental" study that meets some, but not all, of the requirements for true experimental research. For example, the experimental and control groups may not be randomly constituted.

A study by Paul Farrand, Fearzana Hussain, and Enid Hennessy (2002), is virtually a prototype of the standard use of experimental methods in applied research. All three researchers were at the University of London when they did the study, and their work was published in the journal, *Medical Education*. The basic problem these authors addressed was the huge amount of information that medical students are expected to learn. They did not, however, approach the solution of that problem directly, as they might in an action research study. Instead, they organized their efforts around a theory. There are many theories about how memory works, and the implications of one particular theory were used to guide this study. The particular theory these researchers used is called Levels of Processing Theory. The most popular theory of memory today hypothesizes that there are three "buffers" or storage mechanisms that lead to storage of information in the human brain. As shown in Figure 7.3, new data flows first into Sensory Memory, then into a Short Term Memory (STM), and finally into Long Term Memory.

Sensory Memory stores an exact copy of the sensory data—a sound, image, and so forth—for a very brief period. To survive, the data must be transferred into the Short Term Memory buffer. STM differs from Sensory Memory in several ways. First, Sensory Memory is essentially a way of very briefly storing *all* the sensory data a person receives through the various senses. It is stored in Sensory Memory as raw sensory data with no processing or modification. The transfer to STM, however, is selective. Only some of the data is transferred. That is generally referred to as the process of attention. We "pay attention" to some sensory data which means it is transferred to STM while most sensory data never makes it out of Sensory Memory and is lost forever.

While Sensory Memory can hold data for only a brief moment, it has virtually unlimited capacity and stores all the incoming sensory data. STM, on the other hand, can store data for a longer period of time, but it has a very limited capacity. Some versions of memory theory assert that it can only hold about seven pieces of data at a time. STM also begins to process the data it receives and to organize it into meaningful units or "chunks." These chunks are not based solely on the sensory origins (e.g., sounds, im-

Figure 7.3 Diagram of the dominant model of memory today.

ages, tactile sensations, and so on). Instead, they are organized into meaningful units of information—such as information about how to quickly fix the transmission shift mechanism on a 1948 Chevrolet sedan when it locks up, or what Nietzsche meant when he attacked organized religion. These chunks of information are then transferred into Long Term Memory (LTM) which is a bit like an organized warehouse where new chunks of information are stored with other chunks on the same topic.

The warehouse metaphor breaks down at this point, however, because you can only store new arrivals at the warehouse with one type of similar product. Pepper may be stored with other spices for example, but once stored there it cannot be stored with items from India, ingredients for soups, and so on. Contemporary memory theories assume that human memory is organized into "nodes" of information that are linked to other nodes in a series of complex networks or "schemas." Thus, in this more flexible storage system, a pepper node could be a part of the schema for spices as well as the schemata for soups, products from India, and many, many more. There is, of course, much more involved in contemporary theories of memory but this overview will give you an idea of the theoretical framework used in many research studies on human memory.

An alternative theory is the Levels of Processing Theory. It proposes a very different model for how new information is organized and stored. Proponents of the Levels of Processing Theory question assumptions of the traditional model. For example, they are not so sure that the capacity of what is called STM is limited to around seven items, especially since there is little agreement on what "seven" refers to—it could be seven numbers such as 6, 9, 2, 12, 19, 56, and 91 or it could be *Money Magazine*'s of the seven best places to raise a family (e.g., Ames, Iowa, and so on). The seven items may even be much more complex pieces of information. Levels of Processing Theory rejects the memory model that assumes there are three separate and distinct buffers where data is stored before being transferred to the next buffer. It proposes, instead, that there are different levels of processing—from relatively shallow to very deep processing. Shallow processing involves learning surface characteristics such as the shape and pattern of the letters in a text passage, sounds in speech, and the meaning of specific words that have been spoken or read. Deep processing involves extracting more sophisticated meaning from the incoming data. For example, it is shallow processing if you read a short sentence and only process that data to the point of knowing the meaning of some of the words in the sentence. For example, each word in this sentence has individual meaning—"There is a strong smell of gas in the kitchen." Taken individually there is nothing particularly threatening about these words. However, there is much more meaning to be derived from the sentence taken as a whole and acquiring that meaning involves deeper processing.

Levels of Processing Theory assumes that we will remember new information longer if we process it deeper. Two ways this may happen is that deeper processing of new data means it is linked to more networks of knowledge or schemas in the brain. Deeper processing may also cause new data to be more distinctively remembered so that it stands out from the "background" of other stored information. Finally, these two assumptions also lead to a conclusion about the "encoding process"—the conversion of new data into information that will be stored in memory for an extended period of time. For more deeply processed data, the encoding process will include things like the form of the data—text, spoken word, visual images, and so on. And, if deeply processed data involves multiple methods of representation so much the better because that means there will be more links to other pieces of information in memory. More links is important because that means there are more pathways to recall and use that information.

It is this aspect of Levels of Processing Theory that Farrand, Hussain, and Hennessy used as the foundation for their applied research. This theory of memory is the basis for a study technique that is supposed to enhance retention and recall of the information being studied. It is a technique called "mind mapping." Students are required to take the information they are to learn and convert it from textual information into diagrams that include key words that serve as memory triggers for the information being studied. A typical mind map (e.g., a visual diagram) will have an image representing the main topic of study in the middle. Then, "extending from this central image are several major branches containing keywords representing the topic subheadings, which are accompanied by an image whenever possible. The important detail included under each subheading is written upon smaller branches projecting from the subheadings with more detailed information being connected to this information.... Information initially contained within passages of text becomes hierarchically organized, with the most general information being presented in the center of the mind map and material of increasing detail being presented at the extremes" (p. 426). The process of organizing the information, and the use of different media to convey the information—imagery, color, and a "visual-spatial arrangement" should all enhance recall according to Levels of Processing Theory.

To test this implication of the theory, the researchers had medical students study a 600-word passage taken from an article in the *Scientific American* about a topic related to transportation that would not likely be familiar to any of the medical students. After studying the passage for 10 minutes using any study method they wished, the students completed another activity for 5 minutes that served as a buffer between studying and assessment. Then they took a short test based on the information in the passage.

All students in the study completed the initial study-and-test phase, and none of them used a study method remotely resembling mind mapping. Many, for example, wrote down key words, re-read the passage, or underlined parts of the text. Then the students were randomly assigned to one of two conditions:

- Mind Map. After being taught the method, they were required to use the mind map technique when they studied the passage again.
- Self-selected Study Method. Students in this group again used whatever methods they wished to study the passage a second time.

Students in the Self-selected Study Method condition left the experimental setting and returned after 30 minutes. Students in the Mind Map condition spent the 30 minutes being taught to use this study method (using content unrelated to the *Scientific American* article).

After the 30 minute break, or the Mind Map training session, depending on the group, students were given ten more minutes to study the passage, worked for 5 minutes on a buffer task, and then took another version of the test. Then, one week later, the test was administered for a third time. Students did not study the passage before this third testing and they were tested using a version of the test they had not used before.

To improve the ability of their statistical analysis to distinguish differences between the two groups (Self-selected Study Method and Mind Map) the researchers uses an analysis of variance procedure that included each medical student's first test score as a "covariate." A covariate in analysis of variance is a variable you expect to be highly related to the dependent variable. In this study the dependent variable was the scores students made on the second test, after they had studied the passage for a second time. A second dependent variable was scores on the third test. Students who made a high score on the first test, when they used whatever study method they preferred, would likely also make high scores on the second and third tests regardless of the treatment condition they were in. So, to reduce the influence of differences between students that were not associated with method of study, the researchers used the first test as a covariate. ANCOVA, analysis of covariance, statistically removes the impact of the covariate. In this study, the ANCOVA process generated a new set of tests scores based on a hypothetical group of students who all scored the same on the first test. ANCOVA procedures then look at whether there is a difference between groups based on these statistically simulated scores.

In this study the ANCOVA did not find any significant differences between the Self-Study and the Mind Map groups. However, some differences in favor of the Mind Map group on the third test "approached significance." Naturally, the researchers were probably disappointed with the outcome because they believed the Levels of Processing Theory had implications for teaching and learning. And, like thousands of researchers before them, they looked for ways of salvaging their preferred theory and the treatment method they were evaluating. In this case they looked at a measure of motivation for studying the passage. A motivation question was asked after the second study/test phase. That was the phase in which one group of students used the mind mapping procedure. Students were asked how "motivated" they were to study the material and they marked options from *1—Very Unmotivated* to *5—Very Motivated*. The Mind Map group reported significantly lower levels of motivation (a mean of 2.8 versus 3.2 for the Self-selection group). Farrand and his colleagues then reanalyzed the data using the motivation data as another covariate. In this analysis the Mind Mapping group did score significantly better than the Self-selection group on both the second and third tests.

As is typical of traditional experimental research in the social sciences, this study was done to test the implications of a particular theory. The study technique, mind mapping, is derived from the implications of a particular theory of memory, and positive results are typically treated as support for both the particular treatment studied (e.g., mind mapping) and the supporting theory. That was the case here. The authors concluded that "the mind map technique has the potential for an important improvement in efficacy" (p. 429) and they also concluded that "it is likely that mind maps encourage a deeper level of processing than that obtained when the other, more conventional study techniques adopted in the self-selected study technique. A deeper level of information processing has been associated with better academic performance by medical students. . . . It has also been acknowledged, however, that fostering a deep level of learning is very difficult because students do not spontaneously adopt strategies that foster such learning" (p. 430). Thus, the focus of these researchers was on the effectiveness of the treatment and on the link between the treatment and the underlying theory that guided its development. The positive outcome of the study is support for the study technique and the authors virtually assume that the theory of memory that is the foundation for the technique is true.

The conclusions reached by the researchers, and the implications they draw from those conclusions, are not, however, the only ones possible. Keep in mind that the researchers did not make a straightforward comparison between the test scores of the two groups of students. Instead, they used a covariate, scores from the first test administration, to increase the ability of the statistics to detect a difference between the Self-selected and the Mind Map groups. That is not unusual. The logic underlying this method of improving accuracy is very similar to the logic a physician uses when she or he instructs you to eat nothing after midnight and to come in for tests the next morning before eating breakfast. The physician wants to eliminate the impact of recently digested foods on the planned tests in order to determine whether other conditions are having an impact on the test results. Often the purpose of the medical test is virtually impossible to accomplish without requiring the patient to undergo a period of fasting. Using a covariate in an analysis of variance procedure tries to do essentially the same thing.

Using the first test as a covariate meets all the requirements of ANCOVA. We have every reason to suspect that those scores are an indication of a student's ability to do a good job of studying complex written text, and to extract information from that written material. We know that students differ considerably on this ability, and those differences are one reason scores may vary considerably from one student to another. Eliminating the impact of individual differences in this ability will reduce the variability in a group of scores and help us see a difference between groups that might otherwise be statistically invisible or obscured by the variation in test scores due to the varying study abilities of students.

Keep in mind, however, that when scores on the first test were used as a covariate, there were no significant differences between the two groups. It was only when a measure of motivation was used as a second covariate that significant differences were found. Is the motivation measure the same type as the first test score? No, it is not. The researchers did not take the motivation measure until *after* the Mind Mapping group had been taught to use this study technique and had actually used it to study the passage. Had the measure been taken after the passage was read for the first time, and before mind mapping was taught and used, there might be some justification for using it as a covariate. Perhaps, by accident, the random assignment of students to the Self-selected or Mind Mapping groups might have resulted in more students with low motivation in one or the other group. But that is not what happened. Students were asked to rate their motivation just *after* one group had used mind mapping. Thus, the measure of motivation may not be a measure of some intrinsic characteristics of the student. The significant difference between the Self-selected or Mind Mapping groups on motivation may have been due to the mind mapping technique itself. Many students in the Mind Mapping group may not have liked this study technique and thus may not have been very motivated to study the passage. Using as a covariate a measure of motivation that is quite possibly influenced by the treatment being used is a bit like eliminating all the students from a group who say they don't like to practice the piano and then concluding that a piano teaching method based on lots of practice works best because the students left in that group did better than a control group! I suspect the authors waited until after the mind mapping training to gather data on motivation because they expected motivation to be higher in that group. If it had been significantly higher than in the Self-selected group, they might have concluded that mind mapping was such a good study technique that it actually enhanced motivation to study—which would be one more reason to use it widely. However, when the reverse happened, the researchers used it as a covariate, which assumes that it is a characteristic of the individuals being studied that was not influenced by the treatment.

I have made an extended analysis of this study because it illustrates the enormous difficulties of using experimental research methods in education. Even in a study that was well above average in the quality of its planning, execution, and analysis, problems in interpretation are still apparent. The authors' conclusion that "This paper has shown the efficacy of using mind maps as a study aid, even when use has been limited to a single exposure" (p. 430) cannot be confidently supported by the results nor can the recommendation that "before mind maps were recommended as a study technique, a way of providing effective training would need to be established so that students were encouraged and enthusiastic about adopting the approach in preference to other more conventional study techniques. With this in mind, one possibility would be the incorporation of a mind map training course into the first few terms of the medical curriculum" (p. 430). This study and the implications drawn from it by the authors illustrate a serious issue in most experimental research in education. Such research, when conducted on humans, involves many, many decisions that are open to more than one interpretation. Our prior experiences, our biases, our expectations, and our hopes can all influence both our interpretations and the meaning we draw from the research. Objective research on humans, even when very well done, is still subjective because humans make their subjective decisions about things, whether they are subjects in the research study or researchers conducting the research.

My comments on the difficulties of drawing uncontested conclusions from experimental research apply to studies in which the basic guidelines for control group-experimental group research have generally been met. It is even more difficult to confidently draw conclusions from studies that are generally called "quasi-experimental" research. The term "quasi-experimental" means that the one or more of the requirements of experimental research have blatantly been violated or ignored. Most of the control group-experimental group research done in education, and in the field of educational technology, is quasi-experimental because it is often virtually impossible to meet all the requirements of experimental research when working with humans. Thus, while the American government has, under the George W. Bush administration, taken the position that experimental research is the gold standard in education, the result has not been a new period of enlightenment and advancement in education. That is due to two reasons. First, even well done experimental research does not provide us with definitive answers to the real problems of education and educational technology. Second, conducting experimental research that meets all the criteria for valid studies is rarely possible. And when it is, it is often because we elect to study less important questions, or do the research in artificial settings and thus erect barriers to generalizing the findings to the real world of learning. My advice, therefore, is to consider experimental research as one option among a great many rather than the only acceptable choice when trying to do "real research." There are many forms of "real" research in education and educational technology.

Normally, a discussion on experimental research methods would end with quasi-experimental designs. Established wisdom says that if you are doing an experiment, you must be comparing the performance of at least two groups. There is, however, another way to do experiments. That is to study the behavior of one person or animal under different experimental conditions.

SINGLE SUBJECT RESEARCH

This group of research methods is so distinct and different from other quantitative methods that I separated them from other quantitative methods in Figure 7.1. B. F. Skinner, a behaviorist professor of psychology at Harvard University for much of his professional career, was the leading figure in one major effort to bring positivism into psychology. He also introduced and championed the detailed study of one living organism at a time. Skinner's favorite animal to study was the pigeon, in part because it was easy to set up a shiny aluminum disk the pigeon was supposed to peck. In Skinner's experimental chamber for the study of pigeon behavior, a switch closed each time the pigeon pecked the disk and equipment automatically counted the number of pecks. Skinner is the founder of the experimental analysis of behavior movement. The *Journal for the Experimental Analysis of Behavior*, which was created when established journals would not accept the research papers of Skinnerians, is still publishing today. Once the experimental analysis of behavior was established, many young psychologists and graduate students were attracted to the field. Some began applying Skinner's theories and methods to the real world problems of humans. This led to the creation of the *Journal of Applied Behavior Analysis* that is also still publishing. The Applied Behavior Analysts, or ABAs, developed and perfected several research designs for studying individuals or small groups. Tim Stocks (2000) at Michigan State University, has created a web site that is a brief orientation to these research methods. He describes four commonly used designs (see http://www.msu.edu/user/sw/ssd/issd01.htm). The two most common are ABA and multiple baseline.

Figure 7.4 is an example of the typical type of data presentation for an ABA design. It was adapted from Tim Stocks web site. The first or A phase

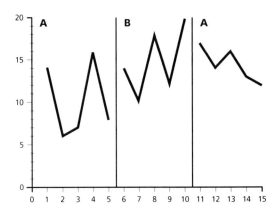

Figure 7.4   Example of an ABA single subject design (from Stocks, 2000).

of an ABA design is Baseline. You observe a student for several periods of time and count a particular behavior. That behavior may be the percentage of class time spent on task, the number of problems completed, number of verbal outbursts, or any other important behavior that can be easily counted. It could even be key clicks on a keyboard. Once a baseline of the behavior is established, the treatment phase begins (the B phase). In applied behavior analysis research, the treatment is often the systematic delivery of some form of reward but other treatments are also studied. If the behavior being measured seems to change with the initiation of treatment (the B phase) then there is reason to believe the treatment is effective. However, it is always possible that some other factor was the real cause of the change in behavior. To test for that possibility, a second A phase is established—sometimes called the Reversal phase. The treatment is withdrawn while the behavior continues to be counted. If behavior changes for the worse, that is strong evidence that the treatment is the causal factor in improvement. The ABA method illustrated in Figure 7.4 could be extended to another treatment condition. This version of single subject research, which includes a baseline (A), treatment (B), withdrawal or reversal (the second A phase), and another treatment (B) phase is called an ABAB study.

The other popular design in this group of single subject research designs, is multiple baseline. It is illustrated in Figure 7.5.

Each of the three graphs in Figure 7.5 represents the behavior of a separate individual or group. In essence these are three separate ABA studies. The topmost graph has the shortest baseline before treatment is instituted. However, when treatment is instituted for one individual or group, the other two individuals/groups are still in a no treatment or baseline condition. If the undesirable behavior decreases in the top graph but not in the

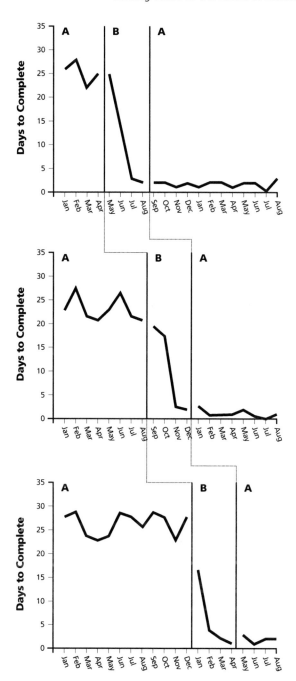

Figure 7.5 Example of the results of a multiple baseline study (from Stocks, 2000).

second and third, that is evidence the treatment is the causal factor. Later, treatment will be started for the second individual/group, and even later for the third individual/group. Every time behavior changes for the better when treatment is introduced, that is more evidence the treatment is effective. Figure 7.5 shows a second A condition (e.g., treatment was withdrawn) but many multiple baseline studies do not include this phase. Instead, they rely on the data from the staggered A and B phases to convince a reader that the treatment was effective. In Figure 7.5 the data suggests the treatment administered in the B phase had a "permanent" impact because the undesirable behavior did not increase in the second A phase. Note, by the way, that both ABA and multiple baseline studies often rely on graphic representation of the data for analysis. No statistical tests are used in most of these single subject studies.

ALTERNATIVES TO THE QUANTITATIVE APPROACHES

Quantitative approaches to research dominated education and educational technology for most of the 20th century. However, at the beginning of the 21st century, there are a number of very strong alternatives to the quantitative model. The difference between the alternatives and the established quantitative approach is not primarily what type of data is gathered—quantitative or non-quantitative. The most critical differences are in the paradigms or ideologies that serve as the foundation for research. The chapters that follow this one will explore qualitative approaches to research, approaches that have emerged from the humanities and the arts, philosophical inquiry, and a special form of applied research that developed in the field of educational technology—instructional design or ID. As you read about each of these cultures of research, you will see that while they often use unique and interesting methods, the paradigms that support the methods are often at the core of what makes them different from other approaches to research.

IN SUMMARY

This chapter has presented a structured but flexible framework for how to think about research and scholarship. The meaning of the terms research and scholarship depend on who is making the meaning but I suggest that one productive way of thinking about these two terms is to treat them as referring to essentially the same process. Under the broad umbrella of research and scholarship, there are many different families or cultures of scholarship. One large family is the quantitative research methodologies and they are often guided by positivist and postpositivist ideologies and theories. (However, quantitative methods are also used by interpretive and critical researchers as well.) Qualitative approaches make up another large family of research methods and this family is influenced primarily by interpretive and critical ideologies. (However, there are many positivist/ postpositivist researchers who also used qualitative methods.) Qualitative approaches will be discussed in the next chapter.

Discussions of methods of research and scholarship in the social sciences and education often end with these two large families—quantitative and qualitative. However, in education, and educational technology research, this restriction is due primarily to the historical influence of psychology on acceptable research methods in education. The dominant brands of American psychology in the 20th century privileged quantitative methods and began grudgingly to accept qualitative methods as the century came to an end. However, both the humanities and philosophy have also developed a number of research methods that have much to recommend them. Education, and particularly educational technology, has tended to ignore these methods because they have not been part of the mainstream methods of American psychology—which may still be coping with envy of the status of the natural sciences by trying to import the research methods of the natural sciences into the social sciences. In later chapters we will explore some of those neglected methods that come from underused and under-respected disciplines such as the humanities and philosophy.

This chapter concludes my exploration of quantitative methods in this book. However, there are thousands of books on standard and not-so-standard quantitative methods. Even in the specialized area of single subject research methods, books like Skinner's (2005) *Single-Subject Designs for School Psychologists,* and *Single-Subject Research: Applications in Educational and Clinical Settings* (Richards, Taylor, Ramasamy, & Richards, 1998) offer very good overviews of both the underlying concepts and practical procedures for using single subject research methods.

Quantitative methods dominated the research values of education and educational technology for much of the last half of the 20th century and it is still virtually impossible to complete a graduate degree in education without completing at least one, if not many, course(s) on quantitative research. In fact, there are still some professors, like the accountant quoted at the beginning of this chapter, who equate research with quantitative methods and relegate all other types of inquiry to the less prestigious category, in their opinion, of "scholarship." However, as the work of the Commission on Research at Emory University illustrates, the increasingly dominant model of research and scholarship adopts a landscape of research and scholarship that is very broad where many communities prosper and grow. You will learn more about several of these communities in the following chapters.

REFERENCES

Boyer, E. (1990). *Scholarship reconsidered: Priorities of the professoriate.* San Francisco: Jossey-Bass.

Farrand, P., Hussain, F., & Hennessy, E. (May, 2002). The efficacy of the "mind map" study technique. *Medical Education, 36*(5), 426–431.

Jensen, B. (2000). *ACCT 5342 Project.* Retrieved May 17, 2007 from http://www.trinity.edu/rjensen/acct5342/proj00.htm

Kadijevich, D. (2006) Achieving educational technology standards: the relationship between student teacher's interest and institutional support offered. *Journal of Computer Assisted Learning 22*(6), 437–443.

Pierce, R., Stacey, K. & Barkatsas, A. (February, 2007). A scale for monitoring students' attitudes to learning mathematics with technology. *Computers & Education, 48*(2), 285–300.

Hewitt, J. & Brett, C. (December, 2007). The relationship between class size and online activity patterns in asynchronous computer conferencing environments. *Computers & Education, 49*(4), 1258–1271.

Ropp, M. (Summer, 1999). Exploring individual characteristics associated with learning to use computers in preservice teacher preparation. *Journal of Research on Computing in Education, 31*(4), 402–424.

Proctor, R., Watson, G., & Finger, G. (2003). Measuring information and communication technology (ICT) curriculum integration. *Computers in the Schools, 20*(4), 67–87.

Richards, S., Taylor, R., Ramasay, R. & Richards, R . *(1998). Single-Subject Research: Applications in Educational and Clinical Settings.* Belmond, CA: Wadsworth.

Skinner, C. (2005). *Single-subject designs for school psychologists.* Binghamton, NY: Haworth Press.

Sterk, C. (2004, February-March). Exploring tenure and research at Emory: A view from the inside. *Academic Exchange.* Retrieved May 17, 2007 from http://www.emory.edu/ACAD_EXCHANGE/2004/decjan/sterk.html

Sterk, C. (2002). *Making the most of our intellectual passions: The Commission on Research at Emory.* Retrieved May 17, 2007 from http://www.emory.edu/ACAD_EXCHANGE/2002/febmar/sterk.html

Stuve, M. & Cassady, J. (2005). A factor analysis of the NETS Performance Profiles: Searching for constructs of self-concept and technology professionalism. *Journal of Technology and Teacher Education, 13*(2), 303–324.

Stocks, T. (2000). Introduction to single subject designs. Retrieved May 21, 2008 from http://www.msu.edu/user/sw/ssd/issd10d.htm

READINGS FOR CHAPTER 7

Reading 7.1

U.S. Department of Education. (December, 2003). *Identifying and implementing educational practices supported by rigorous evidence: A user friendly guide.*

Washington, DC: Institute for Education Sciences, U. S. Department of Education.

When the George W. Bush administration took over the Department of Education it created a new entity, the Institute for Education Sciences. Although the Institute included a number of existing units within the Department of Education, its creation involved much more than rearranging the chairs in a large bureaucracy. The Institution for Education Sciences was created to support an effort to make positivist research paradigms and positivist research methods the dominant, if not the only, methods that were acceptable in the Department of Education. A fundamental assumption of the leaders in the Institute for Education Sciences is that empirical research, especially control-experimental group research, is the primary way to improve education in America. Researchers should concentrate on this type of research, and educators should base their decisions about how to practice, on what that type of research tells them is the Right or Best way to do things. This brief booklet was developed for the Institute to help educators make scientific or "evidence-based" decisions in education. As you read it, try to answer these questions. What are the acceptable and preferred sources of knowledge about how to educate children? What, therefore, are unacceptable or weaker sources of knowledge? What philosophical assumptions (about the nature of reality, epistemology, how, specifically, human behavior can be studied, and how what we learn can be linked to how we practice a profession) are implicit in this booklet, whether they are stated or not? Would other, widely held, beliefs on these same questions lead us to different conclusions about how we should decide what is worth paying attention to or not? Explain and defend your answer.

What types of data are privileged by the Institute of Education Sciences approach to deciding what is worth paying attention to and what is not? Do the types of data that are preferred tend to favor certain approaches to education over others? Do the general criteria for "strong evidence" tend to favor certain approaches to teaching and learning over others?

Reading 7.2

Wanstreet, C. (2006). Interaction in online learning environments: A review of the literature. *The Quarterly Review of Distance Education, 7*(4), 399–411.

Few scholars, regardless of their particular ideological or philosophical preferences, believe that the findings of a single study are definitive. Too many things can go wrong in a particular study to depend totally on it for answers to an important question. There may have been problems with the dependent or independent variables and how they were measured, problems in the way subjects were selected, mistakes or errors in the statistical or qualitative analysis of the data, conclusions that are not well supported by the data, and a host of other potential sources of error. The possibility that any particular study is flawed has led to another type of scholarship—*a review of the literature.* The general purpose of a review of the literature is to combine the results and conclusions of all the available scholarship that meets the reviewer's criteria for inclusion and make conclusions based on the combined evidence in the available research rather than relying on one study. There are many ways to do a review of the literature, including a procedure called a meta-analysis that involves a statistical analysis of the results of the individual studies reviewed. Meta-analyses have their place, but that is not the approach Dr. Wanstreet used in her review of the literature.

However, her review is clearly situated in the positivist tradition of scholarship. The positivist tradition, which relies on the scientific method, is relatively predictable when it comes to how reviews of the literature are conducted. For example, positivist reviews tend to be very focused on a carefully selected and well specified question. Dr. Wanstreet certainly does that in her paper. She is concerned with how the concept of interaction is defined and measured in studies on online learning environments. Thus, unlike many reviews of the literature that focus on questions related to whether this or that treatment is effective, she is concerned with whether there are agreed upon definitions, and ways of measuring, "interaction" in the distance education literature. As you read this paper can you find evidence of other characteristics of a positivist approach to reviewing the literature:

- An emphasis on the technical aspects of meaning such as carefully defining what each major term means.
- A tendency to use rigorous criteria based on the current definition of "good" scientific research to select the studies to be included in the review. Most of the studies published are often rejected because they do not meet the criteria for "scientific research."
- A detailed description of the process used to analyze studies and draw conclusions. This is because positivist approaches emphasize the importance of being able to replicate the findings of studies—whether they be individual research studies or reviews of the literature. To do that, the researchers must provide others with enough detail to allow them to do the study again using the same criteria and methods.
- A tendency to emphasize "one Right answer" as opposed to accepting that different scholars may take different approaches to crucial concepts such as the meaning of "interaction" and how it is measured.

Readings 7.3

Readings 7.3 is not one but a number of readings that all focus on a billion dollar program, Reading First, that was funded by the Bush administration to enhance the reading skills of American school children. There has long been a debate in the field of literacy about whether a set of approaches that have generally be referred to as "whole language" methods are better for teaching reading, or if what some call a "discrete skills" approach is better. Whole language methods emphasize learning in context and learning in ways that are immediately meaningful to the child. Discrete skills approaches tend to break the task of reading down into elemental skills and to teach those skills separately. Discrete phonics instruction is a hallmark of discrete skills instruction. Reading First is based on the assumption that the discrete skills approach is the Right way to teach reading. Reading First funds may not be used to support whole language approaches to reading instruction. Reading First has been described by some as "the most effective federal program in history" and by others as "one of the most egregious of scandals." Essentially, the conflict is over whether the Bush administration's Department of Education, despite the supposed emphasis on "evidence-based education," created and funded the program in a way that benefitted insiders, friends and supporters while systematically keeping other promising methods of teaching reading from receiving funding. As you read these articles and papers, develop your own view. Is Reading First, despite a few small problems, a breakthrough example of how evidence-based decision-making in education can revolutionize American education? Or, is it a prime example of how bad administrators and leaders can subvert the goals and purposes of even a powerful idea such as making decisions about education by relying of empirical evidence? Or is it an example of what can often happen when the narrow focus on empirical evidence is used to justify decisions that are, at their base, guided by ideological and political beliefs rather than data? Or?

Barbash, S. (Summer, 2008). The Reading First controversy: Promises and perils of federal leadership. *Education Next*, 46–53.

Education Next is a conservative journal on education that is sponsored by the ultra-conservative Thomas B. Fordham foundation, among others. This article is a conservative explanation of what happened with Reading First that concludes it is an excellent example of the type of program that is much needed in American schools. Be sure to read the sidebar on page 49 that explains why the "scandal" about improper influence was a tempest in a teapot.

Paley, A. (Saturday, April 21, 2007). Key initiative of 'No Child' under federal investigation: Officials profited from Reading First program. *Washington*

Post, A01. Available: http://www.washingtonpost.com/wp-dyn/content/article/2007/04/20/AR2007042002284_pf.html

This brief article is a broad summary of the situation in April of 2007 from a more liberal source.

Scathing, Scorching, Blistering—Oh My! [online Blog]. (September 25, 2006). Available: http://d-edreckoning.blogspot.com/2006/09/scathing-scorching-and-blistering-oh.html.

This is a summary of a Department of Education report on Reading First by a conservative critic of American education. It was published on the blog, D-Ed Reckoning.

Office of the Inspector General. (September, 2006). *The Reading First Grant Application Process: Final Inspection Report.* Washington, DC: Office of the Inspector General, U. S. Department of Education. Available: http://www.ed.gov/about/offices/list/oig/aireports/i13f0017.pdf

This is the official 51-page report based on an internal study of the Reading First program that was conducted by the Department of Education's Office of the Inspector General. It is, to put it mildly, scathing. It concludes that the Department violated many regulations governing the grant-making process and it proposes many corrective actions to redress the errors found in the Reading First Program.

Thomas B. Fordham Foundation. (March 10, 2008). Fordham demands investigation into the real Reading First scandal. Available: www.nrrf.org/fordham_investigation_RF3–10-08.htm

This press release describes the foundation's response to the Democrat-dominated congress' decision to cut funding to Reading First. The Fordham Foundation presents the decision as part of a wider plot to sabatoge the Reading First program.

Toppo, G. (May 5, 2008). Study: Bush's Reading First program ineffective. *USA Today.* Available: http://www.usatoday.com/news/education/2008-05-01-reading-first_N.htm

This newspaper article is a summary of a large study conducted by the Bush administration's Institute for Education Sciences on the Reading First program. The result, in essence, was that Reading First, which emphasizes discrete skills instruction, did not work. If you would like to read the entire report, it can be downloaded from http://www.ies.ed.gov/ncee/pubs/20084016/index.asp

Reading 7.4

Phillips, D.C. (2006). A guide for the perplexed: Scientific educational research, methodolatry, and the gold versus platinum standards. *Educational Research Review, 1*(1), 15–26.

D. C. Phillips, who is a professor at Stanford University, has a long history of interest in the philosophical underpinnings of research in education. A devotee of postpositivism as a guiding framework for educational research, he is also well known for his sharp, sometimes biting, critiques of scholars who work on the other end of that continuum. This paper is one of many papers and books over the past three decades that attempts to set us on the path to right thinking about the reasons and rationales for doing good educational research. In essence Phillips is a defender of traditional positivist/postpositivist values in educational research, and he sees the scientific method as a highly desirable model in our field. He questions the quality and the accuracy of attacks on that position by interpretivists who question the possibility of discovering Truths about human behavior through empirical, "scientific" research, and by critical theorists who argue that supposedly objective scientific research is often conducted to keep the dominant group in power and prevent oppressed groups in society from (1) realizing they are oppressed, and (2) trying to do something about the oppression.

Phillips organizes the different paradigmatic positions on what good educational research is along a continuum. The right end of the continuum is anchored by positivists, and the left hand is anchored by an assortment of skeptics who question the right end of the continuum and advocate various solutions. (I would organize this "left end" group into several distinct families—the interpretivists, the critical theorists, poststructuralists, advocates of a phronetic approach to social science, and the postmodernists, for example. You will read about all of these variations in the chapters that follow this one.) In the middle of the continuum Phillips puts himself and other fellow postpositivists who generally advocate a kinder and gentler form of positivism.

After you have carefully read Phillips' paper, write a critique of the paper and take a stand on the major and fundamental issues he raises about educational research. Then, after you have read the remaining chapters in this book, write a critique of your critique. Did any of your positions change? Why or why not? Did any of your reasons for supporting your position change? How? Why?

CHAPTER 8

QUALITATIVE RESEARCH METHODS

In addition to the large and diverse family of quantitative research methods discussed in Chapter 7, there is also an equally large and even more diverse family of qualitative research methods. Figure 8.1 graphically represents the current families of qualitative research methods that are particularly applicable to educational and educational technology research. This represents my own view of how to organize qualitative research methods and does not necessarily represent some generally agreed upon framework. My interests in educational technology research certainly colors the structure I have created as does my background as a psychologist and applied researcher.

The three main families of qualitative research methods are traditional methods, applied methods, and emancipatory methods. As Figure 8.1 shows, each family has a number of research methods associated with it.

TRADITIONAL QUALITATIVE RESEARCH METHODS

All of the traditional methods of qualitative scholarship were nurtured and developed in one of the social sciences. Figure 8.2 outlines the four groups of qualitative research methods that are already well established. They involve observing in the field, asking questions or interviewing, doing historical research, and conducting case studies.

Qualitative Research Methods in Education and Educational Technology, pages 199–256
Copyright © 2008 by Information Age Publishing
199

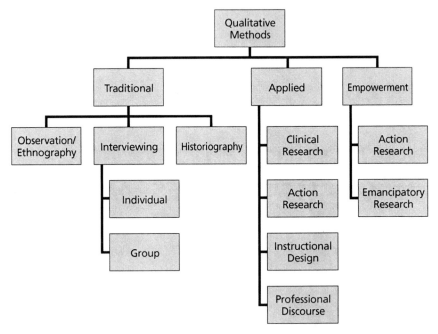

Figure 8.1 A general framework for qualitative research methods.

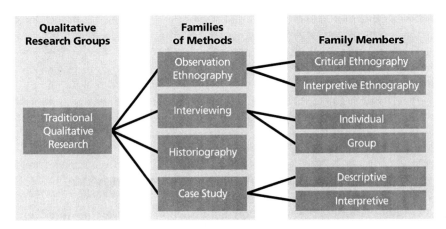

Figure 8.2 Traditional qualitative research methods of interest to educational technologists.

Ethnography/Observation

Ethnography (observation in the field) has been a major research method of anthropology for over 100 years. Ethnographic methods have reached a very advanced level of sophistication and many different variants are now in use. The second edition of David Fetterman's (2007) book, *Ethnography: Step by Step,* is one of many useful guides to doing this type of research. It provides detailed examples and procedures for beginning ethnographers. In the first edition, Fetterman (1998) described ethnography this way:

> Ethnography is the art and science of describing a group or culture. The description may be of a small tribal group in an exotic land or a classroom in middle-class suburbia. The task is much like the one taken on by an investigative reporter, who interviews relevant people, reviews records, weighs the credibility of one person's opinions against another's, looks for ties to special interests and organizations, and writes the story for a concerned public and for professional colleagues. A key difference between the investigative reporter and the ethnographer, however, is that whereas the journalist seeks out the unusual—the murder, the plane crash, or the bank robbery—the ethnographer writes about the routine, daily lives of people....Ethnographers are noted for their ability to keep an open mind about the group or culture they are studying. This quality, however, does not imply any lack of rigor. The ethnographer enters the field with an open mind, not an empty head. (p. 1)

This form of research involves spending considerable time in the field—a classroom, a school, a community center, a school district central office—to observe and learn. Fetterman's text takes a relatively straightforward approach, and the focus of his book is on "how to" topics. While helpful, doing good ethnographic research also involves understanding the broad conceptual context in which ethnographic research is situated. A more comprehensive introduction to ethnographic scholarship is the *Handbook of Ethnography* (Atkinson, Delamont, Coffey, & Lofland, 2007). And, for educational technologists interested in using digital technologies to do ethnographic research a valuable resource is *Qualitative Research and Hypermedia: Ethnography for the Digital Age* by Dicks, Mason, Coffey, and Atkinson (2005).

There are also a number of web sites with excellent resources on ethnographic methodology. These include QualPage (http://www.qualitativeresearch.uga.edu/QualPage/) which is a very large and useful site for information on virtually all forms of qualitative methodology. Click the *Ethnography* link on the left side of the home page to view many resources on the topic.

A "quick guide" to ethnographic methodology is available at http://www.sas.upenn.edu/anthro/CPIA/methods.html and a very useful synthesis of ethnographic methods by Michael Genzuk is at http://www-rcf.usc.edu/~genzuk/Ethnographic_Research.html.

If you would like to see what a course on ethnography might look like, you can take advantage of the Massachusetts Institute of Technology's Open-Courseware project. It makes courses developed by MIT faculty available to anyone for downloading. You can download the anthropology course, *Seminar on Ethnography and Fieldwork,* from http://ocw.mit.edu/OcwWeb/ Anthropology/21A–112Fall2003/Readings/index.htm.

A more specialized web resource is CHARM, *Choosing Human-Computer Interaction Appropriate Research Methods* at http://www.otal.umd.edu/hci-rm/ ethno.html. The site introduces ethnographic methods for this type of re-search and discusses several ways ethnography can be used in Human-Com-puter Interaction (HCI) research (e.g., to understand user needs). And per-haps reflecting the pace of work in software development projects, there are discussions of "quick and dirty" and "rapid" ethnography on this site.

As shown in Figure 8.2 there are both critical and interpretive approach-es to field research involving observation and there are many resources for learning to do ethnographic research (which is also referred to as field observation and participant observation). If you are interested in the use of ethnography within a critical theory perspective, D. Soyini Madison's (2005) book, *Critical Ethnography: Method, Ethics and Performance* is a very good place to start. It covers critical approaches to ethnography using three case studies to illustrate methods, procedures, and common issues. Unfor-tunately, none of the cases are about education or educational technology, but the principles of critical ethnography are there. An older book writ-ten specifically about critical ethnography in education is Levinson, Foley, and Holland's (`1996) *The Cultural Production of the Educated Person: Critical Ethnographies of Schooling and Local Practice.* This, however, is not a methods book. Instead, it is an edited text with 13 chapters that report critical ethno-graphic research on topics such as "rural schooling in Mexico" and "batch produced children in French and U. S. classrooms."

Those interested in interpretive ethnographic methods have several books on methods to choose from, including Norman Denzin's (1996) *In-terpretive Ethnography: Ethnographic Practices for the 21st Century* and a book edited by Troman, Jeffrey, and Walford (2005) titled *Methodological Issues and Practices in Ethnography,* which is part of the *Studies in Educational Ethnog-raphy Series.* In this last book, Dennis Beach (2005) introduces ethnography in education as an outgrowth of anthropology and says it is important in education because we want to know "about how understandings are formed in instruction, how meanings are negotiated in classrooms, how roles and relationships are developed and maintained over time in schools and how education policy is formulated an implemented" (p. 1).

The result of such research is often stories.

Ethnographers produce storied versions of these things. These stories reveal, interpret and represent every day encounters, which ethnographers some-times use in order to develop new education theory....These stories are based on the minute-by-minute, day-to-day social life of individuals as they interact together and develop understandings and meanings by engaging in joint action and adapting to situations. (Beach, 2005, p. 1)

Beach's description of how ethnographic scholarship works, and what it produces, reminds me of narrative inquiry that was discussed in a previous chapter. One of the complications of understanding the landscape of qualitative inquiry is that scholars doing the same thing—observing in the field and writing notes about what they observe—may call it many different things—critical narrative inquiry, ethnography, participant observation, interpretive narrative inquiry, and so on. The different terms do have different meanings—they are not all synonyms for each other—but there is also a great deal of overlap in how data is gathered and what is produced. Often, for example, the term used reflects how a particular scholar came to be doing a certain type of research (e.g., doing narrative inquiry—observing in a school—because hermeneutic theories pointed in that direction or doing ethnography—observing in a school—because that is what anthropologists who study schools call it). The narrative inquiry section of the previous chapter, and the books referred to in that section, are therefore useful resources about ethnography as well.

There are also many examples of the use of ethnography/observation in the educational technology literature. For example, Wang and Yuen (2004) used ethnography to study student patterns of communication in a graduate course using video conferencing while Schmertzing and Schmertzing (2001) used ethnographic methods to study how students adapted to an interactive television course. Finally, for an example of the use of ethnographic methods to study the use of technology-supported teaching methods see Jörgenson, Sinclair, Braham, and Balka (1998).

Asking Questions—Interviewing

Few methods of research are conducted in so many ways, and for so many purposes, as interviewing. They range from the very structured questioning of a subject that yields little more than Yes and No answers to pre-structured questions, to wide open interviews with very limited structure and few restrictions on the content of questions or answers. In general, interviewing research in educational technology is often best served, in my experience, by more open, flexible interviewing methods that allow the person being interviewed to take part in the decision making about where the interview goes and what topics are discussed. The "structured interviewing" methods used in market research and political polling produce less useful data in educational technology scholarship. Chapter 3, Common Qualitative Methods in the online textbook developed by the National Science Foundation (http://www.ehr.nsf.gov/EHR/REC/pubs/NSF97–153/CHAP_3.HTM) is a very good introduction to collecting data using open, flexible interviews (called "in-depth interviews" in this text). The chapter also introduces ethnographic methods and the Focus Group method, which is a way of doing group interviewing.

Interviewing is sometimes considered a rude and intrusive and aggressive approach to research, in part because it may invoke the image of a television news reporter who sticks a microphone in the face of a disgraced politician or a fallen celebrity and asks rude questions, hoping for a sound bite of an answer that can lead the six o'clock news. Or, it reminds us of the numberless episodes of TV crime dramas were detectives ask staccato structured questions of eye witnesses and potential suspects. In the traditions of qualitative research I prefer, interviewing—asking questions—is more like a conversation with a friend or colleague. That concept of interviewing was captured nicely in Foley and Valenquela's (2005) explanation of how they gathered data for a study of Chicano civil rights activities in one city:

> Like most good ethnographers, we developed a set of intimate, trusting relationships with several highly knowledgeable key community residents. These relationships helped us develop an "insider's" perspective on local life. At times, these relationships evolved into friendships, and some local residents became our "anthropological confidants" or "collaborators." They helped us focus and correct our understanding of local events and relationships. We often shared our interpretations with these locals, and as the relationships developed, we shared more of our mutual biographies. The point here is that good cultural critiques usually are based on a number of intimate, "collaborative" relations with research subjects.
>
> Second, we used a conversational or dialogic style of interviewing, which encouraged the subjects to participate more. We interviewed in a very informal manner, and at times we shared more personal information about ourselves than do conventional interviewers. When these free-flowing conversations were transcribed, they often were shared with the respondents. That provided key informants with the opportunity to see how their own speech objectified and represented them. If they did not like their self-representations, they were free to edit their comments. This, of course, led some informants to censor their negative remarks, but sharing the interviews clearly enhanced local confidence in our intentions to be fair. In short, a more open-ended, conversational interviewing style generated more engaged personal narratives and more candid opinions. It also tended to humanize the interviewer and diminish her power and control of the interview process. (p. 223)

Foley and Valenzuela are writing from a critical ethnography perspective but their open, collaborative, and informal approach to interviewing also applies to interpretive approaches as well. In the quote, the authors distinguish between the informal conversations with local "informants" or "collaborators" who had become friends and confidants, and the conversational interviews that were transcribed (e.g., recorded and then converted to printed texts). (Note: The availability of small, high quality digital recorders that save audio files in standard computer formats such as MP3 or WAV makes it very convenient to record interviews and conversations today. Some digital recorders can record over 30 hours of data before the batteries need to be replaced. Also, portable digital music players like Apple's IPod are also good digital recorders when an inexpensive microphone is plugged into the microphone input.)

I consider both the informant conversations and the transcribed interviews to be "interviewing." The informal conversations that were not recorded and transcribed may be documented with field notes written shortly after the conversation. Those field notes can also be shared and corrected, edited, and revised by participants. Both types of conversations are illustrations of the open, flexible types of dialog that are outstanding sources of data that help the scholar understand the local context better. And, field notes written after a conversation as well as verbatim transcripts of recorded conversations, are both acceptable forms of data collection. If you would like more information on open, flexible styles of interviewing there are several good resources. A book by Rubin and Rubin (2006) *Qualitative Interviewing: The Art of Hearing Data* covers the type of interviewing I am advocating here (which they call *open ended, unstructured interviews*) as well as semi-structured or *focused* interviews and even more tightly structured interviews. While I do not agree with all the theoretical perspectives taken by Rubin and Rubin, their book is a good introduction to the "family of qualitative interviews," to how different types of interviews can be conducted, and how the data gathered can be analyzed and interpreted. Another very good resource of information on how to conduct and analyze unstructured or open interviews is an online document, *Interviewing in Qualitative Research.* It introduces the many forms of qualitative interviewing and also presents a number of guidelines and suggestions. It is available at http://fds.oup.com/www.oup.co.uk/pdf/0–19–874204–5chap15.pdf. The chapter is part of a book published by Oxford University Press titled *Social Research Methods,* 2nd edition, by Alan Bryman (2005). Another useful book on interviewing is *Interviewing as Qualitative Research: A Guide for Researchers in Education and the Social Sciences* (Seidman, 2006).

Group Interviews

To this point in the discussion of interviewing, the emphasis has been on interviewing individuals. Group interviewing is also popular in qualitative inquiry and it can be as simple as an informal, on-the-fly conversation with several people that is documented in field note. There are, however, two much more structured approaches to group interviews—Focus Groups and the Delphi Technique.

Focus Groups. The basic format of this method is to bring together a group of participants and ask them to discuss some questions that are posed by a moderator. There are many versions of the focus group method—from very structured to open, informal conversations. The various forms of focus group methodology have been used for an amazing range of purposes, as Kamberelis and Dimitriadis (2005) note:

> Focus groups have been used for a wide range of purposes over the past century or so. The U.S. military..., multinational corporations, Marxist revolutionaries..., literacy activists..., and three waves of radical feminist scholar-activists, among others, all have used focus groups to help advance their concerns and causes. These different uses of focus groups have overlapped in both distinct and disjunctive ways. (p. 887)

Kamberelis and Dimitriadis consider focus groups from a critical perspective and see this method as a form of "critical pedagogical practice" that, in the hands of activists like Paulo Freire in Brazil and Jonathan Kozol in America, was used to help oppressed peoples to begin "imagining and enacting the emancipatory political possibilities of collective work" (p. 889). They contrast this purpose with the uses of propagandists and market researchers who use focus groups to "'extract' information from participants, that is, to figure out how to manipulate them more effectively" (p. 889). In addition to the critical use of focus groups, there are interpretivist uses that generally have one of two purposes. One purpose is understanding. You might, for example, run a focus group of parents to understand their views on the roles of technology in education. Another purpose is planning and decision-making. For example, a group of parents might participate in a focus group to help develop plans for launching a district-wide technology integration project. Focus groups are particularly useful when the give and take of a group conversation is likely to help shape and construct more useful conclusions or recommendations. There are many resources on how to conduct focus groups but quite a few are designed for purposes such as market research or propaganda. One relatively informal and easy-to-read guide to focus group methods is Kruger and Casey's (2000) *Focus Groups: A Practical Guide for Applied Research*. Another good resource is *Focus Group Research in Education and Psychology* (Vaughn, Schumm, & Sinagub, 2005). There are also many online resources about focus group methods, but a great many of them are for market researchers. One particularly useful online resource for educational technologists is Jakob Nielsen's (1997) paper on using focus groups as part of the software design process or to look at user design issues. It is available at http://www.useit.com/papers/focusgroups. html. A good overview of focus group methods is Anita Gibbs' paper at http://sru.soc.surrey.ac.uk/SRU19.html as is Jenny Kitzinger's paper from the *British Journal of Medicine* which is at http://www.bmj.com/cgi/content/ full/311/7000/299. There is also an online version of a book published by the International Nutritional Foundation for Developing Countries in cooperation with the World Health Organization and the World Bank. *A Manual for the Use of Focus Groups* is available online at http://www.unu. edu/Unupress/food2/UIN03E/uin03e00.htm. While the directions in this book are too structured and focused for me (e.g, the authors emphasize the need to carefully create detailed objectives) the book does make you aware of the many details that must be attended to if you are to run a successful focus group. Another good online manual was created at the University of Southern Maine. It is aimed at social services professionals who will be do-ing focus groups with low income families. Development of *The Focus Group Manual* was supported by the Ford Foundation and it is available at http:// muskie.usm.maine.edu/focusgroupmanual/.

Finally, while most focus groups involve face to face meetings there is increasing interest in online or "virtual" versions of focus group methods. Several commercial companies, for example, have systems that allow you to create online focus groups and run them on the company's servers(e.g., www.zoomerang.com; www.e-focusgroups.com). For a discussion of online focus groups in qualitative research see Rezabek, 2000.

The Delphi Technique. Another popular method of group interview is the Delphi technique. Skulmoski, Hartman, & Kran (2007) describe the method this way:

> The Delphi method is an iterative process to collect and distill the anonymous judgments [note: participation is not always anonymous] of experts using a series of data collection and analysis techniques interspersed with feedback. The Delphi method is well suited as a research instrument where there is incomplete knowledge about a problem or phenomenon.... The Delphi method works especially well when the goal is to improve our understanding of problems, opportunities, solutions, or to develop forecasts.

The authors, who are writing for the Information Science and Informa-tion Technology community, recommend the method particularly to grad-uate students who will be doing theses or dissertations. I think it is most useful when you want to summarize knowledge that has not been codified into formalized sets of rules and statements. Much of professional practice knowledge, for example, is this type of knowledge. To get at that knowledge you need a way of involving a group of professional practitioners who are the reservoirs of that knowledge. You also need a method that helps the participants share their expertise, refine and revise it through collaboration, and reach, hopefully, a consensus. One method for doing just that is the Delphi method. It begins with a set of questions submitted to the panel of experts who have been selected because they have relevant expertise or experience. For example, Hayden (1999) used the Delphi technique to study how video conferencing technology, and instructional strategies suited to video conferencing, can facilitate and support constructivist learning experiences. She used a group of experts who had expertise in education, videoconferencing, and educational technology to develop a set of characteristics and support strategies for encouraging K–12 constructivist learning environments.

When the experts receive the questions, they respond to them and the moderator takes the answers and attempts to synthesize what the experts have said. Usually, there are points of agreement as well as points of disagreement. The moderator formulates additional questions to address the points of disagreement and then distributes a synopsis of what has been agreed upon as well as questions about areas of disagreement as well as areas where the group's views are not clear. This second round ends with another set of responses submitted to the moderator who proceeds through additional rounds until there is consensus among the experts or no further progress toward consensus. The report of a Delphi study is basically a summary of the process and the results. In their paper Skulmoski, Hartman and Kran (2007) discuss issues such as how broad or narrow the initial questions should be, how to select participants, how much time should be devoted to each round, whether the group should be homogenous or heterogenous, how to decide when to stop, and which medium of interaction should be used. In terms of medium, most Delphi studies today use either e-mail, online surveys or questionnaires that can be completed by participants, or groupware that supports the Delphi method. In their paper Skulmoski and his colleagues offer an 11-step procedure for completing a Delphi study.

Historiography

The first edition of the *Handbook of Research for Educational Communications and Technology* (Jonassen, 1996) included a very good example of historical research in educational technology. Written by Ann De Vaney and Rebecca Butler (1996), it is a study of the founders of the field of educational technology. Titled *Voices of the Founders: Early Discourses in Educational Technology*, the chapter uses a variety of sources to tell about the people in the first half of the 20th century who created the foundations for what today we call the field of educational technology. The authors summarize their work this way:

Heterogeneous texts...provide a rich account of objects of study, theories engaged, methods employed, and audiences included. The written and oral texts considered here disclose a set of common goals but are diverse projects whose structures are contingent on historically accepted concepts and values. They reflect prevailing notions of learning theory and pedagogy, research methods, economic, military, and political values, and other elements of the social milieu in which they were produced....The rhetoric with which they spoke and the discourses that spoke through them energized an audience of scholars, educators, and students to participate in a new field, educational technology. (p. 3)

The De Vaney and Butler chapter, and the edited book by Gary Anglin (2007), *Instructional Technology: Past, Present, and Future,* are both valuable sources of historical information about the field as well as exemplars of how to do historical research. Two useful books on the methods of doing historical research are *From Reliable Sources: An Introduction to Historical Methods* (Howell & Prevenier, 2001) and the sixth edition of *Short Guide to Writing About History* (Marius & Page, 2006).

In his paper on doing history research in educational technology, Jan Januzweski (1996) proposes that "history can be viewed as an interaction. It can be the interaction between the empirical and the hermeneutical (the intent to understand), the interaction between science and art, the interaction between analysis and expression, or even the interaction between events and thoughts." He justifies the study of the history of educational technology by quoting Duffy (1988) on the valuable contribution a knowledge of history makes to the development of perspective, "the ability to see people, values, ideas, institutions, or events against a larger canvas of antecedents, related situations and relevant principles" (p. 460). While these are very important reasons for studying the history of our field, historical scholarship is not often undertaken. The De Vaney and Butler chapter mentioned earlier is a rare but very valuable example of historical research in the field of educational technology. Over the last 30 years disciplines such as the history of science, the history of technology, and the history of ideas have flourished and have had a significant impact on many disciplines. Educational technology has largely been bypassed by the increased interest and activity in history, however. Gary Anglin (2007) and Paul Seattler (2005) have carried much of the responsibility for documenting the history of educational technology. Seattler's book, *The Evolution of American Educational Technology,* is the latest in a series of books that began with *A History of Educational Technology* in 1968. Occasionally, other authors take a historical look at the field, for example, Johnson and Maddux's (2003) *Technology in Education: A Twenty Year Retrospective.* However, historical methods remain underused.

To better understand our field we need many more studies using the scholarly methods of history to link the theoretical, practical, and cultural conditions of the past to our current practices and theories. If you are interested in exploring the methodologies of history there are several good introductions to historiography in addition to those mentioned already:

- Conal Furay and Michael Salevouris. (2000). *The methods and skills of history: A practical guide*, 2nd ed. Wheeling, IL: Harlan Davidson.
- Anthony Brundage. (2002). *Going to the sources: A guide to historical research and writing*. Wheeling, IL: Harlan Davidson.
- Richard Marius & Melvin Page. (2006). *Short guide to writing about history*, 6th ed. Longman.
- Michael Bentley. (1999). *Modern historiography: An introduction*. New York: Routledge.

Case Study Methods

The final *method* to be discussed in this section is case study, but you could argue that it really isn't a research method, or that it is really a lot of methods gathered up carelessly and bundled into one lumpy bag labeled "case study." As Stake (2005) put it, "Here and there, researchers will call anything they please a case study" (p. 445). However you approach case study, it is different from the qualitative methods discussed thus far. Ethnography, interviewing, and historiography all define the type of data you are going to gather. You cannot do interviewing, for example, without asking questions and getting answers. Case studies, in contrast, don't have a specific type of data associated with them. In fact, they typically involve the collection and analysis of several types of data, including all the standard forms discussed thus far. As one of the authorities on case study method, Robert Stake (2005) put it, "Case study is not a methodological choice but a choice of what is to be studied." Stake argues that it is "the case" that is studied rather than larger or smaller units. For example, a case study might look at the development of a curriculum to prepare students for careers in the digital music industry in one college or university. However, on a broader scale, a policy paper, or a Delphi study, might take a much broader look at the issue of what should be in the curriculum of any institution that offers such a program. On a smaller scale, a paper might look at questions such as which sound and video editing software students in such programs should master. Stake is, I think, correct, that the focus of a case study is a *case,* and that means what you look at a phenomenon holistically and in its natural context. That does not mean there is no analysis of the components of the phenomenon; there often is. What it does mean, however, is that the analysis of elements or components of a phenomenon contributes to the case study report that gives us a better understanding of the phenomenon *in context.*

I think a case study is more a method of organizing and reporting the results of your study than it is a method of collecting data. In fact, saying you're going to do a "case study" does not give much of a hint about the type of data you will collect, except that whatever you collect will likely come from a real world setting rather than the research rooms of a university psychology department.

In spite of the fuzziness of just what a case study is, Robert Yin (2002) has written many good books on how to conduct case studies. In his most recent book, he explains case study this way:

> The case study is but one of several ways of doing social science research. Other ways include experiments, surveys, histories, and the analysis of archival information. Each strategy has peculiar advantages and disadvantages, depending on three conditions: (a) the type of research question, (b) the control an investigator has over actual behavioral events, and (c) the focus on contemporary as opposed to historical phenomena.
>
> In general, case studies are the preferred strategy when "how" or "why" questions are being posed, when the investigator has little control over events, and when the focus is on a contemporary phenomenon within some real-life context. Such *explanatory* case studies also can be complimented by two other types—*exploratory* and *descriptive* case studies. (Yin, 2002, p. 1)

A great many questions in educational technology are either "how" or "why" questions. "How do you design an effective instructional module to teach X to students who have characteristics Y and Z?" "Why has the availability of technology in most American schools not led to more integration across the curriculum?" The work of educational technologists is typically done in settings where the technologist has very little control over what happens. Schools, school districts, colleges and universities, agencies, businesses, and training centers are all work settings where the educational technologist is one of many professionals working in an existing setting in which one of the responsibilities of the organization is teaching and learning. It is not surprising that in a number of fields like educational technology, management information systems, and information technology, the case study method is very popular.

> As a research strategy, the case study is used in many situations to contribute to our knowledge of individual, group, organizational, social, political, and related phenomena. Not surprisingly, the case study has been a common research strategy in psychology, sociology, political science, social work, ... and community planning. (Yin, 2002, p. 1)

Note that Yin talks about case study as a *research method*. It is also a *teaching method*. Many professional fields, including education, medicine, pharmacy, law, and business, use cases as a way of preparing students to be successful professionals. Harvard's use of cases in the business school is legendary, for example. There is even a web site of Harvard Business Cases (http://harvardbusinessonline.hbsp.harvard.edu/b02/en/cases/cases_home.jhtml). Here, I will focus on case study as a research method but it is important to remember that in education and other professional fields, the case method is increasingly used as a form of pedagogy.

For interpretivists and critical theorists alike, one of the advantages of the case study as a research method is that it allows the scholar to take a holistic approach to studying a phenomenon in its natural setting. For example, the impact of implementing an integrated learning system (ILS) into all the middle schools of a urban school district should not rely on one piece of data—such as scores on achievement tests before and after the ILS is implemented. A significant effort to change teaching and learning practices across a district is a phenomenon with multiple and interacting factors at many levels. A good understanding of what happened, and why, calls for collecting many types of data and for a careful analysis of that data so that the interactions across levels (e.g., district, school, teacher, student), across steps in implementation (e.g., planning, pre-implementation professional development, implementation, ongoing support, formative evaluation, and so on), and across the different stakeholder groups (e.g., school board, central administration, building level administrators, teachers, parents, community, student, state policy makers, and so on). For complex, ongoing projects like this, a case study is often the only viable alternative. Even when the phenomenon being studied is simpler—such as how high school science teachers created a "technology-enriched and supported" science curriculum—the case study method is often one of the finalists when it comes to choosing a research method.

Case study methodology is also popular today among proponents of all three of the guiding research paradigms active in the social sciences today: positivism/postpositivism, interpretivism, and critical theory. Practitioners of research from all three paradigms use case study methods, but for different purposes. Three types of case studies have been mentioned already in a quote from Yin:

- **Explanatory**—Looks for reasons why a phenomenon happened the way it did. When the case study looks at a particularly unique or unusual situation it is sometimes called a critical instance case study. In such studies the researcher does not expect readers to generalize the findings broadly because the situation studied is so unique. However, the information gained from a detailed case study is valuable because the case being studied, though rare or relatively unique, is very important.

- **Exploratory**—An effort to develop more knowledge about a particular phenomenon with the expectation that the information gathered will be used to guide and shape additional research. Exploratory case studies are often abbreviated studies that are done to improve the focus and format of larger, more extended studies that may also be case studies or may use some other method. These are sometimes called pilot case studies.
- **Descriptive**—The purpose is to describe in some detail the setting and the phenomenon. Generalization and implications are typically left to the reader rather than undertaken by the researcher. A similar term is illustrative case study. For example, you might do a case study on one high school chemistry class that integrates many forms of educational technology to provide an example or illustration of how such a class works.

Various authors have described additional types of case studies, some of which overlap with Yin's three types:

- **Program Evaluation**—Case studies are often used as all or part of the process of understanding whether a particular project or program was "effective." When done from a positivist perspective the goal may be to determine whether "it worked" or not. Critical program evaluation tends to focus on whether "it worked" or not from the perspective of those in the program who are not in power. For example, a program that uses technology to teach poor, inner city residents to qualify for jobs in a local factory might be considered a success in a positivist case study because many participants were hired by the factory. A critical case study of the same program might conclude it is a failure because it prepared participants for dead end and boring jobs where the workers are treated as cogs in the machine without power over their lives and without a voice in how the work situation is structured. An interpretive case study on the same project might present "multiple perspectives"—those of the factory managers, community leaders, the participants, local activists, and area politicians.
- **Program Implementation**—Some case studies focus on the impact of a project or program. A related type of case study, program implementation, looks at the process of implementation rather than just the impact. Often done from an interpretive or critical perspective, program implementation case studies are in-depth looks at how an innovation, reform, change, or even a reduction in services,

occurs. Positivists also sometimes use program implementation case studies to establish whether the official program adopted by an organization was ever actually implemented by the practitioners, such as teachers. Critical and interpretive scholars may do a program implementation study to better understand the process of implementation and to identify barriers, problems, and issues as well as strengths of the implementation process.

- **Positivist**—In positivist case studies the goal is generally to use a single instance of a phenomenon (e.g., the progression of one teenage delinquent through the school, social service, and legal system of his or her community) to develop theories that can be generalized to other delinquents and other settings. Positivist case studies may also start with an existing theory and try to validate it by demonstrating that the case "fits" the theory.

- **Intrinsic**—Intrinsic case studies are one of three types identified by Stake (2005). A case study is intrinsic "if the study is undertaken because, first and last, one wants better understanding of this particular case. It is not undertaken primarily because the case represents other cases or because it illustrates a particular trait or problem, but instead because, in all its particularity and ordinariness, this case itself is of interest. . . . The purpose is not to come to understand some abstract construct or generic phenomenon, such as literacy or teenage drug use or what a school principal does. The purpose is not theory building—though at other times the researcher may do just that. Study is undertaken because of an intrinsic interest in, for example, this particular child, clinic, conference, or curriculum" (p. 445).

- **Instrumental**—Calling a case study instrumental (which is Stake's second type) is appropriate "if a particular case is examined mainly to provide insight into an issue or to redraw a generalization. The case is of secondary interest, it plays a supportive role, and it facilitates our understanding of something else. The case is still looked at in depth, its contexts scrutinized and its ordinary activities detailed, but all because this helps us pursue the external interest."

- **Cumulative**—A cumulative case study involves the use of more than one case. For example, in program evaluation case studies, five or six participants might be studied and each of their case studies could illuminate the program. The result might be several themes that seem to cut across the cases, or the resulting study and report might illustrate how different the impact of the project is on different participants. Stake calls this multiple case study or collective case study. "It is instrumental study extended to several cases. . . . [Cases] are chosen because it is believed that understanding them will lead to better understanding, and perhaps better theorizing, about a still larger collection of cases" (p. 446).

The types of cases listed above do not exhaust the possible options; there are other lists in the literature with different types. Also, the types are not exclusive. A case study may well meet the criteria for several types. Perhaps the most important thought to take from reading the list is that one reason case studies are so popular in qualitative social science scholarship is their versatility and flexibility. They can accommodate a wide variety of purposes and incorporate a wide range of data sources.

Doing Case Study Research

There are many formats for case study research and formats are often tied to the underlying paradigm that will guide the study. Critical theorists will do a case study differently than a positivist, and an interpretivist will do one a bit differently than either critical theorists or positivists. One relatively general and flexible set of guidelines for doing a case study are described in Stake's (2005) chapter in the 3rd edition of the *Handbook of Qualitative Research.*

For qualitative researchers a case study "concentrates on experiential knowledge of the case" and close attention must be paid to "the influence of its social, political, and other contexts" (p. 444). Stake has five requirements for a case study:

- **Issue Choice.** A first step in planning a case study involves choosing the issues of interest. "A case study has (as has research of all kinds) some form of conceptual structure. Even an intrinsic case study is organized around a small number of researcher questions. Issues are not information questions, such as 'Who initiated their advocacy of regional forestry planning?' or 'How was their hiring policy announced?' the issues or themes are questions such as 'In what ways did their changes in hiring policy require a change in performance standards?' or 'Did the addiction therapy, originally developed for male clients, need reconceptualization for women'" (p. 448)?
- **Triangulation.** While the traditional idea of validity—that the data gathered represent the Truth of the situation studied—is tempered by a recognition that all observations will have a subjective component, Stake still sees a need to give the reader some assurances that he or she can trust the case study. This is in spite of the recognition among qualitative researchers that all understanding is subjective, and that there are always multiple perspectives. "However accuracy is

construed, researchers don't want to be inaccurate, caught without confirmation. Counterintuitive though it may be, the author has some responsibility for the validity of the readers' interpretations" (p. 453). Stake applies the general concept of triangulation to the idea of believability. Conclusions, descriptions, impressions, and explanations in the final report (which is also called a case study) can be checked by requiring more than one source, often at least three. Those sources can be different people, different types of data (e.g., observation, interviews, and artifacts), or different time periods, to name a few. "Good case study research follows disciplined practices of analysis and triangulation to tease out what deserves to be called experiential knowledge from what is opinion and preference" (p. 455). However, the effort to justify by showing multiple confirmations should not be allowed to squeeze out unique or diverse views and impressions that may be as important as views shared by many participants.

- **Experiential Knowledge.** The idea of experiential knowledge is at the heart of Stake's ideas about how we learn from a case study. Experiential knowledge is knowledge gained from experience and that is the major contribution of a case study. "Case study facilitates the conveying of experience of actors and stakeholders as well as the experience of studying the case. It can enhance the reader's experience with the case. It does this largely with narrative and situational descriptions of case activity, personal relationship, and group interpretation" (p. 454). While some forms of knowledge, especially abstract theoretical knowledge, can be difficult to grasp, Stake believes experiential knowledge is easily taken on board by readers. "When the researcher's narrative provides opportunity for vicarious experience, readers extend their perceptions of happenings. Naturalistic, ethnographic case materials, at least to some extent, parallel actual experience, feeding into the most fundamental processes of awareness and understanding" (p. 454). Stake calls this naturalistic generalization. The case study is a way of helping us make naturalistic generalizations.

- **Contexts.** "The case to be studied is a complex entity located in a milieu or situation embedded in a number of contexts or backgrounds. Historical context is almost always of interest, but so are cultural and physical contexts. Other contexts often of interest are the social, economic, political, ethical, and aesthetic" (p. 449). Stake also highlights the problem with thinking of the events and conditions in a case study as having causal relationships that can be discovered. He recommends, instead, that the case be organized and thought of as Tolstoy thought of events in *War and Peace*— "multiply sequenced, multiply contextual, and coincidental more than causal. Many find the search for cause as simplistic. They describe instead the sequence and coincidence of events, interrelated and contextually bound, purposive but questionably determinative. They favor inquiry designs for describing the diverse activities of the case" (p. 449).

- **Activities**. The activities of a scholar doing case study research are diverse, but they include collecting data and going through multiple iterations of reflection on that data. The data itself comes from extended periods of time spent in the environment of the case, where the researcher will likely gather many forms of data.

When it comes to how you conduct a case study, Stake's advice is short and sweet, "Place your best intellect into the thick of what is going on" (p. 449). He provides more details, but this is not a bad summary because it emphasizes the fact that the researcher is the primary means of data analysis. The method of data analysis is reflection. "In being ever-reflective, the researcher is committed to pondering the impressions, deliberating on reflections and records—but not necessarily following the conceptualizations of theorists, actors, or audience....Local meanings are important, foreshadowed meanings are important and readers' consequential meanings are important" (pp. 449–450). Often the data that is reflected upon is primarily observation, but it can include data from interviews, historical study, an analysis of artifacts, visual and structural information, and virtually any other form of data that seems relevant. Sometimes this data is coded in some way so that data relevant to particular issues or questions can be easily located. Or the researcher may take a more holistic approach to interpreting the data. In either case, the researcher will make multiple passes through the data, engage in reflection and re-reflection about the data, and keep in mind the need for validating the impressions and understandings that emerge from the case study. "Qualitative case study is characterized by researchers spending extended time on site, personally in contact with activities and operations of the case, reflecting, and revising descriptions and meanings of what is going on" (p. 450).

Before concluding this section on case study methods I would like to discuss another viewpoint on case studies, that of Bent Flyvbjerg.

Flyvbjerg's Five Misunderstandings About Case Study Research

As Flyvbjerg developed his concept of a social science based on Aristotle's phronetic knowledge, he came to favor narrative inquiry and case study methodology for his new form of social science. However, he (2004) found that "conventional wisdom" about the case study method "if not directly wrong, is so oversimplified as to be grossly misleading" (p. 430). To address this question, he wrote a paper to justify his heavy reliance on case studies and to refute the common, but inaccurate, criticisms of the method. He makes the point that case study methods are often criticized from a positivist perspective that assumes the only way to understand a particular instance or case, is through the theory-implications link. That is, you must use a theoretical framework and the implications of that framework to analyze the specific case. If there is a match, the case supports the theory. Flyvbjerg rejects this line of argument and organized his discussion around five "misunderstandings."

General, theoretical (context-independent) knowledge is more valuable than concrete, practical (context-dependent) knowledge. Flyvbjerg approaches this misunderstanding by arguing that "in the study of human affairs, there appears to exist only context-dependent knowledge, which thus presently rules out the possibility of epistemic theoretical construction" (p. 421). This is his argument for practical, context-dependent phronetic knowledge rather than epistemic knowledge as the goal of social science. Flyvbjerg concludes that case studies are a very good way to develop concrete, context-dependent knowledge which is a better goal for research than trying to discover context-independent knowledge and failing over and over again.

One cannot generalize on the basis of an individual case; therefore the case study cannot contribute to scientific development. Flyvbjerg points out that if one good study goes against a law of human behavior that is grounds for rejecting the law because it supposedly applies to all cases. One case in which it does not apply is enough to say the law is not a law. This is the essence of Sir Karl Popper's idea of *falsification*—that a theory can be disproved by one instance of failure, but it can never be proven beyond a shadow of a doubt. Flyvbjerg also argues that if you choose cases that include "ideal" examples of a particular phenomenon and such a case refutes a theoretical law, we can generalize that less ideal examples are also likely to break the law as well. I don't find these arguments very convincing. For example, falsification on the basis of one study is problematic because it would have to be a "perfect" study that has eliminated all the possible reasons for failure except the theory. I don't think we can ever exclude all the alternatives—poor measurement, improper sampling, researcher bias, and so on. However, another of Flyvbjerg's arguments is more acceptable. "Generalization, be it on the basis of large samples or single cases, is considerably overrated as the main source of scientific knowledge. . . . Thomas Kuhn has shown that the most important precondition for science is that researchers possess a wide range of practical skills for carrying out scientific work. Generalization is just one of these. In Germanic languages, the term 'science' (Wissenschaft) means literally 'to gain knowledge'. And formal generalization is only one of the many ways by which people gain and accumulate knowledge. That knowledge cannot be formally generalized does not mean that it cannot enter into the collective process of knowledge accumulation in a given field or in a society. A purely descriptive, phenomenological case study without any attempt to generalize can certainly be of value in this process and has often helped cut a path towards scientific innovation" (p. 424). Although Flyvbjerg does not mention it, analogical reasoning is one form of knowledge that is supported by case studies. Analogical reasoning does not look for certainties or laws; instead it looks for understanding and similarities. It is similar to abductive reasoning that leads to tentative acceptance of knowledge rather than the more confident acceptance that characterizes positivist models of knowing. These are only two of several forms of knowledge that are more context-dependent and more tentative than epistemic knowledge. Aristotle's phronesis comes to mind as a general term for these practical and more contextual forms of knowing.

The case study is most useful for generating hypotheses, that is, in the first stage of a total research process, while other methods are more suitable for hypotheses testing and theory-building. This view is often expressed by positivist scholars who want to be charitable to qualitative researchers. It gives qualitative methods like case study a place in the grand scheme of science—that of the brush clearer that goes into the rough and unexplored wilds to clean things up enough so that real research can be conducted. Flyvbjerg uses several arguments to attack this view but most of them focus on the importance of proper selection of cases. Random selection of cases, for example, eliminates systematic selection biases. However, "the *extreme* case can be well suited for getting a point across in an especially dramatic way. . . . A *critical* case can be defined as having strategic importance in relation to the general problem" (p. 425). There is also the *paradigmatic* case which can serve as an exemplar or metaphor for a particular phenomenon. While Flyvbjerg's arguments for using case studies for hypothesis testing and theory building are well reasoned, I don't find them very comforting. That is perhaps because I think they are trying to play the positivist's game when there is another game to be played. If we are not going to be able to build highly valid and general theories of human activity, as the positivists still hope to do, there is less reason for emphasizing hypothesis testing and theory building. Why not emphasize that case studies provide us with experiential knowledge and add to the general, phronetic, foundation of understanding upon which we make our professional decisions? Building theories and doing hypothesis testing belongs to another system of epistemology—one in which we can discover laws of human behavior and then apply them to other settings in a technical-rational way.

The case study contains a bias towards verification, that is, a tendency to confirm the researcher's preconceived notions. Flyvbjerg attacks this misunderstanding in two ways. First he points out that all forms of research are prone to this tendency. It is "a problem that all researchers must deal with in some way" (p. 428). Thus, it is not something particularly special to case study methods or to qualitative research in general. Then he argues that qualitative methods like case studies are better at avoiding subjective bias "because the case study has its own rigour, different to be sure, but no less strict than the rigour of quantitative methods. The advantage of the case study is that it can 'close in' on real-life situations and test views directly in relation to phenomena as they unfold in practice" (p. 428). I think Flyvbjerg has a point here, but I do not think that we can be so confident as qualitative researches as to feel comfortable ignoring this issue. Clandinin and Connolley's (2000) comments about narrative inquiry included suggestions about how to check our interpretations and understandings (e.g., by asking participants to read and comment on our field notes and interpretations) are relevant here as well. However, I hasten to add that I agree with Flyvbjerg that traditional positivist social science has tended to ignore many possibilities for subjective bias in quantitative research. All forms of social science scholarship call for careful attention to this possibility.

It is often difficult to summarize and develop general propositions and theories on the basis of specific case studies. Flyvbjerg comments that "Case studies often contain a substantial element of narrative. Good narratives typically approach the complexities and contradictions of real life. Accordingly, such narratives may be difficult or impossible to summarize into neat scientific formulae, good propositions, and theories" (p. 430). This is considered a major weakness by critics but Flyvbjerg quotes Nietzsche that "one should not wish to divest existence of its *rich ambiguity*" (p. 430). Flyvbjerg argues that instead of summarizing and condensing the knowledge in a case study down to a theory, we should keep the rich details of the case and avoid summarizing the results in an abstract theory. As he put it,

> I avoid linking the case with the theories of any one academic specialization. Instead I relate the case to broader philosophical positions that cut across specializations. . . . The goal is to allow the study to be different things to different people. I try to achieve this by describing the case with so many facets—like life itself—that different readers may be attracted, or repelled, by different things in the case. Readers are not pointed down any one theoretical path or

given the impression that truth might lie at the end of such a path. Readers will have to discover their own path and truth inside the case. (p. 430)

From an intepretivist perspective this is a worthy goal for case studies.

I find Flyvbjerg's explanations of the five misunderstandings mostly compelling and share his view of the high value of case study methods. In addition to the books and papers mentioned thus far there are many other useful resources on case study methodology. One relatively comprehensive online guide to doing case studies is at Colorado State University. *Writing Guides: Case Studies* is at http://writing.colostate.edu/guides/research/casestudy/com2b2.cfm. A briefer introduction to case study methods is a paper by Dan Bachor (2000) at http://www.aare.edu.au/00pap/bac00287.htm. In addition, a web site at the University of British Columbia in Canada has a list of linked, online resources about different qualitative methods. There are many excellent ones on case study methods. The web site is at http://www.slais.ubc.ca/resources/research_methods/case.htm. Another site with links to papers on case study methods is at Southampton University in the UK (http://www.solent.ac.uk/library/subject/page210.stm). To get to the links for material on case study methods, click the *Electronic Resources for Information Research Methods* link and then click the drop down menu at the top of the page and select *2.3 Case Studies*. This site also has links for information on other qualitative methods.

A Summary of Traditional Qualitative Research Methods

Many of the traditional forms of qualitative research have been used for decades in educational technology. However, as these methods have matured they have become even more useful and more appropriate for educational technology research. Qualitative case studies are a powerful way of developing alternative forms of knowledge—abductive, phronetic, practical, context-dependent, and they are also a convenient way of organizing research that involves collecting and interpreting a range of data, both quantitative and qualitative. When viewed from the perspective advocated by Flyvbjerg, case studies are often a better "fit" with the conditions and restrictions of research in professional settings such as schools than traditional experimental methods, and they have the additional advantage of providing the researcher with a way of developing an understanding of what happened from several levels (e.g., the community, school district, school, classroom, teacher, student) and from multiple perspectives (e.g., school board, community leaders, administrators, teachers, parents, students).

APPLIED QUALITATIVE RESEARCH

I have divided qualitative research into traditional methods, applied methods, and emancipatory methods. This second division, applied qualitative research, is a rich and growing source of methods for education and educational technology. The two main paradigms of qualitative research, interpretivism and critical theory, both emphasize the importance of doing research "in context." Perhaps that is one reason why the distance between basic and applied research is not great when it comes to qualitative scholarship. Another reason for the closer relationship between basic and applied research in the interpretive paradigm is that the fundamental goal of basic research in the positivist paradigm—discovering universals or laws of human behavior—is not a fundamental goal of interpretivist basic research. Interpretivism eschews the idea of ever finding absolute and universal truth. Instead, it strives for local truth, hermeneutic understanding, multiple perspectives, phronetic knowledge, or some other form of limited, context bound, and conditional knowledge. Such goals for basic research are much closer to the goals of applied research within any paradigm. Thus, particularly within the interpretive framework, many qualitative research methods can be used to accomplish basic as well as applied goals, or both at the same time. There are, however, a number of qualitative methods that are clearly aimed at addressing a problem or issue of professional practice. The goal is not simply understanding, or the development of local knowledge, it is to find ways of solving a problem or improving practice. I will introduce four applied qualitative research methods in this section: clinical research, action research, instructional design, and professional practice discourse. While all four of these methods share the goal of addressing a problem or issue of professional practice, they approach it in very different ways. Clinical research, for example, is typically used to evaluate the suitability of a solution that has already been developed. The classic exemplar of clinical research is testing a new drug to determine if it is effective against the disease or health issue it was designed to cure. Much work on the drug will have already been done before human clinical trials begin. A clinical study typically comes near the end of an extensive development process. In contrast, action research methods are typically undertaken to both select a potential "cure" and to evaluate whether it works or not. Action research is often done by practicing professionals who have identified an issue or problem of practice for which they do not have a clear solution. Part of the action research process involves searching for potential solutions. Once a likely candidate is identified an action research study moves to an implementation stage where the solution is "tried out" in professional practice and evaluated.

Instructional design (ID) focuses on yet another process of finding solutions to professional practice problems. This research methodology focuses on the process of developing solutions. Advocates of different approaches to ID believe the quality of the solution developed is at least to some extent, dependent on the process used to design and develop it. Over the last 60 years many models of ID have been proposed, and there are significant differences between them.

The final type of applied qualitative research to be discussed in this section, professional practice discourse, is less a method of doing research and more a way of communicating the knowledge developed through practical experience.

CLINICAL (APPLIED) RESEARCH

In Figure 7.1 I separated clinical applied research from other forms of qualitative research. That is because clinical research methods have a different history from most of the other methods of applied qualitative research. Clinical research methods have generally been nurtured and developed in the health sciences rather than in the various disciplines of the social sciences. In the various fields of health care, clinical research has been commonplace for decades. Clinical research is an effort to study the impact of a therapeutic intervention in a real world setting. For example, a hospital might participate in the clinical trials of a new drug by prescribing it to patients with a particular disease. Most of the literature on clinical research is in the health care literature but Nelson and Quintana's (2005) paper on "Qualitative Clinical Research With Children and Adolescents" is a good overview of both the design of clinical research and the typical types of data that may be collected. The authors tend to emphasize the contribution of qualitative clinical research to theory building, but the methods and strategies they discuss can also be adapted to qualitative clinical research based on interpretive or critical theory paradigms, and the goal of enhancing professional practice. A source that does emphasize interpretive and critical perspectives on clinical research is Miller and Crabtree's (2005) chapter in the 3rd edition of the *Handbook of Qualitative Research*. There are, however, few examples of the use of clinical methods in either education or educational technology research. There are, however, versions of action research that are sometimes referred to as "clinical action research" to indicate their use of research methods adapted from the methods pioneered in health care research. The many forms of action research have become very popular in education over the past fifteen years and the number of action research studies in educational technology is also growing. That form of applied qualitative research is the focus of the next section.

ACTION RESEARCH

Although action research has existed since the late 1940s, it was often treated as a poor country cousin by adherents of the positivist paradigm that dominated the social sciences and education for much of the 20th century. That is because action research does focus on answering broad theoretical questions and it does not emphasize the discovery of universal truths. Instead, action research identifies real world, practical problems or issues and tries to develop and validate solutions or answers to them. Another reason why action research received very little respect among positivists is that it emphasized relevance over technical requirements. Positivist researchers tend to consider research invalid and unworthy unless it meets the many criteria for empirical research set down by modern versions of the scientific method. Action research methods, on the other hand, tend to emphasize collaboration and research within the workplace. Action researchers also tend to put what they learn to immediate use. If they are in the middle of a study of a new way of teaching Americnan history using collaborative writing software and they realize there are problems with the collaborative projects, they do not stop the study and start again from the beginning. Instead, they make the needed changes and proceed with the study. Many action research projects go through this process several times as the researchers try something out, realize it needs improvement, make the revisions, and then continue to evaluate the revised procedure or approach. Action research thus tends to be subjective, flexible, iterative, and very context bound. The goal is to figure out how to improve professional practice in a particular context. None of these characteristics are desirable features of positivist research and some of them are even considered negative characteristics.

Doing Action Research

Most models for action research have four to six phases or "moments" that are organized into an iterative spiral. A complete action research project may progress through several spirals of the four to six moments. The four-moment model of action research depicted in Figure 8.3 is based on the models proposed by two well-known Australian action research pioneers, Kemmis and McTaggart (1988), and Seymour-Rolls & Hughes (1995).

Reflection. Action research begins with reflection on the issues of interest. In this phase discussions with colleagues and collaborators as well as thoughtful reflection brings the group that is doing the action research study to a consensus on that the issues/problems are and what the goal of the action research should be. All this is tentative and may change many times over the course of the project, but it is the beginning point for think-

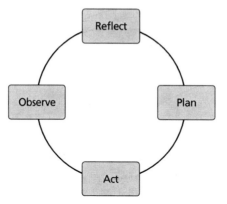

Figure 8.3 A conceptual framework for Action Research.

ing about other steps in the action research project. Although some forms of action research make one teacher the sole initiator and researcher, most models emphasize the need for collaboration and cooperation in doing action research. While I see some value to action research as a model for individual professional development I think it will be much more effective as a collaborative process. Thus, in my view even an individual computer coordinator who has decided to do an action research study of ways to enhance the support provided technology-using teachers will want to involve others in the action research process.

Plan. Once there is at least an initial and tentative understanding of the goal of the action research (AR) project, the next step involves exploring ways to address the problem that is the reason for doing the study. This step may involve many forms of information gathering—from literature reviews and conference attendance to consulting with colleagues and experts as well as visiting other sites that appear to have successfully dealt with problems and issues similar to those the AR project is addressing. In the end, however, the AR project group will discuss the options and develop a plan for addressing the problem. This plan is not likely to be the simple adoption of a solution developed and used elsewhere. It may reflect the team's awareness and appreciation of plans and solutions developed elsewhere but it will probably be different in many ways, which is a reflection of the fact that each professional situation is different—be it a school, middle grades social studies class in the year 2012, or a computer coordinator's four schools in an inner city school district.

Act. A third moment is action. The plan is implemented.

Observe. The change, whether it be a new pedagogy, new ways of integrating technology into the classroom, or new assessment procedures, is carefully observed and evaluated. The data gathered, which may include everything from quantitative scores of objective achievement tests to teacher and student reflections to assessments by stakeholders and experts, is used to decide whether the change was effective or not. That, however, occurs in a new reflective moment. AR rarely ends with one cycle through the Reflect–Plan–Act–Observe cycle. A change worth trying is rarely done well the first time; it requires adjustments, improvements, and enhancements. Several iterations of the AR cycle may be needed before the AR team is pleased with the results.

Note that there are no arrows in Figure 8.3. There is no arrow pointing, for example, from Reflect to Plan. Moving sequentially from Reflect to Plan to Act to Observe makes sense, but there will be times when work on a Plan results in a return to Reflection. The process is thus not a rigid, linear cycle; it is flexible and allows for movements backward and forward as well as in other directions. In fact, in actual practice, an AR team may be working on several moments at once.

If you would like to explore action research methods in more detail there are hundreds of resources on using action research in education. The newer books tend to be somewhat specialized which is an advantage if you know the type of AR you want to pursue. For example, the third edition of Geoffrey Mills' (2006) book, *Action Research: A Guide for the Teacher Researcher*, was written for teachers interested in doing research in their own classroom or department. Richard Sagor's (2004) book, *The Action Research Guidebook: A Four-Step Process for Educators and School Teams* also emphasizes the teacher as action researcher but also covers some aspects of team-based, collaborative AR. In contrast to the emphasis on individuals doing action research found in many textbooks, a book by Clauset, Lick, and Murphy (2008) titled, *Schoolwide Action Research for Professional Learning Communities*, puts the emphasis on collaborative AR. These are but three of hundreds of publications on AR and there are also several journals, such as *Educational Action Research* and online resources.

Because some forms of AR are also empowerment forms of qualitative research I will explore this versatile form of applied research again in the last section of this chapter.

Instructional Design

A third form of qualitative applied research is one that originated in the field of instructional technology. Instructional design—the systematic design, development, and deployment of instructional materials and resources—has been, from the beginning, a core activity of the field of instructional technology. Until recently, virtually all the models and theories of instructional design (ID) were based on a positivist paradigm and relied on behavioral theories of learning. However, over the past 20 or so years, many established ID models have broadened their theoretical and pedagogical bases, and new models that use interpretive foundations and constructivist instructional models have appeared. Qualitative ID models are discussed in more detail in Chapter 11. Papers on qualitative ID models based on interpretivist/constructivist theory include Karagiorgi and Symeou (2005), Willis (1995), Willis (2000), and Willis and Wright (2000).

Professional Practice Research and Professional Practice Discourse

The traditional relationship between professional practice and research has been hierarchical. Researchers discovered truths that were translated into implications for professional practice. The job of the practitioner was to use the findings and implications of research to improve practice. Today that relationship has been challenged. Professional practitioners are now engaging in research themselves as well as becoming involved in defining what should be studied and how the results of research should be used in professional practice. Chapters 8–11 all include information on research and scholarly methods that practitioners can use to analyze their own practice and share the results of their analysis with others. Narrative inquiry, philosophical inquiry, participatory action research, and constructivist-instructional design are a few of the methods professionals are using today to improve and enhance their own practice and that of others.

Professional practice research is simply another term for research:

- Conducted by professional practitioners
- In the setting where they practice—community, school, classroom, computer lab, and so on
- To address problems and issues of professional practice

Another aspect of the growing role of professionals in the research process is the increasing respect for voices from the field. The discourses among practitioners have always been an important channel of influence on professional practice. However, this channel has not always been respected, or even acknowledged, by traditional university-based researchers in spite of the fact it is often more influential and more powerful than the typical research article. Today, information technologies such as blogs, forums, and wikis are joining the traditional channels of professional discourse such as teacher lounge conversations, conferences, and workshops. Both traditional and technology-enhanced methods of professional discourse are today more likely to be valued and highly regarded by practitioners and academic researchers alike. Chapter 9 on research methods from the humanities and Chapter 10 on philosophical inquiry both contain information that will be useful in deciding how to make contributions to the dialogs on professional practice. However, Chapter 12 deals specifically with how to communicate the results of your research and your reflections on professional practice to relevant audiences. That chapter covers both traditional channels of communications such as journal articles and electronic methods of dissemination such as blogs and web sites.

EMPOWERMENT RESEARCH

The final type of research to be discussed in detail in this chapter is also the newest when it comes to achieving respectability within the social sciences and education. In fact, it might be premature to say that empowerment research has become respectable. Many conservative social scientists, and even more conservative politicians, would not consider some forms of empowerment research to be research at all. They would call it political action, social activism, interference, or any of a number of derogatory terms.

The concept of empowerment research emerged from critical theory. It is a natural application of the basic principles of critical theory—that some groups in society have power and use it to both maintain the group's power and to keep other groups in weaker and subjugated positions. The goal of some forms of empowerment research is to identify those power relationships, break them up, and replace them with more equitable and democratic social, cultural, economic, educational, and political systems. However, empowerment research is now practiced by many scholars who are not primarily identified as critical theorists. For example, Vivienne Smith (2004) described her work with reading teachers as a process of empowerment. Smith, who teaches at the University of Strathclyde in the UK, wanted to help literacy teachers "change their practice in such a way as to empower the children in their care, rather than enculture them into the rather more passive and compliant practices of school literacy" (p. 413). Smith views the acquisition of literacy, including the ability to read, as a means of empowerment. "In a lettered society, it is quite clear that those people who cannot read are at an enormous disadvantage" (p. 413). However, Smith believes that many forms of literacy education sanctioned by the state and society do not contribute to empowerment. Rather, they help produce a "compliant workforce" that does not cause trouble or even realize they have been disempowered. Smith proposes another form of literacy education, critical literacy, which is "a set of ideas and practices that grew out of the literacy education programmes first developed by Paulo Friere for the Brazilian underclass from the early 1960s" (p. 414). (Henry Giroux is a contemporary proponent of this type of empowerment or emancipatory education. Giroux gave up an endowed chair at Pennsylvania State University and moved to McMaster University in Canada a few years ago when he became disgusted with America after George W. Bush won a second term as President.) Professor Smith believes that the National Literacy Strategy in England is taking the country further away from critical literacy, and her study is an effort to address that process. She used ethnographic methods (participant observation in classrooms) to gather information on ways reading was taught in three schools. She learned from her observations that literacy education rarely if ever had a goal of empowering children, and her interviews with teachers indicated they felt powerless themselves. In the second phase of her research, Smith used action research methods to help teachers examine their own beliefs and methods. In the end Smith and her research assistant used many methods, some of them part of the action research paradigm and some not, to help teachers, and students, become more empowered and more involved in a critical approach to teaching and learning literacy skills. Smith's efforts at the emancipation of both teachers and students were a limited success, at best. At worst, they were a total failure. One of the most valuable aspects of her study, however, is her analysis of why she failed and what is required to do emancipatory research in schools. In the remainder of this section I will explore two forms of empowerment research: *emancipatory* and *action research.*

Emancipatory Research

While some forms of empowerment research do not rely heavily on critical theory, emancipatory research typically does. The goal of empowerment research is to (1) make both the power relationships, and the methods used to maintain them, public, (2) to help powerless groups overthrow the ways of thinking and acting that actually help to keep them in subjugation, and (3) help those without power acquire it and develop a society that is more democratic, equitable, open, and free. If the only goal of a particular study is to achieve the first goal—make power relationships and the means used to maintain them obvious and public, the term "critical research" is typically applied to it. If a study includes goals 2 or 3, or both, the term emancipatory research is more commonly used.

Oliver (1992) explained emancipatory research this way:

> The development of such a paradigm stems from the gradual rejection of the positivist view of social research as the pursuit of absolute knowledge through the scientific method and the gradual disillusionment with the interpretive view of such research as the generation of socially useful knowledge within particular historical and social contexts. The emancipatory paradigm, as the

name implies, is about the facilitating of a politics of the possible by confronting social oppression at whatever level it occurs. (p. 110)

Oliver, like most advocates of emancipatory research, argues that there is considerable disillusionment about pursuing the traditional goals of discovering eternal truths as the positivists propose. He is also not particularly pleased with the goal of developing contextual understanding as the interpretivists suggest. He argues that confronting and defeating oppression is the highest goal of research (Oliver, 1997). He tempers his view somewhat by saying that his advocacy of emancipatory research "was never intended to be an argument against the pursuit of knowledge per se, whether that knowledge be absolute, socially useful or whatever; but rather an assertion that it is not possible to research oppression in an objective or scientific way.... You cannot be independent... you are either on the side of the oppressors or the oppressed" (p. 17).

Emancipatory research thus tends to have a strong ideological foundation in the critical theory tradition and the questions of power, social equity, and emancipation are naturally the focus. Oliver is a researcher in the area of disabilities at the University of Greenwich in the UK, and much of contemporary emancipatory scholarship deals with helping disabled children and adults empower themselves and take more control of their lives and their roles in society. However, emancipatory research is found in virtually every area of the social sciences and education.

An example of emancipatory research in educational technology is the work of Malewski, Phillion, and Lehman (1995). They helped preservice teachers working in schools to use internet-based videoconferencing to develop classroom approaches that addressed the need for multicultural education. They used the emancipatory pedagogy of Paolo Freire as a foundation for the field experiences of the preservice teachers in an inner city elementary school. The paper, which was published in the open access journal, *Contemporary Issues in Technology and Teacher Education,* describes both work with the preservice teachers and the teachers' work with the children in their classrooms.

An issue many emancipatory researchers struggle with is the degree to which the researcher should try to determine what the participants should come to believe about their situation. Should the researcher determine that, or should he or she help participants develop their own individual understanding of the situation. Traditional Marxist approaches could become little more than efforts at indoctrination in the tradition of the *re-education camps* used by Communist governments in China and North Vietnam after military victories brought them to national power. The movie, *The Last Emperor,* contains a segment on re-education camps after the Communist victory in 1950 over the Nationalist faction in China. While those examples are extreme, the issue of how much authority the researcher assumes in an emancipatory research study is real. For example, Debra Freedman (2006) wrote about her concerns in efforts to work with pre-service teachers about their pre-conceptions and misconceptions of education as portrayed in the media. After considering the data gathered during the study, Freedman wondered: "Did she force her critical stance upon this group of pre-service teachers or did she allow them the space to negotiate with [the media images of education] in relation to their group discussions" (p. 87)? Vivienne Smith (2004) whose work on critical literacy was discussed earlier, made a conscious decision to impose her beliefs and conclusions on the teachers who volunteered to work with her on improving literacy instruction.

This is a choice all emancipatory researchers must make and the decision is based on their answer to the question of whether strongly advocating a particular view, opinion, or ideology is appropriate or not. Freedman (2006) had serious worries because she may have dominated the process designed to help emancipate the teachers she was supporting. On the other hand, Nastasi et al. (2000) described an approach they call Participatory Intervention Research or PIM. It is an approach they propose for school psychologists who are developing interventions in schools. PIM is similar to participatory action research (PAR), which is discussed in the next section. However, like Smith (2004), Nastasi and her colleagues seem much more comfortable than PAR advocates in taking an "expert" role and in expecting other participants in follow their lead in efforts to deal with problems of professional practice. PIM seems to have at its foundation, a positivist view of how research and practice relate. The researcher is an expert and has special knowledge and it is the role of practitioners in the local context to take the implications of that knowledge and use it to improve their practice. However, the PIM approach might be appealing to critical theorists because it emphasizes the need to involve local stakeholders in creating the local version of the treatment or solution. PIM advocates emphasize the need to consider local culture and context. This emphasis will appeal to interpretivists as well. Less appealing is what seems to be the major reason for adopting this approach. The purpose does not seem to emphasize integrating local expertise into the process of developing solutions to a problem; rather, the involvement of local stakeholders seems to be primarily to give them a feeling of involvement and ownership that will ensure they buy into the project and are willing to use the solutions that have basically been developed by the researchers. That is indicated by the subtitle of the article: "A framework for conceptualizing and promoting intervention acceptability."

Another current issue about emancipatory research comes from its recent popularity. The meaning of the term *emancipatory* has lately been watered down considerably as it is applied to many studies that do not have liberation, in the critical sense, as a goal. For example, a number of projects to enhance the teaching skills of educators have been called emancipatory even when those skills do not necessarily have much to do with emancipation.

A third issue about emancipatory research is the basic question of whether it is research at all. There are three answers to this question, one from each of the three major research paradigms in the social sciences:

- **Positivistm.** No it is not. It is not objective but to the contrary is very subjective. It does not try to discover universal truths, instead it is an effort to help a particular group improve their own circumstances or to change the political, social, or economic situation so that it is more favorable to an individual or group. "Emancipatory research" may be a lot of things—social services, social action, social change, activism, social action, among other things—but it is not research.
- **Interpretivism.** It may be a form of applied research. Some forms of emancipatory research are designed to help individuals and groups in a particular context. The goals are to understand that context better and to improve participants' lives or the lives of others. That is an acceptable goal for research, and if emancipatory research has goals like those two, it is perfectly acceptable research. On the other hand, some forms of emancipatory research are really nothing more than indoctrination designed to convert participants to a particular view of the world and of their place in that world. When emancipatory research is an attempt to impose the view of the research leader on others, and to force individuals, organizations, and institutions to accept a particular ideology and way of operating, then the result is not research but just another form of authoritarianism. To be truly emancipatory, and truly research, the process must be voluntary, open, participatory, and democratic. If the conclusions of the research and the solutions are already known by the researcher before emancipatory research begins the process is not research.
- **Critical Theory.** Emancipatory research is not only an acceptable form of research, it is an example of what all research should be—an effort to help build a more enlightened, free, equitable, and democratic society. Emancipatory research may seek to accomplish that with one individual or group, but it often attempts to impact a broader swath of society including organizations, systems, policies, and groups.

There is clearly no single answer to the question of whether emancipatory research is "real" research because the definition of what constitutes real research depends on the paradigm that determines the definition. Oliver (2002) made a similar point in his paper on the emancipatory model

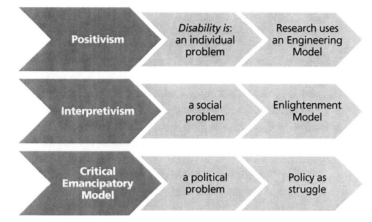

Figure 8.4   Forms of disability research based on the foundational paradigm. Adapted from Oliver, 2002.

of disability research. In his view the three dominant paradigms lead us to three different types of research as shown in Figure 8.4.

Oliver is critical of both the positivist paradigm and the interpretive paradigm. He concludes that "many disabled people have become alienated from both the process and product of social research. In this I would suggest that they are not alone. In recent years other minority or oppressed groups from women, black people, the poor, gay men and lesbians and people from other parts of the world have all voiced similar criticisms in one way or another." Oliver criticizes positivism's "fetishism on methodology" among other things and he criticizes interpretivism's approach to disability research about as harshly. His solution is emancipatory research based on several basic principles:

- **The Researched Must be in Control.** "My own view is that the critical issue in developing more useful and less alienating research is that of control." Oliver explains that "This isn't just about making researchers more accountable but of giving over ultimate control to the research subjects. . . . I have referred to this as the 'changing of the social relations of research production.'" The implications of this shift to control by those who, under a positivist mode, are the "subjects" of the research are extensive, including the need to create a language of research that is not exclusive and inaccessible to those who are the "researched" rather than the "researcher."
- **Emancipatory Research is Scholarship and Partisianship.** Some view the ideal scholar as a detached, objective, non-involved, neutral observer who can be the arbiter of what is true and what is not. That is

virtually the opposite of the partisan who is invested, subjective, and participating in the effort to bring about change. Oliver argues that aspects of both roles are critical to the emancipatory research effort but that the concept of research must change. "I have now made that transition from seeing research as an attempt to investigate the world to seeing research as action involved in producing the world." He thus makes the interpretive argument that we are constructors of our reality, not simply seekers out to discover reality. "Once one takes that cognitive leap, not only is research never the same again but neither is the world itself." At some level, several thinkers—from Marx to Foucault, and several modern movements, including post-modernism and post-structuralism, have made the same point—that we do not discover reality through research, we create it.

- **Research is Not Simply Investigatory, it is Creative.** As Oliver put it, "As researchers then, we labour to produce ourselves and our worlds. We do not investigate something out there, we do not merely deconstruct and reconstruct discourse about our world. Research as production requires us to engage with the world, not distance ourselves from it . . . and we must struggle to produce a world in which we can all live as truly human beings. Thus the research act is not an attempt to change the world through the process of investigation but an attempt to change the world by producing ourselves and others in differing ways from those we have produced before, intentionally or not."

- **Research is a Political Act.** Oliver's other major point is that research, and the researcher, cannot remain separate from the political and social processes that shape both us and the world we live in. Research as an act of creation, or production, is a part of those processes and to pretend otherwise, or to do research as if that were not true, is to do research poorly. "Increasingly as oppressed groups such as disabled people continue the political process of collectively empowering themselves, research practice based upon the investigatory discourse and utilizing 'tourist' approaches by 'tarmac' professors and researchers will find it increasingly difficult to find sites and experiences ripe for colonization." Oliver has in mind a very different framework for research. It involves research based on the "discourse of production" rather than the "discourse of investigation" (e.g., of discovering reality). His framework would also take "much more seriously the experiential knowledge that oppressed groups produce about themselves." However, in an effort to keep from falling into the very deep epistemological pit of total subjectivism, Oliver does not accept the idea that there is no reality to be found. This is in opposition to his advocacy of research as production instead of research as investigation and discovery. He quotes Oakley (2002, p. 298) who says "If there are really no such things as 'facts' about the way people are treated, then there is no such thing as discrimination or oppression." Oliver adopts the critical rather than the interpretive paradigm. He believes there is discrimination and oppression to be discovered and rooted out. For him, "the real challenge therefore for research in the 21st century is how to build an enterprise that exposes the real oppression and discrimination that people experience in their everyday lives without merely contributing to the classification and control of marginalized groups who seek nothing more than their full inclusion into the societies in which they live."

If we consider for a moment how the conceptual framework presented in Figure 8.4 applies to educational technology, one inescapable conclusion is probably that much of the research in educational technology journals is of the positivist-engineering type. That is, the studies describe ways of technically enhancing our ability to do what has already been decided is important to do. This can take many forms—from building a new literacy curriculum because students are not doing well on reading achievement tests to creating new educational software to support the state's high school science objectives. Most of the remaining research in the mainstream educational technology journals is based on the interpretivist enlightenment model. It seeks to help us understand a particular context of technology use or need. Critical, emancipatory research is relatively rare in the educational technology literature, especially when it involves, as Oliver suggests, a political and social struggle to influence and change policy.

In my own view, both the engineering model and the enlightenment model make important contributions to the field of educational technology. However, the emancipatory research also has a great deal to offer the field and it is currently underused. That is particularly true of one way of doing emancipatory research—participatory action research from a critical perspective.

Action Research

At this point you may be thinking that this book should have been more closely edited because action research has already been discussed in this chapter. The quality of editing is not the reason action research appears twice. Action research is a very popular form of applied professional practice research that is often done from an interpretivist perspective. That aspect of action research was discussed earlier. At the same time, action research, or AR, is a second form of empowerment research that is often guided by the critical paradigm. One form of AR, *Participatory Action Research*, emphasizes the necessity of involving stakeholders in the entire process of the action research process and it is often the variant used when the goal is empowerment.

Even as a research approach with the goal of empowerment, the term action research typically applies to efforts to solve a professional practice problem, or to enhance professional practice. Some scholars believe the very nature of participatory action research—that it involves the stakeholders fully in the process; that it is conducted in the real world rather than in laboratories or specially developed situations, that AR's primary purpose is improvement rather than theory development or discovering ultimate truths—makes it by nature an empowering or emancipatory process. Boog (2003), who teaches at the University of Groningen in The Netherlands, is one proponent of that view. "Right from the start, action research was intended to be emancipatory research, and it still is" (p. 426). He believes that all forms of action research are "supported by a participatory worldview and are meant to be a double-sided process of research, self research and education directed at individual empowerment and collective empowerment and/or emancipation" (p. 426). Boog's paper is an exploration of the history of action research as an emancipatory practice and it includes a number of recommendations about how to make AR a more effective method of empowerment and/or emancipation. Boog believes all approaches to AR tend to share six characteristics:

1. The research process involves cycles or iterations. AR is not a one shot process of identifying a problem, searching for a solution, implementing the solution, and then evaluating the impact of the solution. It is, instead, an onging series of such cycles.
2. The purpose of AR is individual and group emancipation, empowerment, a more equitable society, and greater participatory democracy.
3. The "theoretical and methodological stance of action [research] theory is inherently critical and grounded in an emancipatory worldview. Active experiential learning is fundamental to the notion of the human being as the active creator of his or her world" (p. 432).
4. An important assumption underlying AR is that new "knowledge in social research is basically gained through a process of mutual understanding, a so-called double hermeneutic process. Researchers interpret an already interpreted world; researched subjects comment on that interpretation, and so on. In the process of mutual understanding, the research partners try to get to know and trust each other as equals in self-knowledge about their other-ness" (p. 433).

5. The resulting relationship between participants in an AR project is more subject-subject than the typical subject-object relationship that often characterizes positivist research in the social sciences.
6. All forms of AR "share a co-generative research assessment procedure" (p. 434). That is, both intended and unintended outcomes of the research is assessed collaboratively by the participants. Further, at both the individual and the group or social level, the ultimate goals of emancipation and empowerment must be kept in mind.

Boog's six characteristics conflict with some of the approaches to empowerment research discussed already—such as Smith's work with literacy teachers. Boog, for example, emphasizes the collaborative construction of meaning by all participants much more than some critical theorists do. In spite of his insistence that AR is predominantly a critical form of research, his approach might best be considered a blend of interpretive and critical paradigms. However, the importance of the collaborative construction of meaning is at the heart of the issue discussed already—how authoritative a researcher should be and how far researchers should go in imposing their own ideologies and interpretations on other participants in the AR process. That Oliver (2002) manages to come down on both sides of this issue in a relatively short article highlights the difficult and complicated nature of this question.

Boog is one of many AR specialists who view action research as an expression of a particular paradigm. However, as used in the field today, action research is the general term used for systematic efforts to enhance professional practice through careful study in the context of practice. However, while he operates from a critical perspective, some of his conceptual underpinnings are interpretive. His use of the idea of a collaboratively developed and agreed upon statement about reality is more interpretive than critical, yet it has become a core belief of many, if not most, forms of participatory action research. The term *participatory action research*, or PAR, signifies action research conducted by the practitioner working collaboratively within a group that supports and contributes to the research effort. For example, Ditrano and Silverstein (2006) described a participatory action research project with parents of children classified as having emotional disabilities. They describe PAR as "a process in which researchers and participants operate as full collaborators in creating action projects that are designed to meet specific needs of the participants. PAR provides opportunities for researchers and participants to co-construct knowledge, unsettling the power dynamics between outside experts and local community insiders.... The goal of PAR is transformation—transformation of the field of psychology to accept collaborative inquiry as a legitimate form of research and pedagogy and transformation in terms of social action (i.e., empowering citizens and communities)" (p. 360). Ditrano and Silverstein base their approach to PAR on critical theory, particularly the work of Brazilian educator Paulo Freire. They emphasize the need for teachers, psychologists, and other traditional "experts" to abandon their expert role and to develop a dialogue that allows participants to "ask critical questions about their place in society." And as the participants become aware of the social injustice built into the culture in which they live, they begin to think about how to redress the injustice. That phase of enlightened understanding or *critical consciousness* is followed by a phase of action. They see themselves "as empowered actors creating their own destiny" and they initiate actions designed to improve their situation. In their case study report Ditrano and Silverstein tell how parents of children needing special education services developed an understanding of both the details of the way the education and mental health bureaucracies operate and they also became aware of the reasons why "schools and mental health agencies have frequently failed to establish meaningful partnerships with families." The reasons revolved around the fact that "the professional staff and the families come from different socioeconomic, ethnic, and racial backgrounds."

Ditrano and Silverstein divide PAR into three overlapping and iterative phases—developing a collaborative relationship, education, and action. Their paper tells the story of a group of parents who progress through these three phases as they work with schools and other agencies to develop better services for their children.

In the AR and PAR literature a surprisingly large number of terms are sometimes used interchangeably with AR and PAR. They include action learning, action science, applied research, classroom action research, collaborative inquiry, emancipatory research, participatory inquiry, participatory research, PIM or participatory intervention model, and many more. There are real differences between the core meanings of some of these terms, and the meanings also vary from one part of the literature to another. However, a common characteristic is that the research occurs in the real world of practice, addresses a real-world problem of practice, and attempts to develop a working solution. PAR always includes the practitioner and other stakeholders in the research process.

Doing Participatory Action Research

In this section I will introduce one conceptual framework for doing PAR from a critical perspective. The framework was proposed by Stephen Kemmis and Robin McTaggart (2005) in the third edition of the *Handbook for Qualitative Research.* Kemmis and McTaggart are Australian scholars with a long history of work both as developers of the concept of PAR and as researchers who use the PAR framework.

Kemmis and McTaggart's chapter on PAR is an attempt to reconceptualize this approach to research and also to correct some misconceptions that have developed over the years. These authors take some of the responsibility for some misconceptions and misapplications because the view they hold today is not always congruent with their prior scholarship on PAR. The chapter is thus a good overview of how the thinking of two critical theorists changed over the years.

In a section on the history of AR Kemmis and McTaggart trace the development of action research through four generations. The first was an American effort in the fifties to define AR within the then dominant framework of positivism. In their view, "this led to a temporary decline in its development there" (p. 560). Another reason for the decline of AR in America during the mid-20th century was the widespread view that AR was leftist, even "Communist." That was the McCarthy era when many careers and lives were ruined in the right wing efforts to suppress virtually any opinion or action that was not approved by the ideological Right. Action research that attempted to empower people to take more control over their lives seemed subversive. In today's Internet era there are still web sites and publications about the Tavistock Institute in London that describe it as part of a vast left wing conspiracy.

The Tavistock Institute helped a second generation of AR emerge in the UK. Second generation AR put a strong emphasis on practical problem solutions, often at the organizational level rather than at the level of individual practitioners. The idea of changing institutions, organizations, and political/social systems through AR is one reason the institute is still accused of being part of a world-wide system of power and thought-control.

Kemmis and McTaggart believe the third generation of AR began in Australia with efforts to base AR more explicitly on critical and emancipatory foundations. That goal and the increasing use of critical theory as a foundation for AR spread to Europe and to a lesser extent, to America, during this phase.

The current or fourth generation of AR "emerged in the connection between critical emancipatory action research and participatory action research that had developed in the context of social movements in the developing world, championed by people such as Paulo Freire, Orlando Fals Borda, . . . as well as by North American and British workers in adult education and literacy, community development, and development studies . . . Two key themes were (a) the development of theoretical arguments for more 'actionist' approaches to action research and (b) the need for participatory action researchers to make links with broad social movements" (p. 560). Kemmis and McTaggart relate what they now refer to as Critical Participatory Action Research to movements such as liberation theology among the Catholic clergy in South America, neo-Marxist community development projects, and the human rights movement. In making those associations Kemmis and McTaggart are also making it clear that there is an important political component to their form of AR. They also put an emphasis on Aristotle's "sense of practical reasoning [e.g., phronesis] about how to act rightly and properly in a situation with which one is confronted" (p. 561).

Kemmis and McTaggart have their own model of PAR. It is a spiral of six recursive stages:

- Planning a change
- Acting and observing the process and consequences of the change
- Reflecting on these processes and consequences
- Replanning
- Acting and observing again
- Reflecting again, and so on… (p. 563)

Doing PAR Does Not Focus on Following Rules. Despite their use of stages and diagrams to represent PAR, Kemmis and McTaggart consider PAR "only poorly described in terms of a mechanical sequence of steps" (p. 563). They are not even sure PAR should be represented as an orderly sequence of planned steps that lead, hopefully, to a solution. In practice PAR is much more chaotic than the diagrams and steps represent. "The stages overlap and initial plans quickly become obsolete in the light of learning from experience. In reality, the process is likely to be more fluid, open, and responsive. The criterion of success is not whether participants have followed the steps faithfully but rather whether they have a strong and authentic sense of development and evolution in their practices, their understanding of their practices, and the situations in which they practice" (p. 563). Kemmis and McTaggart propose a set of guiding principles that, in their view, are more central to PAR than a set of sequential steps:

- PAR is a social process. It "explores the relationship between the realms of the individual and the social" and it acknowledges that, quoting Habermas, "no individuation is possible without socialization, and no socialization is possible without individuation" (p. 566). Further. "the object of PAR is social, . . . directed toward studying, reframing, and reconstructing social practices. If practices are constituted in social interaction between people, changing practices is a social process" (p. 563).

  Kemmis and McTaggard put a great deal of emphasis on the social. Existing practices, which are not working,
  – were developed socially,

- they are practiced in a social context,
- they will be examined by a collaborating group that uses the PAR process as a forum to explore current practices through communication within what Habermas called *open communicative space.* That is, the participants join the discussion voluntarily and collaboratively develop their view of current practices as well as ideas for new practices. This happens through communication both among members of the PAR project and with others who are not participants but who have an interest in solving the problem.
- Collaborative learning leads to an agreement about what practices need to be changed and ideas about what should replace current practices.
- Implementing the changes is best accomplished by a group that has collectively come to the conclusion that these changes should be made and the group is committed to implementing and evaluating them.
- Often, the changes needed will not be within the power of the PAR group. That group must influence others, often policy makers, to agree to and to create the conditions for making the changes. This is a political aspect of PAR that was not always recognized as vitally important in the early PAR literature.

• PAR is participatory. "Each of the steps . . . in the spiral of self-reflection is best undertaken collaboratively by coparticipants" (p. 563). "All individuals in a group try to get a handle on the ways in which their knowledge shapes their sense of identity and agency and to reflect critically on how their current knowledge frames and constrains their action . . ." (p. 567). PAR is also participatory in the sense that "people can only do action research 'on' themselves, either individually or collectively. It is not research done 'on' others" (p. 567). Kemmis and McTaggart also argue that participation should be broad. For example, in educational PAR, "it is not only teachers who have the task of improving the social practices of schooling but also students and many others (e.g., parents, school communities, employers of graduates)" (p. 579).

• PAR is practical and collaborative. Kemmis and McTaggart believe a major difference between PAR and other forms of social science research is the tenacity with which it emphasizes the particular instance and situation over the general idea or theory. Participatory action researchers "may be interested in practices in general or in the abstract, but their principal concern is in changing practices in 'the here and now'" (p. 564). PAR "involves the investigation of actual practices and not abstract practices" (p. 563–564). "Focusing on practices in a concrete and specific way makes them accessible for reflection, discussion, and reconstruction as products of past circumstances that are capable of being modified in and for present and future circumstances. . . . "Participatory action researchers aim to understand their own particular practices as they emerge in their own particular circumstances without reducing them to the ghostly status of the general, the abstract, or the ideal—or, perhaps one should say, the unreal" (p. 565).

Another part of this guiding principle is that PAR is collaborative. Kemmis and McTaggart also use the term collective to refer to the necessity for working as a group to bring about lasting change. They believe AR should be collective rather than individualistic in part because it generates better decisions through group communication and decision making, and the implementation of plans for change is easier if a group is committed to making change happen. Kemmis and McTaggart even recommend that PAR groups or collectives "include 'critical friends,' . . . build alliances with broader social movements, and . . . extend membership across institutional hierarchies . . . as a way of enhancing the understanding and political efficacy of individuals and groups" (p. 571).

- PAR is emancipatory. It "aims to help people recover, and release themselves from, the constraints of irrational, unproductive, unjust, and unsatisfying social structures that limit their self-development and self-determination. It is a process in which people explore the ways in which their practices are shaped and constrained by wider social (cultural, economic, and political) structures and consider whether they can intervene to release themselves from these constraints—or, if they cannot, how best to work within and around them" (p. 567).

The traditional concepts of emancipation and empowerment focus on individuals or groups and the struggle to free themselves from unhealthy controls . However, Kemmis and McTaggart have recently modified their view of emancipation or empowerment. They do not see it as a process that leads to individuals and groups that are completely autonomous, self-regulating, and self-controlled. "It turns out that neither individual actors nor states can be entirely and coherently autonomous and self-regulating. Their parts do not form unified and coherent wholes but rather must be understood in terms of notions such as difference, contradiction, and conflict as much as unity, coherence, and independence" (p. 594). Within this perspective, "it is difficult to create a believable myth in which PAR is a process for empowering the mistreated group by wresting power from the powerful but misguided. Instead, the best that empowerment can achieve is to enhance the "capacity for individuals, groups, and states to interact more coherently with one another in the ceaseless process of social reproduction and transformation. At its best, it names a process in which people, groups, and states engage one another more authentically and with greater recognition and respect for difference in making decisions that they will regard as legitimate because they have participated in them openly and freely, more genuinely committed to mutual understanding, intersubjective agreement, and consensus about what to do" (p. 594). "We came to understand empowerment not only as a lifeworld process of cultural, social, and personal development and transformation but also as implying that protagonists experienced themselves as working both in and against system structures and functions" (p. 593). In formulating this new version of empowerment, they use Habermas' ideas of lifeworld and system. A major purpose of Habermas' theory building was to explain what is happening in late capitalist societies of the West. Essentially, the normal integrative roles of communication in society no longer work. In earlier times the communicative processes of a society helped citizens to both understand the structures and functions of society and, more importantly, to believe that they were desirable and necessary to a smoothly functioning society as well as beneficial to them. However, in late capitalism, the channels of communication have been high jacked or "colonized" for other purposes. Consider, for example, the now widespread view that different national news services, such as CBS, CNN, and Fox, are not "fair and balanced" purveyors of the news. Instead, they select, produce, and present the news in ways that support particular political and social ideologies. The colonization of communications channels, such as television news networks, means the function of communication to help citizens reach a consensus of belief in the goodness of society's regulating systems has been lost. We do not always believe government operates in our interests; that corporations have the best interests of consumers in mind, or that schools are run in ways that maximize the benefits to students. The result is a "crisis of legitimation." People no longer have a strong faith in "the system." The concept of system in Habermas' thinking means the organized and structured procedures that have been developed to achieve economic and bureaucratic goals (e.g., "money and power"). Lifeworld refers to the set of shared assumptions, beliefs, and values that citizens of a society develop through "communicative action." However, in late capitalist societies, Habermas believes too many channels of communication have been co-opted by those who seek money and power rather than the development of a society based on a shared set of beliefs and values.

He thus proposes that creating environments (public spheres) in which communication for that purpose is unhindered by forces focused on money and power. Kemmis and McTaggart see the PAR group as an example of that type of public sphere. In this view of PAR, empowerment is more than changing the lifeworld. That is certainly necessary because the way we view the world and our place in it is part of the oppression that disempowers us. For example, it is not uncommon for a battered woman's to believe that she may "deserve" to be treated that way. That belief, which can be supported an encouraged by cultural and social practices, is part of the web of oppression that keeps her from acting to improve her lot. Thus, changing the lifeworld is crucial in change efforts. However, PAR, and other efforts to make desirable changes, must also make changes in the system. Sometimes that may involve opposing or fighting the system, but at other times the most effective approach is to use the system to bring about changes in it and the lifeworld.

Kemmis and McTaggert thus view empowerment as a process of changing both the lifeworld and systems. Further, the process of becoming empowered or emancipated is not one great effort that happens in the last reel of the movie, followed by a lifetime of happiness and contentment. Instead, it is an ongoing and continuous process of communicative action and exploratory action. These two terms will be discussed in more detail a little later.

- PAR is "reflexive (e.g., recursive, dialectical)." PAR "aims to help people investigate reality in order to change it . . . and . . . to change reality in order to investigate it. In particular, it is a deliberate process through which people aim to transform their practices through a spiral of cycles of critical and self-critical action and reflection. . . . It is a deliberate social process designed to help collaborating groups of people to transform their world" (p. 567).

- PAR "aims to transform both theory and practice." Unlike some models of PAR, Kemmis and McTaggart's view emphasizes the role of both theory and practice in the process of action research. They do not see theory or practice as the dominant component in the theory-practice relationship. Instead, they see both as standing on the same level and they see both as being important, actually essential, to the other. Their form of PAR "does not aim to develop forms of theory that can stand above and beyond practice" . . . "nor does it aim to develop forms of practice that might be regarded as self-justifying, as if practice could be judged in the absence of theoretical frameworks" (p. 568). They use the terms "reaching out" and "reaching in" to emphasize the need of going from "specific practices in specific contexts" to broader viewpoints such as theories and also to go from "standpoints

provided by different perspectives, theories, and discourages to explore the extent to which they provide practitioners themselves with
a critical grasp of the problems and issues they actually confront in
specific local situations" (p. 568).

Kemmis and McTaggart are more hopeful of broad theories and frameworks than I am, but that probably reflects the difference in their foundation—critical theory—and mine—interpretivism. Critical theory has always
had a set of core beliefs about how the world really is that guides both practice and research while interpretive approaches often urge us to give up on
foundational truths and accept that whatever reality we have is a socially
constructed reality.

The critical perspective of Kemmis and McTaggart is also obvious in what
they see as their mistakes, and the path their thinking has taken with more
experience. Today they have less faith in basic AR procedures yielding the
personal empowerment they hoped for in the beginning. They believe "it
was a mistake not to emphasize sufficiently that power comes from collective commitment and a methodology that invites the democratization of the
objectification of experience and the disciplining of subjectivity" (p. 569).
That is, they do not see AR freeing individuals from the restrictions of current practices without the influence of the collective mind—the shared
exploration of practice that limits the influence of individual, subjective
decision-making while enhancing the influence of the group on interpreting experience.

They also worry more about the "facilitator," consultant, or outside expert (particularly university professors) in the PAR process. Such a role is
prone to be misunderstood and perhaps misused. Outsiders who come into
a practical professional setting such as a school or classroom cannot and
should not try to play a role as neutral arbitrator of what is right or correct,
nor should they present themselves as technical experts in the process of
PAR. Both roles tend to put the outsider in a superior position to the practitioners in that context, which is undesirable. They also tend to limit the
ability of the group to democratically explore and understand the influence
and control of local practice by wider social movements and frameworks,
history, and traditions. Finally, they can also blind you "to the way in which
practice is constituted as a 'multiple reality' that is perceived differently by
different participants in and observers of practice (e.g., professionals, clients, clients' families and friends, interested observers)" (p. 570).

Other issues that are clearer to Kemmis and McTaggart today include
the need to accept that PAR involves research, activism, and theory. Activism has always been a part of PAR but Kemmis and McTaggart "find significant understatement of the role of theory and theory building in the
literature of action research. . . . Our experience suggests that there should

be both more theory and more action in action research. Political activism should be theoretically informed just like any other social practice" (p. 570). On the research side of PAR, they advocate using a range of research methods and approaches because different research methods tend to lead us naturally to certain types of conclusions and perceptions. Using multiple methods helps us keep that in mind and highlights the subjective nature of all research methods.

Kemmis and McTaggart's newest PAR theories move away from a confrontive "us versus them" mentality that often portrayed PAR participants as the revolutionaries fighting the entrenched power of "the establishment" and its bureaucratic functionaries. Instead, following Habermas, they argue that there really is no monolithic establishment that makes uniform policy and practice decisions that are then routinely and rigorously implemented. There are "not unified systems but rather complex sets of subsystems having transactions of various kinds with one another economically...and administratively" (p. 579). From this perspective they urge participatory action researchers to make an effort to both influence and work with different "subsystems" in efforts to bring about change. However, when making the point that there is no monolithic "system" that opposes change, they also note that PAR groups are also not monolithic. All members do not hold the same viewpoints or advocate the same actions. PAR groups are "internally diverse, they generally have no unified 'core' from which their power and authority can emanate, and they frequently have little capacity to achieve their own ends if they must contend with the will of other powers and orders" (p. 580).

This view of PAR groups and the relevant systems, individuals, and organizations outside the PAR group leads Kemmis and McTaggart to propose a revised view of how PAR works. Using Habermas' theories of communication and social structure they propose that "the most morally, practically, and politically compelling view of participatory action research is one that sees participatory action research as a practice through which people can create networks of communication, that is, sites for the practice of communicative action. It offers the prospect of opening communicative space in public spheres of the kind Habermas described. Based on such a view, participatory action research aims to engender practical critiques of existing states of affairs, the development of critical perspectives, and the shared formation of emancipatory commitments, that is, commitments to overcome distorted ways of understanding the world, distorted practices, and distorted social arrangements and situations" (p. 580).

This new perspective of PAR is summarized in Figure 8.5. PAR provides participants with a public sphere. For Habermas, public spheres are contexts where people could come together to discuss social problems. They are a form of participatory democracy and Habermas sees them as a power-

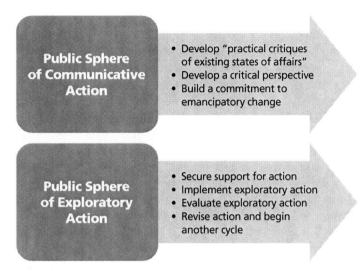

Figure 8.5   A diagram of Kemmis and McTaggart's 2006 framework for PAR.

ful way of giving people back some control over the direction of the society in which they live. In PAR the public sphere for communicative action allows participants to develop a shared understanding of the social problems they face and the reasons for them. A clearer understanding of social problems and their causes is often hampered or even prevented by established rules, structures, traditions, influence groups, and power structures. Thus, a primary goal of PAR is to help participants recognize those barriers, reduce or eliminate their influence, and develop a clearer, shared view of the problems and their causes. The emergence of this shared view is part of the second outcome of communications work in the public sphere—the development of a shared, critical perspective that links cause and effect, power and oppression, and so on. The third outcome is the development of a commitment on the part of the PAR community to a plan for emancipatory action.

The top half of Figure 8.5 focuses on the process of communication that occurs in PAR. People discuss, debate, explore, exhort, and share through an open, democratic process. The goal is educational rather than to initiate action. Participants should come to view their world differently. PAR thus "aims to change the researchers themselves as well as the social world they inhabit" (p. 578). In this process each participant's viewpoint and experience is respected, and input from outside the PAR group may often be sought and used. However, in the end the goal is a group that has both a desire to do something different and an idea of what that difference should be.

The bottom half of Figure 8.5 focuses on action. Once the PAR group has both the will to act and a shared view of what action should be taken, efforts to implement that action are undertaken. Kemmis and McTaggart call this *Exploratory Action* because it is considered only a tentative and potentially useful change. It must be implemented in an exploratory manner that involves careful observation of the impact of the action—both in terms of expected and unexpected effects, including unanticipated negative effects. If the action proposed is within the power of the PAR group, they may implement the exploratory action, carefully evaluate it, and complete one cycle of the PAR process by revising the action before beginning another cycle. Keep in mind, however, that this exploratory action is undertaken by a group that has already developed a more sophisticated and shared view of one or more social practices. Exploratory action is an attempt to change that practice for the better.

If the exploratory action is not within the power of the PAR group, there may be an extended period of work to influence decision makers and policy groups to make the exploratory action possible. This involves a third type of change. In addition to changing "practitioner understanding", PAR must change "social practices," and "the situations and circumstances in which [the PAR participants] practice" (p. 586). This third type of change may emerge from exploratory action or changing the situations and circumstances of practice may be necessary before practice can change. Kemmis and McTaggart seem to feel that many needed changes will not be within the control of a PAR group and that political action in the sense of building coalitions and influencing decision and policy groups will be necessary more often than some AR proponents seem to realize.

Of course, a diagram like Figure 8.5 oversimplifies the PAR process. The two processes, communicative action and exploratory action, overlap considerably and the processes of each interact and intertwine.

To summarize the discussion of PAR, it is probably best thought of, not as a particular methodology of research with a set of prescribed procedures for doing valid research, but as a way of thinking about applied research that emphasizes several important concepts such as the critical nature of participation, the importance of empowerment and emancipation as goals, and the privileging of practical outcomes in a particular setting over broad, abstract theorizing.

IN SUMMARY

Just what does the term "qualitative research" really mean? One way of pinning down what it means is to compare it to quantitative research and say that all qualitative research collects and analyzes non-quantitative data while all quantitative research analyzes numeric, quantitative data. That approach doesn't help very much. In fact, you can find "qualitative" researchers who use quantitative data and vice versa. Another approach is to define qualitative research as any research based on a paradigm other than the dominant positivist approach. Again, this is problematic because the alternatives to positivism do not always "hang together" as a meaningful group or family that shares something other than rejecting positivism. Yet another approach is to define qualitative research as any research that uses one of a particular collection research methods such as ethnography, action research and emancipatory research. Here again, there is a problem because these methods can be used by people who have very different goals and who use the methods in very different ways. It can seem at times that when it comes to "qualitative research" there is "no there there", as Gertrude Stein is supposed to have said about her home town, Oakland, California.

My solution to this muddle is to say that each of the three types of definitions offered are part of what the philosopher Ludwig Wittgenstein would have called a "family resemblance." That is, they point to something that tends to be a characteristic of qualitative research but that are not present in every instance of qualitative research. They are family resemblances, not required characteristics of everything you call qualitative research. For convenience, I have organized this chapter around three families of qualitative research methods—traditional methods that are well established, applied methods that are emerging as popular alternatives to traditional methods, and methods of empowerment that are not yet widely accepted as scholarly or research methods but which represent the cutting edge of yet another redefinition of what it means to be a scholar and a researcher in the social sciences and education. In education, the acceptance of traditional qualitative methods is relatively complete. Well done research using any of the traditional qualitative methods can be published in hundreds of journals today. Applied research is less widely accepted but there are still a number of journals where clinical and action research as well as professional discourse and instructional design research can be published. However, qualitative applied research still has difficulty being accepted in "mainstream" journals though that is changing rapidly.

Empowerment research is even less accepted in education today and is often restricted to a small community of journals and conferences where like-minded scholars and professional practitioners have made a new home for themselves. However, when this was written in the summer of 2008 (when you could fry not only an egg, you could cook an entire chicken on the sidewalk in New York City) you could find the occasional empowerment paper in a mainstream education journal. Academia changes slowly, but it is changing today, and the direction of change is in two, opposing directions. The Bush administration has allied with conservative scholars in what might be called a "back to the basics" movement in research. They advocate a positivist ideology that privileges empirical research in the experimental tradition of the natural sciences. However, at the same time, the broader field of educational research is expanding the boundaries of what counts as research. More and more journals, conferences, organizations, and individual scholars are accepting qualitative methods, qualitative scholarship, and qualitative contributions to our understanding of education and learning.

Unfortunately, the situation in the field of educational technology is not as optimistic. However, traditional qualitative research methods are accepted in a number of educational technology journals, and there are outlets for applied research studies. Outlets for empowerment scholarship is more restricted. The situation in educational technology is due, in part, to the continuing dominance of the positivist model of research. That is changing, but at a much slower rate than in the broader field of education. But, on an optimistic note, it is changing.

REFERENCES

Archie, L. & Archie, J. (2004). *Reading for Philosophical Inquiry: A Brief Introduction to Philosophical Thinking, An Open Source Reader, ver. 0.21.* Retrieved 05/18/2007 from http://philosophy.lander.edu/intro/introbook-links.html.

Boog, B. (2003). The emancipatory character of action research, its history and the present state of the art. *Journal of Community Applied Social Psychology, 13*, 426–438.

Bromley, H. & Apple, M. (Eds) (1998). *Education/technology/power: Educational computing as a social practice.* Albany, NY: SUNY Press.

Campbell, C. (1997, May 1). Rhetoric and the Art of Design, (book review). *Technical Communication, 44*(2), 189.

Clandinin, D. J. & Connelly, F. M. (2000). *Narrative inquiry: Experience and story in qualitative research.* San Francisco: Jossey-Bass.

Clauset, K., Lick, D., & Murphy, C. (2008). *Schoolwide action research for professional learning communities.* Thousand Oaks, CA: Corwin.

Ditrano, C. & Silverstein, L. (2006). Listening to parents' voices: Participatory action research in the schools. *Professional Psychology: Research and Practice, 37*(4), 359–366.

Dowler, L. (1993). Technology, scholarship, and the humanities: The implications for electronic information. The Coalition for Networked Information. Retrieved –5/18/2007 from http://www.cni.org/docs/tsh/Dowler.html

Freedman, D. (2006). Reflections on the research process: Emancipatory research or emancipatory zeal? *Reflective Practice, 7*(1), 87–100.

Fitzpatrick, J., Sanders, J., Worthern, B. (2003). *Program evaluation: Alternative approaches and practical guidelines, 3rd ed.* Boston: Allyn and Bacon.

Gross, A. & Keith, W. (1997). *Rhetorical Hermeneutics: Invention and Interpretation in the Age of Science.* Albany, NY: SUNY Press.

Gaonkar, D. (1996). The idea of rhetoric in the rhetoric of science. In A. Gross & W. Keith (Eds), *Rhetorical hermeneutics: Innovation and Interpretation in the age of science* (pp. 25–87). Albany, NY: SUNY Press.

Greene, J. (1994). Qualitative program evaluation. In N. Denzin & Y. Lincoln (Eds), *Handbook of Qualitatative Research*, (pp. 530–545). Thousand Oaks, CA: Sage.

Jörgenson, L., Sinclair, N. Braham, S. & Balka, E. Experiments in premature adoption of constructive educational technology. Burnaby, British Columbia: Simon Fraser University. Retrieved 05/18/2007 http://www.cecm.sfu.ca/~loki/Papers/IPS/FULL/

Kaufer, D. & Butler, B. (1996). Rhetoric and the Arts of Design. Mahwah, NJ: Lawrence Erlbaum.

Kemmis, S. & McTaggart, R. (1988). *The action research planner* (3rd ed.). Geelong, Australia: Deakin University.

Karagiorgi, Y. & Symeou, L. (2005). Translating constructivism into instructional design: Potential and limitations. *Educational Technology & Society, 8*(1), 17–27.

Malewski, E., Phillion, J., & Lehman, J. (2005). A Freirian framework for technology-based virtual field experiences. *Contemporary Issues in Technology and Teacher Education* [Online serial], *4*(4). Available: http://www.citejournal.org/vol4/iss4/general/articles1.cfm

McCloskey, D. (1997). Big rhetoric, little rhetoric: Gaonkar on the rhetoric of science. In A. Gross & W. Keith (Eds), Rhetorical hermeneutics: Innovation and Interpretation in the age of science (pp. 101–112). Albany, NY: SUNY Press.

Miller, W. & Crabtree, B. (2005). Clinical research. In N. Denzin & Y. Lincoln (Eds), *Handbook of qualitatative research* (3rd ed., pp. 605–639). Thousand Oaks, CA: Sage.

Mills, G. (2006). *Action research: A guide for the teacher researcher, 3rd ed.* Englewood Cliffs, NJ: Prentice-Hall.

Nastasi, B., Varjas, K., Schensul, S., Silva, K., Schensul, J., & Ratnayake, P. (2000). The Participatory Intervention Model: A framework for conceptualizing and promoting intervention acceptability. *School Psychology Quarterly, 15*(2), 207–232.

Nelson, M. & Quintana, S. (2005). Qualitative clinical research with children and adolescents. *Journal of Child and Adolescent Psychology, 34*(2), 344–356.

Oakley, A. (2000). *Experiments in knowing.* Cambridge, UK: Polity Press.

Oliver, M. (December 3, 2002). Using emancipatory methodologies in disability research. Paper presented at the 1st Annual Disability Seminar, The Centre for Disability Studies, University College Dublin (December 3, 2002). Available: http://www.leeds.ac.uk/disability-studies/archiveuk/Oliver/Mike's%20paper.pdf

Oliver, M. (1997). Emancipatory research: Realistic goal or impossible dream? In C. Barnes & G. Mercer, (Eds.), *Doing disability research* (pp. 15–31). Leeds, UK: The Disability Press.

Oliver, M. (1992). Changing the social relations of research production. *Disability, Handicap & Society, 7*(2), 101–115.

Rao, V. & Woolcock, M. (2003). *Integrating qualitastive and quantitative approaches in program evaluation.* Washington, DC: The World Bank. Available: http://www.Powerty2.forumone.com/library/view/12930

Sagor, R. (2004). *The Action research guidebook: A four-step process for educators and school teams.* Thousand Oaks, CA: Corwin.

Seymour-Rolls, K. & Hughes, I. (1995). *Participatory action research: Getting the job done.* Retrieved May 9, 2008 from http://www.beh.cchs.usyd.edu/au/~arow/Reader/rseymour.htm

Smith, V. (2004). Empowering teachers: Empowering children? How can researchers initiate and research empowerment? *Journal of Research in Reading, 27*(4), 413–424.

Willis, J. & Wright, K. (March-April, 2000). A general set of procedures for constructivist instructional design: The new R2D2 model. *Educational Technology, 40*(2), 5–20.

Willis, J. (January-February, 2000). The maturing of constructivist instructional design: Some basic principles that can guide practice. *Educational Technology, 40*(1), 5–16.

READINGS FOR CHAPTER 8

Reading 8.1

Kidd, S. & Kral, M. (2005). Practicing participatory action research. *Journal of Counseling Psychology, 52*(2).

This paper explores what it means to practice participatory action research (PAR) in a community setting. As you read this paper ask yourself what these two scholars consider the core principles and practices of PAR? And, what conceptual framework do they use as the foundation for PAR?

Once you have a solid understanding of what PAR is to Kidd and Kral, take their ideas of PAR and apply them to a research project of interest to you in the broad field of education or the narrower field of educational technology. Does the approach of Kidd and Kral to PAR restrict the type of research you can do? How? Why?

What aspects of PAR transfer to your study without any need for adaptation or adjustment? What needs to be modified before it would work in your study? And what do you see as the least likely aspects of PAR to work at all? What are the reasons for that? Is it at the organizational or cultural level? Part of the restrictions imposed by the particular work setting? Is it due to the differences between how professionals and other stakeholders interact in the setting you would study?

Finally, how do you evaluate the balance Kidd and Kral strike between the generation of knowledge and the emancipatory purposes of their version of PAR? Is it reasonable? Why or why not? Is it the best approach? Why or why not?

Reading 8.2

Paulus, T., Horvitz, B., & Shi, M. (2006). "Isn't it just like our situation?" Engagement and learning in an online story-based environment. *Educational Technology Research & Development, 54*(4), 355–385.

This rather long paper is a bit difficult to unpack because it addresses so many different issues of interest to someone studying research methods and educational technology. It is based on a study conducted in a graduate program for instructional designers and it focuses on how to get students engaged with the content of a core course. Engagement is not often considered and even less often studied, but it is a critical aspect of any program that is preparing students to become professional practitioners. The more engaged and involved a student is with important content, the more he or she is likely to get from the experience.

These authors studied engagement and learning in a course on instructional design that organized some of the content around stories. This is another unusual aspect of the study. Narratives or stories are both a way of doing and reporting research as well as a way of teaching. The authors created a "story-centered learning environment" and they provide an extended review of both the research on engagement and the use of story-centered learning environments. Here, a story-based computer-supported collaborative learning tool called Wisdom Tools Scenarios was used to develop a scenario about working in teams. The goal was to help students develop one of the important "soft skills" needed for professional practice—"the ability to work productively in teams."

Although the paper is about an instructional design project—creating instructional resources for a graduate course—it was written as a qualitative case study. As you read this paper, ask yourself what data the three authors collected and used to write different sections of the paper. Is there any information not in the paper that would be helpful to you as a reader? Does "what is missing" depend on the reason you are reading the paper (e.g., you are thinking about using story-centered learning, you want to explore the use of software like Wisdom Tools Scenario in your own instruction, you are interested in methods for teaching instructional design, you are looking broadly for ways to increase engagement in your students, etc.)?

After reading the paper do you consider the scenario the authors used in the *Introduction to Instructional Design* course more likely to encourage engagement than a simulation based on the same concept that required students to make decisions that determined what happened next in the simulation? Each of the "critical incidents" could have been a choice point for the players in the simulation, for example. Why did you select the scenario over the simulation, or vice versa? How important do you think the small group asynchronous discussions were in facilitating engagement? Could they be eliminated in the interest of saving time? Why or why not?

The authors say the guiding paradigm for their research was constructivism. What evidence do you see in the paper that that was true? Are there any aspects of the study and the project that seem to go against constructivist theory?

What do you think of the decision to use the scenario in a separate, online experience? Do you think it would have worked better if some of the class time had been spent on it?

Finally, the data in this case study was analyzed using a variation of the constant comparative method. The constant comparative method calls for the researchers to carefully explore and study the data before creating a scheme for coding it. Then, the data is coded, researchers make notes about relationships and tentative conclusions about what the data is telling them. An explanation (e.g., a theory) of what happened gradually emerges from the data and the relationships between different coded segments. That explanation is revised and improved through further exploration of the data and the codes (which may change and evolve over the data analysis phase). Once you have a feel for how the authors analyzed their data, write a one page description of a study in which you could use a similar procedure to study a topic of interest to you.

Reading 8.3

Glazer, E., Hannafin, M., & Song, L. (2005). Promoting technology integration through collaborative apprenticeship. *Educational Technology Research & Development, 53*(4), 57–67.

This paper is an effort to convince the reader that a process of professional development the authors call *Collaborative Apprenticeship* is a desirable way to help teachers learn both information and educational technology skills and the ability to integrate technologies into learning environments. Because the concept of collaborative apprenticeship is not well know, the authors spend several pages on two topics: why traditional methods of professional development such as workshops/seminars are ineffective and the conceptual and theoretical foundations that support and encourage using collaborative apprenticeships. According to the authors, what are the reasons traditional professional development activities such as workshops held in the summer or presentations by guest experts are not effective? Do you agree with their assessment of the situation? Why?

What about the conceptual and theoretical foundations for collaborative apprenticeships? What are they according to this paper? Do they "hang together" as a sensible foundation for this approach? Why?

What about the approach itself? What do you consider the most important aspects of collaborative apprenticeships? Why? Is the ongoing and intense working relationship with a knowledgeable technology-using educator important? How? Why? Is the close linking of the apprenticeship with day to day practice in the classroom important? How? Why? What about the creation of a community of peers who support each other? Would it be better to have outside experts available to teachers on a regular basis? Why or why not? What about the idea of creating a community of practitioners in the work context? Wouldn't that be happening already? Why or why not? And, wouldn't one on one support be more private and more comfortable for many teachers than this group approach?

What about the apprenticeship process itself? How does it differ from a traditional inservice workshop model of professional development and are the differences likely to make it more successful? Easier or more difficult to implement? What about the four phases of an apprenticeship, especially as they apply to technology integration? Are they phases all apprenticeships go through, most go through, one among many possibilities? Defend your answer.

Think about how this model of professional development would fit into your preferred career path? Would it be something you could or should use often? For what purposes and in what circumstances? Occasionally? Rarely? Explain your answers.

Finally, is this an example of qualitative research in your opinion? If it is, what type of qualitative research is it? The only type this seems to fit in my opinion is professional practice discourse. The paper is written by professional practitioners and scholars who have used collaborative apprenticeship and who understand the underlying theoretical and conceptual support for it. While they summarize the research of others, they do not present "data" from a new study they conducted. They based the paper primarily on their thoughtfully analyzed and considered experience. What is your opinion? Is this "research" or not? Defend your answer.

Reading 8.4

Raingruber, B. (2003). Video-cued narrative reflection: A research approach to articulating tacit, relational, and embodied understandings. *Qualitative Health Research, 13*(8), 1155–1169.

This article is about how to use a particular qualitative methodology, one that has not been discussed in detail in the chapter on qualitative research methods. Dr. Bonnie Raingruber is a professor of nursing and her focus is on how to do research on professional practice. More specifically, she is interested in how to explore and understand the types of crucial but difficult-to-get-at professional thinking that characterizes much of the foundation for day-to-day decision making in professional practice. Her focus is on the practice of health care professionals but the approach she presents applies equally well to educators and educational technology professionals. In the title of her paper she includes three terms for the type of knowing that interests here—*tacit, relational,* and *embodied* understandings. Tacit knowledge or understanding cannot be fully articulated or "objectivized," and it is a very contextualized type of knowledge. Developing relational understanding, as defined in this paper, involves looking at interactions between the professional and others such as patients, students, or colleagues. Embodied understanding is understanding that develops and has meaning primarily in a context rather than understanding at an abstract level.

The research methodology she introduces in the paper, video-cued narrative reflection, is a way of getting at the thinking processes of professionals as they explore their "lived experiences"—in this case, their day to day professional practice. The primary means of gathering data on lived experiences is to ask professionals to reflect on their work. What Raingruber proposes is that the person reflects while observing videotaped segments of their professional practice experience.

If reflections on the part of participants are a valid form of data for qualitative research, do you feel that data collected via video-cued narrative reflection will have the advantages suggested by the author? Are there any problems or difficulties you foresee in this method? What about the goal of relational understanding? The reflections of more than one person in an interaction can be compared to those of another participant. How does this contribute to the phenomenological goals of the research method?

How could this method be transferred to research in education or educational technology? What adaptations or revisions might need to be made? What additional precautions might need to be taken? Briefly describe a study of interest to you where this research method would be appropriate. How would you organize the interview where participants do their narrative reflection? Would you do several interviews as Raingruber did? Why? Would you take a similar approach to the author when analyzing your data or would you use a different method? Why?

CHAPTER 9

METHODS OF SCHOLARSHIP FROM THE HUMANITIES

In previous chapters we have explored many ways of thinking about the scholarship of educational technology. For example, most contemporary educational technology scholarship is based on one of three guiding paradigms: positivism/postpositivism, critical theory, or interpretivism/constructivism. These three families have other names and there are a great many subgroups, offshoots, cults, special interest groups, clusters, factions, knots, bands, and invisible colleges within each. However, I believe there is enough of a common "core" of shared beliefs that it makes sense to talk about these three paradigm families as if they were real.

There are also two great traditions in the scholarship of the social sciences. One comes down to us from Aristotle and is based on the simple idea that we can best learn what is True by studying the material world around us. I have referred to this as empiricism, but related terms include *materialism, naturalism, realism, sensism, positivism, and objectivism.* If this were a book on advanced philosophy, the different meanings of these terms would have to be carefully explored, but for our purposes it is enough to say that they are all members of the same family.

The second great tradition is the Platonic tradition of *rationalism*. Related terms include *Idealism* and *Intellectualism*. In this tradition, thinking is the critical activity for making sense of what is. In some versions, including Plato's, this involves thinking to get closer to a Divine mind which has per-

Qualitative Research Methods in Education and Educational Technology, pages 257–296
Copyright © 2008 by Information Age Publishing
All rights of reproduction in any form reserved.

fect knowledge of the Truth of all things. In other versions, rational human thought is simply the best tool we have to seek knowledge.

If we combine the two metaframeworks discussed thus far, a graphical representation might look like the one in Figure 9.1 which depicts the approved methods and approved approaches to data analysis of the three dominant paradigms. Positivist approaches to research in a field like educational technology are somewhat limited in the types of methods that are accepted. For a strict positivist all research methods must be empirical and adhere to the requirements of the scientific method. On the other hand, both interpretivist and critical paradigms are open with regard to acceptable research methods. Both will accept methods used in the natural sciences, the social sciences, and the humanities as well as philosophy. Positivism imposes a similar limitation when it comes to the question of what types of analyses are acceptable. Positivists use a combination of empirical data analysis based on established statistical procedures, and rational analysis based on pre-specified forms of logic. For example, "If the experimental group's mean score is significantly higher (at the .05 level or better) than the control group's mean score, then the null hypothesis is rejected." Analyzing data in the positivist tradition is very much a technical procedure with many rules and requirements.

On the other hand, critical theorists and interpretivists may use the same procedures as positivists but not always for the same purpose (e.g., discovering universal laws). Interpretivists, especially, tend to be looking for local understanding rather than universals, and both alternatives to positivism are very comfortable with the use of the methods of philosophical analysis as well as a wide range of rational approaches to analysis, including those drawn from modern literary criticism. This broader range of methodological and analytical options for critical theorists and interpretivists tends to turn even the process of selecting methods (and forms of analysis) into an artistic rather than a technical process.

Positivism
- Empiricist methods
- Empirical analysis
- Rational analysis

Critical Theory
- Open inquiry
- Empirical analysis
- Rational analysis
- Philosophical analysis

Interpretivism
- Open inquiry
- Empirical analysis
- Rational analysis
- Philosophical analysis

Figure 9.1 Characteristics of the three most popular paradigm families in educational technology today.

Figure 9.1 seems to indicate that critical and interpretive paradigms are very much alike while the positivist paradigm is quite different. It is true that the positivist tradition is the most different. It has developed a definitive framework for doing "good" scholarship, a clearly defined purpose for doing research (the search for universals), an enormous and growing culture of research methods, an equally large assortment of statistical procedures for analyzing data, and a very well articulated set of rules for deciding whether a piece of research is reliable and valid. Figure 9.2 represents the

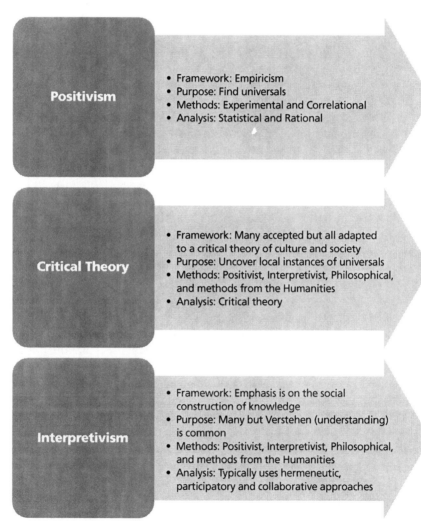

Positivism
- Framework: Empiricism
- Purpose: Find universals
- Methods: Experimental and Correlational
- Analysis: Statistical and Rational

Critical Theory
- Framework: Many accepted but all adapted to a critical theory of culture and society
- Purpose: Uncover local instances of universals
- Methods: Positivist, Interpretivist, Philosophical, and methods from the Humanities
- Analysis: Critical theory

Interpretivism
- Framework: Emphasis is on the social construction of knowledge
- Purpose: Many but Verstehen (understanding) is common
- Methods: Positivist, Interpretivist, Philosophical, and methods from the Humanities
- Analysis: Typically uses hermeneutic, participatory and collaborative approaches

Figure 9.2 An overview of the three major guiding paradigms in educational technology.

much less organized and definitely less systematized situation in which interpretive and critical theorists operate.

In contrast to the very positive and definitive answers positivism provides to adherents on many questions, critical theory and interpretivism do not have well-defined set of concrete answers and methods. Both families will accept quantitative methods such as control group-experimental group research on one end of the research continuum as well as poetry on the other end of that continuum. Thus, in terms of the methods considered acceptable, critical theory is like interpretivism. However, in terms of purpose, critical theory is more like positivism. Critical theory also looks for Truths but they are defined by critical theory's vision of how the sociocultural world of human beings operates—that is, in a context where there is typically oppression and the use of power to privilege one group over another. Positivism, on the other hand, is often criticized by critical theorists as tending to do research that supports those in power instead of the oppressed groups so often championed by critical theorists.

Interpretivists also diverge from critical theorists on purpose. They do not always look for universals, even the universal that those in power suppress those without power. Instead, they frequently seek a richer understanding of the local context. However, even scholars seeking local understanding may offer "theories" based on their research. These theories are more like useful fictions that others may consider using rather than the Truths proposed by both positivists and critical theorists.

The two other aspects in Figure 9.2 are Framework and Analysis. Both alternatives to positivism are looser and less structured here as well. Many general frameworks are acceptable to the alternative paradigms but there are restrictions. Critical theory requires that the framework used be adapted to the deterministic assumptions of the theory—there are power relationships and oppression to be uncovered, and the job of the critical theorists is to uncover them (and to help redress them). Interpretivism insists that the framework used be adapted to a relativistic assumption about knowledge. That is, absolute knowledge or truth is not available to humans and any knowledge developed is thus the shared belief of a community of *knowers* rather than a discovery of universal laws. This interpretivist restriction applies particularly to knowledge about how humans behave and think because humans are conscious decision makers who influence, and are influenced by, their experiences and the social and cultural environments in which they live. The restrictions on frameworks by critical theorists and interpretivists also apply to the types of analysis that are acceptable. That is, critical theorists tend to use research methods that help them confirm in a local context the universal assumption that patterns of power and oppression will be present. Interpretivists tend to use research methods that help bring to light multiple perspectives on the issues under study and that facilitate communication and under-standing across different stakeholder groups and different ideologies.

THINKING ABOUT RESEARCH METHODS IN EDUCATIONAL TECHNOLOGY

Both critical and interpretive approaches to educational technology research favor accepting a broad range of methods. That breadth is, however, both a blessing and a curse. The range of methods available means that educational technology scholars have many options to choose from when it comes to de-ciding how to approach a particular question or issue. On the other hand, the number of options is almost overwhelming. Few, if any, scholars are capable of doing good scholarship in all the traditions or using all the methods. It is difficult even to become familiar with so many possibilities. The very weight of books like the *Handbook of Qualitative Research* is intimidating, as are the thousands of pages of very small print. In Chapter 7, I began an exploration of the most important families of research methods. In this chapter and the next two I will continue that exploration. This chapter explores methods from the humanities, which have not been discussed to this point in any detail.

METHODS OF SCHOLARSHIP FROM THE HUMANITIES

Figure 9.3 presents the major forms of inquiry from the humanities that can be fruitfully applied in educational technology.

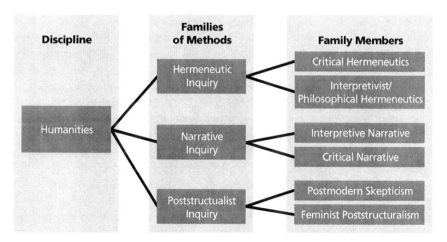

Figure 9.3   Humanities methods of scholarship that are applicable in educational technology.

HERMENEUTIC INQUIRY

Hermeneutic scholarship is an effort to derive meaning from texts (broadly defined) by a wide range of methods that take into consideration the context in which the text was created. Gadamer's (2004) *Truth and Method,* originally published in German in 1960, has become a classic statement of hermeneutic theory and practice:

> In the nineteenth century, the hermeneutics that was once merely ancillary to theology and philology was developed into a system and made the basis of all the human sciences. It wholly transcended its original pragmatic purpose of making it possible, or easier, to understand written texts. It is not only the written tradition that is estranged and in need of new and more vital assimilation; everything that is no longer immediately situated in a world—that is, all tradition, whether art or the other spiritual creations of the past: law, religion, philosophy, and so forth—is estranged from its original meaning and depends on the unlocking and mediating spirit that we, like the Greeks, named after Hermes: the messenger of the gods. It is to the rise of historical consciousness that hermeneutics owes its centrality within the human sciences. (p. 165)

Gadamer based his hermeneutics on the assertion that humans live in a world of sociocultural traditions that we have become alienated and estranged from and that hermeneutics helps us both understand ourselves and our traditions. In fact, we cannot understand ourselves without understanding our traditions and their history. Understanding is also mediated by language which means we must understand the critical roles of language in both constructing and carrying meaning. Gadamer emphasizes the importance of dialog and conversation in the search for understanding, and his discussions with students influenced his own writing. Gadamer often used art in his examples as he built a case for hermeneutics. One of his major points was that *"all encounters with the language of art is an encounter with an unfinished event and is itself part of this event"* (p. 99). Gadamer used the German word, *dasein,* or "being in time" to emphasize that humans are understood within their place in the flow of history and experience.

Gadamer both studied and made use of the ideas of Plato and Aristotle. His emphasis on dialog or dialectical thinking—the exchange of questions and answers - comes from Plato's dialogs as a method of working out ideas and communicating them. Following Heidegger he also gave Aristotle's concept of phronesis an important role in his theories. "Thus Aristotle sees ethos as differing from physis in being a sphere in which the laws of nature do not operate, yet not a sphere of lawlessness but of human institutions and human modes of behavior which are mutable, and like rules only to a limited degree. The question is whether there can be any such thing as philosophical knowledge of the moral being of man and what role knowledge

(.i.e., logos) plays in the moral being of man. If man always encounters the good in the form of a particular practical situation in which he finds himself, the task of moral knowledge is to determine what the concrete situation asks of him. . . . In contrast to the theory of the good based on Plato's doctrine of ideas, Aristotle emphasizes that it is impossible for ethics to achieve the extreme exactitude of mathematics. . . . What needs to be done is simply to make an outline and by means of this sketch give some help to moral consciousness" (pp. 312–313).

For Gadamer, phronesis is a foundation for hermeneutics:

> Practical knowledge, phronesis, is another kind of knowledge. Primarily, this means that it is directed towards the concrete situation. Thus it must grasp the "circumstances" in their infinite variety. . . . The Aristotelian distinction refers to something other than the distinction between knowing on the basis of universal principles and on the basis of the concrete. Nor does he mean only the capacity to subsume the individual case under a universal category—what we call "judgment." . . . The grasp and moral control of the concrete situation require subsuming what is given under the universal, that is, the goal that one is pursuing so that the right thing may result. Hence, it presupposes a direction of the will—i.e., moral being (hexis). That is why Aristotle considers phronesis an "intellectual virtue." He sees it not only as a capacity (dunamis), but as a determination of moral being which cannot exist without the totality of the "ethical virtues," which in turn cannot exist without it. Although practicing this virtue means that one distinguishes what should be done from what should not, it is not simply practical shrewdness and general cleverness. The distinction between what should and should not be done includes the distinction between the proper and the improper and thus presupposes a moral attitude, which it continues to develop. (pp. 21–22)

It is a bit ironic to be including Gadamer and hermeneutics in a section on research methods because Gadamer was not very concerned with step-by-step methods. He was more concerned with the broader ideas about how we come to understand. For him it involves a dialogical process (Plato) and it helps us to acquire phronesis (Aristotle)—knowledge that is practical and contextual.

Critical and Interpretive Hermeneutics

While I have discussed hermeneutics as a unitary concept, there are actually many types of hermeneutic scholarship and many different applications of this method in the social sciences and education. Two of the three forms of hermeneutic inquiry listed in Figure 8.3 refer to an underlying theory that guides the hermeneutic process—critical theory or interpretive theory. One way of thinking about the difference is Jurgen Habermas' (1968) divi-

TABLE 9.1 Habermas' Types of Human Interests and the Associated Research Methods

Human Interest	Research Method	Outcome
Technical	Empirical-Analytic (Positivist)	Instrumental Knowledge
Practical	Interpretive Hermeneutics	Practical Knowledge
Emancipatory	Critical Hermeneutics Emancipatory Research Methods	Emancipatory Knowledge and Procedures

sion of human interests into three general categories. In his book *Erkenntnis und Interesse* (Knowledge and Human Interest) Habermas proposed that humans have technical interests, practical interests, and emancipatory interests (See Table 9.1)

Most of the content of Table 9.1 will be familiar to you from previous discussions. Habermas' critical theory foundations are illustrated by his placement of Aristotle's phronesis in a secondary position to the more important emancipatory interests that are the focus of critical hermeneutics. Though sharing many positions, Habermas and Gadamer disagreed on others and had an ongoing debate that lasted for decades. Part of that debate was over phronesis (McGee, 1998). Habermas, who helped built a critical social science, had two foundational commitments (McGee, 1998, p. 16):

> First, any acceptable social theory must contribute to the emancipation of both the thinker and humanity in general. The most prominent feature of society is its system of constraints, and the imperative duty of the social critic to minimize the effects of those constraints which cannot in reason be eliminated.... Second, any acceptable social theory must be amenable to bringing "empirical-analytical" thinking (social science) and "historic-hermeneutic" thinking (human science) "under one roof." This coexistence would not entail choosing causal analysis over interpretive understanding, or vice versa, "but of criticizing any pretension to universal and exclusive validity on the part of either, and of finding some sort of higher synthesis in which both have a place" (McCarthy, 1978, p. 140)

Habermas thus situates his perspective solidly within the paradigm of critical theory and interprets everything else in ways that support his worldview. His hermeneutics is a *critical hermeneutics*. Gadamer, on the other hand, has more faith in the possibility of understanding, including shared understanding between individuals and groups, which can come from engaging in "conversations" or dialogs between people who begin the conversation with different views. Gadamer's approach is not so dominated by the critical paradigm and it is not as skeptical as Habermas' view. Habermas, for example, believed that it was difficult, if not impossible, to engage in the types of dialog Gadamer advocated because the strongly held ideologies of the participants would cause them to artificially engage in dialog without actually buying into the goals of dialog in a free and open manner. Without that, there would not be the possibility that they would change their beliefs through the process of dialog. Gadamer's approach is called *philosophical hermeneutics* but it could also be called *interpretive hermeneutics*.

Literary Criticism and Literary Theory

Although not all literary criticism/theory is hermeneutic I have included it here because much of modern literary theory is a part of the hermeneutic tradition. Considering the origins of hermeneutics, it is, itself, a literary theory. Literary criticism, once primarily the domain of tweedy English professors and their studious graduate students, has become a major force in the social sciences, and society in general. So much so, that Bressler (2007) began his book on literary criticism with this quote from Thomas McLaughlin:

> Literary theory has permeated our thinking to the point that it has defined for our times how discourse about literature, as well as about culture in general, shall proceed. Literary theory has arrived, and no student of literature can afford not to come to terms with it.

Some literary theories have already been discussed in earlier chapters. The divergent views of Plato and Aristotle are still important to contemporary discussions, for example. There has been a long line of literary theorists since then. The British Romantic poet, Percy Shelly, for example, wrote *A Defense of Poetry* in 1821. In it he takes an idealistic stance and defends poetry as a way of achieving Plato's ultimate truths (e.g., Ideal Forms) that are not physical but spiritual Truths. Shelly rejects the rationalism of the Enlightenment and supports creativity, imagination, feeling and emotion. Poetry was for Shelly a superior path to eternal knowledge that goes beyond some more limited sources of knowledge such as science.

In the remainder of this section I will use Bressler (2007) as my main source to introduce some contemporary literary theories and methods of literary criticism. Modern literary criticism in the West began with a movement called New Criticism. It could be thought of as the literary equivalent of positivist social science.

New Criticism. This movement emerged in the first part of the 20th century and involves a detailed or "close reading" of literature. It "provides readers with a formula for arriving at the correct interpretation of a text using—for the most part—only the text itself. Such a formulaic approach gives both beginning students of literature and academicians a seemingly objective approach for discovering a text's meaning. Using New Criticism's clearly articulated methodology, any intelligent reader, say its adherents (called New Critics), can uncover a text's hitherto so-called 'hidden meaning' " (Bressler, 2007, p. 55). A primary characteristic of New Criticism was that it tended to ignore or minimize the importance of context and history in understanding literature. With no more than New Criticism's research methods and a novel, you could spend a weekend at the lake and do literary criticism!

Reader-Oriented Criticism. Another movement, which came to prominence in the 1970s, was called Reader-Oriented Criticism (ROC). However, the origins of ROC are much older. Concerns about the reader's response to a poem or novel, or an audience's response to a play, were an issue for both Aristotle and Plato. Aristotle, for example, talked about the cathartic effect of Greek tragedy on the audience. The modern expression of ROC began in the 1920s with the work of L. A. Richards at Cambridge University. It matured and developed through the 20th century. While there are several variations of Reader-Oriented Criticism, Bressler (2007) sees a common core:

> What differentiates . . . all reader-oriented critics from other critical approaches (especially New Criticism) is their purposive shift in emphasis away from the text as the sole determiner of meaning and toward the significance of the reader as an essential participant in the reading process and in the creation of meaning. Such a shift negates the Formalists' assumption that the text is autonomous and can, therefore, be scientifically analyzed to discover its meaning. No longer, then, is the reader passive, merely applying a long list of learned, poetic devices to a text in the hope of discovering its intricate patterns of paradox and irony, which, in turn, supposedly leads to the one correct interpretation. For reader-oriented critics, the reader is an active participant along with the text in creating meaning. It is from the literary experience (an event that occurs when a reader and print transact), they believe, that meaning evolves. (pp. 79–80)

Bressler points out that most reader-oriented critics use one of three methods of scholarship: *structuralism, phenomenology,* or *subjective criticism.* Structuralism has already been discussed in an earlier chapter. "The proponents of structuralism . . . look for specific codes within the text that allow meaning to occur. These codes or signs embedded in the text are part of a larger system that allows meaning to occur in all facets of society, including literature. . . . According to structuralist critics, a reader brings to the text a predetermined system for ascertaining meaning (a complex system of signs or codes similar to the sirens and the red light [that are well known codes/signs to someone who drives a car]" (p. 82). Phenomenology "is a modern philosophical tendency to emphasize the perceiver. Objects can have meaning, phenomenologists maintain, only if an active consciousness (a perceiver) absorbs or notes their existence. [So now we know whether that tree falling in the forest makes a noise when no one is around.] In other words, objects exist if, and only if, we register them in our consciousness. . . . The true poem can exist only in the reader's consciousness, not on the printed page" (pp. 85–86).

Perhaps the most radical of the ROC is *subjective criticism.* "For these psychological or subjective critics, the reader's thoughts, beliefs, and experiences play a greater part than the actual text in shaping a work's meaning. . . . These critics assert that readers shape and find their self-identities in the reading process" (p. 86). While ROC was radical for its time, a major shift occurred in the 20th century that led to even more radical literary theories. That shift was postmodernism.

Literary Criticism and Postmodernism

There are also genres of literary criticism based on psychoanalysis, Marxism, and Feminism, to name but a few of the broad theories that have been applied to literary criticism. However, many of the contemporary theories could be organized under the general category named postmodernism. Modernism is a legacy of the Enlightenment that embodies two major assumptions, "that reason is humankind's best guide to life and that science, above all other human endeavors, could lead humanity to a new promised land" (p. 96). Using modernism as a foundation, theories like structuralism looked for truths, enduring ways of deriving meaning, from literature. For example, the French anthropologist Claude Lévi-Strauss studied myths and proposed that myths are made up of basic components called *mythemes.* A myth has meaning because these mythemes are organized into a mythic structure. This is both a modern and a structural approach to literature. Postmodernism, in many forms, attacked, and some say destroyed, the supposedly secure foundations of modernist thought. Deconstruction, one of the foundations of postmodernism, will be discussed next.

Derrida, Deconstruction and Poststructuralism. In the middle of the 20th century both modernism and structuralism were attacked by approaches that rejected the search for underlying and universal codes, rules, and structures. This movement helped redefine the sources of meaning not only of literature but of all forms of culture. One of the leaders in this attack was the French theorist Jacques Derrida. He rejected the Platonic underpinnings of traditional Western modernism that assumes there is one truth, one correct interpretation, one right answer, to most important questions. Derrida also rejected the structuralist idea that you can find rules that let you uncover the hidden but true meaning of literature. Often, structuralism proposes a general coding system that can be applied to a particular piece of literature or culture to find its true essence. Claude Lévi-Strauss' development of the idea of *mythemes* is an example. As a postmodernist, Derrida argued that there is not one true meaning. Instead, there are many meanings in all types of text that can be uncovered through a process called *deconstruction.*

> Deconstruction theory asks a different set of questions, endeavoring to show that what a text claims it says and what it actually says are discernibly different. By casting doubt on most previously held theories, deconstruction declares that a text has an almost infinite number of possible interpretations.... With the advent of deconstruction and its challenge to structuralism and other prior theories, a paradigmatic shift occurs in literary theory and criticism. Before deconstruction, literary critics—New Critics, some reader-oriented theorists, structuralists, and others—found meaning within the literary text or the codes of the various sign systems within the world of the text and the reader.... Underlying all the predeconstructionist suppositions about the world is a set of philosophical, ethical, and scientific assumptions we dub modernity that provided the bases for the beliefs held by Western culture for about 300 years. With the emergence of deconstruction, however, these long-held beliefs were challenged by poststructuralism, a new basis for understanding and guiding humanity. (p. 117)

Deconstruction in literary theory has parallels to the interpretive tradition in the social sciences. Both reject the idea that humans can acquire some sort of objective truth (called *logocentrism* by Derrida) and both emphasize that for any major social issue there will be multiple perspectives. A goal of deconstruction is to understand the "center" of a text that allows it to say that such and such is true. That center can take many forms—from a belief in a particular religion to a belief in rationalism or the scientific method. The goal of deconstruction is to "decenter" our understanding and open up the possibility of seeing alternatives. Derrida blames our current tendency to see things from an either/or perspective (which he calls *binary opposition*) on Aristotle and "his principle of non-contradiction: A thing cannot both have a property and not have a property. Thanks to Aristotle, maintains Derrida, Western metaphysics has developed an 'either/or' mentality or logic."... He therefore wishes to dismantle or deconstruct the structure such binary operations have created. Derrida asserts that the binary oppositions on which Western metaphysics has been constructed since the time of Plato are structured so that one element will always be privileged (be in a superior position) and the other unprivileged (in an inferior position). In this way of thinking, the first or top elements of the pairs in the following list of binary oppositions are privileged: man/woman, human/animal, soul/body, good/bad" (p. 121).

One important implication of deconstruction is that meaning emerges from the process of reading a text; it does not reside in the text itself. A second implication is that what the author intends to say is not necessarily what is communicated. There may be many, often contradictory, messages in a text. Bressler (2007) boils the deconstructive process down to six habits of thought:

- Discover the binary operations that govern a text.
- Comment on the values, concepts, and ideas beyond these operations.
- Reverse these present binary operations.
- Dismantle previously held worldviews.
- Accept the possibility of various perspectives or levels of meaning in a text based on the new binary inversions.
- Allow meaning of the text to be undecided (p. 128).

While this list is presented in a linear fashion, the process of deconstruction is not. It is nonlinear, and different components may operate at the same time or in a different order than presented in the list.

Deconstruction was not met with unabashed and universal enthusiasm, to put it mildly. "Such a reading strategy disturbs most readers and critics because it is not a neat, completed package, whereby if we follow the steps A through Z, we arrive at *the* reading of the text. Because texts have no external referents, their meanings depend on the close interaction of the text, the reader, and social and cultural elements, as does every reading or interpretative process. Denying the organic unity of a text, deconstructors declare the free play of language in a text. Language, they assert, is reflective, not mimetic. We can therefore never stop finding meaning in a text, whether we have read it once or a hundred times. . . . By examining the text alone, deconstructors hope to ask a set of questions that will continually challenge the ideological positions of power and authority that dominate literary criticism. Furthermore, in the process of discovering meaning in a text, deconstructors declare that criticism of a text is just as valuable as the text being read, thereby inverting the text/criticism hierarchy" (p. 129).

Cultural Poetics (New Historicism). Deconstruction acknowledges the role culture and context plays in the meaning of texts, but as a method of scholarship it focuses tightly on the text at hand. Another movement in literary theory takes a broader focus and emphasizes that all truths are relative. They are therefore best understood within a historical and cultural context:

Appearing as an alternate approach to textual interpretation in the 1970s and early 1980s, Cultural Poetics—often called New Historicism in America and Cultural Materialism in Great Britain—declares that all history is subjective, written by people whose personal biases affect their interpretation of the past. History, asserts Cultural Poetics, can never provide us with the objective truth of or give us a totally accurate picture of past events, persons, or eras nor the worldview of a group of people....Cultural Poetics declares that history is one of many discourses, or ways of seeing and thinking about the world. By highlighting and viewing history as one of many equally important discourses such as sociology and politics and by closely examining how all discourses (including that of textual analysis) affect a text's interpretation, Cultural Poetics claim that it provides its adherents with a practice of literary analysis that:

- Highlights the interrelatedness of all human activities.
- Admits its own prejudices.
- Gives a more complete understanding of a text than does the old historicism and other interpretative approaches. (p. 214)

New Historicism thus "formulates its own readings of history and interpretative analysis. Literature, they decree, should be read in relation to culture, history, society, and other factors that help determine a text's meaning" (p. 215). It also broke down some of the barriers between different forms of scholarship. For example, when history is interpreted in such a relativist manner, the distance between history and literature is not so large. Both are subjective and both are grounded in a historical and cultural context. Thus, they are both voices, or forms of discourse, to be listened to, not to find truth, but to understand. "Because Cultural Poetics critics view history, literature, and other social activities as forms of discourse, they strongly reject the old historicism, which sees history as necessary background material for the study of literature. They view a work of art, a text, as they would any other social discourse that interacts with its culture to produce meaning. No longer is one discourse superior to another, but all are necessary components that shape and are shaped by society. No longer do clear lines of distinction exist among literature, history, literary criticism, anthropology, art, the sciences, and other disciplines. Blurring the boundaries among disciplines, Cultural Poetics investigates all discourses that affect any social production" (p. 225).

One of the founders of New Historicism, or Cultural Poetics, is Stephen Greenblatt, who taught at the University of California Berkeley for many years before recently moving to Harvard. He tells many stories about his life, and one story involves how he might have a very different career than his profession as a literary theorist. While working as a camp counselor he sang songs and played the guitar with a fellow counselor who wanted him to meet a friend so they could sing together. Greenblatt decided to go to college instead of pursuing a singing career. He completed his graduate work at Yale and Cambridge University. The fellow camp counselor was Art Garfunkle and the friend he wanted Greenblatt to meet was Paul Simon. The famous duo of Simon and Garfunkle might have been the trio Simon, Garfunkle, and Greenblatt.

In lieu of becoming a pop singer, Greenblat, with Svetlana Aplers, launched the journal, *Representations* (http://www.representations.org/vision_board.php) in 1983, and it has become one of the major publication outlets for New Historicism. Greenblatt and other New Historicists have been heavily influenced by postmodern thinkers like Michael Foucault who made a career of questioning received views of how the world is, as well as critical and Marxist theorists. In fact, the British version of New Historicism, which is called *Cultural Materialism,* is avowedly Marxist in orientation. However, the American version is more in the interpretive tradition and even claims some of the same ancestors as interpretive qualitative research. Clifford Geertz, a cultural anthropologist, is the father of "thick description", the guideline of qualitative research that insists we must provide a great deal of detail in order for readers to situate the knowledge being communicated in qualitative scholarship. He is often quoted in both the qualitative research and the New Historicism literature.

Stephen Greenblat has recently become concerned about "the crisis in scholarly publishing." That crisis is one of access because of rising costs. Commercial journal publishers are raising the prices of journal subscriptions to levels that many college libraries cannot afford, which means that more and more people do not have access to those journals. Some scholars believe the healthy profits regularly reported by commercial journal publishers come at a cost of limited access to the ideas and knowledge that was, after all, developed by scholars who are not paid anything for publishing in a journal. Their goal is to disseminate their work as widely as possible, but the rising costs of subscribing to journals are limiting access. Greenblat is a supporter of an international collaborative of scholars called the Open Humanities Press. In 2008 Open Humanities Press was publishing six humanities journals that were "open access"—they charge no subscription fee and are available to anyone with access to the Internet. See the organization's web site for more information and access to the journals (http://www.openhumanitiespress.org).

Standpoint Theory or Cultural Studies. In the social sciences the term *standpoint theory* is often used to indicate scholars and scholarship written from the perspective of a particular group. Feminist theory, for example, is one of the most established of the standpoint theories, but there is also African-American theory, Hispanic theory, Queer theory, Postcolonial theory, and many others. One of the founders of standpoint theory, Sandra Harding (1993), in *Rethinking Standpoint Epistemology: What is "Strong Objectivity"?* argued that the acceptance and inclusion of standpoint scholarship, the views of outsiders in a community, will result in a *strong objectivity*. That is, through standpoint scholarship, a community's understanding of its own biases, prejudices, and oppression, will be better understood. Thus, it is important to give the views of marginalized groups a place of influence in the scholarship of a culture.

In literary theory, the term Cultural Studies embraces much the same territory as standpoint scholarship in the social sciences. One result of the postmodern revolution in literary theory was the displacement of the dominant view in a particular culture as *The* correct view. It became one of many, although it often defined what was considered right and wrong, true and false, in that culture. However, with the rise of postmodernism, the weaknesses of the foundations upon which this dominant or hegemonic view rested became obvious. The result was twofold—members of the dominant groups within the culture began to question things that had been taken for granted as true, and members of other groups (the Other) began to reject the imposed truths from the dominant culture and offer truths from their own cultural perspective. Toni Morrison, the Nobel prize winning African American author, is but one of many examples of authors who communicate with both minority and majority elements of American culture. In his discussion of the role of Hispanic-American literature, the Cuban American novelist Virgil Suarez (2000) introduced the topic this way:

> In an autobiographical sketch written in 1986, the respected Chicano American novelist Rudolfo Anaya observed that "if I am to be a writer, it is the ancestral voices of...[my]... people who will form a part of my quest, my search."

> Ancestral voices are very much a part of Hispanic American literature today, a tradition harking back more than three centuries that has witnessed a dramatic renascence in the past generation. As the Hispanic experience in the United States continues to confront issues of identity, assimilation, cultural heritage and artistic expression, the works of Hispanic American writers are read with a great deal of interest and passion.

> In a sense, the literature functions as a mirror, a reflection of the way Hispanic Americans are viewed by the mainstream culture—but not always the majority. Readers and critics alike tend to celebrate this literature. It is rich, diverse, constantly growing, blending the history that infuses it with an impassioned feeling of contemporaneity.

> In essence, the boom in the literature today is being forged in English, by people who live and work in the United States—not in Spanish, as was the case with writers of generations and centuries past. This is a key difference, and a point of departure.

> True, there are still some very real issues and problems facing Hispanic American writers in terms of finding outlets and venues for their work, as there are for other multicultural artists and, to be sure, writers in general. Although

more work is being issued each year by major publishing houses, most of the interesting and engaging literature comes from small, independent presses that rely upon U.S. Government, private and university grants for stability. Literary journals and reviews always have been an outlet for Hispanic American voices, and some of the best work is coming from such sources. Increasingly, though, with the recognition associated with the nation's most prestigious literary awards—the Before Columbus Foundation Award, the National Book Award and the Pulitzer Prize—Hispanic American authors are being courted by the publishing establishment.

This is both a statement of some of the roles of Hispanic-American literature and an expression of optimism about its present and future. Today the literature of cultural studies is playing an increasing role in our efforts to understand ourselves and others. That applies as well to educational technology. One impressive example of the use of cultural studies methods to study educational technology is Hank Bromley and Michael Apple's (1998) book, *Education/Technology/Power: Educational Computing as a Social Practice.* Apple, a critical theorist who frequently focuses on the undesirable consequences of current practices in educational technology, has written many books and papers that use the methods and framework of cultural studies to examine important topics related to the use of information and educational technologies in education.

And on that note, the increasing importance of standpoint theories and cultural studies literature, it is appropriate to shift our focus to another type of scholarship that has come to us from the humanities. Narrative inquiry involves telling stories, and it has already established itself in education as a valuable method of scholarship.

NARRATIVE INQUIRY

In the last 20 years it has become fashionable to talk about the "narrative turn" in the social sciences. This is one reflection of the movement away from the search for universal truths and toward a search for more contextualized understanding of human experiences. Narrative inquiry certainly supports the new goal. In their book, *Narrative Inquiry: Experience and Story in Qualitative Research,* Jean Clandinin and Michael Connelly (2000) lay out three roles for narrative:

- As an epistemological framework within which to do scholarship.
- As a method of doing research.
- As a method of scholarly discourse.

While these three roles are different they are also strongly interrelated and I will explore all three of them in this section.

Narrative, like hermeneutic inquiry, emerged from the humanities where it has a long and valued history. It has been mentioned several times already but has not been explored in any detail. Narrative, or storytelling, is a form of expression in the humanities, with the short story and the novel being the most familiar form of narrative. However, narrative is not simply a literary form:

> We make narratives many times a day, every day of our lives. And we start doing it almost from the moment we begin putting words together. As soon as we follow a subject with a verb, there is a good chance we are engaged in narrative discourse. "I fell down," the child cries, and in the process tells her mother a little narrative. (Abbot, 2002, p. 1)

Many scholars believe narrative, telling stories, is the most fundamental way of communicating knowledge in human societies. That is illustrated in the ancient origins of the word. It is derived from the Sanskrit word *gna* that means *know* (Abbot, 2002, p. 11). Narrative comes in many forms—from novels, anecdotes, and epics to films, plays, poems, and songs. Of course, not all poems or songs are narratives but many are. The country-western singer, Marty Robins, for example, was a master of narrative songs. His classic, *El Paso,* tells the story of a cowboy's love for Felina who dances in a cantina.

But narratives are not simply entertainment. In education, a novel written by Jean Jacques Rousseau in 1762 , *Emile,* detailed how he would educate a child from infancy to adulthood. It is still in print and still read today. It begins with the sentence, "God makes all things good; man meddles with them and they become evil." The sentence sums up Rousseau's idea that 18th century European societies were corrupting the natural, inborn goodness of the citizenry, and the book lays out a plan for how to combat the undesirable effects of *civilization*. More recently the novel form has been used to communicate on socially relevant topics. Bebe Moore Campbell's (1995) novel, *Your Blues Ain't Like Mine,* is a good example. It is fiction based on the murder of Emmett Till, a young black man from Chicago who in 1955 was murdered in Mississippi while visiting his grandparents.

While the natural sciences (and the social sciences) have generally rejected the novel as a source of "knowledge" in the way an empirical study is a source of knowledge, several forms of postmodern thought have elevated narrative to a level equal to, or even superior to, other traditionally accepted forms of knowledge. Some theories of literature argue that narrative gives us a way of making sense of our lives that many other forms of knowledge do not. Because we are in the middle of living our lives, it is difficult for us to stand outside that life in order to understand it better. Stories are one way of "stepping outside" ourselves because we can identify with the characters and situations in the stories. When we do that, we begin to see ourselves through the narrative. Stories or narratives have been a way of communicating history and culture, and a way of understanding ourselves as well as the world we live in, at least since Homer's *Odyssey* and the *Iliad*. However, the story fell on hard times when modernism severely restricted our "acceptable" sources of knowledge and understanding. Modernism privileged more objective, structured, and "scientific" sources of knowledge, and it often relegated to the garbage bin of epistemology many very personal and subjective sources of knowledge such as stories. Bonnie Sunstein (2000) illustrated that with a story of her own:

> A few years ago, among the browned and dusty papers in my mother's storage cartons, I found an old report card. "Bonnie tells too many stories," my second grade teacher wrote in perfect 1950s cursive. "She is a smart girl, but she needs to stop telling stories and get to her real work." The remainder of my school years reflected this concern among my teachers and taught me that stories did not blend very well with the "real work" of school.
>
> As a new college student in a very selective Honors English 1 class at the University of Pittsburgh, I turned over the onionskin of my first weekly essay to view my professor's response. I'd read the assigned book, crafted an essay on my new graduation typewriter, and submitted the package with swollen freshman expectation and a fancy paper clip. "This is a narrative piece. Your mind wanders all over it. It is too creative; not a critical analysis of the work in question. This is not the business of an English class. D."
>
> More than three decades later, I've finally collected the knowledge and given myself the courage to recognize that my teachers may have been mistaken, that my "real work" is tied to telling stories. And for all those years, my "real work" has been, in fact, the "business of an English class." Despite my teachers' efforts to socialize me into the rules of school appropriateness, I've never been able to stop myself from telling stories and writing them—personal ones and professional ones, despite the humiliations they've afforded me. And I've never been able to stop listening and reading those of others. Stories have shaped my skills as a teacher, a writer, and a researcher. (p. ix)

Bonnie Sunstein is an English professor at the University of Iowa, and her story is an excellent example of the power of narrative, of storytelling. Today it is emerging as a powerful method of doing qualitative social science scholarship, and it is a very important thread of scholarship in education, though not very well established in educational technology. However, as Sunstein (p. xi-x) points, out, it has a history.

> Using narrative for learning is not a new idea; stories are essential to the human condition. Folklorists have long known that people use stories to both

teach and resist tradition, whatever their culture. Verbal art...and performance theory...are terms used in anthropology and sociology to describe the symbolic features of storytelling. Stories, like other cultural events, present and represent a culture of itself....Performance of verbal art invites participation in symbolic experience. (p. 461)

At the end of the 20th century the social sciences and education became interested in the use of narrative as both a form of inquiry and a form of communicating the results of scholarly study to others. My focus here will be on narrative as a form of inquiry in social science and education. There is a growing literature of narrative scholarship that deals with a wide range of topics in education. Reading some of that literature is one of the best ways to learn to do narrative inquiry. That is because there is no hard and fast set of rules on how to do narrative inquiry. For every rule you could make, someone else could point to examples in the scholarly literature of very successful narrative studies that violate that particular rule. As Clandinin and Connelly (2000) put it in their book on narrative inquiry, "Our approach is not so much to tell you what narrative inquiry is by defining it but rather to show you what it is by creating a definition contextually by recounting what narrative inquirers do" (p. xiii).

While showing is better than telling when it comes to teaching about narrative inquiry, there are some important theoretical foundations. For example, Iran-Nejad, McKeachie, and Berliner (1990) describe two approaches to scholarship in education. One is *simplification by isolation,* which is a foundation of positivist research. You keep everything constant except the one variable you want to study. This is a guiding assumption underlying much of the research in educational technology, but the authors argue that this has not worked. Often the result is research conducted in artificial environments on artificially constructed variables such as nonsense syllables. Iran-Nejad, McKeachie, and Berliner propose an alternative: scholarship based on *simplification by integration.* That is, instead of removing what we are interested in studying from the natural environment where it lives and develops, we should acknowledge that removing it breaks the critical connections it has with other aspects of that context. Removing it changes its nature and destroys the possibility of knowing it in the rich and multifaceted way that will be most useful. Work in the natural environment allows us to maintain those connections and to understand them. That conclusion leads us inevitably to the notion that narrative inquiry is a valuable method of research. Narrative inquiry is one of the major ways of doing the scholarship of *simplification by integration.*

Another foundation of narrative inquiry is the work of psychologist Donald Polkingborne. In his book, *Narrative Knowing and the Human Sciences* (1988), Polkingborne justifies narrative inquiry this way:

Narrative is the fundamental scheme for linking individual human actions and events into interrelated aspects of an understandable composite. For example, the action of a narrative scheme joins the two separate events "the father died" and "the son cried" into a single episode, "the son cried when his father died." Seeing the events as connected increases our understanding of them both—the son cares for his father, and the father's death pains the son. Narrative displays the significance that events have for one another. (p. 13)

Narrative as Method

While I have used examples of narrative from literature, such as novels, the fictional novel form is not often used in qualitative research. More often narrative scholarship is presented to readers in other forms—a case study, biography, autobiography, narrative ethnography based on observations in the field, and narrative papers based on the stories told by several teachers, students, or parents. It is somewhat confusing to say that the result of narrative inquiry is narrative, but it is nevertheless true. Narrative is both the name of a method of scholarship and the name of the results. "Narrative inquiry entails a reconstruction of a person's experience in relation to others and to a social milieu" (Clandinin & Connelly, 2000, p. 39). Here I will focus on narrative as inquiry, as method.

There are two very active communities of narrative research in education today. I will use the terms *Interpretive Narrative Inquiry* (INI) and Critical Narrative Inquiry (CNI) or *Counternarrative Inquiry.* Counternarrative is a term used to indicate people who write narratives are often trying to overcome and replace a more dominant narrative that defines them in ways they do not accept. These dominant narratives are sometimes called metanarratives because they exert control over members of a particular community or society. For example, in a culture with a strong metanarrative of male dominance and privilege, the metanarrative will influence not only the attitudes of men toward women but women toward themselves and their relationships to men.

There is no generally agreed upon term for these two families of narrative scholarship. Interpretive narrative inquiry (INI) is based on a foundation of interpretive theory that emphasizes the importance of the context, and multiple perspectives, in the search for meaning. Knowledge and knowing is local, relativistic, and social. One of the best introductions to this form of narrative scholarship is Clandenin and Connelly's (200) book, *Narrative Inquiry: Experience and Story in Qualitative Research.* It is based on scholarship in schools conducted primarily by teachers.

Critical Narrative Inquiry (CNI) or Counternarrative, is based on critical theory, especially standpoint theories in the critical tradition such as feminist inquiry. One of the best introductions to counternarrative in educational scholarship is Joy Ritchie and David Wilson's (2000) book, *Teacher Narrative as Critical Inquiry: Rewriting the Script.*

These two books both introduce narrative inquiry, both make heavy use of the work of the authors' students in colleges of education, and both believe narrative inquiry is a powerful way of both developing knowledge and of communicating the understandings developed to others. There are, however, a great many differences in the suggestions and guidelines these two books offer.

Reaction Against. There are times when what you are against is as important as what you are for. Sometimes it is *more* important. Both books are, to a greater or lesser extent, responding to what they see as limitations in the way both the scholarship of teaching, and teaching itself, is structured and organized. The Clandinin and Connelly book (which will be referred to as INI - for Interpretive Narrative Inquiry—from now on) responds to two restrictions—*reductionist thinking* and *formalistic boundaries.* Formalistic boundaries are restrictions on the way knowledge can be sought. Only some ways are sanctioned by formalists. "Formalists begin inquiry in theory, whereas narrative inquirers tend to begin with experience as expressed in lived and told stories. . . . Narrative inquiry characteristically begins with the researcher's autobiographically oriented narrative associated with the *research puzzle* (called by some the research problem or research question) . . . . The tension of the place of theory exists not only at the beginning of inquiry but throughout. . . . [Dissertation] committee members frequently wish theory to appear as a separate chapter, designed to structure the inquiry, identify gaps in the literature, outline principal theoretical lines of thought, and generate potential research possibilities. Our own narrative inquiry students, on the other hand, frequently write dissertations without a specific review chapter. They weave the literature throughout the dissertation from beginning to end in an attempt to create a seamless link between the theory and the practice embodied in the inquiry" (p. 40–41). INI opposes the idea that theory should be used as a "structuring framework" that guides the research. INI scholars prefer a structure that is more like a conversation, a story, a narrative. INI also rejects the idea that the proper outcome of inquiry will always be a contribution to a particular theory or to the implications of a particular theory for practice. The narrative result of inquiry "is more often intended to be the creation of a new sense of meaning and significance with respect to the research topic than it is to yield a set of knowledge claims that might incrementally add to knowledge in the field" (p. 42). Thus, "the narrative inquirer does not prescribe general applications and uses, but rather creates texts that, when well done, offer readers a place to imagine their own uses and applications" (p. 42). This is a very important guideline of INI - the responsibility for deciding what is helpful in a narrative is the job of the reader. It is a very different definition of both generalization and the process of generalizing from a study to professional practice than is typical of the model in positivist scholarship.

The other tradition that INI responds to is reductionism. Clandinin and Connelly distinguish between narratives and *grand narratives* or *metanarratives*. One definition of a metanarrative is something like critical theory, feminist theory, psychoanalysis, structuralism, postmodernism, and a hundred other paradigms that tell a scholar what to look at, what to expect, and how to interpret the data gathered. Though they accept this type of scholarship as legitimate, that is not what Clandinin and Connelly see as the goal of narrative inquiry:

> A person is a member of a race, a class, a gender, and may be said to have varying degrees of power in any situation. Part of the tension for a narrative inquirer is to acknowledge these truths while holding to a different research agenda. (p. 45)

The narratives of INI are thus the products of unique individuals rather than just examples of a female teacher, or a Black-American teacher in a suburban school, and so on. INI also opposes the reduction of the teaching process to the application of predefined rules (e.g., a *technical-rational* approach) and instead emphasizes reflective approaches to practice. This is another thing that sets INI scholars apart. They are not looking to tell stories that demonstrate how powerful any particular, prepackaged teaching approach is. Instead, their stories, their narratives, tend to illustrate how complex and convoluted the teaching and learning environment is, and how important it is for the teacher to make on-the-fly decisions about what to do next. Good practice is not so much following predefined rules; it is making good decisions based on a sophisticated understanding of the unique situation the teacher finds herself or himself in at the moment.

Ritchie and Wilson (2000) (which will be referred to as Critical Narrative Inquiry or CNI) see narrative inquiry in a very different way. They are also responding to two major trends they view as harmful, if not destructive, to education. One is positivism and the other is teaching methods based on behaviorism. Citing critical theorists of education like Michael Apple, Henry Giroux, Paulo Freire, and Donaldo Macedo, CNI takes for granted that "the practice of education in America is part of a larger social narrative that promotes a positivist ideology of knowledge, teaching, and learning, one that continues to conserve and reproduce the status quo" (p. 30). Not only does positivism support the undesirable inequalities of the status quo, it "presents knowledge as authoritative and 'given' and thus conceals the power relations in which it has been produced" (p. 31) while "progressive perspectives make the relationship between the knower and the known more visible and indeed part of the process of inquiry" (p. 31). Behavioral approaches to teaching and learning also contribute to the status quo and reduce teaching to a mechanical process. "Education programs in this country are dominated by an orientation that breaks learning into skills and then focuses on methods to teach mastery of those skills. . . . Despite reformist rhetoric and process pedagogies, little seems to have changed in many schools and classrooms. . . . Teaching is reduced to method, activity, and management: lecture, study guides, quizzes, worksheets, tests, grades, discipline" (pp. 36–37).

CNI's and INI's Agendas. As an antidote to behaviorism and positivism, CNI proposes a focus on "progressive reforms" "shaped by such varied perspectives as social constructionist, cognitive psychological, poststructuralist, critical, feminist, and cultural theory" (p. 31). While this is a relatively ecumenical list of alternatives, CNI is clearly focused on a foundation of critical theory. For example, CNI discusses the theories of Bakhtin on how competing ideologies presented in popular and professional culture influence and control the beliefs and attitudes of individuals. They then comment that "in our teaching each of us sought to acknowledge and work against ideological narratives surrounding masculinity and femininity, for example. Feminist and gay and lesbian rights issues . . . brought us to this political understanding" (p. 11). Overcoming positivism and behaviorism is the major negative goal of CNI's version of narrative inquiry. Put positively the goal is *transformation*. That is, the purpose of critical narrative inquiry is to help participants undergo a transformation that helps them (1) become aware of how detrimental theories like positivism and behaviorism have deceived them and (2) adopt more "progressive, student-centered, feminist, or critical paradigms" (p. 50). These goals are best accomplished through personal experiences like writing and sharing narratives.

The agenda of INI is less clear and more open. The stories of INI may include threads related to race, gender, and ethnic biases, but INI generally emphasizes the development of an understanding within a particular context and through a particular individual rather than from the standpoint of a group such as female teachers or African-American males in high school.

The Operating Framework. CNI sees teachers as coming to teacher education programs already having been influenced by the dominant ideologies of the culture. The authors talk about "dual apprenticeships" that represent "conflicting narratives." There is the *deliberate apprenticeship* that teacher education programs organize and provide to students planning to become teachers. (In their book, Ritchie & Wilson (2000) focused on a group of students preparing to be teachers of English.) But "there is another 'accidental' apprenticeship that plays a much more significant role in determining preservice teachers' understandings of writing, reading, and language learning; their understanding of themselves as teachers; and their visions of education. This other apprenticeship is longer, extending from preschool to young adulthood" (pp. 29–30). In the CNI framework, the *deliberate apprenticeship* is an effort to use narrative writing and other experiences in college to bring about a transformation in students that involves the adoption of the theoretical perspective the authors feel is most appropriate (e.g., against positivism and behaviorism; for progressive education, postmodern perspectives, and critical theory). The conflicting narratives of the accidental apprenticeships that children and adults experience may expose them to some aspects of the preferred approach, but they are, for the most part, anchored in competing ideologies. "Powerful cultural and personal narratives surround prospective teachers and shape their emerging identities as teachers.... In fact, the accidental apprenticeship is no accident. It is only accidental to teacher education. It is not accidental in the culture; it's part of an ideology of regulation and control, part of our socialization in very specific epistemologies and discourses surrounding schooling and literacy....A 'good' teacher is a veritable warrior for standards, order, and control, and a self-sacrificing saint. This and other similar caricatures project contradictory visions of teaching that our [teacher education] students clearly have internalized" (p. 33–34).

The framework for INI is quite different. Yet the differences are often more in degree of emphasis than in foundational differences. For example, INI also views narrative inquiry as a means of professional transformation and change. INI scholars use Donald Schön's ideas of *reflection in action* and *knowing in action* to emphasize this point. INI rejects the idea that all professional or practical knowledge is "technical" (or *techne* to use Aristotle's term). Instead INI's concept of professional practice knowledge is much closer to Aristotle's *phronesis*. It is less certain, and more context driven than techne, but less authoritative than episteme.

CNI tends to see personal narratives as ways of relating metanarratives and theories to personal practice. INI tends to look at narrative as an expression of the uniqueness of the individual and the context. INI goes not put a high value on the goal of linking metanarratives to personal narratives. "One of the ever-present and strongest tensions is how to understand the place of people in inquiry. One of the simplest ways of saying this is that in formalist inquiry, people are looked at as exemplars of a form—of an idea, a theory, a social category. In narrative inquiry, people are looked at as embodiments of lived stories. Even when narrative inquirers study institutional narratives, such as stories of school, people are seen as composing lives that shape, and are shaped by social and cultural narratives" (p. 43).

INI is much less focused on the ideas of power and control than CNI. They are there in the stories told by INI scholars, but they do not play the dominant role they do in CNI. For INI scholars narrative inquiry is a means of developing understanding of the lived world. That understanding can be shared with others. It is a process that informs and enlightens those who do narrative inquiry, but in INI a major goal is also to share findings with a broader community. CNI, as expressed in the Ritchie and Wilson book, is primarily shared with a group of like-minded colleagues who provide support and encouragement to each other. When the narratives are shared with wider audiences the goal is often to help that audience learn how to do CNI in their own setting.

CNI's use of the idea of two apprenticeships as an organizational framework helps focus on the way competing metanarratives influence and control individuals. INI uses a different organizational framework to further the goal of emphasizing the uniqueness of individuals and contexts. The INI research framework is "the *three-dimensional narrative inquiry space* and the 'directions' this framework allows our inquiries to travel—*inward, outward, backward, forward,* and *situated within place*" (p. 49). Figure 9.4 illustrates this narrative inquiry space graphically:

As illustrated in Figure 9.4, when narrative inquirers do their work Clandinin and Connelly suggest they keep three dimensions in mind. One is the *Interactive Space* which is anchored on one end by inward focused concerns

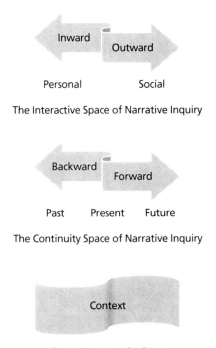

Figure 9.4   The Three-dimensional narrative inquiry space.

such as "feelings, hopes, aesthetic reactions, and moral dispositions" (p. 50) and on the other by the interactions between individuals and groups (the social, or as the authors put it, "toward the existential conditions, that is the environment" (p. 50)). Another dimension is *Continuity Space,* which deals with time—past, present, and future. The third inquiry space which I will call *context,* but the authors refer to as *place,* is the social, cultural, and physical environment in which the story being told takes place.

In INI, the three-dimensional narrative inquiry space serves a number of functions:

- It provides "directions or avenues" that can be pursued in narrative inquiry. All narrative inquiry must consider all of the spaces, but different studies will have different patterns of emphasis.
- "We might imagine the terms as an analytic frame for reducing the stories to a set of understandings" (p. 53). This is another way the concept of inquiry space helps scholars organize their work.
- "We could think of them [the inquiry spaces] not so much as generating a list of understandings achieved by analyzing the stories, but rather as pointing to questions, puzzles, fieldwork, and field texts of different kinds appropriate to different aspects of the inquiry" (pp. 54–55).

While Clandinin and Connelly acknowledge that the first two functions are useful, they emphasize the third. INI work generally means a scholar spends a great deal of time in the field. They arrive *in the midst* of their lives and the "participants also enter the inquiry field in the midst of living their stories. Their lives do not begin the day we arrive nor do they end as we leave. Their lives continue. Furthermore, the places in which they live and work, their classrooms, their schools, and their communities, are also in the midst when we researchers arrive. Their institutions and their communities, their landscapes in the broadest sense, are also in the midst of stories" (p. 75). Clandinin and Connelly criticize "blitzkrieg ethnography" that involves a quick foray into the field, because it does not get beyond the surface of issues. Instead, they argue that "it is being in the field, day after day, year after year, that brought forth a compelling sense of the long-term landscape narratives at work. This too is one of the things that narrative inquirers do in the field: they settle in, live and work alongside participants, and come to experience not only what can be seen and talked about directly but also the things not said and not done that shape the narrative structure of their observations and their talking" (p. 67–68). Being in the field involves many ongoing actions and responsibilities—negotiating relationships, negotiating purposes, negotiating transitions, especially entry and exit; "negotiating a way to be useful" (p. 75), and "getting a feel for it" (p. 76).

The idea of finding a way to be useful requires some comment. Critics of INI often focus on the assertion that the inquirer co-opts the voice of the participants. Clandinin and Connelly believe the opposite is often true— the inquirer becomes so much the "voice" of the participants that "the narrative inquirer may feel silenced and voiceless on matters about which he or she feels passionate" (p. 75). The process of negotiating how to be useful (e.g., helping participants acquire their "voice") can be difficult.

Being in the field also involves finding places where the inquirer can communicate and exchange ideas with a supportive group. "We encourage narrative inquirers to establish response communities, ongoing places where they can give accounts of their developing work over time. As the explaining takes place, clarification and shaping of purpose occurs" (p. 73).

The primary interest of INI "is the growth and transformation in the life story that we as researchers and our participants author. . . . We imagine, therefore, that in the construction of narratives of experience, there is a reflexive relationship between living a life story, telling a life story, retelling a life story, and reliving a life story" (p. 71). This rather fuzzy but useful explanation of INI distinguishes it from simply going into the field and conducting a set of interviews that are tape recorded and then transcribed for presentation to readers. INI is not that. "Through the reflexive process of interpreting and understanding the lived experiences of participants and ourselves, INI adds value to the literal, unexamined stories told through raw interview transcripts. "Narrative inquiry is much more than 'look for and hear story.' Narrative inquiry in the field is a form of living, a way of life. . . . [It is a way] of trying to make sense of life as lived. . . . One may observe a teacher in a classroom and count the number of student utterances and the number of teacher utterances or any sophisticated version of kinds of utterances one might be interested in. But the narrative inquirer hardly knows what to make of this without knowing the narrative threads at work. Those narrative threads are complex and difficult to disentangle" (p. 78). This requires the development of positive and caring relationships between the inquirer and the participants. Clandinin and Connelly even talk about "falling in love" to distinguish INI from "cool observation." "Narrative inquiry is relational. [Inquirers] must become fully involved, must 'fall in love' with their participants, yet they must also step back and see their own stories in the inquiry, the stories of the participants, as well as the larger landscape on which they all live" (p. 81).

The Process of Inquiry. INI is not a process of structured, preplanned data gathering to test a hypothesis where "the researcher is in charge" (p. 76). Instead, an INI "researcher tends to be at the other end of the continuum from the controlled-plot hypothesis tester. Here, the researchers enters a landscape and joins an ongoing professional life. One thing that narrative inquirers do is quickly learn that even if they are familiar with the kind of landscape—perhaps even members of that landscape, as teachers on sabbatical doing a thesis might be—there is a great deal of *taken-for-grantedness* at work in the moment-by-moment relationships and happenings on the landscape" (p. 76). INI requires being involved and engaged in the field for an extended period—long enough to work through and past our taken-for-granted assumptions that defined what we see, and long enough to become "a sensitive reader of and questioner of situations in an effort to grasp the huge number of events and stories, the many twisting and turning narrative threads that pulse through every moment and show up in what appears to the new and inexperienced eyes of a researcher as mysterious code" (p. 77).

The primary means of moving from mysterious code to understanding, while being in the field, is what Clandinin and Connelly call *field texts*. While in the field the inquirer writes extensively about the experience. Writing is part of the process of experiencing, reflecting, and growing. "The inquirer scribbles in a notebook, dictates into a Dictaphone, or types onto a screen a flood of descriptively oriented field experience observations. These are a mixture of you and me, the participant and researcher—notes on what you did, notes on what I did with you, notes on what was around us, notes on where we were, notes on feelings, notes on current events, notes on remembrances of past times" (p. 83). These field texts become a core of data that help you remember, reflect, and reconstruct when you move from writing field texts to writing a narrative for readers who will learn from your work. "Field texts help fill in the richness, nuance, and complexity of the landscape, returning the reflecting researcher to a richer, more complex, and puzzling landscape than memory alone is likely to construct" (p. 83). However, INI does not view field texts as truths. INI does not view them as totally relative either, with the implication that "all have their own interpretation of events and each is equally valid" (p. 85). While field texts cannot be trusted to be "the truth" in any absolute sense, they are valuable guides to developing understanding. "Mere relativism will not do. Field texts need to be kept and continually referenced by narrative inquirers" (p. 86). Field texts often typically contain two general types of data—descriptions of inner experiences such as "feelings, doubts, uncertainties, reactions, remembered stories and so on" (p. 86) and "notes that record the existential, outward events" (p. 87).

While field texts are critical to INI, there is no prescribed format for them. They can take many forms, "teacher stories; autobiographical writing; journal writing; field notes; letters; conversation, research interviews; family stories; documents; photographs; memory boxes; and other personal-family-social artifacts; and life experience - all of which can make valuable field texts" (p. 93). However, regardless of the form, "all field texts are inevitably interpretive texts" (p. 94); we never come face to face with the un-interpreted and pure "truth of the matter."

INI's approach to data analysis and to moving from field text to "research texts" that will be disseminated to others as the outcome of INI is a flexible process in which art and on-the-fly decision making plays a more important role than prescribed formats, rigid structures, and inviolable rules.

I will turn now to the process of doing CNI. There are many differences in the way INI and CNI approach and do narrative inquiry. Both see narrative inquiry as a way of producing change and transformation, but INI is more focused on developing an understanding of a particular lived experience. That lived experience may be the experience of an individual, a group, or an organization, but the emphasis is on understanding, or *verstehen* to use the German word often used by hermeneuticists. CNI, on the other hand, is more focused on using narrative inquiry to foster and support transformation.

In fact, CNI does not really separate inquiry from action and change. It thoroughly integrates them and views the creation of narratives as a very important part of the process of teacher change and transformation. CNI tends to use excerpts from the written narratives of teachers to illustrate major points or generalizations. For example, the Ritchie and Wilson book includes a long narrative written by a lesbian teacher about how she gradually began to develop ways of dealing with sexual orientation in her English classes. One section of the narrative tells a story about one of the books her high school students were reading that semester—Fannie Flagg's *Fried Green Tomatoes at the Whistle Stop Café*:

> One day Lori came up to me, breathless, shouting, "Ruth and Idgie were lesbians, weren't they?" She said that Sandy [a student the teacher thought was lesbian but not yet ready to accept it] didn't think they were, but she did. I went with Lori to find Sandy, and we talked about possibilities. Could the two main characters have been lesbians? What is a lesbian? There were no sex scenes between the two women in the book; were there other things about Ruth and Idgie and their relationship we could look at to answer the question? We talked about it for about 20 minutes.
>
> Afterward I wondered what I would have said if I had read *Fried Green Tomatoes* when I was in high school. I would have had absolutely no context for even questioning whether Ruth and Idgie were lesbians. I was glad that I had the chance to help provide some of that context for Sandy and Lori. (p. 165)

As used in the book, this passage is an example of how a teacher used storytelling or narrative to work through her beliefs and ideas. However, the preservice and practicing teachers who write the narratives are using them for something different. The process of writing the narrative is an action that can lead to growth and development. CNI takes the position that when we write narratives, share them in a supportive group, and are encouraged to think about them, narratives are a powerful path to development. "As teachers and scholars, we value the material, experiential, local, daily lived experience; we believe that attention to practice is important" (p. 14). CNI does not stop there, however. Writing narratives about experience is not enough. Experience, "whether in our personal lives or in our classrooms—does not provide us with 'authentic' uncontested truth. All experience is interpreted, valued, and felt through particular perspectives" (p. 15). Then CNI moves to a core issue that separates it from INI. "The problematic relationship between theory and experience/practice has also remained a constant question in this study. In academic circles over the past decade, theory has often held a privileged position over experience or pedagogy in literacy and English studies, and too much attention to experience has been demeaned for its lack of critical rigor. . . . Our study has helped us see how this binary [theory versus practice] also shapes the dilemmas that arise for students and teacher educators. It has become more crucial for us to attempt to establish a reciprocal, dialogic relationship between theory and experience in the opportunities we attempt to provide our students. The problem is not that experience—either in the accidental apprenticeship or the deliberate apprenticeship in teacher education . . .—is too personal or local, and therefore invalid. The problem is that experience is often left un-theorized. Without the opportunity for critical analysis of experience, teachers and students have no way to see how their experience is itself constructed in and through language and through institutional and cultural ideologies. Indeed, it is a central premise of this book that the reconstruction and reconsideration of experience through narrative is crucial for teachers to achieve critical literacy" (p. 15). CNI goes on to argue that a theoretical language is necessary. For example, one of the teachers whose narrative is in the book "needed the authoritative language of theory to critique the authoritative theories that attempted to shape her pedagogy as a beginning teacher, just as she needed feminist theories to help her critique the narratives that situated her as a female in the culture. (p. 15). Therefore, "it is when experience is theorized and scrutinized that it can become an important source of knowledge about teaching" (p. 68).

CNI thus situates narrative in a larger process that involves learning and using metanarratives like feminist theory to interpret and act on personal narratives. The CNI book was based on work at the University of Nebraska—Lincoln. That program for English teachers was designed to provide students with experiences, theories, and many opportunities for writing and sharing their narratives in a supportive environment of fellow students and faculty. One of the reasons for emphasizing the theory-practice link was the danger "that students continued to believe in an autonomous, unified self" (p. 51). It was important that students "acknowledge that their experience and even their reading, or writing of a text are also shaped by their histories in particular social and political contexts, by their race, gender, and social class" (p. 51).

Unfortunately, when Ritchie and Wilson followed up their graduates as they left the university and entered the teaching profession, they found the transformation they sought to encourage in their students was often incomplete—students seemed able to think and teach like behaviorists one week and like progressive, student-centered teachers the next, without seeing the contradictions inherent in that. And, even when the transformation seemed complete at graduation, teachers who took jobs in schools where the norms were positivist and behavioral often slipped back into patterns of teaching and relating to students they would have rejected outright when they graduated from the teacher education program. Ritchie and Wilson (pp. 53, 61, 65) came up with a number of reasons why this might happen:

- Many of our students' formal educations had been devoid of successful mutual, collaborative, "conversational" learning.
- Students had been given few—generally no—opportunities to reflect on and question their educations or the status quo of their lives.
- Without ongoing critical dialogues between their old and new assumptions . . . their new assumptions could not become fully transformative. . . . Genuinely transformative knowledge would be critical and reflexive about what seemed 'given' and natural in our students' experience
- Their education had not taught them to be critical consumers who might ask: For what purpose are personal narratives being used? How do these stories function in a given context? What is its intended effect on listeners or readers. . . . We were hoping that students would be able to make more carefully examined distinctions and build learning theories and pedagogies based on close, critical examination and dialogue between competing assumptions about learning.
- We also began to understand the powerful pull of socialization, of the ways in which the culture of school and community can undermine even well-crafted and examined beliefs.

The result was that "rather than revising their understanding of teaching, learning, and literacy, our students were often merely adding on new, alternative notions to their existing, and often unexamined, assumptions, and they did so with little apparent sense of tension or conflict" (p. 55). To be effective as a transformative process, narrative inquiry needs to be, from the critical perspective of Ritchie and Wilson:

- Part of a long-term process that includes opportunities to share narratives with supporting colleagues, and to analyze and critique both personal narratives and those of others through the lens of appropriate theories,
- Develop caring and loving relationships with others who constitute groups where you are a valued "insider,"
- Use marginalization and an "outsider" position as a foundation for resisting the hegemony of the dominant values of school and society.

The theory underlying this approach has a number of important assumptions:

- As stories are shared, examined, and critiqued they become "a lens through which to examine" classroom practice, "to reflect on the experiences" of students and the teacher's efforts to "resist and revise the conservative socializing narratives" encountered in a typical teaching situation. "Carol's [one of the teachers featured in CNI) own storytelling allowed her to bring together reflection and critique of her personal life and her professional life. Rather than being locked into the murmured stories and scripts that constrained her personal and professional identities, Carol used her examined experience to resist and rewrite earlier scripts and stories that had defined her, thus redefining herself" (p. 87).
- "Narratives like those that Carol composed and recomposed, create multiple potential meanings and even contradictions, and therefore create spaces for rethinking and resisting old interpretations. In this process, Carol came to understand that 'there are other ways,' that therefore there is no single answer" (p. 87).
- "The scripting power of ideology is never unified or absolute. Individual identity is never singular. There are 'gaps' and discontinuities in the ideologies that control us and define us. "And [through] exposure to these gaps ... [transformation] becomes possible in the moment when the individual begins to name her own experience, to interpret it in relationship to wider cultural/political narratives. This process makes possible the recognition that cultural narratives about who one ought to be and how one might live are not monolithic or homogeneous. When individuals begin to see the multiple and often conflicting nature of those narratives, it becomes possible to hold them up to scrutiny to resist them, to break their hold over us" (p. 88).
- Traditional approaches to explaining and understanding teaching and learning tend to "compartmentalize knowledge", to depersonal-

ize it, and to disconnect it from the lives of teachers and students. What is needed is a more holistic and integrated way of understanding that combines personal and professional experience, theory and metanarratives, and critical reflection. "Instead of taking on what Bakhtin (1981) calls 'authoritative discourse,' accommodating themselves to the critical perspectives of authoritative critics, theorists, or university professors and teachers, [preservice teacher education] students were being asked to set their own 'internally persuasive' narratives in dialog with theoretical narratives of teaching and learning. As we watched this occur, we began to see more clearly that the convergence of narrative experiences had the potential of providing preservice and practicing teachers with ongoing opportunities for critical reflection that could help them resist and revise confining narratives of teaching and learning. Theory and practice are not decontextualized abstractions; students were enacting and critiquing them in tandem" (p. 88–89).

- "Simply 'having theories' is not enough. Nor is blind action useful. What is necessary is reflection and action." This can be done "with narrative as a critical practice linking reflection and action in the communities that [participants] help to sustain through their participation" (p. 89).

For Joy Ritchie and David Wilson, critical narrative inquiry is primarily a means of emancipating those engaged in the narrative process from the restrictions and controlling influences of ideologies that are deeply embedded in the culture of society and the culture of school. It is an example of the general approach of critical theorists to emancipation that involves two steps:

- Developing awareness and then overthrowing the false beliefs and ideologies that control us and cause us to restrict ourselves through the "false consciousness" they create in us. "Groups often actively maintain and nurture beliefs and practices that oppress them and support those in power over them" (Willis, 2007, p. 232).
- The second phase of the emancipatory process is praxis. This involves using the understanding that has developed to "overcome the oppression and develop a fairer and more equitable social structure; the process of making that change is called praxis" (p. 232).

While the use of narrative as a "therapeutic" or emancipatory process is an important concept in CNI, the narratives created by participants can also become part of an effort to help others learn from what happened in a particular context. For example, a teacher or group of teachers may include excerpts from their narratives in a paper or book written for others to read. This is "storytelling" at another level where the goal is still emancipation but of others who have not been a part of the story being told. Also, a narrative scholar may use the narratives of several teachers (or students or parents) in a narrative paper or book to tell the story of a particular effort at emancipation and empowerment. Thus, as a part of Critical Narrative Inquiry, narrative can be both the "treatment" and the means of communicating the results of "treatment."

CNI or INI?

There are major differences in the way narrative inquiry is conducted from a critical versus an interpretive perspective and there is certainly room for both approaches in the scholarship of education as well as educational technology. However, both critical and interpretive approaches put a premium value on developing stories, narratives, of life and work in the context of education. Narrative, which was relegated to a secondary or inferior role in the scholarship of education for much of the 20th century, is emerging in the 21st century as a valid and desirable way of knowing. Deciding to do narrative inquiry is a major step; deciding whether to use a critical or an interpretive framework for your narrative inquiry will probably depend on the paradigm you prefer and on your purpose for doing the research.

POSTSTRUCTURALIST SCHOLARSHIP

At the beginning of this chapter Figure 9.3 presented an orderly way of thinking about the methods of humanities research. From the humanities, three families of methods emerged: hermeneutic inquiry, narrative inquiry, and poststructuralist inquiry. Both hermeneutic methods and narrative inquiry have been explored in some detail. Also, in a somewhat disorderly way, I have already explored aspects of poststructuralism. Poststructuralism is one component of the general postmodern trend toward doubting that many of the Truths proposed by modernist methods of scholarship in the social sciences are really universals. Poststructuralists may still look for patterns, structures, and organizing frameworks but they are not likely to accept Freud's division of the mind into Id, Ego, and Superego as a universal. Rather, poststructuralists are much more likely to think of any organizing structure, typology, or categorical scheme as a construction of creative humans who were influenced by their culture, their context, and their purposes. Structuralism becomes poststructuralism when postmodern skepticism is added to the intellectual foundations and the result is a healthy skepticism about anything proposed as universal and eternally true.

A second poststructuralist method, deconstruction, has also been discussed in the section on literary theory. It also emphasizes the skeptical characteristic of postmodernism because postmodernists doubt the truth value of any type of proposed structure or pattern that purports to explain or define the basic nature of cultural or social life. Even when an author intends to convey a particular message to readers, deconstructionists are likely to find competing and conflicting messages in the author's work.

The third poststructuralist approach, *poststructuralist feminist theory,* involves applying the skeptical values of postmodernism, and the rejection of universal frameworks, to issues specifically related to the lives of women:

> The post-structuralist feminist group denies any possibility of defining "woman" at all. Any attempt at definition (whether it comes from a misogynist male, a cultural feminist, or anyone really) is impossible without, according to post-structuralist thinking, reinvoking "mechanisms of oppressive power". For post-structuralist theorists, the idea of a subject being some basic anything is dependent on prevailing discourses that construct us creatures this way or that way, even to the point of constructing us in such a way as to have us believe we are in control—that (for many today "infamous") autonomous, coherent subject that is the product (construct) of humanist discourses. (McMahon, 2003)

Thus, when postmodern skepticism is applied to women's studies to combat efforts to define in any universal way what it is to be woman, that is feminist poststructuralism. It is one example of how poststructuralist theory can influence virtually any standpoint theory.

IN SUMMARY, HUMANITIES RESEARCH METHODS IN EDUCATIONAL TECHNOLOGY

In this chapter I have introduced three families of scholarly methods from the humanities: hermeneutics, narrative inquiry, and poststructuralist inquiry. In each, there are at least two subfamilies of related methods, one based on critical theory and one based on interpretive theory. The extended discussion of narrative inquiry from the critical and interpretive perspectives illustrates the application of these two frameworks to scholarship in general. In education, there are examples of scholarship based on all three of the families discussed in this chapter, and both critical and interpretive paradigms are regularly used as guiding frameworks.

The use of humanities research methods in educational technology is not, however, so common as in the general field of education. As a field we remain closely linked to positivist epistemologies and to natural science methods of research and scholarship. How can the methods of poststructuralist feminist theory, for example, be applied to important instructional technology research questions? And, perhaps even more important, how might poststructuralist feminist theory change the types of questions that are considered important in educational technology research? These an similar questions must be asked about all the forms of humanities research presented in this chapter. The questions are very difficult to answer because we are just beginning to think seriously about how the methods and the questions of humanities research can be applied in the field of educational technology. To help you explore those options, the readings for this chapter are exemplars of the way these methods have already been used in our field. By reading the papers carefully you will see how the theoretical frameworks, the methods, and the data analysis procedures of the humanities can be applied to the field of educational technology. This chapter was written in 2008. By 2028 I believe the use of research methods from the humanities will be much more commonplace in educational technology. Perhaps some of your scholarship will be in that literature.

REFERENCES

Bakhtin, M. M. (1981). *The dialogic imagination* (C. Emerson & M. Holquist, Trans.). Austin: University of Texas Press. (Original work published in Russian in 1975).

Bressler, C. (2007). *Literary criticism: An introduction to theory and practice, 4th ed.* Upper Saddle River, NJ: Pearson Prentice Hall.

Bronner, S. (1998). *Following tradition: Folklore in the discourse of American culture.* Logan, Utah: Utah State University Press.

Campbell, B. (1995). *Your blues ain't like mine.* New York: One World/Ballantine.

Gadamer, H.-G. (2004). *Truth and method,* 2nd revised ed. New York: Continuum.

Harding, S. (1993). Rethinking Standpoint Epistemology: What is "Strong Objectivity"?" In L. Alcoff & E. Potter (Eds.). *Feminist epistemologies* (49–82). New York: Routledge.

Iran-Nejad, A., McKeachie, W., & Berliner, D. (1990). The multisource nature of learning: An introduction. *Review of Educational Research, 60* (4), 509–515.

McGee, M. (1998). Phronesis in the Gadamer versus Habermas debates. In J. Sloop & J. McDaniel, (Eds.). *Judgment calls: Rhetoric, politics, and indeterminancy* (pp. 13–41). Boulder, CO: Westview Press.

McMahon, M. (2003). Cultural and post-structuralist feminism. Retrieved May 28, 2007 from http://webpages.ull.es/users/mmcmahon/textos/feminisms.htm

Richards, S., Taylor, R., Ramasamy, R., & Richards, R. (1998). *Single-subject research applications in educational and clinical settings.* Belmont, CA: Wadsworth.

Ritchie, J. & Wilson, D. (2000). *Teacher narrative as critical inquiry: Rewriting the script.* New York: Teachers College Press.

Suarez, V. (2000). *Hispanic American literature: Divergence and commonality.* Retrieved May 26, 2007 from http://usinfo.state.gov/journals/itsv/0200/ijse/latino1.htm

Sunstein, B. (2000). Foreword. In J. Ritchie and D. Wilson (2000). *Teacher narrative as critical inquiry* (ix–xii). New York: Teachers College Press.

READINGS FOR CHAPTER 9

All the readings for Chapter 9 are illustrations of how methods and concepts from the humanities can be applied to important questions in the area of educational technology. There are examples of hermeneutic research, narrative inquiry, and poststructuralism. There is also a paper on how Aristotle's concept of phronesis can serve as the theoretical foundation for pedagogical reflection.

These are only a few of the growing number of papers on educational technology that use methods from the humanities. In fact, the most creative and innovative applications of humanities methods in our field are probably in our future. As a field, educational technology has not yet paid much attention to the types of questions humanities research can address. Methods from the humanities promise to enlighten many of the traditional areas of scholarship in educational technology *and* open up new and important topics to careful study. As you read these papers consider how the research methods might be used to explore other questions in the field of educational technology. For each method, write a concept paper, about a half a page in length, that describes how the method could be used to study a question that interests you.

Reading 9.1: Hermeneutic Dialog (Conversation)

Tella, S., & Mononen-Aaltonen, M. (1998). *Developing dialogic communication culture in media education: Integrating dialogism and technology.* Media Education Publications #7. Available: http://www.helsinki.fi/~tella/mep7.html

Reading 9.2: Hermeneutic Phenomenology

Robinson, P. (2000). The body matrix: A phenomenological exploration of student bodies online. *Educational Technology & Society, 3*(3). Available: http://ifets.massey.ac.nz/periodical/vol_3_2000/c05.html

Reading 9.3: Interpretive Phenomenology and Hermeneutics

Conroy, S. A. (2003). A pathway for interpretive phenomenology. International Journal of Qualitative Methods, 2(3), Article 4. Available from http://www.ualberta.ca/~iiqm/backissues/2_3final/pdf/conroy.pdf

Reading 9.4: Deconstruction

Dwight, J. (2001). *Looking for the hype in hypertext: An essay deconstructing pedagogical assumptions associated with online learning and instructional design.* ERIC Document # ED470131. Available: http://eric.ed.gov/ERICWebPortal/custom/portlets/recordDetails/detailmini.jsp?_nfpb=true&_&ERICExtSearch_SearchValue_0=ED470131&ERICExtSearch_SearchType_0=eric_accno&accno=ED470131

Reading 9.5: Poststructuralism

Foley, A., & Voithofer, R. (2003). Bridging the gap? Reading the No Child Left Behind Act against Educational Technology Discourses. Available: http://education.osu.edu/rvoithofer/papers/nclb.pdf

Reading 9.6: Narrative Inquiry

Hung, D., Looi, C.-K., & Koh, T.-S. (2004). Situated cognition and communities of practice: First-person "lived experiences" vs. third-person perspectives. *Educational Technology & Society, 7* (4), 193–200.

Reading 9.7: Narratives and Cases

Bearman, M. (1998). *Narratives and cases: Implications for computer-based education.* Paper presented at the 1997 ASCILITE Conference. Available: http://www.ascilite.org.au/conferences/perth97/papers/Bearman/Bearman.html

Reading 9.8: Narrative Analysis

Peters, M., & Hume, W. (2003). Educational futures: Utopias and heterotopias. *Policy Futures in Education, 1*(3). Available: http://www.wwwords.co.uk/pdf/viewpdf.asp?j=pfie&vol=1&issue=3&year=2003&article=1_Editorial_PFIE_1_3_web&id=68.11.168.36

Reading 9.9: Phronesis and Reflection

Birmingham, C. (September/October, 2004). Phronesis: A model for pedagogical reflection. *Journal of Teacher Education, 55*(4), 313–324.

CHAPTER 10

THE METHODS OF
PHILOSOPHICAL INQUIRY

The word philosophy comes from the Greek word *philosophia* (φιλοσοφα) which means "love of wisdom" or "love of knowledge." Over the centuries there are been many forms of philosophical inquiry. One useful way of thinking about philosophical inquiry is to think about its purpose. Core concerns over the ages have been (1) what it means to be "good" (ethics), (2) what really exists (metaphysics and ontology), and (3) how we can come to know something as well as what knowing itself is (epistemology). Beginning with Aristotle, another aspect of philosophy has been (4) the search for reliable principles for thinking (logic). All four of these purposes for doing philosophical inquiry are relevant to scholarship in education and educational technology. Although they have not been the focus of many educational technology publications the questions of ethics, metaphysics and ontology, epistemology, and logic have been, and continue to be, serious topics in the field. Positions on these topics have more often been assumed and implicitly accepted than explicitly discussed and debated.

Qualitative Research Methods in Education and Educational Technology, pages 297–314
Copyright © 2008 by Information Age Publishing
　　　　　　297

ARCHIE AND ARCHIE'S APPROACH
TO PHILOSOPHICAL INQUIRY

I have based some of the format for my treatment of philosophical inquiry on the work of Lee Archie and John Archie (2004) who are writing *Reading for Philosophical Inquiry: A Brief Introduction to Philosophical Thinking.*

Archie and Archie are using an open source format that allows anyone to go to their web site (http://www.lander.edu/intro/introbook2.1/book1. html) and download the book's chapters. Readers are also encouraged to comment on the text and to submit any errors they find to the authors. It is thus a "work in progress" that is continuously being revised and updated. Of interest to educational technologists is that the files for the book are formatted using the Open Source DocBook schema. DocBook is available for several formats including XML and is an effort to provide authors with a predetermined structure that includes virtually all the common, and un-common, elements of a book. DocBook is not like the templates in Micro-soft Word, for example, that define a Heading in specific terms—such as "Centered, Bold, 18 point type, Times New Roman, with 20 points of space above and 16 points of space below." Instead, DocBook defines material by the role it plays in the book (e.g., author name, title, and so on). DocBook is thus a level of abstraction above that of the formats in a Word template. Because of that, DocBook can be used to format the document differently for different media. For example, it allows the document to be displayed on the screen of a cell phone, produced in printed form, or displayed on a computer monitor. A Word template cannot do this because it "hardwires" the display characteristics of different elements in a book. If a heading were printed in 18 point type, for example, a few letters would fill the screen of a cell phone. DocBook was designed to support the use of different display options. If you would like more information on DocBook, see the website http://www.docbook.org.

Archie and Archie (2004) use a simulated conversation to explain what philosophical inquiry is all about:

> One reasonably good beginning characterization of philosophy is that phi-losophy is the sustained inquiry into the principles and presuppositions of any field of inquiry. As such, philosophy is not a subject of study like other subjects of study. Any given field of inquiry has philosophical roots and ex-tensions. From the philosophy of restaurant management to philosophy of physics, philosophy can be characterized as an attitude, an approach, or per-haps, even a calling, to ask, answer, or even just comment upon certain kinds of questions. These questions involve the nature, scope, and boundaries of that field of interest. In general, then, philosophy is both an activity involving thinking about these kinds of ultimate questions and an activity involving the

construction of sound reasons or insights into our most basic assumptions about the universe and our lives.

Quite often, simply asking a series of "why-questions" can reveal these basic presuppositions. Children often ask such questions, sometimes to the annoyance of their parents, in order to get a feel for the way the world works. Asking an exhaustive sequence of "why-questions" can reveal principles upon which life is based. As a first example, let us imagine the following dialogue between two persons as to why one of them is reading this philosophy book. Samantha is playing "devil's advocate."

> **Samantha:** Why are you reading *Reading for Philosophical Inquiry*?
> **Stephen:** It's an assigned book in philosophy, one of my college courses.
> **Samantha:** Why take philosophy?
> **Stephen:** Well, philosophy fulfills the humanities elective.
> **Samantha:** Why do you need that elective?

At this point in the dialog, a growing resemblance to the insatiable curiosity of some children is beginning to be unmistakable. We continue with the cross-examination.

> **Stephen:** I have to fulfill the humanities elective in order to graduate.
> **Samantha:** Why do you want to graduate?
> **Stephen:** What? Well, I'd like to get a decent job which pays a decent salary.
> **Samantha:** Well, why, then, do you want that?

Undoubtedly, at this point, the conversation seems artificial because for some persons, the goal of graduating college is about as far as they have thought their life through, if, indeed, they have thought that far—and so for such persons this is where the questioning would have normally stopped. Other persons, however, can see beyond college to more basic ends such as Stephen's want of an interesting vocation with sufficient recompense, among other things. Even so, we have not yet arrived at the kind of basic presuppositions we have been talking about for Stephen's life, so we continue with Samantha's questioning.

> **Stephen:** What do you mean? A good job which pays well will enable me the resources to have an enjoyable life where I can do some of the important things I want to do.
> **Samantha:** Why do you want a life like that?
> **Stephen:** Huh? Are you serious?

When questions finally seem to make no sense, very often, we have reached one of those ultimate fundamental unquestioned assumptions. In this case, a basic principle by which Stephen lives his life seems to be based on seeking happiness. So, in a sense, although he might not be aware of it at the moment, he believes he is working toward this goal by reading this textbook. Of course, his choice of a means to obtain happiness could be mistaken or perhaps even chosen in ignorance—in which case he might not be able to obtain what he wants out of life. If the thought occurs to you that it is sometimes the case that we might not be mistaken about our choices and might actually be choosing knowledgeably and even so might not achieve what we desire, then you are already doing philosophy.

If we assume that Samantha is genuinely asking questions here and has no ulterior motive, then it is evident that her questions relate to a basic presupposition upon which Stephen is basing his life. Perhaps, she thinks the quest for a well-paying job is mistaken or is insufficient for an excellent life. Indirectly, *she* might be assuming that other fundamental values are more important. If the questioning were to continue between Samantha and Stephen, it quite possibly could go along the lines of attempting to uncover some of these additional presuppositions upon which a life of excellence can be based.

In philosophy these kinds of questions are often about the assumptions, presuppositions, postulates, or definitions upon which a field of inquiry is based, and these questions can be concerned with the meaning, significance, or integration of the results discovered or proposed by a field of inquiry.

The authors go on to say that the meaning they have arrived at here "omits what are sometimes termed the 'antiphilosophies' such as postmodernism, a philosophy opposing the possibility of objectivity and truth, and existentialism, a group of philosophies dismissing the notion that the universe is in any sense rational, coherent, or intelligible. The characterization of philosophy proposed in the text is provisional and is used as a stalking horse for the discipline."

I agree with the general tenor of this definition of philosophical inquiry. It involves studying "basic" or "fundamental" issues that are often so deeply embedded in our thinking that we are unaware that they exist and have an influence on us. Keep in mind, however, that the study of "fundamental issues" may be carried out by someone who does not believe there are any "fundamentals" or reliable foundations from which to think about those issues.

The forms philosophical inquiry take when it is expressed for others are very diverse—from long and dense books, to stories and conversations, to poetry, to focused discussions of the implications of this or that view for practice. Most of those diverse products of philosophical inquiry are based on three broad modes of scholarship.

MODES OF PHILOSOPHICAL INQUIRY

Figure 10.1 illustrates the options when it comes to methods of dealing with philosophical topics, including those related to theory. Before looking at particular methods, however, it might, be appropriate at this point to dis-

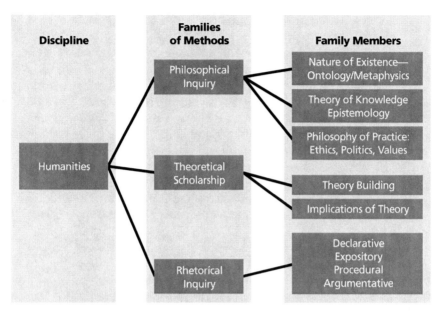

Figure 10.1 Methods of Philosophical Inquiry that are particularly useful in educational technology.

cuss the differences between the questions philosophical, theoretical, and rhetorical methods address. I suggest that philosophical inquiry addresses "foundational" questions. These are questions that must be answered, at least tentatively or implicitly, before other questions can even be asked, much less answered.

For example, suppose you have decided that all this talk about hermeneutics and being in the world is a crock. The Right answer to the question of how you do research is the scientific method, and that is how you can learn things about the world. Figure 10.1 lists three types of philosophical inquiry: metaphysics, epistemology, and the philosophy of practice. If the adoption of the positivist scientific method is to make any sense whatever, it *must* be based on certain answers to questions that are the focus of philosophical inquiry:

- **Metaphysics.** Metaphysical questions ask about the nature of what is. For you, as a proponent of the scientific method, the nature of things is entirely physical. Nothing exists that is not physical. But if it does, the nonphysical does not interact or influence the physical. Materialism is the correct metaphysics; there is no spiritual or mental world separate from the physical. In addition, the material world is knowable by humans if we use the correct methods, That, however, is an answer to another target of philosophical inquiry - epistemology.

- **Epistemology.** Epistemological questions ask about how we can learn things about the "real" world (whatever that real world is). A proponent of the scientific method would naturally argue that the way to know things is to carefully study the physical world. Aristotle would, therefore, be correct, we can find universal knowledge by systematically observing and manipulating the physical world.
- **Philosophy of Practice.** Questions in this sphere have to do with values. Why should we do and why should we do it. A scientific method proponent might say that the way we make decisions in life, what we value, find beautiful, and what we consider right or correct must be based on the universal laws we discover through the scientific method.

Each of the three major paradigms that are active in educational technology today—positivism, interpretivism, and critical theory—are based on specific answers to these three philosophical issues. You cannot adopt the philosophical foundations of positivism, for example, and then adopt and use the assumptions and methods interpretive hermeneutic research methods without being logically inconsistent. As scholars and practitioners, our beliefs can be organized into three rough levels: philosophical, theoretical, and practical as illustrated in Figure 10.2.

The three levels—philosophical, theoretical, and professional—vary primarily in terms of the breadth of the questions that must be answered. At the philosophical level the questions are about things like "What is the nature of truth?" At the theoretical level, they are more specific. "What is the best approach to finding out more about how children learn?" And, at the professional level, questions are even more specific. "Given that I want to study the problems teachers have integrating new learning technologies into the classroom, what is the best research method for me to use?" The questions are different at each level, but they are also interlocked. A person who adopts a positivist philosophy and the scientific method, would have a difficult time justifying to themselves, much less others, that an interpretive narrative inquiry is the "best" way to study the problems of technology integration. The "answers" that seem comfortable to us at each level of this hierarchy of questions are based on the answers we have accepted on the levels below.

Although it is not represented in Figure 10.2, an important factor in this structure is how positive we are about our choices at each level. Positivism, of course, builds into the belief system a requirement of strong belief. Critical theory does as well. Interpretivism is different, however. Its basic belief system requires that statements of truth be conditional and acknowl-

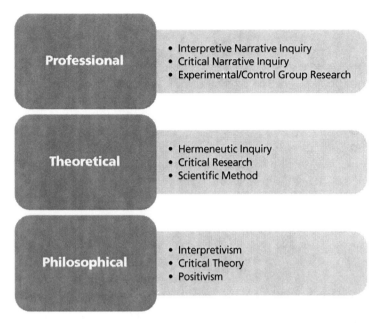

Figure 10.2 Educational technology scholars have beliefs that influence their work on three different levels.

edged as possibly incorrect. These different levels of "positivism" across the three major paradigms are a factor in the attitudes expressed in papers, presentations, and debates. Positivists and critical theorists tend to be more aggressive, more assured, and more hostile toward opposing answers to basic questions. Interpretivists tend to be more accepting, more flexible, and more comfortable with what seems fuzzy or even contradictory answers.

Doing Philosophical and Theoretical Scholarship

In the social sciences, theoretical papers are more common than philosophical papers but the formats of philosophical and theoretical papers are often very similar. A philosophical/theoretical paper will generally:

- Focus on one major issue or a group of related issues.
- Lay out the position being proposed or defended and distinguish it from actual or possible alternatives.
- Marshall the evidence for the favored position. The "evidence" can take many forms—from other philosophical and/or theoretical papers/books, from an analysis of the logic behind the position,

from an analysis of historical cases that seem to support the position, from the opinions of people and organizations who are trusted by the readers, and so on.

- Address the existing and anticipated criticisms. Any important positions will be criticized and it is important to address as many of the major ones as possible so that readers, when faced with them, will already understand their meaning and how proponents of your position deal with them.

- Present any specious arguments in favor of your position and explain why they cannot be used to support the position, or actually detract from its attractiveness.

- Make sure readers understand the weaknesses of the alternative positions.

- Be sure to acknowledge weaknesses in the favored position as well and explain why readers should still favor it.

- Refine your favored position and distinguish it from similar but different positions if that is important. Point out why the position you propose is better than the close alternatives.

- Explain the implications of the position for the targeted readers. If they are educational technology scholars or professionals, what difference will your favored position make in their professional lives if they accept your viewpoint? What will be the "costs" to them if they do?

The points above are relatively abstract but we can use them to analyze a particular paper to see how one author applied the ideas to a published paper. The paper I will analyze is Bent Flybjerg's *Social Science That Matters* which was published in *Foresight Europe* in 2005. If you would like to read the article in full, it is available at http://flyvbjerg.plan.aau.dk/Publications2006/ForesightNo2PRINT.pdf

Major Issue Focus: Flybjerg's focus is clear. The social sciences have failed society because they "pretend to emulate natural science by producing cumulative and predictive theory.... [But] the natural science approach simply does not work in the social sciences. No predictive theory has been arrived at in social science, despite centuries of trying. This approach is a deadend" (p. 38). That is the first part of his focus. The second part is that a social science based on Aristotle's concept of phronesis can actually help society.

Lay Out the Position; Distinguish it from Alternatives. In the paper Flybjerg introduces the epistemic model of scholarship used in the natural sciences and details the core values and beliefs of phronetic social science. He highlights the differences many times. For example, "To sum up the differences: The epistemic or natural science model sees social scientists and social science professionals as technocrats who—through their insight into social theories and laws—may provide society with solutions to its social ills. The phronetic model sees social scientists and social science professionals as analysts who produce food for thought for the ongoing process of public deliberation, participation, and decision making" (p. 39).

Marshall the Evidence and Anticipate Criticisms. In this paper he presents an abbreviated version of some of the arguments for the natural science model, explains why they are wrong, and then relies mainly on his own rhetorical skills to make the case for a phronetic social science. He does a better job of this aspect of philosophical/theoretical inquiry in his book (2001).

Address Existing and Anticipated Criticisms. Flyvbjerg addresses one of the most common criticisms of all relativist theories—that there is no use doing any research if every theory and explanation is *just as good as any other.* "Phronetic social science, like any other social science, is based on interpretation and is open for testing in relation to other interpretations and other research. Thus the results of phronetic social science may be confirmed, revised, or rejected according to the most rigorous standards of social science, in relation to other interpretations. This does not mean that one interpretation can be just as good as the next, as relativism would have it, for each interpretation must be based on validity claims. It does mean, however, that phronetic social science will be as prepared to defend its validity claims as any other research" (p. 41)

Deal with Specious Arguments in Favor of Your Position. Flyvbjerg, in this paper, does not deal with any arguments in favor of his position that are actually detrimental or unsupportable.

Make Readers Aware of Weakness in Alternative Positions. The author draws a bead on epistemic social science and hammers his point home over and over that it has failed to produce the expected result because it is based on a failed epistemology and a failed theory (scientific method).

Address Weaknesses in Your Position. Flyvbjerg does not deal with any perceived weaknesses. Others, however, have offered many criticisms that probably should be dealt with by Flyvbjerg. For example, some feel his discussion of research methods for a phronetic social science is problematic because he argues that method is not important; that phronetic social science is "problem driven" rather than based on one family of methods. Another important criticism is that his idea of dialog, in an interpretive hermeneutic sense of the word, is carrying much of the responsibility for problem solving in his version of social science. "This work is dialogical in the sense that it incorporates, and, if successful, is incorporated into, a polyphone of voices. No one voice, including that of the researcher, may claim final authority. The goal is to produce input to dialog and praxis in social affairs, rather than generate ultimate, unequivocally verified knowledge"

(p. 41). This, however, is a short paper and he does address some of the criticisms in his book and in other papers.

Distinguish Your Position from Similar Perspectives. Flyvbjerg does not do this in the paper. He is essentially proposing that social science emphasize problem-based scholarship and favor interpretive narrative inquiry. There are other forms of qualitative research and other paradigms, such as critical theory, that share some, but not all of his core beliefs. He does not attempt to differentiate his position from any that might be distant or close relatives. His target for criticism is always the epistemic social science model borrowed from the natural sciences.

Explain the Implications. Flyvbjerg does a good job of addressing the implications of his theory for organizational researchers who will read this journal. For example, he says that "Insofar as organizational situations become clear, they are clarified by detailed stories of who is doing what to whom. Such clarification is a principal concern for phronetic organization research, which explores current practices and historic circumstances to find avenues to praxis" (p. 41). He even goes on to propose a three-step action plan to convert epistemic social science to phronetic social science.

Flyvbjerg's article illustrates the point that the guidelines listed earlier are just that—guidelines and suggestions rather than rules and requirements. While he did not include material on every topic in the list, his paper is a very well written presentation of his theory, particularly considering that is a very short paper.

THE COMPLEXITIES OF PHILOSOPHICAL INQUIRY AND THEORETICAL SCHOLARSHIP

Doing philosophical/theoretical work typically involves becoming very familiar with all three of the levels of knowledge shown in Figure 10.2: philosophical, theoretical, and professional. If you are writing a philosophical paper, it will be important to understand the implications of the philosophical position for theory, and professional practice. And, if you are writing a theory paper on professional practice, the practices you discuss will be based on supporting theories and philosophical positions. You will find it difficult to write an influential paper without understanding the three levels and how they interact. Therefore, theory and philosophy scholarship call for considerable preparation before you start a paper, and writing the paper may call for much more library and online research before you are finished. In fact, as you track down important books and articles relevant to your topic, you are very likely to find that your focus is changing and that your viewpoint may also change. Writing a theoretical or philosophical paper is thus a learning process as well as a process of scholarship and communication. With that in mind, it is important to plan on doing several revisions of the paper and to be prepared to make drastic changes as you, and your thinking, progress. Another important aspect of writing this sort of paper is getting feedback from people who both support and disagree with your position. This can be very difficult to do—people with the necessary expertise are often busy and do not have free time. However, the quality of your paper will very likely be increased significantly by careful and thoughtful critiques from both supporters and opponents. You will gain useful information from both. And, should the first journal (and second, third …) you submit your paper to reject it; the recommendations and comments from the reviewers can be invaluable. You don't have to agree with every suggestion and make the every change proposed, but even when you do not accept a comment or change, the reviewer has highlighted an issue or point in the paper that should be considered for revision to reduce the likelihood of another reviewer or reader making the same criticism.

WHAT ABOUT RHETORICAL INQUIRY?

Perhaps I have been too influenced by Plato but I see rhetorical methods as a system of supporting methods rather than stand alone methods. I can hear essay writers, textbook authors, and many others (who use declarative and expository rhetorical methods), technical writers (who use procedural rhetorical methods) and debaters, opinion page authors, and politicians (who use argumentative rhetorical methods) rising up en mass and pointing out how important the skills of rhetorical inquiry are to untold professions. They are correct. I am even willing to admit that the more rhetorical skill and knowledge you have the better your thinking, and your writing, are likely to be. Still I admit this more with my mind than with my heart. However, there are thousands of resources on how to write and speak better, including hundreds of specialized guides to everything from how to write a good computer manual to how to develop campaign speeches. Scholars who plan on writing and speaking a lot on philosophical and theoretical topics should become skilled in the arts of rhetoric!

One way of making space for rhetoric in our consideration of methods is to place it within another family of methods. Some authors, for example, approach rhetoric as a form of hermeneutics, which was discussed in the previous chapter. In the book, *Rhetorical Hermeneutics: Invention and Interpretation in the Age of Science,* (Gross & Keith, 1997) Dilip Gaonkar (1997) discusses the "current revival of interest in rhetoric" and points out that rhetoric is often positioned "as a hermeneutic metadiscourse rather than as a substantive discourse practice" (p. 25). For example, a study of the discourse on how computers should be integrated into classrooms might lead to the conclusion that that the discourse is part of the capitalist metanarrative that promotes the preparation of citizens for mind-numbing jobs that benefit the capitalist class but leads to unfulfilling lives for workers. (This analysis, of course, might be done by a critical theorist.) The author, however, is not pleased with the new role for rhetoric. As Deidre McCloskey (1997) put it, "The rhetorical studies of biology, economics, and mathematics over the past twenty years have used this tactic, reading even scientific text rehetorically. Gaonkar does not like it, not one bit. He wants to keep Science distinct from the rest of the culture. He wants rhetoric to stay in its cage. He is a Little Rhetoric Guy" (p. 101). Gaonkar might be echoing the thoughts of Plato when he asks "What does it tell us about a culture that it finds interpretive solace in rhetoric rather than in religion or in economics or in science" (p. 25).

Gaonkar's treatment of rhetoric involves differentiating ancient and contemporary rhetoric. "Contemporary rhetoric differs from its classical counterpart in two important ways. First, we have extended the range of rhetoric to include discourse types such as scientific texts that the ancients would have regarded as falling outside its purview" (p. 26). He argues that Aristotle limited rhetoric to a narrow role—that of being a means to an end in the area of civic action (e.g., politics) "despite the sophists' attempt to promote an enlarged vision of rhetoric" (p. 26). Then he traces the history of rhetoric to a very sad end:

> [Rhetoric] remained as a cultural practice bound to the civic realm and later, with the erosion of the public sphere in the classical world, rhetoric migrated to the realm of the arts and aesthetics. Here, once again, rhetoric failed to establish its hegemony as the generative grammar of artistic prose. . . . Rhetoric, after Quintilian, now domiciled within the pedagogical institutions and driven by changing cultural needs . . . found itself progressively reduced in scope from an idealized medium of "general culture" to a regimen for training of bureaucrats for the state and the churches, and then to a technical study of stylistics, and finally to a brittle taxonomy of tropes and figures. . . . [According to some scholars] taxonomically ossified rhetoric finally died in the early nineteenth century with the emergence of the Romantic aesthetics that privileged genius and spontaneity as opposed to the classificatory order and stylistic conformity characteristic of rhetorical instruction." . . . [However,] rhetoric [today] is everywhere. Never before in the history of rhetoric, not even during its glory days of the Italian Renaissance, did its proponents claim for rhetoric so universal a scope as some postmodern neosophists do today. . . . The rhetoric of science is simply one manifestation of this contemporary impulse to universalize rhetoric. (p. 26)

While the use of rhetorical hermeneutics to find metanarratives even in the supposedly "non-rhetorical" writings of science is abhorrent to Gaonkar (he comments at one point, "If science is not free of rhetoric, nothing is."), as a constructivist and an interpretivist I am convinced that looking rhetorically at scientific writing, including writing in educational technology, is not only appropriate but very fruitful. Science is not free of rhetoric. Many of the authors in the Gross and Keith (1997) book agree. Gaonkar is displeased that "we have reversed the priority the ancients accorded to rhetoric as a practical/productive activity over rhetoric as a critical/interpretive activity. As academics, we are more interested in rhetoric as interpretive theory than as cultural practice" (p. 27). But in her defense of rhetorical hermeneutics McCloskey (1997) advocates more use of rhetoric as a way of interpreting and understanding different aspects of our culture, including science. "The Platonic distain for how we actually persuade each other is the central absurdity of our culture" (p. 104).

One particular chapter in Gross and Keith (1997) is of particular interest to educational technologists. It is titled *From Tekhne to Technique: Rhetoric as a Design Art* (Kaufer, 1997). Kaufer suggests the two definitions of rhetoric as a means of persuasion and as a means of hermeneutic interpretation can be bridged through a middle ground. "Classifying rhetoric as a lowly practical art makes it seem vulnerably thin, open for 'rehabilitation' as a hermeneutic art.... As an alternative ..., I suggest rhetoric is more profitably understood as a design art.... Traditionally, Platonists have rejected rhetoric for its imprecision, its sense of praxis with no foundation in a structured art or *techne.* Rhetoric comes to be identified with a practical art in the lowest sense of that term, far too thin, eclectic, and opportunistic to support a systematic hermeneutic.... The charge being made is that rhetoric does not live up to the internal standards of coherence of a true techne, a true art of design, where praxis is carefully regulated by techne, where a theory of reception is closely monitored and informed by a theory of production..." (p. 248). Kaufer goes on to make a case for rhetoric as a *design art* that merits the responsibility placed on it. He expanded that argument in *Rhetoric and the Arts of Design* (Kaufer & Butler, 1996). Rhetoric is like other types of design such as architecture and instructional design. Design arts are not based on rigid rules but on a more open, flexible approach that should lead to a product that serves its purpose and is appealing to the human users. In his review of the book, a technical communications professor (Campbell, 1997) commented that "Where Aristotle uses Homer and contemporary playwrights for occasional illustrations, Kaufer and Butler use the Lincoln–Douglas debates."

SUMMARY

If you sample the pages of five or six randomly selected journals in education and educational technology, you will likely find at least a few papers that are best characterized as philosophical or theoretical. These may even be the most interesting papers in the issue you peruse! That fact makes it even more surprising that most graduate programs in both education and educational technology do very little to help students become either sophisticated consumers or talented producers of this type of scholarship.

However, reading this form of scholarship is an important aspect of professional practice, and writing it can be a major aspect of a scholar's contribution of the knowledge base in a discipline. I commend this form of scholarship to you and urge you to explore it both as a source of understanding and as a vehicle for communicating what you have to say to others.

REFERENCES

Beach, D. (2005)From fieldwork to theory and representation in ethnography. In G. Troman, B. Jeffrey & G. Walford. *Methodological issues and practices in ethnography,* (pp. 1–18). San Diego, CA: Elsevier.

Bentley, M. (1999). *Modern historiography: An introduction.* New York: Routledge.

Brundage, A. (2002). *Going to the sources: A guide to historical research and writing.* Wheeling, IL: Harlan Davidson.

Bryman, A. (2005). *Social research methods, 2nd ed.* Oxford, UK: Oxford University Press.

Denzin & Y. Lincoln, (Eds). *Handbook of Qualitative Research,* 3rd ed (pp. 217—234). Thousand Oaks, CA: Sage.

Denzin, N. (1996). *Interpretive ethnography: Ethnographic practices for the 21st century.* Thousand Oaks: Sage.

Duffy, R. E. (1988). Why History? *Social Education, 6,* 460–462.

Flyvbjerg, B. (October 2005–March, 2006). Social science that matters. No. 2. Foresight Europe, 38–42. Retrieved May 31, 2007 from http://flyvbjerg.plan.aau.dk/Publications2006/ForesightNo2PRINT.pdf

Flyvbjerg, B. (2004). Five misunderstandings about case-study research. In C. Seal, G. Gobo, J. Gubrium, & D. Silverman (Eds.). *Qualitative research practice* (420–434). Thousand Oaks, CA: Sage.

Flyvbjerg, B. (2001). *Making social science matter: Why social inquiry fails and how it can succeed again.* Cambridge, UK: Cambridge University Press.

Foley, D. & Valenzuela, A. (2005). Critical ethnography: *The politics of collaboration.* In N. Furay, C. and Salevouris, M. (2000). *The methods and skills of history: A practical guide, 2nd ed.* Wheeling, IL: Harlan Davidson.

Hayden, K. (1999). *Videoconferencing in K–12 education: A Delphi study of characteristics and critical strategies to support constructivist learning experiences.* Unpublished doctoral dissertation, Pepperdine University.

Januszewski, A. (1996). History in educational technology. In *Proceedings of Selected Resarch and Development Presentations at the 1996 National Convention of the Asso-*

ciation for Educational Communication and Technology (Indianapolis). Retrieved June 1, 2007 from http://eric.ed.gov/ERICWebPortal/custom/portlets/recordDetails/detailmini.jsp?_nfpb=true&_&ERICExtSearch_SearchValue_0=ED397800&ERICExtSearch_SearchType_0=eric_accno&accn o=ED397800

Johnson, D. & Maddux, C. (Eds) (2003). *Technology in education: A twenty year retrospective.* Binghamton, NY: Haworth Press.

Kamberelis, G. & Dimitriadis, G. (2005). Focus groups: Strategic articulations of pedagogy, politics, and inquiry. In N. Denzin & Y. Lincoln, (Eds). *Handbook of qualitative research* (3rd ed, pp. 887–914). Thousand Oaks, CA: Sage.

Kruger, R. & Casey, M. (2000). *Focus groups: A practical guide for applied research.* Thousand Oaks, CA: Sage.

Madison, D. S. (2005). *Critical ethnography: Method, ethics, and performance.* Thousand Oaks: Sage.

Marius, R. & Page, M. (2006). *Short guide to writing about history, 6th ed.* Longman.

Rezabek, R. (2000, January). Online focus groups: Electronic discussions for research. *Forum: Qualitative Social Research, 1*(1). Retrieved January 6, 2007 from http://www.qualitative-research.net/fqs-texte/1-00/1-00rezabek-e.htm

Rubin, H. & Rubin, I. (2006). *Qualitative interviewing: The art of hearing data,* 2nd ed. Thousand Oaks, CA: Sage.

Schmertzing, L. & Schmertzing, R. (2001). Domains of adaptation in technologically mediated classrooms: An ethnographic report. In C. Crawford et al. (Eds.), *Proceedings of Society for Information Technology and Teacher Education International Conference 2001* (pp. 2424–2429). Chesapeake, VA: AACE.

Seattler, P. (1968). *A history of educational technology.* New York: McGraw-Hill.

Seattler, P. (Ed.) (2005). *The evolution of American educational technology,* 2nd rev. ed. Charlotte, NC: Information Age Publishing.

Skulmoskis, G., Hartman, F., & Krahn, J. (2007). The Delphi method in graduate research. *Journal of Information Technology Educaton* [on-line], *6.* Retrieved June 1, 2007 from http://jite.org/documents/Vol6/JITEv6p001-021Skulmoski212.pdf

Stake, R. (2005). Qualitative case studies. In N. Denzin & Y. Lincoln, (Eds). *Handbook of qualitative research* (3rd ed., pp. 443–466). Thousand Oaks, CA: Sage.

Troman, G., Jeffrey, B. & Walford, G. (2005). *Methodological issues and practices in ethnography.* San Diego, CA: Elsevier.

Vaughn, S., Schumm, J. & Sinagub, J. (2005). *Focus group research in education and psychology.* Thousand Oaks, CA: Sage.

Wang, S. & Yuen, S. (2004). An Ethnographic Study on a Video Conferencing Class. In G. Richards (Ed.), Proceedings of World Conference on E-Learning in Corporate, Government, Healthcare, and Higher Education 2004 (pp. 1007–1012). Chesapeake, VA: AACE.

Yin, R. (2003). *Case study research: Design and methods.* Thousand Oaks, CA: Sage.

READINGS FOR CHAPTER 10

Reading 10.1

Olssen, M. (May–June, 2006). Understanding the mechanisms of neoliberal control: lifelong learning, flexibility and knowledge capitalism. *International Journal of Lifelong Education, 25*(3), 213–230.

Mark Olssen's paper is an example of how philosophical issues can be linked to educational issues, in this case the postmodern theories of Foucault and others and the concept of lifelong learning. Please evaluate this paper using the format used in the chapter to critique a paper by Brent Flyvbjerg. Also, ask yourself how this paper differs in purpose and approach to the one by Flyvbjerg.

What if someone asserted that Olssen's paper is simply an effort to rehabilitate Marxist theory after the failure of the Soviet Union? Would you agree? Why or why not? What about Olssen's view of the dominant concept of lifelong learning? Does it really serve as a way of keeping the powerful in control? And what about his ideas about how lifelong learning could be made to serve progressive and emancipatory goals through linking it to "egalitarian politics and social justice?" Does this make sense? And what critical assumptions must be true if it does make sense? Finally, what is your view of this paper as an effort to link philosophy to education? Is it too broad? Too narrow? To theoretical? Too practical? Explain your view.

Reading 10.2

Dwight, J., & Garrison, J. (June, 2003). A manifesto for instructional technology: Hyperpedagogy. *Teachers College Record, 105*(5), 699–728.

The authors believe the educational promise of hypertext and hypermedia is so great they can lead to a virtual revolution in education. The problem, they believe, that keeps this from happening is that the new tools are "encrusted within concepts borrowed from traditional curriculum theory and instructional design." In their paper, they propose to (1) make the hidden philosophical assumptions of existing educational theory apparent, and (2) propose an alternative foundation upon which to build a new approach to teaching and learning—hyperpedagogy.

How to you evaluate Dwight and Garrison's critique of the philosophical foundations of education? Are they correct in their assertions about what those foundations are? Are they correct that those foundations lead to undesirable results? Why? How? For example, they say one of the "serious errors" of "conventional curriculum theory and instructional design" is the assumption that you can determine objectives before developing the curriculum. Do you agree? Why? Is this an important issue? Why?

What about the alternative foundations they propose? Why is poststructuralism so important? Why is critical theory important?

Finally, if you fully accepted the assertions of this article, what would be the most important changes in the way you work as an educator, an educational technology specialist, a scholar? How are these changes related to the alternative paradigm of hyperpedagogy and its supporting philosophical theories?

Reading 10.3

Solomon, D. (2000). *Philosophy and the Learning Ecology: The Meaning of Learning Project.* Presidential Session at the Association of Educational Communication and Technology Annual Conference, Denver, Colorado, October 25–28, 2000. *Note:* This reading was also assigned for Chapter 3. It has been repeated here because of its relevance to philosophical inquiry.

David Solomon is one of a few leading educational technology scholars who seriously focuses on philosophical issues as they relate to educational technology. In this paper he focuses on postmodernism as a movement in philosophy and as an influence on educational technology. Do you find his explanation of postmodernism as a philosophy convincing? Why? Does it make sense to consider all the theories and movements he associates with postmodernism as part of a single meaningful whole? Or are they really different movements with different purposes and foundational assumptions? If they are all "postmodern" in one way or another, what is it that ties them together and makes them all postmodern?

Which of the 8 assumptions of postmodernism do you consider most important for education? Why? Which do you consider the weakest or least supportable assumption? Why? Do these assumptions "hang together" as a whole? How?

Do you find his analysis of how postmodernism relates to educational technology convincing? Why? Which of his applications of postmodern assumptions would cause the most significant changes in educational technology? How? Why?

Reading 10.4

Carter, M. (January/February, 2004). From Aristotle to Advocacy: Critical reflections on the philosophy and practice of social science research. *Educational Researcher,* 35–39.

In this book review published in the AERA publication, *Educational Researcher*, Dr. Carter reviews in some detail two books—one on the idea of anti-racist scholarship and the other on how to make social science inquiry meaningful and relevant. While the topics are quite different, the two books have a number of things in common. Carter points those out and analyzes the two books from her vantage point as a qualitative researcher interested in the history of African-American education. Neither of the books nor Dr. Carter's review are focused on the implications of educational technology. After you read the review, read it again and develop your response to the following questions. If the basic ideas in these two books were adopted by the majority of educational technology scholars and practitioners, what would change and why? And, which of your implicit or explicit assumptions do either of these two books challenge most seriously? How? Why?

CHAPTER 11

DESIGN AS SCHOLARSHIP

Instructional Design, or ID, has a long history in educational technology. At least one course on ID is part of virtually every graduate degree program in educational or instructional technology offered in North America and in most of the rest of the world. ID, however, has an interesting and somewhat puzzling history.

THE TWO MEANINGS OF ID: PEDAGOGICAL ID AND PROCESS ID

As you read the scholarly literature on ID, you will find two related but very different uses of the term. Both have the core idea that ID involves the creation of instructional materials and educational resources. However, one use of the term ID is to indicate the theories of learning, principles of teaching and learning, and the pedagogical strategies that should be used in creating those educational materials and resources. In this tradition, the core responsibility of the instructional designer is to make the "right" choices about

- Guiding theories of learning (e.g., behaviorism or constructivism, or?),
- General strategies for teaching and learning (e.g., direct instruction, student-centered instruction) and

Qualitative Research Methods in Education and Educational Technology, pages 315–348
315

- Pedagogies (e.g., problem-based learning, anchored instruction, tutorials, simulations, and so on).

This use of the term ID I will call *Pedagogical ID* because it emphasizes the responsibility of the instructional designer to choose, or help choose, the right way to teach the content that has been selected. In the Pedagogical ID literature, the instructional designer is someone (see Figure 11.1):

- With knowledge of scientifically proven theories that tell us what teaching strategies should be used to teach each type of content,
- Who uses a technical-rational approach to designing instructional materials, and
- Who serves as the leader and expert on the design team because the designer has special knowledge that others do not

The work of the designer is in the technical-rational tradition because it involves using scientifically established rules about which learning theories, and what types of teaching strategies, are best for teaching various types of content to various types of students. In the Pedagogical ID tradition this is at the heart of what it means to design instructional materials. The underpinnings of the Pedagogical ID perspective are concisely expressed by M. David Merrill and the ID2 Research Group (1996) at Utah State University:

The Discipline of Instructional Design
- There is a scientific discipline of instructional design.
- The discipline of instructional design is based on a set of specific assumptions.

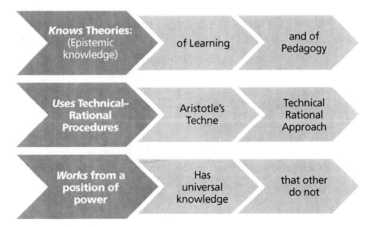

Figure 11.1 Characteristics of a designer from a pedagogical ID perspective.

- The discipline of instructional design is founded on scientific principles verified by empirical data.

Those persons who claim that knowledge is founded on collaboration rather than empirical science, or who claim that all truth is relative, are not instructional designers. They have disassociated themselves from the discipline of instructional design.

Instruction and Learning

- Instructional design is a technology for the development of learning experiences and environments which promote the acquisition of specific knowledge and skill by students.
- Instructional design is a technology which incorporates known and verified learning strategies into instructional experiences which make the acquisition of knowledge and skill more efficient, effective, and appealing.
- While instruction takes place in a larger organizational context, the discipline of instructional design is concerned only with the development of learning experiences and environments, not with the broader concerns of systemic change, organizational behavior, performance support, and other human resource problems.
- Instruction involves directing students to appropriate learning activities; guiding students to appropriate knowledge; helping students rehearse, encode, and process information; monitoring student performance; and providing feedback as to the appropriateness of the student's learning activities and practice performance. (Merrill and ID2 Research Group, 1996)

This view of ID is widely held and often used as the unstated but implicitly accepted framework for a great many papers, especially case studies that describe a particular instructional design project. The definition below, which is widely quoted on the Internet, is also a definition of Pedagogical ID:

Instructional Design is the systematic process of translating general principles of learning and instruction into plans for instructional materials and learning. (Retrieved from http://www.elearnspace.org/Articles/InstructionalDesign.htm)

A case study that takes for granted the framework of Pedagogical ID is Gordon Hensley's (2005) article on creating a hybrid college course. Hensley describes the revision of a popular humanities course at Appalachian State University, *Introduction to Theatre*. To deal with the problem of too many students wanting to take the course and not enough classrooms to handle the load, Dr. Hensley decided to create a hybrid version of the course that met face to face only a few times a semester and worked online the rest of the time. In his paper he summarized his prior experience teaching online and reviewed the relevant literature. He found "there are several theories in support of hybrid learning and ample supporting research available." In designing his course at Appalachian State University he used studies of hybrid courses at the University of Central Florida and the University of Wisconsin-Milwaukee as well as the *exemplary* courses on the WebCT site (http://webct.com/exemplary) to guide his thinking. He also attended workshops at Appalachian State on Dreamweaver and WebCT to develop the technical skills he needed to create his online course web. Essentially, he transferred his face-to-face course to the online site. "I created a simple web site of materials to be covered. I then created study sheets for the quizzes, walked through all of my PowerPoint presentations to make sure the written text was self-explanatory, and wrote a few informal articles on topics—I basically wrote out my lectures in a brief and informal way." He put the course web site on a CD-ROM and distributed the CD to students because many had slow internet access at home. Then he created a set of "discussion posts, live chats, and personal student web pages [as well as] quizzes and assignments for the class in WebCT." Finally, Dr. Hensley created "a small support site to introduce students to hybrid learning."

In the article Dr. Hensley basically starts with the theoretical foundations he used to create his hybrid course. Then he tells us the end result of his design work. (Hensley does not, however, tell us very much about the design process that he used.) The article ends with an overview of what worked, what failed, and some suggestions for other designers who want to create hybrid courses. Figure 11.2 illustrates how Hensley's approach to design fits the pedagogical ID definition.

Hensley's paper is an illustration of how ID is considered from the perspective of pedagogical ID. It involves the technical-rational application of known truths about teaching and learning to a new but familiar problem that has been addressed before by many others. Those who have come be-

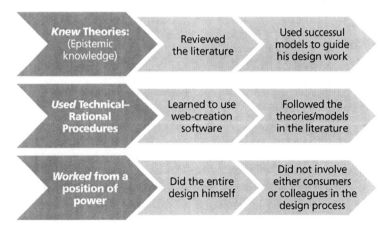

Figure 11.2   Hensley's case study as an example of pedagogical ID.

fore have developed and validated general theories, specific models, and detailed teaching strategies that can be applied to the *new but familiar* design job. From a pedagogical ID perspective, anyone wanting to criticize the work of Dr. Hensley would do so by questioning the choice of teaching methods, content taught, or technology deployed. There is, however, another way of thinking about id—the process approach.

ID as a Process

The other use of the term ID is to indicate the *process* by which educational materials and resources are developed. This general definition of ID as a process for accomplishing design work does not refer directly to learning theory or instructional strategies. They are, of course, important to an instructional designer, but they are *not* design. ID is the *process* of designing learning materials, and one aspect of a designer's work is the use of knowledge and theories from many different disciplines. Theories of learning and pedagogy are part of the tool set that instructional designers use, but there is a difference between designing and the tools a designer uses. We do not equate nailing with being a carpenter or knowledge of the load bearing capacities of beams with architecture. The definition below, which is compatible with a view of ID as a process, is from Christa Harrelson at the University of Georgia:

> When people ask me what instructional technology is, instructional design is a large part of the definition. Instructional design is the process by which instruction, computer-based or not, is created. Instructional design provides a framework for the creative process of design, and ensures the learners' needs are met. (Retrieved from http://ttc.coe.uga.edu/christah/clhport/themes. htm#id)

I am going to use the view that ID is a process and reject the narrower (and, I believe, confusing), use of the term ID to emphasize the use of certain psychological and instructional theories in creating instructional material. *ID as Pedagogy* is much too narrow a definition, and it completely ignores the idea that the translation of learning and instructional theory into an instructional resource is not a simple or obvious process. ID is a rather complex process and quite a few models have emerged over the past sixty years to guide that process.

I suggest that doing ID involves (1) developing and using phronetic (local, contextually constrained) knowledge, (2) using a range of technical knowledge and expertise, and (3) working collaboratively with a team of stakeholders. (See Figure 11.3.) However, I have actually committed an error that I sometimes criticize in others. The figure does not actually repre-

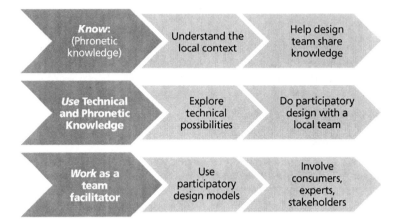

Figure 11.3   ID as a participatory process.

sent the general idea of ID as a process. Instead, it presents ID as a *constructive-interpretive* process. Many of the definitions of ID in the literature are like that. They purport to provide a general definition of ID but are actually advocating a definition that is heavily laden with the preferred theoretical and epistemological positions of the authors. In my case the constructivist-interpretive paradigms are the foundations for my view of ID as a process. I have also framed the view of ID with and emphasis on two of Aristotle's types of knowing: phronetic and technical. Most of the traditional definitions of ID put an emphasis on Aristotle's third type of knowing—epistemic knowledge that is universal and eternal.

The quote from Merrill and the ID2 group given earlier, for example, defines ID within a framework that emphasizes both the existence and use of epistemic knowledge. It would take a very long article to unpack all the implicit but foundational assumptions and beliefs that are inherent in the definition presented by Merrill and his colleagues. To illustrate, consider the statement:

> The discipline of instructional design is founded on scientific principles verified by empirical data.

There are at least three implicit assumptions in this statement and all of them are hotly contested in education and the social sciences today. The first is that:

- Human behavior can be subjected to scientific research that leads us to laws or law-like generalizations—expressed in theories—that are portable. They travel well from one context to another and are the most important type of knowledge a designer must know.

Many of the other design fields have moved beyond this positivist model of how we come to understand human behavior. A second implicit but fundamental assumption of the Merrill definition is that:

- Variations from one setting to another are of little importance compared to the value of the law-like generalizations that scientific research has given us. Thus, when it comes to creating instructional materials, it is the general truths, not the local truths, that are the most important. This means that a well prepared designer is an expert with special knowledge who must make sure that the right theories and instructional strategies guide the development of the instructional materials being created.

A third implicit assumption in the statement is that:

- As a scientific discipline, ID may not be perfect now but it becomes better and better as new scientific research tells us more and more about how students learn and how teachers should teach. Thus, ID will change over the decades and become better and better as new knowledge is added to the already substantial foundation of established truths that guide it today.

All three of these foundational assumptions are the subject of intense criticism in education, social science, and educational technology today. There is no body of scientific research that proves these assumptions. And, that brings into question the statement that "*The discipline of instructional design is founded on scientific principles verified by empirical data*" because all three of the assumptions noted above *must* be true before we can accept the statement as even possibly true. As Brent Flyvbjerg (2001) has pointed out, the social sciences (including education) have yet to come up with a single law of human behavior that is reliable and generalizable in the way that laws in physics and chemistry are considered reliable and general (and there is some debate today in the sciences about whether the "natural science" model fits even the research and knowledge of the natural sciences!). The assertion that a particular teaching method, or way of designing instructional materials, is "scientifically proven" is simply not true today, and may never be true. Similarly, criticisms of another approach on the grounds that it is "unscientific" because it is not supported by empirical research lacks foundation because little, if any, of what we believe we know about human behavior, human learning, and teaching is clearly supported by empirical research. As social science moves away from the idea that there are solid, empirical foundations for our theories and beliefs about human behavior, it becomes less and less acceptable to take an aggressive and fundamentalist perspective about any position. We simply do not have that type of research. One of the reasons I say that is because the second implicit assumption noted above is also wrong. When it comes to human behavior, the local context is important. It is often more important than the general laws proposed by experts, and many of the failures of reform and transformation efforts in education have foundered on this very point—the failure to understand the local context and how important that context is. And, if the laws positivists are so confident of, turn out to be less dependable than they believe, then instructional designers do not have such a strong hold on the title of Expert. They might better consider their role as one of facilitator and organizer than of expert. (Note how I have strongly criticized ID positivists for their almost absolute confidence in certain truths and in the scientific method while doing exactly the same thing myself—claiming that what I happen to believe is *really* the truth and not what opponents say. I do not believe any of us can take a fundamentalist view that we are obviously correct and thus the other is obviously wrong. There is much more in the literature about this particular issue and it is up to you as a participant in the ongoing and extensive dialog to make up your own mind. Hopefully you will do it from an informed perspective so that you understand the various positions taken by different scholars before making your own decision.)

The idea that ID is a discipline based on results of scientific research has also been questioned by other educational technology scholars, including Thomas Reeves (2000) at the University of Georgia. A respected and widely read scholar, Reeves commented on the position paper by Merrill and his colleagues this way:

> Not everyone in or out of academe shares Professor Merrill's positive assessment of instructional design as a scientifically valid technology. . . . There is an enormous gap between Merrill's identification of instructional design as a robust technology derived from the science of instruction and Resnick's conclusion that instructional design is a field that does not seem to contribute to the solution of educational problems.

The Resnick that Professor Reeves refers to is Dr. Lauren Resnick from the University of Pittsburgh. He quoted from her 1999 AERA discussion after a presentation:

> We don't have a well-developed design field in education, . . . I've looked around at the field called instructional design in which people can get degrees, and so far have not been interested in hiring any of the people with

those degrees who have crossed my path. Just didn't look like they were going to add much.

Reeves goes on to point out that many other scholars, in our field and outside the field, have very little confidence in ID and educational technology research in general.

THREE CONTEMPORARY THREADS IN ID

In the first decade of the 21st century, three broad movements are active in the area we call Instructional Design or ID, and they are not all going in the same direction. The three movements are:

- **Traditional ID Scholarship Based on Positivist Epistemologies.** The most popular example of this movement is the Dick and Carey (Dick, Carey, & Carey, 2004) model of ID. The Dick and Carey ID model is the most popular example of a type of ID model often referred to as ISD or "instructional systems design." It is also a specific example of a generic ID model called ADDIE that has five sequential phases: Analysis, Design, Development, Implementation, and Evaluation. A great many ID models in use today are variations on the ADDIE model.
- **The Design-Based Research (DBR) Movement.** This is an effort to integrate design and research in ways that advance both our basic or theoretical knowledge and at the same time create high quality educational resources. Special issues of *Educational Researcher* (Vol. 32, No. 1, 2004) and *Educational Technology* (Vol. 45, No. 1, 2005) contain articles that define DBR and what it attempts to do. The book edited by a group of scholars at the Universities of Twente and Utrecht in the Netherlands (Akker, Gravemeijer, McKenney, & Nieveen, (2006) is one of the first book-length treatments of DBR. What sets DBR apart from other approaches to ID is that it tries to solve a local problem by designing effective instructional resources or procedures while also trying to create knowledge that has a broader application than the local context. DBR is thus positivist in its view, and advocates typically remain optimistic that the positivist agenda of finding law-like truths about human behavior is possible.
- **Constructivist-ID Models (C-ID).** ID models based on interpretive epistemologies and constructivist theories of teaching and learning have begun to appear in the last two decades (Cennamo, Abell, Chung, & Hugg, 1995; Cennamo, Abell, & Chung, 1996; Duffy &

Cunningham, 1996; Johari, Chen, & Toh, 2005; Lebow, 1993; Willis, 1995, 2000; Willis & Wright, 2000; Wilson, 1997).

In an earlier paper (Willis, 1995) I suggested that traditional (e.g., *objective-rational*) ID models like the one developed by Dick and Carey share a number of important "family characteristics" (See Table 11.1) and that C-ID models also share "family characteristics (see Table 11.2)

These two tables illustrate the many differences between the traditional and C-ID models but the great majority of them are related to two choices—the preferred epistemology and the preferred theory of learning and teaching.

I will return to C-ID models later, but at this point it is important to explore the other relatively new influence on contemporary ID scholarship, Design-Based Research (DBR).

TABLE 11.1   Family Characteristics of Objective-Rational Instructional Design (ID) Models

1. **The Process Is Sequential and Linear**	The design process is sequential, objective, and focused on experts who have special knowledge.
2. **Planning Is Top Down and "Systematic"**	Begin with a precise plan of action including clear behavioral objectives. Proceed through the instructional design process in a systematic, orderly, planned manner.
3. **Objectives Guide Development**	Precise behavioral objectives are essential. Considerable effort should be invested in creating instructional objectives and objective assessment instruments
4. **Experts, Who Have Special Knowledge, Are Critical to ID Work**	Experts, who know a great deal about the general, universally applicable principles of instructional design, are needed to produce good instruction.
5. **Careful Sequencing and the Teaching of Subskills Are Important**	Break complex tasks down into subcomponents and teach the subcomponents separately. Pay particular attention to the sequence of the subskills taught as well as the events of instruction.
6. **The Goal Is Delivery of Preselected Knowledge**	Emphasis is on delivery of 'facts" and enhancement of skills selected by experts, which favors drill and practice, tutorial, and other direct instruction methods. The computer takes the roles of a traditional teacher-information deliverer, evaluator, recordkeeper.
7. **Summative Evaluation Is Critical**	Invest the most assessment effort in the summative evaluation because ft will prove whether the material works or not.
8. **Objective Data Are Critical**	The more data the better, and the more objective the data the better. From identifying entry behaviors to task and concept analysis, pretests, and posttests, this model emphasizes collection and analysis of objective data.

TABLE 11.2   Family Characteristics of Constructivist-Interpretivist Instructional Design (C-ID) Models

1. The ID Process Is Recursive, Non-linear, and Sometimes Chaotic	Development is recursive or iterative; you will address the same issues such as learner analysis and instructional objectives many times. Development is also non-linear. There is no required beginning task that must be completed before all others. Some problems, improvements, or changes will only be discovered in the context of design and use. Plan for recursive evaluations by users and by experts. Plan for false starts and redesigns as-well as revisions.
2. Planning Is Organic, Developmental, Reflective, and Collaborative	Begin with a vague plan and fill in the details as you progress. "Vision and strategic planning come later. Premature visions and planning can blind" (Fullan, 1993). Development should be collaborative. The design group, which includes many who will use the instructional material, must work together to create a shared vision. That may emerge over the process of development. It cannot be "established" at the beginning. "Today, 'vision' is a familiar concept in corporate leadership. But when you look carefully, you find that most 'visions' are one person's (or one group's) vision imposed on an organization. Such visions, at best, command compliance-not commitment. . . . If people don't have their own vision, all they can do is 'sign up' for someone else's." (Senge, 1990, 206–211)
3. Objectives Emerge from Design and Development Work	Objectives do not guide development. Instead, during the process of collaborative development, objectives emerge and gradually become clearer.
4. General ID Experts Don't Exist	General ID specialists, who can work with subject matter experts from any discipline, are a myth. You must understand the "game" being played before you can help develop instruction. If specialists are used, they should be immersed in the environment of use before assisting with design. However, for much ID development, the "citizen legislator" model, as opposed to the "professional politician" model, is preferred. Citizen legislators are developers who know and understand the content or context of practice and who pick up the ID skills needed. Professional politicians are ID specialists who are not situated in the learning context or the content knowledge, domain.
5. Instruction Emphasizes Learning in Meaningful Contexts (The Goal Is Personal Understanding Within Meaningful Contexts)	Standard direct-instruction approaches that focus on teaching content outside a meaningful context often result in "inert' knowledge that is not useful. The instructional emphasis should be on developing understanding in context. This approach favors strategies such as anchored instruction, situated cognition, cognitive apprenticeships, and cognitive flexibility hypertext.

(continued)

TABLE 11.2   Family Characteristics of Constructivist-Interpretivist Instructional Design (C-ID) Models (continued)

	Also favored are instructional approaches that pose problems and provide students with access to knowledge needed to solve the problems. This favors development of hypermedia/multimedia information resources, electronic encyclopedias, and a wide range of accessible, navigable electronic information resources.
6. Formative Evaluation Is Critical	Invest the most assessment effort in the formative evaluations because they are the ones that provide feedback you can use to improve the product. Summative evaluation does nothing to help you improve the product.
7. Subjective Data May Be the Most Valuable	Many important goals and objectives cannot be adequately assessed with multiple choice exams, and exclusive reliance on such measures often limits the vision and value of instruction. Some things can be shown or observed but not quantified. Many types of assessment, including authentic assessment, portfolios, ethnographic studies, and professional opinions, should be considered. In addition, during the instructional design process, there are many points where informal or qualitative approaches, such as interviews, observations, user logs, focus groups, expert critiques, and verbal student feedback, can be much more valuable than a data from a 10 item, Likert-scale, questionnaire.

TABLE 11.3   The Choices Made by Developers of Objective-Rational and C-ID Models

Family of ID Models	Epistemology	Learning/Instructional Theory
Objective-Rational (e.g., Dick and Carey, ISD, ADDIE)	Positivism, Postpositivism	Behaviorism, Information Processing Theory, Cognitive Science, Instructionism, Direct Instruction
Constructivist Instructional Design Models	Interpretivism, Hermeneutics	Constructivism, Social Constructivism, Student-Centered Instruction

DESIGN-BASED RESEARCH:
A PROMISING MODEL OR MORE OF THE SAME?

In her paper inaugurating a series of articles on how to do research in the field of educational technology, M. D. Robyler (2005) began with the statement "We need a more organized and persuasive body of evidence on technology's benefits to classroom practice." She then discussed the problems of the existing body of research such as "fragmented and uncoordinated approaches to studying technology resources and strategies, methods that lack rigor or are ill-matched to the research questions at hand, and poorly written reports that render problematic subsequent attempts at replication and follow-up." Robyler's analysis of the continuing problems of traditional educational technology research leads her to suggest some solutions. One of them is to acknowledge that the instructional design process is one form of research. Instructional design (ID) has been a major component of the field of educational technology virtually from the beginning, but it has typically been viewed as a professional practice activity which is separate from, and different from, educational technology research. But Robyler believes "the field is beginning to resound with the call for a new educational technology research agenda—one that focuses on capturing the unique impact of technology-enhanced instructional designs, rather than the digital technologies themselves." She describes an approach that suggests five pillars for educational technology research:

1. **The Significance Criterion.** "Every educational research study should make a clear and compelling case for its existence." She advises that in an era when scientific evidence of impact is emphasized by the federal officials and many others, "articles that report research studies with technology-based teaching strategies should begin by making it clear that they address a significant educational problem, as opposed to a proposed technology solution."

2. **The Rationale Criterion.** Failure to "attend to the need for a solid theory base in research" is very damaging to the field. "If we are to make progress in this field or any other, new research must carefully consider previous lines of research, and each study must be built on a foundation of theory about expected effects derived from past work."

3. **The Design Criterion.** "After establishing research questions, researchers must decide on a research approach and methods that are well-suited to capturing and measuring impact on the variables of interest." Robyler rejects the positivist foundations of the No Child Left Behind model of educational research that considers randomized experimental studies as the gold standard. She argues that many research designs are appropriate. "What is essential is a design that is a logical choice for the questions under study." She supports the thoughtful use of both objective, scientific methods as well as naturalistic inquiry which includes a great many traditional qualitative research methods plus methods drawn from the humanities and philosophy.

4. **The Comprehensive Reporting Criterion.** This criterion addresses the problem of how research is to progress toward a goal of better knowledge about important questions and problems. Knowledge should be cumulative across a series of studies on the same issue. Robyler believes that this is often difficult or impossible because many research reports do not provide "enough sufficiently detailed information to allow others to analyze and build on previous work." Well organized and detailed reports of research are needed but often not provided.

5. **The Cumulativity Criterion.** This criterion also addresses the question of how individual research papers can contribute to cumulativity—to "moving the field forward." Robyler advises that "articles reporting research ideally should make it clear that the study is part of a current or proposed line of research, along with proposed next steps in the line."

In the political sphere, when efforts to solve a major problem have not been very successful, the proposals for correction fall into two broad categories (see Figure 11.4).

Some will argue that what has been done in the past was not done well enough, or was not done in the quantity needed. As I write this, the most obvious example of this tendency is President Bush's "surge" answer to the problems of the war in Iraq. When the military solution to Iraq did not work, he sent more troops. On the other side, virtually all of the Democratic candidates for President took the opposite position—remove the combat troops from Iraq. Robyler's solution to the problems of educational technology research falls roughly in the "more and better" tradition of dealing with failure. With the exception of her acceptance of natural inquiry models of research, all of her Pillars are compatible with a positivist model of applied research (and many are also compatible with an interpretivist approach as well). The Pillars and the text of the article emphasize the importance of the *Theory-Implications-Practice* link that is at the heart of positivist thinking. She emphasizes over and over again that we should use research methods that "can help researchers understand the effects of technology on student

Figure 11.4   Two responses to failure.

learning." My reading of Robyler is that she believes that by doing better research we can discover general rules about technology and learning that are robust enough to be transferred from the context of discovery to other contexts of application. This is a positivist goal that is solidly in the tradition of finding universals that can be generalized to other settings.

In a commentary on the Robyler article, Chris Dede (2005) praised the beginning of the series on research methods and commented on one of the types of research mentioned by Robler: "studies of technology-based instructional designs" which she described as "almost non-existent in the existing literature." Dede argued that the reverse is true, "scholars are publishing a growing body of high quality, design-based research studies that address many of the weaknesses of typical scholarship in educational technology." What Dede was referring to is *design-based research* (DBR). He notes that there have been special issues on DBR in the *Journal of Learning Sciences* (2004, Vol. 13, No. 1), *Educational Researcher* (2003, Vol. 32, No 1) and *Educational Technology* (2005, Vol. 45, No. 1). Several authors, including Dede, have used the work of Pasteur as a foundation for DBR. Pasteur's work tended to focus on "difficult, applied, practice-driven questions" that direct the researcher to questions that are, at their base, "fundamental theoretical issues." This idea comes from Stokes' (1997) book about how basic and applied research can be related. Stokes rejected what he considered the simplistic idea that research could be organized by a binary categorization of Basic or Applied. He developed a four quadrant diagram that represented the relative importance of basic knowledge and applied use to the researcher. (see Figure 11.5)

The work of Neils Bohr is an example of a research program that has a High interest in Foundational Knowledge and No interest in Applied Use.

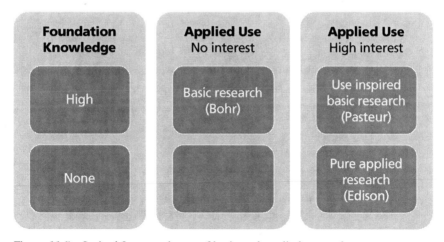

Figure 11.5 Stokes' four quadrants of basic and applied research.

When he developed a description of the atomic structure of the universe, Bohr was searching for basic, foundational knowledge but he had little or no interest in how that knowledge might be applied. Thomas Edison's research, on the other hand, is an example of work with a very High interest in Applied Use and No interest in Foundational Knowledge. When he developed the light bulb and the phonograph, his interest was on developing a useful product. And, while he was quite willing to use foundational knowledge he had little or no interest in developing basic or foundational knowledge in his own work. He was a *consumer*, not a producer, of foundational knowledge.

Stokes (1997) comments that it would be appropriate to call his bottom right quadrant "Edison's quadrant "in view of how strictly this brilliant inventor kept his co-workers at Menlo Park, in the first industrial research laboratory in America, from pursuing the deeper scientific implications of what they were discovering in their headlong rush toward commercially profitable electric lighting. A great deal of modern research that belongs in this category is extremely sophisticated, although narrowly targeted on immediate applied goals" (p. 74).

Many of the educational technology scholars who appreciate Stokes' model, believe the work of Louis Pasteur, not Thomas Edison, is the example we should follow. Stokes suggests calling the upper right quadrant Pasteur's Quadrant "in view of how clearly Pasteur's drive toward understanding and use illustrates this combination of [basic and applied] goals" (p. 74). Pasteur worked from the context of practice. He looked for problems in practice and then tried to understand the origins and causes of the problem. For example, he became concerned with the practical problem of stopping milk and wine from going sour. His research led to his understanding that active and living micro-organisms entered nutrient broths such as milk and wine when they were open to the air. (An earlier explanation was the *spontaneous generation* of living organisms from non-living matter.) He also showed that these microorganisms were the cause of the problem. That was basic knowledge that was not known before his research. He developed the process of pasteurization to prevent the problem, based on his discovery that even microscopic organisms would die if exposed to enough heat. That was his applied contribution in this case.

Stokes' model and Pasteur's Quadrant appeal to educational technologists who want our discipline to be an applied field that makes a difference in education and training *as well as* a field that contributes to basic knowledge about human learning. Pasteur's Quadrant lets the field do just that. Chris Dede (2005) used Stokes model when he proposed that DBR is an example of research in Pasteur's Quadrant.

> DBR resembles the scholarly strategy chosen by the scientist Pasteur, in which investigation of difficult, applied, practice-driven questions demands and fos-

ters studies of fundamental theoretical issues. As one illustration, the research my colleagues and I are conducting on multi-user virtual environments (Nelson, Ketelhut, Clarke, Bowman, & Dede, 2005) tests the efficacy of three alternative pedagogical strategies based on different theories about learning: guided social constructivism, expert mentoring and coaching, and legitimate peripheral participation in communities of practice. We are examining which of these pedagogies works best for various types of content and skills, as well as for different kinds of learners.

DBR is the most common name for this type of scholarship but it is not the only one. Others include *development research, design research, formative research, design experiments* and *educational design research.* All these terms have been used in the literature to refer to design research in Pasteur's Quadrant.

Pasteur's Quadrant is also the focus of some proponents of change in the general field of educational research. Burkhardt and Schoenfelt (2003), for example, cite the "awful reputation of educational research" and use Pasteur's Quadrant to advocate design research based on an engineering model:

> In the educational research community the engineering approach is often undervalued. At major universities only "insight" research in the humanities or science tradition tends to be regarded as true research currency for publication, tenure, and promotion. Yet engineering research has a key role to play in making educational research as a whole more useful. In Pasteur's Quadrant, Stokes (1997) argues that better insights come from situating inquiry in arenas of practice where engineering is a major concern. Stokes's motivating example is Pasteur, whose work on solving real world issues contributed fundamentally to theory while addressing pressing problems such as anthrax, cholera, and food spoilage.... Analogous arguments have been made regarding the potential for such work in education (National Academy of Education, 1999; Schoenfeld, 1999), and serve as a justification for design experiments. Our point is that the same profitable dialectic between theory and practice can and should occur (with differing emphases on the R&D components) from the initial stages of design all the way through robust implementation on a large scale. We also argue that success will breed success: Once this approach is shown to produce improved materials that work on a large scale, more funding will become available for it. Such has been the history in other applied fields, such as medicine and consumer electronics. (p. 5)

Design-Based Research is an example of how Pasteur's quadrant can be used to refocus and reform our approach to research in education and educational technology. As an emerging model for research, many aspects of DBR have not yet been agreed upon, even by those most involved in promoting the approach. However, I believe there is enough agreement to permit a critique of DBR. In the next two sections I will explore desirable and undesirable family characteristics of DBR. I do this from the perspective of an interpretivist and a constructivist and make no pretense at trying to be "objective" about my judgments

Desirable Characteristics of DBR

Two characteristics of DBR seem to add considerably to the possibilities of educational technology research, and particularly to the idea of ID as scholarship.

Emphasize *Use-Inspired Research.* This suggestion, made by Stokes (1997) and many others, makes sense. In education and the social sciences we have failed at the positivist research goal of discovering universals that can guide practice. The result of that failure is the separation of research from practice so that the "success" of a researcher is dependent, not on the contributions made to improving professional practice, but to the judgment of other researchers. When researchers publish mainly for other researchers, and their contributions are evaluated by other researchers, the gap between research and practice becomes wider and wider. One way to narrow that gap is to insist that in an applied field like educational technology, researchers should be encouraged to conduct "use-inspired research." DBR does just that—it focuses research on the design and development of educational resources.

Integrate Research and Development. Reeves (2000) pointed out that there has been a traditional separation of "research" and 'development" (with ID considered development, not research) in our field. It is even evident in the way one of the leading journals is organized. Both the title of the journal, *Educational Technology Research and Development,* and the organization of the journal into two separate sections (one on research, another on development) with different groups making decisions about what is published and what is rejected, highlights the tendency in our field to view research and development as separate and distinct activities. "Some instructional technologists appear to have great commitment to basic research, regardless of whether it has any practical value, perhaps because basic research seems more scientific or they believe that it is someone else's role to figure out how to apply the findings of basic research. Others seem to believe that the value of basic research in a design field such as IT is limited and that IT research should therefore have direct and clear implications for practice" (Reeves, 2000). Reeves proposes that we place ourselves squarely in Pasteur's quadrant and focus on "use-inspired basic research." He justifies his proposal in several ways, but one of the most important is that "in contemporary science, new technological developments often permit the advancement of new types of research, thus reversing the direction of the basic to applied model." Reeves thus does not give up on discovering basic knowledge; he is simply arguing that we approach the task from a different angle. Instead of doing "basic research" in the Niels Bohr tradition, we should emulate another successful scientist, Louis Pasteur, and work on problems that are important to practitioners. In the process of doing "use-inspired basic research" we may discover more basic knowledge than we have discovered using the Bohr or basic research model.

Summarizing Ann Brown (1992) and Alan Collins (1992), Reeves specifies three critical characteristic of the type of design experiments he advocates:

- "addressing complex problems in real contexts in collaboration with practitioners,
- integrating known and hypothetical design principles with technological affordances to render plausible solutions to these complex problems, and
- conducting rigorous and reflective inquiry to test and refine innovative learning environments as well as define new design principles"

These three characteristic represent a radical departure from the traditional positivist approach to educational technology research. For example, the first characteristic acknowledges that work in "real contexts" is more important than maintaining tight control of the study by conducting it in tightly controlled "laboratory" conditions. The first characteristic also acknowledges the critical importance of local knowledge by making collaboration with practitioners a fundamental component of design experiments. The second critical characteristic emphasizes the need to work from an informed position, taking into consideration the relevant professional and scholarly literature. The third characteristic emphasizes the need to carefully and thoroughly study the products of design experiments to determine what works and what does not work. Reeves specifically includes an interpretivist method, reflective inquiry, as an important method of doing that. The only vestige of a positivist approach is his last phrase—"as well as define new design principles." Without this last phase, design experiments as he defines them could just as well fall into Thomas Edison's quadrant of pure applied research as Pasteur's quadrant of use-inspired basic research. However, even here he acknowledges that some people may consider these new design principles not as truths that have been discovered but as ideas readers, rather than the researcher, will decide whether to adopt, adapt, or reject in their own work context. In spite of that concession, Reeves remains enamored with the idea that design experiments will produce generalizable knowledge very similar to the law-like generalizations of positivist research. For example, he describes the work of Jan Herrington and her colleagues at Edith Cowan University as a "long-term effort to develop and apply a model of situated learning theory.... She not only developed a model of the critical factors of situated learning and instantiated these factors in multimedia learning environments, but she tested the model and the technological products in multiple contexts, including pre-service teacher education courses and K–12 schools." This sounds very much like research in the positivist tradition and I believe it reflects Reeves' reluctance to give up on the positivist agenda of finding laws and generalizable truths that can be discovered in one context and generalized to other contexts. His diagram of the process of development research (e.g., design experiments or DBR) also reflects this emphasis (see Figure 11.6).

The second and fourth boxes reflect a positivist heritage in Reeve's model. Requiring that solutions be developed "with a theoretical framework" harks back to the positivist idea that in *real* research the most important thing is to develop and validate theories that represent our current thinking about what is true and generalizable from one context to another. In Reeves model, there is no opportunity to take a pragmatic approach and ignore theory (or take a theoretically promiscuous approach) while trying to design instructional resources that "work" in the local context. In Reeves model, theory comes in early and stays late. In the fourth step of the process, documentation of what happened when the resource was actually used, and reflection on the process and results, come together to produce "design principles" that can be passed on to other designers. Note that the emphasis is on the creation of design principles, which are based on the theoretical framework established in Step 2. The model thus emphasizes the accomplishment of a theoretical goal—the creation of design principles—rather than the accomplishment of a practical goal—the creation of useful resources for use in the local context. This difference is what separates Edison's Quadrant from Pasteur's Quadrant.

Another difference reflects a positivist rather than an interpretivist approach to generalization. It is the researchers doing design experiments

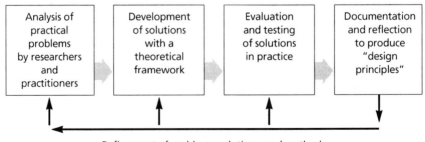

Figure 11.6 Reeves' model of design experiments. (Adapted from Reeves (2000).

who develop the "design principles" and pass them on to practitioners. A more interpretive approach might provide practitioners with enough information about a design experiment to let them make the decision about design principles they want to try out in their own setting rather than accepting those developed by the researcher. Some of Reeve's commentary suggests just that approach, but other comments are more compatible with a positivist model.

Undesirable Characteristics of DBR

Two characteristics of DBR seem likely to generate very undesirable results. One of them has already been mentioned.

Maintaining the Hope of Finding Laws. As noted earlier Reeves' (2000) model of DBR emphasizes the importance of organizing design work within a theoretical framework and using the applied design work to develop "design principles" that are essentially generalizations in the positivist sense of that term. However, he undercuts the possibility of doing that by distinguishing between research in fields like chemistry and biology, and research in education. "Education is a fundamentally different type of science, if it is a science at all, and educational researchers have never produced discoveries even remotely analogous to those in the physical and biological sciences. Educational researchers must confront the sterility of their past labors and make radical steps to conduct inquiry in more productive ways." This is a fundamental contradiction found in much of the DBR literature. The approach insists that a critical component of the work is to find generalizable knowledge, whether it be called "design principles" or something else. Yet, at the same time, proponents of DBR criticize the existing research for its failure to find just those sorts of generalizations. Many, like Reeves (2000, 2006) and Flyvbjerg (2001) also doubt that such a goal will ever be accomplished. Seeking law-like generalizations while also developing locally useful educational resources has the potential to reduce the amount and quality of those educational resources while, at the same time, continuing the tradition of positivist research in the social sciences—investing much to find laws and achieving little.

Rejection of Work Based on Interpretivist and Hermeneutic Paradigms. Much of the work on the conceptual and theoretical foundations of Design-Based Research involves a careful balancing act between harsh criticism of the existing body of positivist research in educational technology, and enthusiastic recommendations to pursue a modified version of the positivist agenda. While it is a thoughtful and useful analysis, Reeves' (2000) paper is a good example of this. After criticizing the "poor quality" of the existing body of research on educational technology, he nevertheless rejects the most radical efforts at reform. Interpretivist studies, which are "focused on portraying how education works by describing and interpreting phenomena related to teaching, learning, performance assessment, social interaction, innovation, and so forth" are criticized as producing little results that can be generalized to other settings. He concludes that "there is little evidence that the increasing popularity of qualitative methods will improve the impact of IT research on practice, especially given that the proponents of qualitative approaches make few claims to generalizability." In making this criticism of interpretive/qualitative research Reeves is using a positivist framework that insists the development of generalizable knowledge is the primary goal of a researcher. He ignores the focus in interpretive research on shifting the responsibility for generalization to the consumer of the research. He also seems to assume that generalization can only occur in the form specified by the positivist research model. That form of generalization involves carefully studying a selected sample of subjects drawn from the population the researcher wishes to generalize the results to. If all the requirements of positivist research are met (which almost never happens) the findings of a study should be generalizable from the sample to the population.

Greenwood and Levin (2005) presented another approach to generalization in their discussion of how universities, especially the academic departments of social science, could be reformed and brought into more relevant contact with the societies around them. These authors follow Flyvbjerg's (2001) approach of situating a discussion in Aristotle's framework of three types of knowledge: epistemic, techne, and phronesis:

- Episteme is "the conventional and favored form of explicit and theoretical knowledge and the form that currently dominates academic social sciences. . . . The sources of episteme are multiple—speculative, analytical, logical, and experiential—but the focus is always on eternal truths beyond their materialization in concrete situations. . . . Episteme accords rather closely to everyday usage of the term theory." (p. 50).
- Techne "is a form of knowledge that is inherently action oriented and inherently productive. Techne engages in the analysis of what should be done in the world in order to increase human happiness. . . . The courses of techne are multiple, [but all of them require] sufficient experiental engagement in the world to permit the analysis of 'what should be done.'" It is craft and art knowledge, and "as an activity it is concrete, variable, and context-dependent. The objective of techne is application of technical knowledge and skills according to a pragmatic instrumental rationality" (p. 50). While Greenwood and Levin acknowledge that "practitioners of techne do engage with local stakeholders, power holders, and other

experts, ... they are first and foremost professional experts who do things 'for,' not 'with,' the local stakeholders. They bring general designs and habits of work to the local case and privilege their own knowledge over that of the local stakeholders" (p. 51).

- Phronesis "is best understood as the design of action through collaborative knowledge construction with the legitimate stakeholders in a problematic situation. The sources of phronesis are collaborative arenas for knowledge development in which the professional researcher's knowledge is combined with the local knowledge of the stakeholders in defining the problem to be addressed. Together, they design and implement the research that needs to be done to understand the problem. They then design the actions to improve the situation together, and they evaluate the adequacy of what has been done. If they are not satisfied, they cycle through the process again until the results are satisfactory to all the parties" (p. 51). I am not sure that Aristotle would recognize this definition of phronesis if through some magical process this quote could be read to him. It is an expansion of Aristotle's ideas into the modern context of qualitative research in complex 21st century democracies, which is no mean feat. However, Greenwood and Levin's characterization is probably defendable if expansive. They go on to say that phronesis involves creating a "new space for collaborative reflection, the contrast and integrating of many kinds of knowledge systems, the linking of the general and the particular through action and analysis, and the collaborative design of both the goals and the actions aimed at achieving them" (p. 51). This is very close to the core ideas of Participatory Action Research but it can also be applied to an interpretivist form of design experiments. The authors also talk about phronesis developing within egalitarian "communities of practice" that collaboratively develop their own core beliefs that lead to an understanding of "knowing how to act to reach certain goals ... in real-world contexts with real-world materials." This is contextual knowledge as Greenwood and Levin point out, but it is also ethical and aesthetic knowledge, which involves making fundamental judgments about what is good for people. This is not emphasized by the authors but it is a part of Aristotle's original conception of phronesis.

Greenwood and Levin prefer *phronesis* over other forms of knowledge and approach the issue of how qualitative research results can be generalized by establishing their position on the role of epistemic knowledge. "'Knowing how' thus implies knowing how in a given context in which appropriate actions emerge from contextual knowing. The conventional understanding of general knowledge that treats it as supracontextual and thus universally applicable is of very little interest to us because we do not believe that what constitutes knowledge in the social sciences can be addressed usefully from the hothouse of armchair intellectual debate" (p. 51–52). The act of generalization in a positivist sense is based on the idea that humans can discover "supracontextual and thus universally applicable" knowledge about humans. Without that foundational assumption, generalization, at least in a positivist sense, is not a concern because it is not possible. Greenwood and Levin argue that social science's inability to discover universal knowledge means that the traditional distinction between basic and applied research is untenable. "We believe this division makes social research impossible. Thus, for us, the world divides into action research, which we support and practice, and conventional social research (subdivided into pure and applied social research and organized into professional subgroupings) that we reject on combined epistemological, methodological, and ethical/political grounds" (p. 53). The authors defend their position against "the dominance of positivistic frameworks and *episteme* in the organization of the conventional social sciences" and against the "hard-line interpretivists" who take a completely relativist position that since nothing is ever known for sure we cannot make sensible decisions about what action to take based on what we have come to know through scholarship.

If universal or epistemic knowledge is not possible in the social sciences, and extreme relativism in which every theory is no better, and no worse, than any other theory, are there any other viable possibilities? There are several, but the one Greenwood and Levin offer is based on a pragmatic philosophy of social science that was nurtured by three American scholars from the 19th and early 20th centuries: John Dewey, William James, and C. S. Pierce. One of the key points of pragmatism is how it defines truth. In a lecture given in 1904 titled *What Pragmatism Means*, William James explained pragmatic truth this way:

> Riding now on the front of this wave of scientific logic Messrs. Schiller and Dewey appear with their pragmatistic account of what truth everywhere signifies.... It means, they say, nothing but this, that ideas (which themselves are but parts of our experience) become true just in so far as they help us to get into satisfactory relation with other parts of our experience, to summarise them and get about among them by conceptual short-cuts instead of following the interminable succession of particular phenomena. Any idea upon which we can ride, so to speak; any idea that will carry us prosperously from any one part of our experience to any other part, linking things satisfactorily, working securely, simplifying, saving labor; is true for just so much, true in so far forth, true instrumentally. This is the 'instrumental' view of truth taught so successfully at Chicago, the view that truth in our ideas means their power to 'work,' promulgated so brilliantly at Oxford.

Messrs. Dewey, Schiller and their allies, in reaching this general conception of all truth, have only followed the example of geologists, biologists and philologists. In the establishment of these other sciences, the successful stroke was always to take some simple process actually observable in operation—as denudation by weather, say, or variation from parental type, or change of dialect by incorporation of new words and pronunciations—and then to generalise it, making it apply to all times, and produce great results by summarising its effects through the ages.

James is saying that "what works" is what is true. This is sometimes referred to as the "cash value" of truth. This is not the epistemic truth of positivists; it is the contextual and constrained truth of craft knowledge (techne) and the practical or praxis knowledge of phronesis. James does talk about the ability to generalize this form of truth, but that generalization is not the same as positivist generalization. For the positivists, a discovered law *must* generalize because it is universally true. Thus, if an effort to generalize a universal truth about how children learn mathematics fails, the most likely targets for blame are the teachers; they *must* have implemented the universal truth incorrectly. The generalization of pragmatists is not so assured because their idea of truth is based on the assumption that all distinctions and boundaries are subjective. The idea of *usefulness* is at the heart of pragmatic truth, not a match between what is said and what exists in the physical world. When the assumption that our understanding of the world is always subjective is combined with the concept of truth as *useful knowledge,* the result is an approach to scholarship that is more likely to question the truth than the implementers of truth when something goes wrong. Based on those foundations Greenwood and Levin propose that we do social science research that:

- Involves the generation of knowledge "through action and experimentation in context" (p. 53)
- Is based on "participative democracy as both a method and a goal" (p. 53)
- Relies on cogenerative inquiry which "aims to solve pertinent problems in a given context through democratic inquiry in which professional researchers collaborate with local stakeholders to seek and enact solutions to problems of major importance to the stakeholders. We refer to this as cogenrative inquiry because it is built on professional researcher-stakeholder collaboration and aims to solve real-life problems in context" (p. 54)
- Combines local knowledge and professional knowledge. That is, cogenerative inquiry involves the collaborative use of both local and professional knowledge and the result is often a unique solution to a problem that relies on that blending of the two forms of knowledge.

Proponents of this approach might argue that positivist approaches tend to privilege professional knowledge too much while interpretivist approaches tend to privilege local knowledge too much.

In advocating this form of scholarship the authors reject the dominant, positivist paradigm of social science research. "This positivist credo obviously is wrong, and it leads away from producing reliable information, meaningful interpretations, and social actions in social research" (p. 53).

A Note on Generalization from a Critical Theory Perspective. In this discussion of how the concept of truth acquires meaning and what generalization involves, I have not spent much time on the viewpoint of critical theory. For critical qualitative research, the issue of generalization is different from that of interpretivism but also at odds with the traditional positivist definition. Critical qualitative research often involves uncovering local instances of a universal phenomenon—oppression and domination. The purpose of critical research is, therefore, to uncover and make obvious the universal characteristics of oppression and domination in a specific local context. Thus, the logic of critical qualitative research does not so much involve taking data from a specific local context and then generalizing to a much broader or universal context. The theoretical foundations of critical theory include the assumption that what you find locally is an example of universal patterns in human relationships. It is a given then that each context will exhibit those universal patterns, though perhaps in different ways, and that emancipation may take different forms in different contexts. However, the need to go from local findings to universal conclusions is not so urgent in critical research as compared to positivist research. For the critical theorist the universals have already been discovered and that knowledge is the foundation upon which research is conducted. On the other hand, successful efforts at emancipation in one setting (e.g., teachers in a district mount a campaign to get better classroom support) will be looked at by other critical scholars who have similar interests. The particular methods used to successfully achieve emancipation are not, however, automatically generalized to other settings. As with interpretive scholarship, the generalization is based on (1) thick description of the original setting that allows us to carefully consider the original and the new context, and for many but not all critical theorists (2) consumer rather than researcher responsibility for deciding what and how to generalize.

BLENDING CONSTRUCTIVIST INSTRUCTIONAL DESIGN AND DBR: AN APPEALING ALTERNATIVE

Traditional instructional design models based on positivist assumptions and behavioral theories of learning are increasingly questioned by both practitioners and ID scholars (Cobb, 2002; Crawford, 2004; Häkkinen, 2002; Willis, 1995; Winters & Mor, 2008).

One of the alternatives, Constructivist Instructional Design, or C-ID, is emerging as an option for many instructional designers as they shift from positivist and behaviorist paradigms to constructivist and interpretivist or critical paradigms. However, C-ID models have been around for less than 20 years and they are still not widely used, nor have they had time to mature through several generations of use and revision cycles. Further, none of the existing C-ID models have as a purpose the positivist goal of finding universals such as the right processes for designing certain types of educational resources, the "best" teaching methods for particular types of content, or the "most effective" pedagogies for gifted, hyperactive, handicapped, immigrant, talented, or learning disabled children. C-ID models may be employed to develop educational resources and curricula for many contexts, but the emphasis is on development work *for the context at hand*. The generalization of design processes, pedagogies, or instructional strategies to other settings is left to those who read about the C-ID projects rather than the scholars and professionals who write papers on those projects. For many instructional technologists this is a weakness. Reeves (2000) is critical of action research because it is "similar to development research (e.g. DBR) except that there is little or no effort to construct theory, models, or principles to guide future design initiatives. The major goal is solving a particular problem in a specific place within a relatively short timeframe. Some theorists maintain that this type of inquiry is not research at all, but merely form of evaluation." Reeves does accept action research as a "legitimate form of research provided reports of it are shared with wider audiences who may themselves choose to draw inferences from these reports in a sense similar to reports of interpretivist research." While hardly providing a ringing endorsement of interpretive, critical, and action research, Reeves does at least make some room for these approaches in educational technology. However, his primary focus is on "developmental research" in the form of "use-inspired basic research." As noted earlier, I find the optimism of DBR proponents that law-like generalizations and universal laws can be discovered about education to be too optimistic given the more than 100 years of failure to make even modest strides toward fulfilling this hope (Flyvbjerg, 2001).

Perhaps there is a way of combining the more open and flexible processes of C-ID models (Willis, 2000; Willis & Wright, 2001) with the goal of generalizable conclusions that are often a goal of design-based research (DBR). C-ID proponents would accept that what they learn in the professional practice of design may be of use to other designers, and DBR proponents would accept the idea that the end result will not be the positivist laws and universals but kinder, gentler suggestions, ideas, and exemplars that can be considered by other designers, but never unthinkingly adopted without thoughtful and reflective consideration of their relevance for a new and different context. This middle ground asks the constructivist-interpretivist to accept that there can be enough commonality from one context to another to justify thoughtful importation (and adaptation) across the contexts. It asks DBR proponents to check their enthusiasm and their hope that universal laws about human behavior can be discovered and articulated.

A related approach was suggested by a National Science Foundation Senior Program Director, Nora Sabelli, and Chris Dede at the Harvard Graduate School of Education (2001):

> The strategy we advocate for increasing the impact of research on education practice goes beyond "transfer" and "action research" towards reconceptualizing the relationship between scholarship and practice...An analogy for understanding a "scholarship of practice" is to consider the levels of experimentation and applied research that take place after scientific research in the physical sciences is conducted and published, and before the results of this research are applied large-scale in society. The field of education does not provide roles akin to engineering for developing research prototypes into robust practices and products. As discussed later, the outcomes of research include people, not just knowledge, and transfer between research and practice is implemented through both scholarly products and human capacity-building.
>
> Stokes' recent book and related policy papers reinforce this perspective by presenting models for relating fundamental and targeted research, strategies largely absent in educational scholarship. These include the use-driven research model successfully applied by NIH to simultaneously:
>
> - provide resources for fundamental biological research and its medical public health applications,
> - resolve persistent problems in medical practice through the adaptation of research findings, and
> - develop public and political support for allocating resources to both basic and applied research.
>
> Stokes argues convincingly for the Pasteur (or NIH) model, in which research on use-driven, applied questions demands and fosters studies of fundamental scientific problems associated with that practice. In fact, "use-inspired" basic research has the same quest for fundamental understanding that is present in "pure" basic research, associated in Stokes's analysis with Bohr's work as the defining paradigm. In contrast, in Stokes's analysis Edison's work is shown as driven solely by considerations of use, without a concomitant quest for fundamental understanding. (p. 2)

Sabelli and Dede's proposal is still too positivist for me. For example, it continues to use the natural sciences as a model for doing research in the human sciences even when a century of research dominated by natural science envy in the social sciences, particularly psychology, has not generated anything like the expected, and promised, outcome. Not one of the contemporary debates over questions such as charter schools, bilingual education, multicultural education, gender bias, phonics versus whole language, evidence-based education, high stakes testing, accountability and a hundred other major issues in education has been settled by empirical research. Like opposing lawyers in a major court case, each side has its favored experts and cites its favored research, but what is surprising from a positivist view is that there seems to be research that supports all the major sides in any significant debate about education! Consider the question of phonics versus whole language. Research has not settled that long and contentious debate. Over the past 60 or so years, there have been shifts in what approach is emphasized in literacy programs, but those shifts are probably linked to shifts in ideology (often liberal versus conservative political ideologies) rather than new empirical research.

Therefore, if we add the goal of generalization to instructional design work based on C-ID models, it is not only reasonable, it is critically important, that the type of generalizations we attempt to make are tentative and contextual rather than assertive and universal. How do we do that? We do it by including in our papers and presentations on ID projects the "thick description" and detail so eloquently called for by Clifford Geertz (1973) so many years ago. Readers cannot make decisions about what to generalize from a study without a rich description of all aspects of an instructional design project. Also, and perhaps even more important, when we write papers about our ID projects we should add to the rich narrative detail about the process, components that take the discussion up a level or two in generality to make suggestions about design procedures that seemed to work well in a particular context (appropriately detailed in the paper), pedagogies and strategies that seemed to work well for students or content or instructional purposes (also all appropriately detailed in the paper). And finally, the third thing we would need to do is make sure we do not fall back into the positivist mode of thinking that allows us to present our generalizations as laws and universals. Presenting them with rich descriptions of the context in which we came to our understanding, and acknowledging the contextual limitations of any generalization about human behavior, models appropriate behavior for readers just as acknowledging that our own biases, beliefs, and prior experiences (again, detailed in our papers to the best of our abilities) have had a major influence on how we interpret the process and results of our design work.

IN SUMMARY

Instructional design has been dominated since its inception by positivist paradigms, empiricist beliefs, and behaviorist theories of learning. Over the past thirty or so years there have been a number of efforts to move beyond Instructional Systems Design/ADDIE models that tend to organize the process of ID into a set of linear steps based on positivist thinking and behavioral learning theory. Many of these models are actually Pedagogical ID models because they emphasize the selection of teaching strategies based on a preferred family of learning theories. Process ID models seem more promising in a field where there has been considerable doubt as to its success and promise. Recently, two alternatives, Design-Based Research (DBR) and Constructivist Instructional Design (C-ID), have emerged as appealing options to ISD. Though different, these two approaches to ID both have strengths. One possible way of harnessing those strengths to (1) develop locally useful educational resources and (2) suggest generalizations that may be applicable in other settings is to combine the approach to ID as a process that comes from C-ID models with the continuing optimism of DBR that we can yet discover useful generalizations about human behavior.

REFERENCES

Akker, J., Gravemeijer, K., McKenney, S., & Nieveen, N. (2006). *Educatonal Design Research*. London: Routledge.

Bressler, C. (2007). *Literary criticism: An introduction to theory and practice, 4th ed.* Upper Saddle River, NJ: Pearson Prentice Hall.

Brown, A. L. (1992). Design experiments: Theoretical and methodological challenges in creating complex interventions in classroom settings. *The Journal of the Learning Sciences, 2*(2), 141–178.

Cennamo, K. S., Abell, S. K., and Chung, M. L. (1996). A "Layers of Negotiation" model for designing constructivist learning materials. *Educational Technology*, July-August 1996, 39–48

Cennamo, K., Abell, S., Chung, M., Campbell, L., and Hugg, W. (1995). *A "Layers of Negotiation" model for designing constructivist learning materials.* Proceedings of the Annual National Convention of the Association for Educational Communications and Technology (AECT), Anaheim, CA, 95, pp. 32–42.

Cobb, P. (2002). Theories of knowledge and instructional design: A response to Colliver. *Teaching and Learning in Medicine, 14*(1), 52–55.

Collins, A. (1992). Towards a design science of education. In E. Scanlon & T. O'Shea (Eds.), *New directions in educational technology* (pp. 15–22). Berlin: Springer.

Crawford, C. (2004). Non-linear instructional design model: Eternal, synergistic design and development. *British Journal of Educational Technology, 35*(4), 414–420.

Dick, W., Carey, L., & Carey, J. (2004). *The systematic design of instruction*, 6th ed. Boston: Allyn & Bacon.

Duffy, T., & Cunningham D. (1996). Constructivism: Implications for the design and delivery of instruction. In Jonassen, D. H. (Ed.), *Handbook of Research for Educational Communications and Technology*, New York: Simon and Schuster, 170–198.

Flyvbjerg, B. (2001). *Making social science matter: Why social inquiry fails and how it can succeed again.* Cambridge, UK: Cambridge University Press.

Fullan, M. (1993). *Change forces: Probing the depths of educational reform.* Bristol, PA: The Falmer Press.

Gadamer, H.-G. (2004). *Truth and method,* 2nd revised ed. New York: Continuum.

Geertz, C. (1973). Thick description: Toward an interpretive theory of culture. In *The Interpretation of Cultures* (pp. 3–32). New York: Harper.

Häkkinen, P. (2002). Challenges for design of computer-based learning environments. *British Journal of Educational Technology, 33*(4), 461–469.

Harding, S. (1993). Rethinking Standpoint Epistemology: What is "Strong Objectivity"?" In L. Alcoff & E. Potter (Eds). *Feminist Epistemologies,* (49–82). New York:Routledge.

Hensley, G. (2005). Creating a hybrid college course: Instructional design notes and recommendations for beginners. Journal of Online Teaching, 2(1). Retrieved June 11, 2007 from http://jolt.merlot.org/vol1_no2_hensley.htm

James, W. (1906). Lecture II: What pragmatism means. Retrieved 06/13/2007 from http://www.marxists.org/reference/subject/philosophy/works/us/james.htm

Johari, A., Chen, C., & Toh, S. (2005, March). A feasible constructivist instructional development model for virtual reality (VR)-based learning environments: Its efficacy in the novice car driver instruction of Malaysia. *Educational Technology Research and Development, 53*(1), 111–123.

Lebow, D. (1993). Constructivist values for instructional systems design: Five principles toward a new mindset. *Educational Technology Research and Development,* 41 (3), 4–16

McDaniel, (Eds). *Judgment Calls: Rhetoric, Politics, and Indeterminancy* (13–41). Boulder, CO: Westview Press.

McGee, M. (1998). Phronesis in the Gadamer versus Habermas debates. In J. Sloop & J. McDaniel (Eds), Judgement Calls: Rhetoric, Politics, and Indeterminancy (pp. 13–41). Boulder, CO: Westview Press.

McMahon, M. (2003). Cultural and post-structuralist feminism. Retrieved 05/28/2007 from http://webpages.ull.es/users/mmcmahon/textos/feminisms.htm

Merrill, M. D. & ID2 Research Group. (1996). Reclaiming the Discipline of Instructional Design. *ITForum.* Retrieved 06/12/2007 from http://itech1.coe.uga.edu/itforum/extra2/extra2.html

Merrill, M. D., Drake, L, Lacy, M, Pratt, J., & the Utah State University ID2 Research Group. (1996). Reclaiming instructional design. *Educational Technology, 36*(5), 5–7. Available: http://www.coe.usu.edu/it/id2/reclaim.html

Reeves, T. (2000). Enhancing the worth of instructional technology research through "design experiments" and other development research strategies. Paper presented at Annual Meeting of the American Educational Research

Association, New Orleans, LA. Retrieved 06/12/2007 from http://it.coe.uga. edu/~treeves/AERA2000Reeves.pdf

Reeves, T. (2006). Design research from a technology perspective. In J Akker, K. Gravemeijer, S. McKenney, & N. Nieveen (Eds). *Educational design research.* London: Routledge.

Richards, S., Taylor, R., Ramasamy, R., & Richards, R. (1998). *Single-subject research applications in educational and clinical settings.* Belmont, CA: Wadsworth.

Senge, P. (1990). *The fifth discipline.* New York: Doubleday.

Skinner, C. (2005). Single-subject designs for school psychologists. Binghamton, NY: Haworth Press.

Suarez, V. (2000). Hispanic American Literature: Divergence and Commonality. Retrieved 05/26/2007 from http://usinfo.state.gov/journals/itsv/0200/ijse/latino1.htm

Willis, J. & Wright, K. (2000, March/April). A general set of procedures for constructivist instructional design: The New R2D2. *Educational Technology, 40*(2), 5–20.

Willis, J. (2000). The maturing of constructivist instructional design: Some basic principles that can guide practice. *Educational Technology, 40*(1), 5–16.

Willis, J. (1995). A recursive, reflective instructional design model based on constructivist-interpretivist theory. *Educational Technology , 35*(6), 5–23.

Wilson, B. (1997). Reflections on Constructivism and Instructional Design. In Dills, C. R. & Romiszowski, A. A. (Eds.), *Instructional Development Paradigms*, (63–80). Englewood Cliffs, NJ: Educational Technology Publications, 63–80.

Winters, N. & Mor, Y. (2008). IDR: A participatory methodology for interdisciplinary design in technology-enhanced learning. *Computers & Education, 50*(2), 579–600.

READINGS FOR CHAPTER 11

Readings 11.1 to 11.4

Willis, J. (November–December, 1995). A recursive, reflective, instructional design model based on constructivist-interpretivist theory. *Educational Technology, 35*(6), 5–23.

Willis, J. (May–June, 1998). Alternative instructional design paradigms: What's worth discussing and what isn't. *Educational Technology, 38*(4), 5–16.

Willis, J. (January–February, 2000). The maturing of constructivist instructional design: Some basic principles that can guide practice. *Educational Technology, 41*(1), 5–15.

Willis, J., & Egeland Wright, K. (March–April, 2000). A general set of procedures of constructivist instructional design: The new R2D2 Model. *Educational Technology, 41*(2), 5–20.

These four papers detail the development of a constructivist instructional design model called R2D2 that I began developing while working on a NASA project at the Johnson Space Center in Houston. The first article contains a conceptual and theoretical framework for both rejecting traditional ID models and developing another one based on a different set of assumptions. The second paper addresses some of the issues still under debate in the literature and suggests what is important enough to the field to continue exploring. The final two papers are, taken together, a major revision of the R2D2 model of ID that is based on the additional experiences of my group from 1995 to 2000.

As you read these papers ask yourself whether the conceptual and theoretical foundations for rejecting traditional ID models are meaningful. What do you think? What about the foundations for constructivist instructional design? Do those foundations appeal to you or do you find at least some of them weak or wrong? Explain and defend your position.

Finally, what elements of the R2D2 model appeal to you? Why? What elements or approaches seem less satisfactory or problematic? Why?

Reading 11.5

Colon, B., Taylor, K., & Willis, J. Constructivist instructional design: Creating a multimedia package for teaching critical qualitative research. *The Qualitative Report*, 5(1/2). Available: http://www.nova.edu/ssss/QR/QR5–1/Colon.html

This is an example of how the R2D2 ID model was used to guide the development of an instructional package for teaching certain qualitative research methods. Did the researchers actually follow the basic concepts of the R2D2 model, or were some of them modified or ignored in this real world project? Explain your answer. If you had been an instructional designer on this project, what would you have changed in terms of the process of design? Why? And, do the changes you would have made fit within the general principles of C-ID, or are they based on other theories, models, or foundations?

Reading 11.6

Chwen Jen Chen & Seong Chong Toh. (2005. A feasible constructivist instructional development model for virtual reality (VR)-based learning environments: Its efficacy in the novice car driver instruction of Malaysia. *Educational Technology Research & Development, 53*(1), 111–123.

This is another study that used a C-ID model to develop instructional material. In this case the project was led by two instructional designers who wanted to use virtual reality technology to enhance the quality of driving instruction in Malaysia. As you read this paper answer the same questions you did for Reading 5.

Reading 11.7

Cennamo, K., Abell, S., & Chung, M.-L. (July–August, 1996). A "layers of negotiation" model for designing constructivist learning materials. *Educational Technology, 36*(4), 39–48.

This paper describes another C-ID model and it also presents a case study in which the model was used to develop some case-based lessons for elementary school science. How does this C-ID model differ from the R2D2 model? Are there different emphases? Explain your answer? Are different procedures recommended or required? Describe them or show how the two models share a very similar framework for doing ID. Finally, describe a ID project that you feel the R2D2 model would be best for, and another for which the Layers of Negotiation model would be the model of choice. Are there ID projects that would not be a good fit for either of these C-ID models? If there are, please describe one of them and explain why there would not be a good fit.

SECTION 4

DISSEMINATION OF RESULTS

CHAPTER 12

FORMS OF COMMUNICATION AND CONVERSATION

Disseminating the Results of Scholarship

Less than thirty years ago a chapter on how to "write up" a study would typically have focused on the process of writing a traditional research paper, with attention to the quirks and needs of the journals in education and educational technology. And, thirty years ago there were so few educational technology journals that the chapter could give some attention to the acceptable styles and formats for virtually every one of them!

That is not the case today. First, there are hundreds of journals devoted to educational technology. The acceptable styles range from requiring traditional research paper formats to flexible requirements that accept anything from dense philosophical papers to narratives, conversations, and poetry. Second, there are thousands of journals devoted to topics in education, psychology, and related fields that accept submissions on educational technology topics, and these journals have an even wider range of formats.

Perhaps the best advice about how to disseminate your work is to consider two options and select the one you are most comfortable with.

- Option 1. Find the journal (or another type of scholarly outlet) that is the best fit for your work. Carefully read the requirements for ar-

Qualitative Research Methods in Education and Educational Technology, pages 351–371
Copyright © 2008 by Information Age Publishing
All rights of reproduction in any form reserved. **351**

ticle submissions as well as many of the papers published recently in the journal (e.g., the last two years). Using that information, write or produce your paper following the guidelines, and the examples of papers in the publication.

- Option 2. Decide the best format or formats for presenting the results of your study. Start to create the report using that format and at the same time look for outlets that will accept submissions on your topic in the format you are using. If necessary, send a brief but informative query to the editor and ask, for example, if a qualitative discourse analysis article organized as a radio play would be considered.

Depending on your project, your preferences, and the range of your comfort zone when it comes to both trying innovative things and handling criticism as well as rejection, either of these options can work.

NO MATTER WHAT, DO THIS

While nothing is universal to an interpretivist qualitative researcher, there are a few suggestions I want to pass on that are based on 35 years of work as a scholar as well as a journal reviewer and editor.

- Make sure you meet the **length requirements** for the journal. Some journals like short, punchy articles while others accept papers that are almost long enough to be monographs. However, most journals prefer papers in the 12 to 25 page range (double spaced). It irritates an editor to receive a paper that will not even be considered because it is too long. If you believe your paper will be accepted despite being twice the maximum length stated in the "Information for Authors" section of the journal's web page, your name had better be as well known in the field as the current American President.
- Make sure you follow all of the **formatting requirements** for the paper. My estimation is that almost 90% of conference proceedings papers and 70% of journal submissions have errors in the formatting. Often the errors involve a failure to follow the APA (American Psychological Association) guidelines for how to do references. Most authors get the citation in the text correctly (e.g., "Jackson & Pollock, 2010), but the references at the end of the article often cause problems. Do you know, for example, whether the APA guidelines require you to put a period after the abbreviation for Editor (e.g., Ed.) or not (e.g., Ed)? Is there a comma between the journal name and the volume (*Reading Journal, 14*(2)) or a period (*Reading*

Journal. 14(2)? And, when you italicize the name of the journal in a citation, do you italicize the volume number too as in the second example, or the volume and issue number (*Reading Journal, 14(2)*? A paper with few, if any, problems with citations and references is welcome in any journal editorial office. There are many online guides to APA formatting for journal papers, and preparing a clean paper is little more than checking the rules and following them (or finding someone else who will do it for you). Two additional areas of formatting that are often mangled by authors are how to cite electronic publications and how to indicate a level 1 or main heading versus a level 2 or second level heading, and a third level heading. All these details are in hundreds of APA formatting guides online as well as in several publications from the American Psychological Association. Finally, tables are also frequently set up incorrectly with solid lines where dotted lines should be, or double lines where no lines at all should be.

- **Correct any inconsistencies** in format. If you have second level headings and sometimes they are centered and bold while at other times they are flush left and run-in, both the reviewers and the editors may have trouble understanding how you have organized your paper. Be consistent when you write and if you will be submitting to a journal that requires the APA format, make sure the headings in your paper are formatted correctly according to APA requirements. Then assume that you were not perfect and get someone else to specifically check for inconsistencies. That someone else should be a person who is a good editor and who will notice problems and tell you about them. Many people cannot do that well. They tend to see what is supposed to be there rather than what is there. Thus, a colleague who does and is willing to help is very valuable.

- Don't submit a paper before it has been **read locally by at least two people** who are familiar enough with the topic to be good critics. Ask them to make any criticisms they want, then think through the suggestions you receive and decide which ones you want to follow. Finding two qualified people who will thoughtfully and thoroughly read a paper is often more difficult than it sounds. Academics and professional practitioners are busy people and it can take several hours to read and critique a paper. When I read other people's papers the thing that most irritates me is finding errors, such as spelling or grammar, or APA format mistakes, the writer should have found and fixed before giving me the paper to read. I would rather spend my time helping with the conceptual problems, with issues about whether the paper is communicating effectively, and whether the conceptual and theoretical points have been effectively made.

There are, however, many people who do not want to do the type of review that I enjoy doing. They prefer to do developmental work which means they do check for APA formatting faux pas, grammar gremlins, and the like. Having both types of readers who are willing to read and critique your work is rare but wonderful—most of us only get that on our dissertation, if ever. One way of cultivating the interest of good reviewers is to help organize a writing group of 4 to 10 people who meet regularly and read as well as make thoughtful suggestions about drafts of papers written by group members.

- **Do use I, we, me, and us** in your paper. Positivists and postpositivists often insist that personal pronouns have no place in scholarly literature of any type. That is true, if you adopt the objectivist stance of positivism. From that perspective, a researcher should not let his or her personality, preferences, or personal experiences intrude on the objective search for truth. But if you use other paradigms as your foundation, you and other adherents may take precisely the opposite position—that all research and scholarship is shaped and influenced by the researcher. From this perspective, there is no way to avoid subjectivity. I tend toward that end of the continuum and feel that in most qualitative studies it may not only be appropriate, it may be important, to use "I" and related terms because it is an acknowledgement of the impact human scholars have had on the study being reported. Hiding that influence behind a façade of third person prose makes the situation worse, not better. It gives the impression of objectivity and masks the intensely subjective nature of much of the research in the social sciences, education, and educational technology. In many studies, different results and conclusions would have been obtained if different researchers had done the study. To illustrate this point I want to summarize an article in *Newsweek* (May 7, 2007, p. 57) by Sharon Begley. Her article was titled "Just Say No—To Bad Science." Her focus was on empirical research in the positivist tradition that dealt with the impact of different forms of sex education. She commented that "for us civilians, it's hard to grasp how much of science is subjective, and especially how much leeway there is in choosing how to conduct a study." She illustrated that point by noting that 153 out of 167 government funded studies of a chemical used in making plastic (bisphenol-A) found "toxic effects in animals" while not a single industry-funded study found any toxic effects. She pointed to one possible explanation: "many industry studies tested this estrogen-like chemical on a strain of rat that is insensitive to estrogen. That's like trying to measure how stress affects lactation . . . using males." Her focus, however, was on sex education research, particularly studies of whether abstinence-only methods are effective. She noted that the conservative Heritage Foundation claimed "that abstinence-only had been proven 'effective in reducing early sexual activity.' " This contrasts sharply with a recent Congressionally ordered study that found students in abstinence-only programs did not abstain any more than students who were not. Begley then explores the differences and finds many possible explanations. For example, several studies reporting positive results for abstinence-only programs used so-called virginity pledges as evidence of success. A student who took a virginity pledge and then reported not having sex was counted as a success. However, as Begley points out, some of those "studies relied on kids' memory. But up to half of kids forget whether they took a virginity pledge, or pretend they never did. Those who fall off the abstinence wagon are likely to 'forget' they pledged, while those who remain chaste might attribute it to a pledge they never made. Both factors inflate the measured efficacy of pledge programs." There is little doubt that the opinions, theories, biases, and beliefs of researchers have an impact on results. One way to acknowledge that is to use "I" and "we" instead of "the researcher" or "the researchers" in your papers. Another is to make your background, beliefs, theories, and biases as clear to readers as you can. Don't pretend to be "objective" about whether digital portfolios are useful or not when you write a paper on a study you conducted. Let the reader know if you are a strong advocate, or an opponent, and explain the reasons for your view.

Before moving on to another topic I want to soften my advice about using "I" and "we" in papers. Many journals still do not accept these words in scholarly papers which means if you want to be published in those journals you will have to follow the journals' requirements or publish elsewhere. However, do not assume that because you to not see papers in the journal using I and we that it is forbidden. Many scholars were taught that writing, "I interviewed the teacher" instead of "The researcher interviewed the teacher" is close to a mortal sin and self-censor their writing. A brief email to the editor should clear up any question about the journal's stance on this and other issues.

These are simple suggestions but they all help improve the paper and create a positive attitude in the minds of the editor and reviewers toward you and your paper.

MASTER YOUR MEDIUM

Another suggestion that could have been added to the list above is that you should develop the skills needed to write the type of paper or report your study requires. Do not, for example, write your first narrative article and submit it to a journal before studying and practicing the narrative genre of scholarly article. Too many qualitative studies submitted by young scholars follow a format that was designed for traditional positivist papers (Introduction, Methods, Data Analysis, Conclusions and Discussion) when a different format would have made the paper much stronger. Possible sources of help include books, online tutorials and articles, a mentor, coauthors, writing support groups, and specialists in other fields who have expertise in writing papers in the genre you have selected.

This advice is especially critical if you decide to communicate the results of your work in a non-traditional format. For example, if you want to report your work in a documentary film, there are probably courses at nearby colleges on film production as well as books, seminars, workshops, film festivals, magazines, and organizations for documentary film makers. There will also probably be people at your institution or in the area who have experience and might be willing to help you develop your skills (or partner with you to do the film). Consider the list below of possible formats for a qualitative research report. It also includes some potential sources of help.

- *Qualitative Research Paper.* A paper can use many different formats. However, most formats for qualitative research reports have been discussed in the literature, and there are examples you can critique and learn from, as well as organizations you can join that may offer several types of support for beginning scholars. For example, established scholar Harry Wolcott (2001) has written a very useful book, *Writing Up Qualitative Research.* Though relatively short at 208 pages, it is a very useful guide for novice qualitative researchers. Even shorter, but covering the entire process of writeup, submission, and revision, Adrian Holliday's (2007) *Doing and Writing Qualitative Research* is another useful resource. A third short book recommended in this category is Karen Golden-Biddle and Karen Locke's (2007) *Composing Qualitative Research.* If you want resources that focus on a specific type of qualitative research, Clandinin and Connelly's (2000) book, *Narrative Enquiry: Experience and Story in Qualitative Research,* has two good chapters on writing the "research text." Also, *Narrative Inquiry,* is one of many journals that publish examples of narrative scholarship, and the website of the Center for Narrative Inquiry (http://www.geocities.com/Athens/Delphi/9759/main02.html) has several helpful resources on writing scholarly papers based on narrative and storytelling. There are examples in the literature of virtually any form for reporting qualitative scholarship. Becoming familiar with the way a particular genre is used will be helpful. For example, two UK doctoral students (Gale & Wyatt, 2006) published a paper about their efforts to write while they are graduate students. The paper is a transcript of the email-based interview that went on between them as one posed questions about writing and the other responded. You would not necessarily want to organize your paper based on interviews the same way, but careful reading of many examples of the genre is helpful. This is particularly true for qualitative research because there are very few, if any, hard and fast rules about any aspect of qualitative scholarship. There is no "standard" format for "interview research" that must be followed. Instead, there are examples that illustrate the diversity of possibilities, mentors who can help you see how they do it, articles/ books that give some guidance, and organizations that can provide collegial encouragement and support.

- *Performance Ethnography.* On the other hand, if the results of your study will be distributed in a form that is established in another field (e.g., a play, drama, music, video, painting) there are publications on everything from how to write a play to how to use digital music software to compose and create everything from 3 seconds of transition music to an entire rap song with musical accompaniment. In most cities of any size, there are also theatre groups, film groups, writers groups, and many other forms of collegial support. Using a genre such as a play or musical performance to communicate the results of your scholarship is often called performance ethnography.
- *Literary Criticism as a Dissemination Format.* The section in Chapter 9 on literary theory and criticism focused on the use of theories developed in the humanities to guide scholarship in educational technology. However, literary criticism and theory can also be used as a framework for disseminating qualitative scholarship. In fact, one education theorist, Eliot Eisner at Stanford University, has developed a model of qualitative scholarship in education that is based on theories and methods from the humanities, especially the arts. Although it has had a number of names, his approach is called Connoisseurship today. Eisner (1997) offers a comprehensive but flexible model for doing qualitative inquiry. He uses the metaphor of a wine connoisseur to illustrate his approach to qualitative inquiry. It involves a knowledgeable scholar studying a topic in depth and then communicating that understanding to others. "Connoisseurship is the means through which we come to know the complexities, nuances, and subtleties of aspects of the world in which we have a

special interest" (p. 68). Eisner's connoisseurship model of qualitative inquiry has not been used very much in educational technology but it has many applications. In terms of dissemination, he recommends considering traditional as well as alternative formats such as plays, musical performances, and theatrical performances. Any of the alternative forms have their own well-developed procedures and processes that a qualitative scholar would need to learn. Fortunately, as with performance ethnographies, there are many sources of information and support. Another point that should be made here is that there are many types of specialized software for creating novels, screenplays, and plays. Programs like Final Draft and Movie Magic Screenwriter are two of many programs for creating scripts for movies. There is also software for writing novels and many other forms of literature. You will also find many different books and articles on writing literary criticism.

- *Documentary Film.* As noted earlier, there are journals, organizations, film festivals, and a host of other sources of help for documentary film making. One short but useful book is Sheila Bernard's (2004) *Documentary Storytelling for Video and Filmmakers.*
- *Philosophical Inquiry, Theoretical Scholarship, and Rhetorical Inquiry.* Few graduate programs in education prepare students to write philosophical or theoretical works and even fewer accept the idea that using the tools of modern rhetoric is an important aspect of being a scholar. There are, fortunately, several useful books on writing philosophy papers. Some of them were written for students in undergraduate and undergraduate courses, but these are also helpful. Some I recommend are:
  - Seech, S. (1999). *Writing Philosophy Papers,* 3rd ed. Belmont, CA: Wadsworth. 160 pages.
  - Vaughn, L. (2005). *Writing Philosophy: A Student's Guide to Writing Philosophy Essays.* Oxford, UK: Oxford University Press. 160 pages.
  - Martinich, A. P. (2005). *Philosophical Writing.* London: Blackwell. 216 pages.

There are fewer guides to writing theoretical scholarship but examples of both good and bad theoretical writing abound in the literature. When it comes to writing rhetorically strong papers and books, there are too many resources to list. For example, there are guides to writing how-to books on technology as well as guides on making arguments, writing narrative, and writing teaching materials.

ELECTRONIC SCHOLARLY COMMUNICATION

Before concluding this chapter and the book, I should comment on the growing number of electronic channels of communication that are being used to disseminate scholarly and professional knowledge today. In addition to electronic journals, which have been mentioned several times already, there are several promising alternatives:

Organizational and Group Web Sites

One way of communicating with other scholars and practitioners is through a web site created specifically for that purpose. One of the best, if not the best, in the field of educational technology is the *Instructional Technology Forum* which is supported and operated by the Department of Instructional Technology at the University of Georgia. The address is http://it.coe.uga. edu/itforum . If you browse this web site you will find a range of resources including active and archived discussions. The *Instructional Technology Forum* is a very valuable resource for faculty and students at the University of Georgia, but it is much more as well—it is a venue for discussion, dissemination, and communication among instructional technology scholars and practitioners all over the world. A web site is one form of electronic scholarly communication that is likely to become more and more relevant and important in the future. If you would like to explore what others are already doing with web sites, the educational technology program at the University of Colorado Denver maintains the *Instructional Technology Connections* site that lists many different web sites about educational technology. The web address is http:// carbon.cudenver.edu/~mryder/reflect/itconn.html.

Blogs

Another type of emerging communication method that is becoming more popular among scholars is the blog. A blog is essentially an online location where you can post messages (posts) and pages. Pages are intended to be relatively permanent parts of the blog where information with a long shelf life can be placed (e.g., information on the blog's purpose and how to use it). Posts usually have a shorter useful lifespan and often deal with current events. In 2007–2009, for example, there were hundreds if not thousands of blogs where people wrote about the U. S. presidential election. On many of these blogs you could only read what the owner of the blog was posting, but on others you could also write a response to any post. Blogs are very useful for disseminating both information and opinions, especially if the content needs a fast dissemination channel because it is time sensitive. Some blogs are open and accessible to anyone while others are restricted only to those who are approved by the blog administrator. There are also variations where a selected group can post to the blog but most people can only read posts.

If you would like to look at some blogs devoted to topics in educational technology, Kathy Schrock maintains a list of them at http://kathyschrock. net/edtechblogs.htm . For example, Alan November, a well-known expert on technology in K–12 schools, maintains a blog at http://nlcommunities. com/communities/alannovember/default.aspx .

If you would like to create a blog yourself, there are hundreds of services as well as many types of blog software that automate the process of creating and maintaining a blog. WordPress is a free blog creation program that is also associated with a web site where you can create your own blog free of charge. The address is http://www.wordpress.com but keep in mind that there are many, many types of blogs and blog software.

Wikis

Another relatively new electronic communications service is a wiki. Whereas a blog lets one person post a document that others can read and perhaps reply to, a wiki is designed to help groups of people coauthor documents. The best known and largest wiki today is the Wikipedia, which is a huge online encyclopedia that is always in the process of being written. Virtually anyone can participate in the process of writing an entry in the Wikipedia—either by adding a new entry or by editing an entry that already exists. For example, there are entries in the Wikipedia on thousands of topics relevant to educational technologists—the educational technology entry is huge, the ADDIE Model entry is very useful, and the instructional design entry is instructive.

Wikipedia is an "open content" publication which means that anyone can go in and change or edit an entry. The idea is that by letting anyone improve an entry the quality of the encyclopedia will increase over time. Critics have claimed that letting anyone write or edit an entry means that all the content is suspect. Critics usually suggest that without a system of peer review by recognized experts (and perhaps limiting authors to those with academic credentials) the Wikipedia will never be a source of valid and reliable information. Scholarpedia is one of several competing online encyclopedia that only allow scholars to write original entries. It also has a refereeing/peer review process. All these competing online encyclopedias are, at present, much smaller than Wikipedia.

There are, of course, some who take advantage of the open content principle to vandalize entries in the Wikipedia, but several studies of the site suggest that it is quite accurate and that when errors do get in, either accidentally or on purpose, they are usually corrected very quickly. However, Wikipedia, and the Wiki movement in general, are viewed with suspicion by many academics who believe that recognized authority should be favored over the consensus approach to deciding what is correct that is used by Wikipedia. Having seen how authority was used in the Soviet Union to promulgate patently false "truths", and after the "weapons of mass destruction in Iraq" debacle of the Bush administration, the luster of authoritative sources of information, especially government spokespeople, has dulled considerably.

Wikipedia is the biggest and most widely used Wiki, but there are thousands of others. For example, the *EduTechWiki* (http://edutechwiki.unige.ch) was established by Daniel Schneider at the School of Education and Psychology at the University of Geneva. It currently has over a thousand entries and is growing. Another educational technology Wiki is *Educational Technology Encyclopedia* which is managed by the San Diego State University Department of Educational Technology (http://coe.sdsu.edu/eet/wikis/articles/index.htm). This encyclopedia is under the general editorship of Bob Hoffman. These are only two of the growing number of public educational technology-related Wikis on the web today. Wikis are also used by restricted groups—such as co-authors of a book or scholarly paper—as a platform for collaborative writing. A *private* Wiki is one way to support a writing group with members who live in work thousands of miles from each other.

A simple search on the web will turn up hundreds of Wikis about educational technology. If you would like to create a Wiki yourself, for public or private use, the entry for "wiki" in the Wikipedia (http://en.wikipedia.org/wiki/Wiki) is a very good overview of the history of Wikis as well as how they work. Another Wikipedia entry (http://en.wikipedia.org/wiki/List_of_Wiki_Farms) includes a list of providers who support Internet servers where you can set up and operate your own Wiki. These are generally called "Wiki farms." Some Wiki farms are free but they often make their money by displaying not-so-subtle advertisements while people use your Wiki. Wetpaint (www.wetpaint.com) is a free service that makes money by displaying ads on Wiki sites. However, one interesting policy of Wetpaint is that it does not put ads on free Wiki sites that are classified as educational. A search using the term "educational technology" in May of 2008 turned up 433 sites on Wetpaint. Other Wiki farms charge a monthly fee but the fees are generally not excessive.

One book I have found very helpful in setting up a Wiki is Mark Choate's (2007) *Professional Wikis.* Another highly rated book is *Managing virtual teams: Getting the most from Wikis, Blogs, and other collaborative tools,* (Huettner,

Brown, & James-Tanny, 2007). It focuses on the use of several types of electronic tools for collaboration from the point of view of someone with responsibility for leading teams in business, industry, or educational settings.

Podcasting

A podcast is a audio, visual, or video communication carried over the Internet. Podcasts come in so many flavors and variations that it is difficult to offer a definition that differentiates podcasts from other forms of communication, without also eliminating some forms of podcasting as well. For example, podcasts are not always carried over the Internet. At least one school in Louisiana uses podcasting software to create a weekly or daily message for parents that is broadcast over a low power radio transmitter like the ones used by real estate agents to broadcast information about a house for sale. Parents dropping off their children, or waiting to pick them up, can listen to the school podcast. In the area of educational technology, podcasting technology has been used primarily to disseminate lectures, discussions, and other types of multimedia materials over the Internet. For example, EdTechTalk (www.edtechtalk.com) is a free online service where educators interested in instructional technology can meet online and discuss issues, exchange ideas and information, and listen to the comments and discussions created by others. The last time I checked this site, for example, there was an ongoing discussion about professional development, another about EarthCast 2008, and many more. Participants can communicate via text, audio via their computers, voice via telephone, and digital video that is uploaded to the site. The audio and digital video formats are variations on the podcast concept. EdTechTalk is one of a number of innovative efforts to expand the channels of professional and scholarly communication.

Virtual Conferences

Another technology-enhanced form of scholarly communication is the virtual conference. Thousands of meetings relevant to education and/or educational technology are held each year in places like Orlando, New York, London, Paris, Tokyo, and Sydney, but as the cost of travel increases to new highs, more and more groups are organizing "virtual conference" that meet over the internet rather than face to face in a particular geographic location. If you do a Google search for "virtual conference" you will probably find several thousand "hits" on the topic (my search produced over 250,000 hits), and if you narrow the search by adding additional restrictions (e.g., "virtual conference" "educational technology") the number of hits may be more manageable (3000+). Virtual conferences generally have the same components as face to face conferences—keynotes, presentations, discussions, and so on—and they often produce proceedings that are distributed via the Internet. The best way to learn about virtual conferences, and decide if this is something your institution or organization might want to sponsor, is to find two or three relevant to your interests and "attend."

Social Networking Sites like Facebook

Over the past ten years another Internet phenomenon has emerged - social networking sites. A social networking site is a place on the Internet where you can establish a presence, develop a group of online friends, and exchange everything from normal chitchat to videos of your last fraternity party. Your site may include information about yourself, your work and personal interests, and the type of friends you are interesting in making. Your site may have all types of data on it - text, video, audio, graphics, animation, and so on. You and your site will also be a part of a flexible and adjustable network of other friends/sites that are linked. Someone may ask to be linked to your site, for example, and you can decide to allow that link or not. And, of course, you can ask to be linked to someone else's site.

Facebook, MySpace, and hundreds of other sites, were initially populated primarily by teens, preteens and college students. And much of the news coverage about social networking sites has focused on the efforts of older men to find underage sexual partners. Teens, and preteens, are at risk when using these sites and there is an emerging consensus on steps they, and their parents, should take to protect themselves from predators. In spite of the dangers, however, these sites have become a major component of Internet use today, and adults have begun to use them as well. A growing number of professors, for example, have put their profiles on a social network site. And, specialized sites are appearing that cater to people with special interests. An example is *Many2Many,* a "group weblog on social software" that has the characteristics of a social networking site and a blog. To use this site go to this address:

http://www.corante.com

Then pull down the "Our Blogs" menu on the top, right of the screen and select ManytoMany under Internet—Technology. It is a bit early to predict just how social networking sites will be used by researchers, scholars, and professional practitioners, but I expect that social networking software may become a part of many online resources created to support individuals and groups who share an interest in a particular area of research and/or practice.

Multimedia-Enhanced Web Resources

For hundreds of years the primary means of scholarly and professional communication has been black ink on white paper. We are so accustomed to scholarly communication in this form that we tend to discount documents that use color and have some design elements that make them more attractive. That may be one reason why even electronic scholarly journals have been reluctant to move much beyond relatively bland text and simple graphics. There are, however, a number of e-journals that accept multimedia as well as text, tables, and basic graphics. That includes audio such as interviews and discussions, video such as classroom clips, and many forms of 3-D graphics as well as animations. One particularly interesting use of video is the InTime project at the University of Northern Iowa (http:// www.intime.uni.edu) . The web site has a large collection of video vignettes from classrooms where teachers and students are using different teaching and learning strategies as well as different types of technology. The classroom videos are supplemented with support materials such as explanations of the lessons and the teaching/learning strategies used, commentaries by the teachers featured in the vignettes, and much more. All this is organized into a database that lets you search for relevant video cases by aspects of the lesson such as grade level, subject, teacher behaviors, teaching approach, and technology use. InTime was supported by a federal grant and is the product of a collaborative effort led by the University of Northern Iowa that included several other colleges of education. It is an example of the type of resource that might not have been considered "research" a decade ago but is now considered as an excellent example of Boyer's "scholarship of teaching" that we need much more of in education and educational technology. An important point here is that the result of the InTime project is not a journal article or even a traditional book. Instead, it is a multimedia resource distributed over the Internet to anyone who wishes to use it. There is no way to estimate the impact InTime has had on education, but my guess is that it has been, and continues to be, a significant influence, both as an exemplar of what can be done via multimedia and the Internet, and as a very valuable resource for preservice and inservice teacher education.

SUMMARY

To summarize, the scholarly and professional practice environment encourages scholars as well as practitioners to disseminate their work in a wide variety of formats. Some of those formats are text-based, some are multimedia-based, some are literary, and some formats come from the humanities and philosophy. Regardless of the format you elect to use, there are resources available that will help you create a stronger report or product of your work.

There are, of course, some "core" knowledge and important skills you need to know in order to communicate your scholarship, regardless of the form that communication takes. However, there is also a great deal of specialized knowledge and expertise associated with different forms. Being able to write a good traditional, quantitative research paper does not, for example, mean you can write a good paper based on a narrative inquiry study or produce a quality documentary film on the same subject. If you are exploring alternative formats for disseminating the results of your scholarship take into consideration the need to learn the basics of that form before using it, or consider taking on a coauthor who is a master of the form and can mentor you while collaborating on the publication.

REFERENCES

Begley, S. (2007, May 7). Just say no—To bad science. *Newsweek,* p. 57.

Bernard, S. (2004). *Documentary storytelling for video and filmmakers.* New York: Focal Press/Elseiver.

Choate, M. (2007). *Professional Wikis.* Indianapolis: Wiley.

Clandinin, D. J., & Connelly, F. M. (2000). *Narrative inquiry: Experience and story in qualitative research.* San Francisco: Jossey-Bass.

Eisner, E. (1997). *The enlightened eye: Qualitative inquiry and the enhancement of educational practice.* Columbus, OH: Merrill.

Gale, K. & Wyatt, J. (2006). Inquiry into writing: An interactive interview. *Qualitative Inquiry, 12*(6), 1117–1124.

Golden-Biddle, K. & Locke, K. (2007) *Composing Qualitative Research.* Thousand Oaks, CA: Sage.

Holliday, A. (2007) *Doing & writing qualitative research, 2nd ed.* Thousand Oaks, CA: Sage.

Huettner, B., Brown, M. K., & James-Tanny, C. (2007). *Managing virtual teams: Getting the most from Wikis, Blogs, and other collaborative tools.* Plano, TX: Wordware Publishing.

Wolcott, H. F. (2001). *Writing Up Qualitative Research.* Thousand Oaks, CA: Sage.

READINGS FOR CHAPTER 12

Reading 12.1

Jones, K. (2006, April). A biographic researcher in pursuit of an aesthetic: The use of arts-based (re)presentations in "performative" dissemination of life stories. *Qualitative Sociology Review 2*(1). Available at http://www.qualitativesociologyreview.org/ENG/Volume3/abstracts.php

I selected this article for several reasons. First, it is written in a style and form that breaks some of the rules of "proper" scholarship in the social sciences. Second, it is a thoughtful piece on the question of how to present the results of biographic narrative research. The author, Kip Jones, presents a strong theoretical framework for thinking about "performative" ways to disseminate the knowledge developed in biographic narrative research. Some of what he says is controversial; all of it is interesting. As a field, educational technology has not been very innovative when it comes to the forms used to disseminate scholarship. Kip Jones' paper has ideas, concepts, and suggestions all of us should at least consider. As you read the paper ask yourself what types of questions of interest to you in education or educational technology are amenable to the type of research he describes.

Reading 12.2

Pryor, J. (2006). *Guidelines on writing a philosophy paper.* Retrieved May 21, 2007 from http://www.jimpryor.net/teaching/guidelines/writing.html

Dr. Pryor is an Associate Professor of Philosophy at New York University and he compiled this set of directions and suggestions for writing philosophy papers. Actually, in his acknowledgements Dr. Pryor gives credit to several others for ideas that form parts of this paper. Although the paper was written for undergraduate students in philosophy courses, it is also very helpful for anyone writing philosophy papers without a graduate degree in the field of philosophy.

There are a few points, however, I want to take issue with in Professor Pryor's advice, as it relates to writing philosophical inquiry papers in the field of educational technology. His advice was written specifically for undergraduate students taking a philosophy course and his suggestions fit that target audience well. For educational technology scholars, I would modify a few of his suggestions. For example, he suggests that "a good philosophy paper is *modest* and makes *a small point.*" Often, when you are applying ideas from a different discipline to educational technology, the implications may actually be very significant. There is nothing wrong with being ambitious and focusing on "big ideas" that, if accepted, would have a major impact on the field.

Another point that I might disagree with is Dr. Pryor's emphasis on making an outline before writing. While that is common advice, even a requirement, in courses from sophomore English composition to advanced graduate courses, I think the reason for that advice may be the personality and preferences of the advisor as much as any inherent characteristic in the content to be written about. When told that they must create an outline for the entire paper before writing, some writers do just that and find that it is a natural thing to do. Others, if they can, will write their papers then create the required outline and find that the natural thing to do. I am in the "write the outline last" group. I start with a fuzzy, often very vague, idea of what I want to say and let it evolve and change over the writing process. However, there are times when I must write an outline. For example, when I send a book proposal to a publisher I can't just tell the editor that I "want to write something about qualitative research." To get a contract to write a book, I must provide the editor with more than that. So, I write a fairly detailed outline of the book and each chapter, not because I need it, but because the editor requires it before offering a contract. Once the contract is offered and I start writing, I do look at the outline I prepared and I do use it while writing. However, I treat it as a general and very flexible framework to begin work. It almost always changes radically before the book is finished. Some chapters are added, some are deleted, some are combined, some are split, and some appear in a different order than specified in the outline. Often I start writing an article without any outline at all. And, when I do have an outline (which may be necessary when coauthoring a paper) I treat it as a general framework that may change at any time.

I'm also of two minds about Dr. Pryor's advice, "Don't shoot for literary elegance." If you have the talent to do that, why not? Yes, simple writing is appealing and it can help communicate your points. However, rich, elegant writing that uses metaphors, examples, illustrations, and has a pleasing feel to it can be a powerful way of communicating your ideas.

I'm also a bit uncomfortable with the idea of pretending your reader is "lazy, stupid, and mean." I see what he means, but most readers who will think seriously about what you say are not lazy, stupid, or mean. However, Dr. Pryor is correct, I believe, in saying that you should not make the reader work any harder than necessary to understand your points. Convoluted sentences that have to be read over and over again are generally signs of bad writing, not complex ideas. Complex ideas can be communicated effectively, but it takes effort on the part of the author. One compact and convoluted sentence may turn into a paragraph or two because you "unpack" the content into more digestible sentences, add a metaphor and a few examples or illustrations, and provide scaffolding the reader can climb to reach your idea. Though longer, this second method is often faster to read and it does not "feel" long and drawn out to the reader because he or she is enjoying the reading. Another point to expand on Dr. Pryor's suggestions is that when you write a paper for educational technology, you should be writing to one or more target audiences. Your audience should help you define what should be included and what should not. For example, if you are writing to faculty who teach computer literacy courses in college or high school, there would be no need to spend a paragraph telling them what PowerPoint is. On the other hand, if you use the concept "open source software" most but not all of the audience will know what that term means. You may want to provide a reference those who do not know can use to find out. And, if you use the words *techne* and *phronesis* to distinguish types of knowledge the computer literacy instructor uses to make decisions about instruction, you can assume almost all of the audience of computer literacy instructors will not be familiar with the meaning and origins of those terms. Thus, the target audience is an important factor in determining what you include in a paper.

Dr. Pryor gives very good advice when he says "Make sure every sentence in your draft does useful work. Get rid of any which don't." I would only add that when I review papers from my graduate students as well as articles submitted to journals, a common problem is transition. When you end discussion of one topic and start another, there should be a sentence or two that helps the reader make that transition. Otherwise, the change is abrupt and calls attention to itself. You want the reader to be focusing on your ideas, not the abrupt shift in topics. Also, there are times when the reader needs an opportunity to take a breath and relax. For example, if you are presenting a complex topic that is hard to explain and even more difficult to demonstrate why it is important in educational technology, don't just finish that effort and move right on to the next difficult and complex topic. Instead, add a few paragraphs of material that give the reader a chance to unwind and stop working so hard to understand the material. An interesting or humorous example, for example, can do that. Or, a metaphor, a link to a myth or cultural tradition, may also fit. The idea is to give the reader something to read that is not filler but not demanding either.

Finally, I will just note that this paper uses the *he* instead of *he or she* and *him* instead of *him or her*. My preference is to rewrite many such sentences that are referring to an undefined person and to make them plural. That gets rid of the gender specificity of the pronoun. However, when that is awkward, I use "her or him" or "he or she" instead of only one, gender-specific word. Others simply alternate and use her one time, he the next.

To get a feel for how you would approach writing a paper based on philosophical inquiry, select a topic that interests you and start work on a paper about it. Begin with the title, then write topic or beginning sentences for each section of the paper and give those sections main headings. Keep Dr. Pryor's advice in mind as you work on each part of the paper and if you decide not to take his advice, write a parenthetical note explaining why. If you are using Microsoft Word to create this assignment, use the Outlining commands to create the headings and topic sentences. Once you have main headings and topic sentences, start thinking about what should come under those main headings. Create second level, and even third level, headings if needed, and write one or two sentences under those as well. As you work on this paper, use the Outline commands of Word to move main and subheads around if your thinking changes, and promote as well as demote headings to higher or lower levels as needed. When you have the main and subheads as well as some beginning sentences for each heading and subhead, you should have a fairly good idea of where your philosophical inquiry is taking you.

Reading 12.3

Deacon, A., & WynScully, C. (2006). Learning from the rhetoric of academics using educational technology. Paper presented at the *e/merge 2006: Learning Landscapes in Southern Africa,* July 10–21, 2006. Retrieved 05/26/2007 http://emerge2006.net/programme.php

The authors of this paper, Andrew Deacon and Catherine WynScully, both work in the Center for Higher Education Development at the University of Cape Town in South Africa. One of their jobs is to develop and deliver services to academics at the university that helps them integrate educational technology into their teaching. In this paper Deacon and WynScully use rhetorical analysis to evaluate the methods used to provide professional development support to academics. As they note, "Formal research communities themselves might not always appear especially collaborative . . . , yet other channels do exist for disseminating some of this knowledge [about the use of educational technologies in higher education]. Staff development activities involve understanding this context and can play an important mediating role in the university organization, exposing academics to best practices, developing skills, fostering collaborative working relationships and offering theoretical foundations. . . . Thus although the information content of the presentations we analyse are not traditionally viewed as especially significant as research, it is their social function in how understandings of educational technology are communicated with peers that is of interest here." The paper is useful from several perspectives: as an example of how to write a paper based on an analysis of your own professional practice, as an exploration of professional development in higher education, as an example of an effort to improve one's own professional practice, and as an example of how rhetorical theory can be used as a framework for scholarship. As you read this paper ask yourself how the methods these authors used might be applied to other questions related to educational technology? What sorts of questions are they? Are there several types of questions that might be addressed, or is rhetorical analysis applicable to only one or two types of research? Why?

Reading 12.4

Webster, J., & Watson, R. (2002, June). *Analyzing the past to prepare for the future: Writing a literature review. MIS Quarterly, 26*(2), xii–xxiii. Retrieved May 26, 2007 from http://www.misq.org/archivist/vol/no26/issue2/vol26n-2index.html

This paper was written for Management Information Systems (MIS) scholars interested in writing publishable reviews of different aspects of the scholarly literature in their field. One of the motivations for writing it was the rarity of literature reviews in the MIS literature. As the authors put it, "A review of prior, relevant literature is an essential feature of any academic project. An effective review creates a firm foundation for advancing knowledge. It facilitates theory development, closes areas where a plethora of research exists, and uncovers areas where research is needed." Webster and Watson believe progress in their field "is impeded" by the lack of literature reviews" and they wrote this paper to encourage scholars to write more literature reviews *and* to write them well. While their approach emphasizes the development of theory, the advice of Webster and Watson can also be adapted to other goals, including interpretive and hermeneutic perspectives. For educational technologists, the paper is well worth reading because our field too is not blessed with an abundance of literature reviews and the quality of those that are published is uneven. After reading this paper, select a topic you feel should be the focus of a literature review, then write a "treatment" about the review. A treatment is a short one to three page overview of the idea with enough details to give the reader a good feel for what is being suggested and how different aspects of the project hang together. "Treatments" are often used in efforts to help sell investors on an idea for a movie. As you write your treatment, assume the target audience is one or two colleagues who would join you in doing the work required to write a literature review on the topic you have selected. Use the advice in this paper to guide your thinking on how the review would be approached and how it would be organized.

Reading 12.5

Glass, G. V. (1999). Commentary—A new day in how scholars communicate. *Current Issues in Education* [On-line], *2*(2). Available: http://cie.asu.edu/volume2/number2/

In this paper, Gene Glass, writes about the transition in scholarly publishing from ink on paper to electronic publication. He is specifically interested in two journals published online at Arizona State University where he teaches. One is *Current Issues in Education,* (http://cie.asu.edu/) which is a project of the College of Education at Arizona State University that is edited by ASU graduate students. The other is *Education Policy Analysis Archives* (http://epaa.asu.edu/), which was begun by Dr. Glass and is now a joint project of the colleges of education at ASU and the University of South Florida. Dr. Glass sees the future of scholarly communication in journals like the two he discusses. Once you have read this paper, develop two ideas—one for a paper that would be submitted to an online journal in educational technology, and the other for an online journal that would fill a gap in the existing scholarly and professional journals in your field. Write about a page on each. Explain why the paper is needed and which online journal it should be submitted to. If you are not familiar with online journals in education, see the list maintained by AERA of online, open access journals in education (http://aera-cr.asu.edu/ejournals) and explain why the paper would be appropriate for that journal. For the one page about a new online journal explain why it is needed and identify online and print journals that cover similar topics but do not meet the need you have identified. You may want to do this assignment in collaboration with others.

Printed in the United States
206287BV00004B/4-42/P